CATULLUS THROUGH HIS BOOKS

Modern readings of the Roman poet Catullus' work have always been constrained by doubts about the surviving text. Does the sequence of our corpus reflect the artistically coherent and meaningful arrangement of the poems? Why are the various parts of the collection so jarringly different in content and emotional tone? To what extent, if at all, can we explain these shifts by appealing to Catullus' famously vivid portrayals of his emotions and life circumstances? *Catullus Through his Books* argues that we possess three separate books of poems designed by the poet himself; at key moments in these books, the poems dramatize the creative activity of their own composition, embedding apparent autobiographical details and purportedly revealing the poet's intentions and goals. These dramas of composition direct us through the poems, integrating our understanding of each part and generating a holistic vision of Catullus as poet of self-destroying longing and irreparable loss.

JOHN K. SCHAFER is a Visiting Assistant Professor at Wake Forest University, North Carolina. He specializes in Republican and Imperial Latin literature, and is the author of numerous articles on Seneca, Vergil, and Horace, as well as the monograph *Ars Didactica: Seneca's 94th and 95th Letters* (2009).

T0381545

CATULLUS THROUGH HIS BOOKS

Dramas of Composition

JOHN K. SCHAFER

Wake Forest University, North Carolina

CAMBRIDGE
UNIVERSITY PRESS

CAMBRIDGE
UNIVERSITY PRESS

Shaftesbury Road, Cambridge CB2 8EA, United Kingdom

One Liberty Plaza, 20th Floor, New York, NY 10006, USA

477 Williamstown Road, Port Melbourne, VIC 3207, Australia

314–321, 3rd Floor, Plot 3, Splendor Forum, Jasola District Centre, New Delhi – 110025, India

103 Penang Road, #05–06/07, Visioncrest Commercial, Singapore 238467

Cambridge University Press is part of Cambridge University Press & Assessment,
a department of the University of Cambridge.

We share the University's mission to contribute to society through the pursuit of
education, learning and research at the highest international levels of excellence.

www.cambridge.org
Information on this title: www.cambridge.org/9781108459174

DOI: 10.1017/9781108559584

First published 2020
First paperback edition 2023

A catalogue record for this publication is available from the British Library

Library of Congress Cataloging-in-Publication data
NAMES: Schafer, John, 1978– author.
TITLE: Catullus through his books : dramas of composition / John Kyrin Schafer.
DESCRIPTION: New York : Cambridge University Press, 2020. | Includes bibliographical
references and index.
IDENTIFIERS: LCCN 2019045017 (print) | LCCN 2019045018 (ebook) | ISBN 9781108472241
(hardback) | ISBN 9781108559584 (epub)
SUBJECTS: LCSH: Catullus, Gaius Valerius – Criticism and interpretation.
CLASSIFICATION: LCC PA6276 .S314 2020 (print) | LCC PA6276 (ebook) | DDC 874/.01–dc23
LC record available at https://lccn.loc.gov/2019045017
LC ebook record available at https://lccn.loc.gov/2019045018

ISBN   978-1-108-47224-1   Hardback
ISBN   978-1-108-45917-4   Paperback

Contents

Acknowledgments

It is slightly terrifying to reflect how deeply indebted I have been, in the writing of this book, to so many loved ones, friends, and colleagues. Above all and by far, to my wife Julie: it isn't fair, how much this book and I have taken from you, and I can't imagine how I could ever make good on your steadfastness and love. Others I now thank collectively, thinking it both needless and impossible to disentangle between those who have been such brilliant intellectual benefactors, such wise professional counselors, and such personally generous friends – most of you have been all of these. And so my deepest thanks to all of you: Kimberly Allen, Eugenie Allen, all the Allens everywhere, David Bird, Tess Cavagnero, Rob Cioffi, Kathy Coleman, Lauren Curtis, Katie Deutsch, Micaela DiLeonardo, David Ebrey, Moa Ekbom, David Elmer, Joe Farrell, Stephanie Frampton, Ana Galjanic, Bill Gladhill, Marina Haworth, Joe Howley, Tim Joseph, Alison Keith, Sasha Kirichenko, Paul Kosmin, Christopher Krebs, Leah Kronenberg, Ben Levine, Cameron Lewellen, Margot Lurie, Jake Mackey, Lisa Mignone, Andy Miller, Michelle Molitor, Micah Myers, Jim O'Hara, Nandini Pandey, Emily Pillinger-Avlamis, Susan Prince, Laura and Jack Schafer, Frannie Schafer, Madeleine and Jacob Schafer, Tim Schafer, all the Schafers everywhere, Marilyn Skinner, Gisela Striker, Sarah Culpepper Stroup, Francesca Tataranni, Richard Thomas, Kate Topper, Jarrett Welsh, Gareth Williams, Alison Witte, and Tom Zanker. I also thank the Loeb Classical Library for supporting this work with a fellowship over the 2014–15 academic year, as well as Cambridge University Press, its anonymous referees, and its Classics editor Michael Sharp.

Cui dono? Eleven years ago, my dear friend and brilliant fellow graduate student, Isaac Meyers, passed away suddenly. About six years ago, hoping to renew the presence of his memory in mine, I found myself looking vaguely around for "something brief but interesting" to say about Catullus 101 – I had always remembered him and worked through my grief for him with those holy words (to me they are that), the unvoiced stop consonants in *mutam nequiquam alloquerer cinerem* have mimed the catch in my throat more times than I can know, and so I thought, a nice act of memory, and maybe a short article. Within a couple months, my plan to write a second book on Senecan prose was on hold, and I was giddy with a new intellectual thrill, lost in the rabbit hole of this work. I wish I could talk to him and tell him how he changed my life. And so, Isaac, *accipe* whatever this is of a book. And, of course, forever, *aue atque uale.*

Introduction

On the matter of Catullan arrangement, scholarly progress has moved glacially and without the impetus of global warming. Yet, after a century and a half, some limited consensus seems to have been reached ... In the next 150 years we may finally see a satisfactory resolution of die Catullfrage. *Or not.*

Marilyn Skinner

All that [sc. uncovering Catullus' literary models and affiliations] *is important for understanding the individual poems and can be done appropriately without supposing that the poems which claim to represent reality or to express the strong and genuine emotions of the poet are "simply" literary constructs ... There is nothing "simple" about the relationship of literature, even the most accessible literature, and life.*

Ian Du Quesnay and Tony Woodman

But there [sc. the quotation above] *– until we find a better way of talking about emotional reality in ancient poetry – the book has to end.*

Gail Trimble

The quotations above are the concluding remarks respectively of Marilyn Skinner's magisterial 2007 overview of the arrangement of Catullus' poems, of Ian Du Quesnay and Tony Woodman's equally authoritative retrospect of their 2012 volume on Catullus, and of Gail Trimble's fine review essay of that volume.[1] These pronouncements are offered as epigraphs marking the points of departure, and to some extent the ultimate ambitions, of this work.

Regarding the traditional problem discussed in the first of these epigraphs, the work immodestly proposes that Skinner's "satisfactory resolution" is at hand, and some 140 years earlier than she dared hope (or not): to the most general and most pressing questions concerning the poems'

---

[1] Skinner (2007) 47, Du Quesnay and Woodman (2012b) 272, Trimble (2013).

arrangement and circulation, it claims, determinate answers can confidently be given. It hastens, however, to add that this resolution proceeds almost entirely from the "limited consensus" already won on this question, and that its sole essential element going beyond that consensus has been repeatedly seen and persuasively argued for, most notably by Skinner herself.[2] This volume, then, does not *resolve* this laborious philological crux so much as *notice* that previous learned studies have already loosed the long-tied knot, if not yet in the same place and at the same time.

On the latter two epigraphs and the notorious problems they address, an apotropaic modesty is even more urgent. Examining the Catullan poems in accordance with this account of their arrangement and circulation does not reveal a "better way" of thinking about ancient authors, their texts, and their worlds in any general sense. It does, however, illuminate the ways in which this particular ancient author focalizes and manipulates those notorious relationships, above all by textually collocating his interest in the poems' own creation, at the seam between his poetry and his lived reality, with the seams internal to the poems: the openings, transitions, and closures of his books. Teasing these out, in turn, yields shifting metapoetic characterizations of the poems, guiding us through their sequence, explaining modulations in their poet-speaker's subjectivity, and globally integrating the parts of the corpus. How does the Catullan personal voice change or develop? To what extent does change or development in the author explain changes in the text? How, and to what extent, does the world of his first-person poems interact with those of his impersonal or less personal ones? How, and to what extent, does the content of the former reflect the lived reality of the poet and his associates? How, and to what extent, do these questions matter? Before readers ever posed these questions of Catullus' text, the text itself posed them to its readers, in pointed ways and with far-reaching results.

This work proposes, in broadest outline, that we can recover from the poems the overarching design for their mode of circulation on papyrus rolls. As this structural thesis develops, however, the work will also examine a series of related exegetical issues, the sum of whose conclusions amounts to a second global claim. That is, Catullus' design transforms how his poems read, above all by textually privileging their depictions of their own genesis and by inviting us to interrogate these depictions and their relation both to other Catullan texts and to purported extratextual realities.

---

[2] Skinner (1981) 80–92.

Three Catullan Books

The Catullan corpus, I claim, consists in three authorially designed books; at the close of one of these is found a short, heterogeneous run of poems, whose status is uniquely problematic. The books and their parts, which will be referred to throughout this work by the accompanying shorthand, are:

A: poems 1–51, consisting of a bipartite first half and a (unitary?) second half:
> 1–14 and 14b–26
> 27–51
> [**Ax:** 52–60]
B: 61–64
C: 65–116, consisting of halves:
> **C1:** 65–68b, itself consisting of halves:
>> 65–67 to Ortalus
>> 68a and 68b to Mallius
> **C2:** 69–116, itself consisting of halves:
>> 69–92
>> 93–116

The problematic run, **Ax,** are genuine Catullan poems, but they are also generically distinct from what precedes (and follows) them, frequently obscure, and apparently ill-fitting.[3] On these poems, I find that available evidence falls short of licensing firm, univocal conclusions about their nature, their relations to other Catullan texts, or the history of their original circulation and later transmission. What is overwhelmingly supported by the evidence, and what my thesis really requires, is the following core claim: there is some sort of textual and/or artistic discontinuity between poems 51 and 52. On different versions of this claim, the discontinuity will either mark **Ax** off as a textual intrusion, an "unauthorized" presence at the conclusion of **A**, or else as a distinct, subordinated "part" or "unit" there, a kind of postscript or annex to **A**.[4] On either option, our inability to pronounce unequivocally on how these poems present

---

[3] The shorthand is adapted from Hutchinson (2003), with the restriction of **A** to poems 1–51 and the coining of **Ax** for 52–60 my own innovation (in part for the cleaving implement many scholars would take to these poems, but more importantly for the view of them I mean to promote: *Appendix Catulliana*). My use of Hutchinson's shorthand does not imply my agreement with his substantive views of the corpus (or vice versa). In fact my thesis shares considerable common ground but departs from his on important points.

[4] On this option, these poems will find a parallel in the role and function I claim for the "unit" consisting of poems 14b–26.

themselves to readers can be plausibly explained by the extensive textual corruption apparent in them, and poem 54 in particular.

All of these claims will be examined fully in what follows; in advance of this, it will already be clear to many readers how little of this picture is new. In brief, a familiar but nonstandard move, the exclusion of poems 52–60, is here adopted (or adapted, if one prefers that **Ax** be kept, but kept separate) and combined with the most orthodox claims for multi-poem unities and points of textual articulation in the corpus. That each of the two consecutive runs of poems 1–14 and 14b–26 bespeaks some sort of artistic unity is widely agreed, the core of Skinner's "limited consensus" just mentioned. Next, a clear metrical break (at least) separates these poems from 27 and following. While there are competing versions, it is entirely mainstream to see the divisions marking off 1–14 and 14b–26 as internal, with a larger affinity tying the two units together (my "bipartite first half"), and a still larger artistic integrity uniting them with some or all of the remaining shorter poems in various meters, 27–60. The artistic unity of these poems can then be seen as that of an authorial book.[5]

The claim that the longer, metrically diverse poems of **B** and the elegiac distichs of **C** are artistic units and/or books is also familiar, though the former is plausibly resisted even by some who accept the latter.[6] If the elegiac poems 65–116 are a book, its division into "long poem" and "short poem" halves, my **C1** and **C2**, is a patent reality; the mediality of this division is apparent from their matching line-counts.[7] My sole novelty here will be to argue for a medial division grouping 65–67 and 68a–68b respectively within **C1**.[8] The articulation of **C2** into 69–92 and 93–116, by contrast, is yet another widely shared claim.

Readers will have rightly detected the rhetorical pose of a modest tinkerer confronting a notorious problem, a humble practitioner quick to admit, and even perversely proud of, the wanting originality of his own thesis. Nonetheless, the same tinkerer proclaims to offer a convincing account of, and even resolution to, the dread *Catullfrage*. How?

---

[5] On the distinction between books and artistic units (and the attractive but problematic inference of the former from the latter), much more will be said.

[6] This includes Hutchinson (2003) 210–11 himself, whose christening of poems 61–64 as **B** I follow. On Hutchinson's view, **B** is a textual unit in the transmitted corpus, four independent longer pieces whose "partness" for us, so to speak, is an accident of transmission arising from their distinctness from the authorial collections preceding and following them. I will scrupulously attempt not to conceal this possibility or beg any questions against it.

[7] 326 lines, and perhaps one or two distichs more, constitute **C1**, while 320 lines, and almost certainly a few distichs more, constitute **C2**.

[8] Even this division, as we will see, is anticipated by Höschele (2009).

The crucial move is the bracketing of **Ax**.[9] The case for the ill-fitting heterogeneity of these poems is powerful in its own right, as my predecessors' studies have shown, and as I will further explore;[10] what is new here is primarily the synoptic investigation of the rest of the corpus, once these poems are bracketed. My most extraordinary claim about Catullan arrangement, I think, is not that the poet composed single-volume works that are as structurally neat (taken individually) and as tightly coherent and mutually illuminating (taken together) as the works of his Augustan successors often are. Rather, it is that we Catullans need only look at a leading variant of our own best account to see it: as soon as we inspect the corpus as a whole from the assumption that poems 52–60 are *definitely* distinct and problematic and *might well* be completely out of place as transmitted, we see that a clear, simple, and pervasive global design ranges over the remaining 97 percent of the text.

That is, the elegiac book **C** constitutes a chiastic responsion to **A** and **B**; **C1** answers to the latter and **C2** to the former, giving the triptych the effective form **A**, **B**, (**B′** + **A′**). Locating the close of the lyric book at poem 51 rather than 60, striking parallelisms abound.[11] The openings and closes of all three books conduct a rich intratextual dialogue; in particular, the end of **A** (poem 50, an epistle on poetic composition and gift-exchange, followed by 51, the translation of Sappho, a key model-text for the book) is mimed *both* by the beginning of **C** (the epistolary 65, followed by the Callimachean translation of 66) and by its end (116, which *refuses* a translated Callimachean poem 117).

Meanwhile, the respective halves of **C2** closely reprise the content and thematic movement of the respective halves of **A**; where studies of Catullan arrangement have fretted over the looser thematic arrangement later on in each collection of short poems, I point out that the structure of each, a thematically tighter first half followed by a looser second half, itself constitutes a pattern.[12] If a pattern of this sort is felt to be a plausible authorial design, but not elaborate enough to rule out nonauthorial recension or chance as explanations, I point out that it is accurate and

---

[9] Throughout this work I use "bracket[ing]" as a mild term of art for what I urge be done with these poems, the genus, as it were, of which the "exclusion" of these poems (from the three-book collection), and their "inclusion as separate part" (of the **A** book) are the species.

[10] Segal (1968b) 307 n. 1, Skinner (1981) 80–92, Hubbard (1983) 220–22 and (2005) 260–62, 269; cf. Richter (1881), Kroll (1924) x, Barwick (1928) 80, Heck (1951) 56 n.1, Clausen (1976) 37–41.

[11] If **Ax** is excluded, of course, poem 51 becomes the last in its line without qualification. But even on the retention of **Ax** as *corpus separatum*, it remains a core element of my thesis that poem 51 recognizably functions as a closural moment, at least for the run of poems beginning with poem 27, and preferably for "the lyric book proper" or some such characterization.

[12] While I do not say that the second halves are merely negative unities, miscellanies marked off by their exclusion from the narrative and other coherences of the first halves, such an account is clearly *possible*, and its possibility is clearly in my favor.

hardly tendentious to describe either **A** or **C2** in the following way: a tighter half focused on Lesbia and on Catullus' erotic rivals, followed by a looser half introduced by political invective, featuring the belated return of Lesbia with a plot of her reconciliation with Catullus, and ending with a drama of poem-translation and gift-exchange. Our Catullan text contains two such poem collections; this, I claim, is patently pattern-like, and hardly the sort of thing we would expect to arise by accident.

Closure at 51 also produces a remarkable correspondence in poem-count. I am rhetorically careful on this score, thinking the case sufficiently persuasive even without this point, on which reasonable people reasonably disagree. Given, however, the orthodox but contested judgments about poem-division I adopt (and share with Mynors' Oxford text and other editions), the number of poems in each half of **A** and **C2** is identical, each internal unity is pentadic in sum, and their collective sum is handsomely round: (15 + 10) + 25 and 25 + 25, for a neat century of Catullan short poems.[13] If this is correct, the well-attested tendency for pentadic and decadic multiples of poems in Augustan poetry books can be backdated to the late Republic and to our earliest extant and intact books of Latin poems.[14] Even for critics who disagree on one or both of the closely contested cases (poems 2/2b and 95/95b), another notable Augustan book feature, the medial break or division, is likewise found in Catullus. There is a clear formal disjunction between poems 26 and 27, and it is widely agreed that the latter programmatically marks a new beginning; on either view of poem(s) 2/2b, poem 27 falls at the middle of 1–51 by poem-count.[15] On the majority view that poem 27 is introductory and programmatic, it is also a "proem in the middle."[16]

Finally and briefly, there remains the question of **B**. I concede from the outset that the burden of proof for these poems' artistic unity is greater than is the case for **A** and **C**: the strictly independent physical realization of each of these poems remains a plausible alternative, and one which has yet to be adequately refuted.[17] Abundant new evidence and argument,

---

[13] Where this claim fits in the persuasive structure of my argument will be spelled out in its turn. In short, it is indeed important, but anyone who argues that the unification of poem 2b with 2 disproves this thesis has not understood it; the same goes for arguments that poem 2/2b unification disqualifies matching poem-counts as evidence of Catullan design.

[14] Port (1926) 456, Skutsch (1963), Griffiths (2002) 67–68. For doubts on this phenomenon, see Heyworth (2012) 221–22.

[15] It is the twenty-fifth of forty-nine or twenty-sixth of fifty poems.

[16] The programmatic reading of poem 27 was first put by Wiseman (1969) 7–8, and has been widely endorsed: Cairns (1975), Skinner (1981) 27–28, Holzberg (2002) 43–45, Gutzwiller (2012) 99. On "proems in the middle," see Conte (1992).

[17] The case for their independent circulation and against their status as a book is elegantly stated by Hutchinson (2003) 210–11.

however, can be presented in its favor. First, the beginning of its first poem, 61, and end of its last, 64, participate fully in the intratextual dialogue conducted by the terminal points of **A** and **C**. Meanwhile, the longer elegiac poems of **C1** not only respond globally to the four long poems of **B**, but do so in ways that resonate with its transmitted sequence. So too do I unearth a provocative case for seeing the poems of **B** foreshadowed, in sequence, in **A**. Finally, the nuptial theme of **B** is anticipated in an authorial **A** ending with poem 51: its Sapphic translation not only looks back on the short and erotic lyrics of **A**, acknowledging Sappho as their preeminent generic model, but also forward to the wedding song – in which genre she is even more preeminent – found in **B**.

Dramas of Composition

Thus my account of Catullus' books. Casting a global eye on the poems so arranged, one sees that a striking metapoetic feature is repeatedly found at terminal and transitional moments in the corpus. Poems 1 (opening **A**), 14 (at the hinge within the first half of **A**), 50 (twinned with 51, closing **A**), 65 (opening **C**), 68a and 68b (and notably its end, at the seam between **C1** and **C2**), and 116 (closing **C**) all feature the Catullan speaker representing and commenting on the artistic intention, conception, creation, textualization, and dedication of the Catullan poems themselves. These are my titular dramas of composition.[18] I argue that these dramas are of signal importance for understanding the poems in that they repeatedly actualize their intrinsic potential to enhance and transform the meaning of the compositions they depict and comment on.

In his seminal 2001 study, David Wray brilliantly put forth the influential but controversial case that poem 50 is a letter of dedication not (only) of *itself*, but (also) of poem 51;[19] depending on how one sees various details, this reframing potentially authorizes a vertiginous shift in one's understanding of that poem and its place in both the Lesbia plot in particular and the poems in general. At first glance, poem 50 appears to be little more than a light vignette, a frivolous occasional piece: "yesterday's" eroticized poetic play between

---

[18] The only clear example not at a transitional space is poem 35, whose importance to this study we will see. A broader characterization would include the poet's reply to his critics in poem 16, poems that dramatize Catullus' reading of *other* authors (22, 44), the drama of convivial poem-performance I read in 27, and poems that merely threaten future verse (e.g. 12 and 40). Reasonable criteria differing from my own are possible, and it suffices to say that the texts I call dramas of composition share certain metapoetically interesting characteristics; I need not and do not claim that any strict set of features defines them as a class.

[19] Wray (2001) 91–99, quietly anticipated by Lavency (1965).

Catullus and his poet-friend Licinius Calvus, followed by a sleepless night and quasi-medical symptoms of erotic longing, then by "today's" composition of "this poem," intended to show Calvus the depth of Catullus' *dolor*. Poem 51, by contrast, conveys the pain of Catullus' absence from Lesbia and the erotic symptoms he experiences in her presence. These we believe in – and respond to sympathetically. But if poem 51 is the referent of "this poem" in 50, and if the pain it brings to light is the erotic longing for Calvus which few would take at face value, does the pain of Catullus' separation from Lesbia in 51 (and potentially elsewhere) lose *its* claim to be taken seriously? Is the meaning of "Lesbia" in this poem (and potentially in all the poems) now subordinated to the homosocial world of Catullan friendship, which we now see aright, as the predominant focus of the poet's interest? And if so, can we countenance that result? Regardless of whether we can comfortably live with it ourselves – on this question I am of those who think our interpretive comfort is irrelevant at best – can we plausibly ascribe it to Catullus?

There are separate questions here, mutually imbricated but distinct. Poem 50 is a drama of composition – but of *which* composition(s)? Certainly, of "yesterday's" improvised polymetric scribblings (whether or not any historical correlate to these existed), and of poem 50 (which plainly does exist). For Wray and others, including me, poem 50 also dramatizes the composition of 51.[20] If that is so, it potentially comments on and alters the other Lesbia poems as well. But what, then, does poem 50 say about the compositions it dramatizes? How does the drama read? From the point of view of poem 51 – and anyone invested in a given understanding of that poem, by itself and on its own – this question is a troubling one. For there is a sense, if not necessarily a totalizing one, in which poem 51 becomes helpless in respect to 50, just as soon as we see 50 pointing down or right on the papyrus roll, gazing at *ille mi par esse*, and saying *hoc*.

To be clear, this is not to deny that a flatly unthinkable reading clearly foisted on a given poem by a given drama of composition would rule out the deictic reference on which it is predicated. On the contrary, opponents of taking "this poem" at 50.16 as 51 on the grounds of its reframing of 51 (and Lesbia) are on my view correct in their assessment of the power of the framing deictic, and they would be right to try to dig in here if they were right that it ruins 51 (and Lesbia). Nor am I claiming that the reframing of poem 51 by 50 interpretively nullifies anything in 51 found

---

[20] The improvised verses were composed "yesterday" (50.1–6), and "this poem" the next day (50.14–17); if 51 is "this poem," 50 was written after it as its cover-letter.

to be incompatible with this reframing. As we will see, this is far from my view. Rather, the point is that 51 loses control over itself once another poem claims the power to speak of it and for it; like the Catullan bride with a one-third voting share in respect to her own maidenhood (62.62–64), it must now negotiate for its own identity, and not from a position of strength.

Nonetheless, the case for seeing this deixis will be the better the more the indicated poem 51 bears it not only as a yoke to poem 50's metapoetic plow, but also as an arboreal prop for its own metapoetic vine. The more interesting, illuminating, and exciting poem 51 becomes, *as* pointed to by 50, the greater our confidence that it *is* pointed to by 50.

In short: what Wray did for the metapoetry of poems 50–51 I mean to do for the metapoetry of the dramas of composition in general, and to do again and differently for 50–51; what he did in revising the deictic referent of poem 50 I mean to do for two other compositional indexicals in Catullus, namely those in poems 14 and 65. From these works we reap rich and comprehensive results. Specifically, a powerful account of how the different parts of the corpus interact and are mutually enhanced is brought to light.

The following table summarizes the picture:

Drama of composition	Referent	Metapoetic characterization
poem 1: dedication to Cornelius Nepos	itself and 2–14 directly, 14b–51 by extension	charming, novel verse
14: epistle to Calvus after Calvus' Saturnalia gift of a poetry book to Catullus	itself and 14b–26	14b–26 as "horrid" invective inversion of 1–14, jocular "revenge" against Calvus
35: Catullus' address to epistolary papyrus, on Caecilius and a drafted poem about Cybele	itself and 63	more ambitious future work now in draft, the work in progress of the represented Catullus
50: Catullus' eroticized longing for Calvus "yesterday," after their eroticized poetic play	itself and 51, the lyric Lesbia by extension	the reality of her extratextual correlate makes writing Lesbia painful
65: Catullus, cut off from the Muses by his brother's death, sends translated Callimachean verse to Ortalus	itself and 66–67 directly, 68–116 by extension	66 and 67 composed before brother's death and for another purpose, now repurposed as gift-poems to Ortalus; all future poems to be tinged by grief

(cont.)

Drama of composition	Referent	Metapoetic characterization
68a: Catullus unable to fulfill Mallius' request for love (and) poetry	itself, its correspondent's prior epistle, the gift-poem it does *not* introduce	68a the unpoetic product of Catullus' grief-stricken poetic incapacity
68b: (the textualization of) Catullus' eventual fulfillment of Mallius' request	itself, 69–116 by extension	*inter alia* (!): poetic content explained by and inseparable from the poet's subjective reading of his life circumstances
116: Catullus had thought to conciliate Gellius with Callimachean verse, now promises invective	itself; 74, 78, 80, 88–91? Future poems?	high-minded intentions and high-genre poetry rejected in favor of low-register invective

Some of these characterizations are Catullan orthodoxy, some less so but familiar in the literature, and others are innovative. The metapoetry of *lepidum nouum libellum* and the like in poem 1 is no novelty.[21] Also familiar is the story that 1–14 and 14b–26 mirror each other;[22] new to these pages is the claim that the poems with which Catullus threatens Calvus at the end of 1–14 just are the upcoming 14b–26. As we will see, the explanatory power and transformational potential of this proposal are considerable. The claim that poem 35 refers not to Caecilius' poem on Cybele but to poem 63, Catullus' own work-in-progress on the goddess, was first put by Giuseppe Biondi (1998), and has been taken up and endorsed by Hunink (2000); for my project of integrating the first-person Catullus with the less personal poems,[23] the importance of Biondi's thesis will be obvious.

My reading of the metapoetics of poem 51 is also new, and its details can be only partially anticipated now; what does bear notice at this point is the presence of Catullus' poet-friend Calvus both at 14, the internal hinge of the first half of **A**, and at its close, the twinned 50–51. Both times,

---

[21] The tradition goes back as far as Baehrens (1885) 66; more recent discussions include Syndikus (1984) 71–72, Batstone (1998), and Feeney (2012) 34–36.

[22] Stroh (1990), Beck (1996).

[23] As we will see, which poems count as less personal and how impersonal each one is are far from self-evident. At this stage it is important to note that they are by no means coextensive with **B** and **C1**, the so-called *carmina maiora*. Poems 62–64 and 66 are surely among the "least personal" Catullan poems, but so are 34 and arguably 45; 65, 68a, and 68b are as fully personal as any of the poems; for different reasons, 61 and 67 pose serious difficulties in this respect.

I find questions about the accuracy (or perhaps "historicity," "reliability," or "truth") of Catullus' self-disclosed "personal information" focalized. In the transitional poem 14, it is the patent jocular unreality of his conceit (that Calvus "tried to kill" him with poetry) that grounds the equivalent metapoetic characterization of its promised verses, 14b–26. At book-end in poems 50 and 51, our knowledge that Calvus (as an internal reader) knows precisely how much lived reality underlies its Catullus/Calvus vignette, and the implausibility of supposing there is no such correspondence, guides our Calvus' interpretation of Catullus' longing and grief over the absence of his love(s).

It is again impractical to anticipate much of the argument for poem 65 here. The most crucial element, that poem 65 characterizes 66–67 as composed before the brother's death, is tied to a reading of the maiden-and-apple simile which concludes the poem. A second key point is the inclusion of poem 67 with 66, as the fulfillment of Ortalus' request. The crucial ground here was broken by Regina Höschele's (2009) demonstration that poem 67 stages a bourgeois Transpadane adaptation of the royal North African backstory to poem 66; given this twinning of the two poems, the initial presumption of a plurality of gift-poems in the dedicatory poem (*haec expressa tibi carmina Battiadae*, 65.16), and the presence of adaptively "expressed" and even literally translated Callimachean elements in 67, I argue that Ortalus receives both poems. Here too Catullus' specular art is brought into a fuller light, comparing the close of his lyric book (50–51) with the opening of his elegiac one (65–67): the programmatic translations proper (51, 66) are both juxtaposed with looser, Romanizing adaptations (50, 67), both featuring differing sorts of gender-inversion from the Greek model-text to both the Latin translation and the Latin adaptation. Remarkably, we also find that in both cases, elements of the Greek text left pointedly untranslated in the translation proper turn up instead in the looser adaptation.

The metapoetics of 68a and 68b (separate poems on my view, with the latter presenting itself as composed some time after the former) are again too complex to sketch out here, and I should make clear that the centrality of these poems to my thesis arises from many factors, some far removed from their status as dramas of composition. In terms of integrating the three-book corpus into an emergent synthesis, two of my claims are most important. On one of these, Catullus' dubious love- and grief-stricken reasoning at the end of 68b explains the emotional savagery to come in **C2**; what Catullus sees as his casual betrayal by Lesbia (beginning in poems 71 and 72) can only devastate him, as now, with his brother dead, he reckons her essentially his sole reason to live (68.135–48, 159–60). On the other claim, the recipient and dedicatee of 68a and 68b (following a long tradition,[24] I take *Allius* in the latter as pseudonymous for *Mallius* in the former) is identical with one of the honorands of poem 61, the bridegroom Manlius Torquatus.[25] On this identification, the specular pair of **B** and **C1** (the so-called *carmina maiora* of earlier scholarship) begins and ends in the same place and almost the same way: with a narrative of a godlike woman's (pseudo-) nuptial entrance, and her embrace of her waiting husband or lover, both times in the same man's house. Once again, the integrative benefit of assimilating poem 61 into the narrative backstory of 68a and 68b, just as poem 63 is assimilated into the drama of composition of poem 35, will be readily apparent. Moreover, the traditional question of whether the contents of the long, impersonal poetry should be read as conditioned by the experiences and subjectivity of the personal-poem Catullus is answered, affirmatively. The first-person Catullus of the composition dramas just tells us so at 65, 68a, 68b.

Finally, Catullus' elegiac book ends with 116 as it began, with a change in poetic plan involving Callimachean verse. I find myself unable to pronounce definitively whether the promised retaliatory invective against Gellius refers back to his earlier appearances in **C2**, forward to a planned work which has not survived, or both;[26] in any case, the mention of Callimachean *carmina* constitutes an elevated, high-genre foil for the lower-register invective with which its addressee is threatened.

Construals and Credence

A signal feature of the dramas of composition is their partially self-defeating staging of the realities putatively external to them. That is to say, while texts like poem 50 ostentatiously lift the authorial curtain, affording us a view of a Roman poet in his study writing *this* poem for *this* reason, only the most naive readers could fail to see the further authorial curtain behind *him*. In one sense, to begin or end a book of

---

[24] From Palmer (1879) and Frank (1914) to Goold (1983) 257, Hubbard (1984), and Skinner (2003) 41–44.

[25] Wiseman (1974) 102–03; see also Forsyth (1987), McKie (2009). That "Mallius" is the addressee of 68a, and that the man in question is identical with Manlius Torquatus in poem 61, are defended in their turn; my practice throughout is to refer to the addressee of poem 61 (both as internal Catullan "character" and presumptive historical personage) as "Manlius" and the addressee of 68a as "Mallius."

[26] So also Gutzwiller (2012) 90 n. 37.

poems with such a gesture at extratextual reality is just to reinforce the fact of the work's artifice. We may compare the self-frustrating opening of *The Adventures of Huckleberry Finn*, whose eponymous hero there intones:

> You don't know about me without you have read a book by the name of *The Adventures of Tom Sawyer*; but that ain't no matter. That book was made by Mr. Mark Twain, and he told the truth, mainly. There was things which he stretched, but mainly he told the truth.

Yet even this assertion of partial factuality by a fictitious speaker succeeds in making contact with extratextual and historical reality: *Tom Sawyer* is a historical document whose historical author "Mr. Mark Twain," or Samuel Clemens, is. So too does a papyrus roll with the words *Corneli, tibi* (1.3) perform the historicity of its dedication of itself to a certain Cornelius. Readers' justified belief in this historical reality (further grounded by the extratextual reality of a second document, the *Chronica* of Cornelius *Nepos* alluded to at 1.5–7) now combines with their knowledge or reasonable suppositions about social practices at Rome to make the historicity of further details in the poem highly likely: Cornelius' historical ownership of the physical book it mentions as unique object, its production under Catullus' direction and at his expense, its polishing with pumice, a specific if unrecoverable day and time and place at which it was presented. The poem's prayer for the perdurance of the book and/as text (1.9–10), like the later address by the Catullan book to its *lectores* (14b), even incorporates posterity into its drama, making verifiably historical Catullan characters of us all.

Questions for us now ramify. How far does this credence of ours go? Do we believe the poem's claim that Cornelius repeatedly thought well of Catullan poetry at the time of his composition of the *Chronica* (1.2–7)? Or do we reinterpret Cornelius' positive thought as historical acts of commendation, by which our aspiring young poet came to the notice of the right literary people? Do we credit the sincerity of the poet's respective characterizations of his own "trifling" and his dedicatee's "learned and laborious" work? Or do we, similarly, reinterpret this sincerity by taking less literally the manner of its expression?

Having read his dedication and the sparrow poems 2 and 3 (which themselves represent implausible human behavior in respect to a dubiously historical sparrow, inviting coded readings of the same without ruling out that the erotic content they somehow encode might have historical correlates), Cornelius Nepos, on my case for the poems' arrangement, will have come to our poem 4. *Phaselus ille, quem uidetis, hospites | ait* (4.1–2): the poet's (credibly) represented guests are (credibly) visually adverted by the poet-host to a yacht, whose asserted speech, instantly self-discrediting of course on a literal reading, is then conveyed in *oratio obliqua*. Still, just as with Twain's fictional overture, the speech conveys putative biographical information about the author which is hard to resist: the journey of yacht and master from Bithynia to Italy seems as reliably biographical as anything in the poems,[27] and the specific itinerary checks out.

Or does it? If we are authorized to read back from poem 31, the dramatic setting of poem 4 is Catullus' villa at Sirmio on Lake Garda/Benacus; on this inference, the previously credible itinerary of a fictional speaker ends dubiously, with the yacht making its way up first the Po, then the Mincius. As scholarship on the poem has repeatedly seen, this claim deeply taxes our credence.[28]

Options, at this point, are multiple. A simple solution is merely to transfer the yacht's claims to Catullus, reducing the yacht's speech to merely a witty conceit. Another is to notice that we also disbelieve that the yacht is literally the fastest of ships (4.2), that Catullus owned the *Millennium Falcon* of the old Roman Republic: if we know the yacht is an exaggerating braggart, spot its delusional comparison of its pedigree with that of the *Argo*,[29] and stress *ait fuisse* (4.2: "it *says* it was . . . "), the yacht might know the itinerary Catullus took, and falsely claim to be the vessel he took it on. Still another solution is to argue that the yacht is not a yacht at all; perhaps the noun in *erum tulisse* ("carried its master," 4.19) is actually a subject accusative ("its master carried it"), and the yacht is a miniature, the model boat which Catullus brought back to Italy, rather than the real boat which brought him back from there.[30] The opening line of the poem, then, would set us readers off in counterpoint to the internal interpreters of the poem, the imagined guests whose privileged sight of the object in question grants them unmediated access to the problem we must solve – if we can – by clever reading.

---

[27] At least, anything which is not self-validating *qua* performative.

[28] On this traditional problem, see Copley (1958) and Kroll (1968) 8–9. Even if such a route was possible – or if a costly overland hauling can be imagined – it seems like a deeply unmotivated and implausible thing actually to do.

[29] Khan (1967).

[30] As originally discussed by Lenchantin De Gubernatis (1928) 9, and revived by Griffith (1983). Feeney's (2012) 33 summary of the mimetic layering here is not to be missed: "if we are being invited to 'see' a model, the representation the poem is offering us would be a presentation of a self-presentation of a representation of a real object."

Answering this sort of Catullan question is in principle beyond this work's remit, and I do not assert that this particular solution is correct; I do think it mostly fits and has considerable attractions. Nor, for that matter, is this the place to say what the sparrow in poems 2 and 3 is or represents.[31] The point, rather, is that not only those critics who endorse allegorical or otherwise coded readings of *passer* and *phaselus*, but also any who seriously entertain these possibilities, have reasons to see in poems 1–4 a repeated and even insistent dialectic between factual and fictitious elements on the one hand, and face-value or coded readings on the other. At face value, every location on our spectrum of credence (certain–likely–possible–unlikely–impossible) is already occupied by Catullan claims;[32] whether we should take a given claim at face value is inseparable from where on this spectrum we take it to lie. The falsity of the statement "the yacht says" on a face-value reading opens up and points to other strategies of reading; at least on one possible solution (that the yacht bears a dedicatory epigram, which the speaker paraphrases),[33] the claim will bend back around and turn out all but true (within the poem's conceit), and even historically credible (why couldn't a yacht with such an epigram have been docked at Sirmio?). And then, what look like all of the most important apparent facts of Catullus' biography in the short lyric poems (that he is a poet in 1, his love for a *puella* in 2 and 3, his Bithynian journey in 4) are introduced in these putatively introductory poems; only the first of these – the one we knew anyway – is found in a text for which a simultaneously factual and face-value reading is even thinkable.

The thinkable factual reading of poem 1, however, is far more than that; as we have seen, much of it is unthinkable to deny, and it seems to me that anyone wishing (for example) to find coded criticism of Nepos in the flattery of poem 1 is accordingly paddling against a strong current of presumption. Catullus the poet, meanwhile, is not *only* a framing device, a figure who disappears within the book. Here Twain's example is contrastive: his novelistic *sphragis* at the beginning points to a historical composition by a historical author, but his fictional speaker Huck

---

[31] See Gaisser (2007) 307–40 for a collection of texts "debating the sparrow," starting with Poliziano. I will take up this issue at the end of this work, after the core arguments have been made.

[32] Ranging from the certainty that Catullus gives a book to one Cornelius, and the likelihood that the latter commended Catullus' work, to the possibility of real correlates of the *puella* and *phaselus*, the unlikeliness of the yacht's upstream voyage, and the impossibility of its speaking Greek-accented Latin.

[33] Courtney (1996).

underlines the fictional nature of its content exactly in his denying it; in Catullus the speaker who successfully vouches for extratextual realities from the outset is called *Catullus* and repeatedly appears under this guise and description, as a poet. The historical truth-telling he does here at the beginning, then, is something he may do again, and habitually do; we have positive warrant to expect so, and none to presume otherwise.

The inference I draw is the assumption I will make throughout the work: the poems display and play on the inextricability of their interpretive modes from the reliability or reality of their claims. They usefully signal that the question matters, but the evidence declines to point in any single direction. This tension is never dropped or resolved. The poems certainly contain and address indisputably historical figures, sometimes in presumptively reliable ways: in the Rome of the mid-50s BCE, to take an important example, the prima facie likelihood that a vicious attack on Julius Caesar reflects genuine sentiment (or at least a real partisan affiliation) is high. Yet some addressees come off as almost certainly fictitious (e.g. the lovers Acme and Septimius in poem 45, and Ipsitilla, the prostitute addressed in poem 32); others are at least suspicious. In one clear index of fictionalization, there are pairs of addressees who are almost entirely Tweedledummed and Tweedledee-ified.[34] Catullus' friend Veranius has but the slightest existence apart from their mutual friend Fabullus – and even that is all but exhausted by the stylized mirror of Catullus' anticipated social reception by the former *chez lui* (poem 9) and of the latter *chez soi* (13). The two friends, we are (not) asked to believe, even contributed jointly in gifting Catullus with the napkins stolen by Asinius (poem 12). My guess, then, is that at least one of these men is at least mostly a fiction. As to their poetic function, I offer an unprovable proposal; it will be the more attractive the more one agrees that the fact/fiction dialectic is the poems' own focalized problem. Perhaps, that is, they are *redende Namen*, interpretively pregnant names, figuratively signifying the opposed generative principles of the poems' world: Veranius and Fabullus as Rosen<u>fact</u> and Guilden<u>fiction</u>.[35]

This may be unprovable fancy; the poems, in any case, are riddled with fictions, lies, and especially jocular insincerity or bullshit.[36] To exemplify

---

[34] Veranius and Fabullus (9, 12, 13, 28, 47), Furius and Aurelius (11, 15, 16, 21, 23, 24, 26), and the paired rivals in **C2**, Rufus (69, 71, 73?, 77) and Gellius (75, 78?, 80, 88–91, 116) – though the final two are more sharply distinguished. To be sure, the *treatment* of characters as intrinsic pairs lacking individual identities does not prove that no historical persons underlie them, but it does point away from realism.

[35] Fabullus, indeed, cannot be linked to any historical personage (Neudling (1955) 65–66).

[36] For "bullshit" in this sense, see the celebrated philosophical analysis of Frankfurt (2005).

all of these, consider the matter of Catullus' finances. His equestrian family maintains at least four residences: the family home in Verona and Catullus' place in Rome (poem 68a), the "Tiburtine or Sabine" *suburbanum* (44), and an enviably situated villa overlooking the Garda Lake, at Sirmio (31). On a face-value reading of poem 4 he will have purchased the *phaselus* which brought him back to Italy – and will have also needed to hire (or own) and feed its crew. Yet he is too poor to provision up for a dinner guest (poem 13), and he lies shamelessly about his purchase of a litter and a team of slaves to save financial face before his friend Varus' girlfriend, who cleverly exposes the lie (10).

Which is it: is Catullus rich or poor? Does the answer matter, and if so, how does it matter? On the former question, the answer is clear: in fact he is rich.[37] On the latter, in arguing that Catullan poetry adverts to and makes use of its own unreliabilities, it helps me considerably that Catullus tells us he is a liar in respect to his wealth (his parenthetical motivation for the lie is given at 10.16–17, the parenthetical fact at 21–23). An opponent, of course, can plausibly resist assigning deeper significance to this fact: not every instance in which a speaker confesses to a lie will be a global index of irony, even in poetry. In this case, however, to read poem 10 with the explicit understanding that Catullus is actually rich is to see that Catullus' lie to Varus and the girlfriend is bound up inextricably with a lie to *us*, his poetic audience or readership: it is the revelation of Catullus' poverty in poem 10 we now see to be false, at least as false as the represented Catullus' self-presentation (to Varus' girlfriend) as wealthy. Poem 10 is a rich man's anecdote about pretending to be rich to impress a woman, who turns out to be too clever to fall for it. How clever are *we*? If we neglect to audit Catullus' financial statement here, to ask whether what he is telling us is true, we fail the test she passes.[38]

Do we laugh with or at Catullus in this poem? Does the *scortum* reveal herself to be witless, as Catullus says (*insulsa*, 10.33), or just the opposite? These are traditional interpretive questions about poem 10 – and will remain good ones on my reading. But thinking through this poem after catching Catullus in his lie about lying also warrants our meta-laughter at

---

[37] Stroup (2010) 47–48, following Wiseman (1982) 39. For readers who resist (as I would) taking the historical wealth of the Valerii Catulli of Verona to settle the literary question, that is, render "Catullus is rich" a sound premise in a literary argument, the reality of the estates mentioned within the poems should itself suffice to do so. In any case, Catullus' aristocratic self-possession or *libertas* and his access to the social elite are also realities within the poems, and are themselves questionably compatible with the poet's alleged penury.

[38] As we will see, poem 10 is marked in its surroundings by its lack of an addressee. Catullus' direct speech addresses the girlfriend, but the narrative frame directs itself to no one but its readers.

whatever first-order laughter the poem elicits. This higher laughter is decisively *with* the poet – and can only be *at* readers more credulous than we happy few. As soon as we catch sight of this we are seated on a privileged interpretive perch, facing the godlike poet as he laughs sweetly and congratulates our critical acumen.

At this point, the purpose of this example is just that: exemplary. The interplay between the question of what Catullus is saying and the question of whether we believe him will be repeatedly examined, and I will claim that this examination pays off repeatedly and in multiple ways. One of its chief benefits is that it clearly attests the existence of Catullan texts we would be remiss not to read, in various ways, against themselves, and in a way that either answers or justifiably sidesteps pressing contemporary concerns about self-subversion, literary persona, and the like.

Such reading strategies, of course, are hardly novel, either in Latin studies in general or Catullus in particular. On both levels, however, voices of reservation or opposition have been powerfully raised; on current standing, such arguments deserve either to be answered or acceded to. Clay (1998) and Mayer (2003) point to the lack of a clear ancient correlate to our concept of the literary persona, that modern universal solvent for unwanted consequences of *sensus litteralis* readings. Du Quesnay and Woodman, in the piece excerpted atop this Introduction, add positive evidence that ancient readers took the poets to be reliably speaking of and conveying information about themselves in their first-person reports (and their example is of a maximally sophisticated ancient reader, Cicero, at that).[39] For Catullus in particular, Wray's work presents a richly detailed and well-supported case for *not* subverting away the meaning of what is probably the perennial leading candidate for such treatment, namely its frequent aggressive content and its menacing, hypermasculine pose.

It is on this point that my results are conspicuously different from and often incompatible with Wray's. The book reconstruction, in bracketing (perhaps the most aggressive) poems 52–60, begins by considerably lowering both the quantity and intensity of aggression in the three-book global design. Next, the claim that the metapoetic deixis of poem 14 points to 14b–26, combined with the metapoetic significance I claim for our disbelief in the sincerity of the conceit of poem 14, undermines and subverts the

---

[39] Du Quesnay and Woodman (2012b) 272. Earlier studies that take Catullus' autobiographical references at face value include Lindsay's (1948) reconstruction of the Catullan biography, and Rothstein's (1923) and Maas' (1942) reordering of the poems based on biographical "sense."

aggressiveness of 14b–26, another conspicuously aggressive run of poems.[40] My arguments for these subversions, I claim, rely on less vulnerable assumptions than traditional appeals to persona theory do and are compatible with a default assumption (whether this is justified or not, I need not and do not say) that Roman poets mean what they say about themselves – whatever that means – unless they give overriding reasons to suppose otherwise. My Catullus does indeed mean what he says, or so I hear him sometimes claiming, but he is also a serial practitioner of deliberately ill-concealed jocular insincerity: in Frankfurtian terms, he is a bullshit artist. Much of the space for the oblique and ironized interpretations I offer is opened up by appealing to this feature of his art.

Narrative Time and Poem Sequence

Here too my thesis about the Catullan books conduces to hearing further voices in the poems, sometimes subversively and sometimes with ethically pregnant implications, over and above the voices and agenda of the poems taken individually. It is easy to see how this could arise, and unsurprising that it does: if the poems are authorially arranged and if a dramatized temporal ordering can be won from them, the various perspectives of the represented Catullus at any given moment will take on new and richer meanings in the light of our access to the ensemble of his temporal perspectives. To give what may be the simplest possible example, Catullus may sincerely think and say opposing things at different times; the ensemble of the poems and the ensemble of their narratives might then enable us to consider why and how we could judge him to have been "right" at one moment and "mistaken" at the other.

What I take to be a clear example of this phenomenon occurs early in our collection. Usefully, it can be convincingly claimed without appeal to authorial poem-arrangement at all, in that it occurs within a single poem. In poem 8, that is, we discover that there has been a rupture in the affair with Lesbia; the poem is a soliloquy in which Catullus clearly vacillates, giving us grounds to suspect the chronic irresolution of his attitude toward his lover, as will later be amply confirmed. His self-suasion to reject Lesbia

---

[40] To be sure, I neither can nor would wish to write the hypermasculinity out of Catullus; if there is a partial sanitizing of Catullus (relative to the mores of our social world) which these arguments bring about, it is only partial and accidental. I do not see Catullus as a "nice man" (Wray (2001) 113), and I agree that a nice Catullus has been seen far too often, and for self-discrediting reasons. Still, my Catullus holds himself more aloof from what many see as his most ethically troubling material than has been realized, and I try to bring this result to light *sine ira et studio*.

in return (8.1–11) ends with the advice to be resolute, firm (*obdura*); Catullus then dismisses Lesbia, or rather imagines himself dismissing her, leading off with a report of his resolution (*uale, puella. iam Catullus obdurat*, 8.12). As his (imagined) address to her continues, though, the fact of Catullus' ongoing irresolution asserts itself; by the end, he must repeat his self-suasion to be resolute (*at tu, Catulle, destinatus obdura*, 8.19).

Poem 8 is not a simple text, and the likely complexity of its ironies should not be elided. My initial point is just this: if Catullus sincerely believes in the resolution he reports (*obdurat*) at the moment of reporting it, he can be "right" in only the most attenuated, fleeting sense, and is "wrong" in any deeper sense. A few moments later, every competent reader knows this, and Catullus probably knows it, too. The conclusion is quite immediate: this alone suffices to show that there are what one typically calls ironies in Catullus, moments in which we find gaping distances between what the text says and what we understand, and the passage of time is a generator of these gaps.[41] Before settling or even asking the hard questions about persona and the like mentioned earlier, it is quite impossible to think through time in this poem (and elsewhere) without conceding that some justification for ironic reading strategies – or some functional equivalent thereof – will have to be granted, if the poems are to be read at all.

To broaden our focus now to the spaces between individual poems, their temporal sequence is of course another traditional Catullan problem, on which any determinate theory of their circulation ought to shed light. The twin theses of book-end with poem 51 and the metapoetic reframing of that poem by poem 50 take on a surprisingly crucial role here as well. The traditional nostrum that the narrative sequence of the Lesbia story (to the extent it exists and can be reconstructed) runs discordantly from the sequence of the poems is deeply undermined by these claims. If poem 51 depicts an initial moment in the story – as is traditionally thought, and as I think it clearly does – its reframing by poem 50 provides its own temporal frame (purporting its composition and dedication the "day after" Catullus' poetry session with Calvus). The two moments need not coincide; the "day after" Catullus of poems 50 and 51 can recall "yesterday" in composing poem 50 and the more remote past time of his initial love for Lesbia in composing poem 51.

Once that possibility is conceded, the sequentiality of the Lesbia plot in **A** becomes far more compelling. The signs of the temporal sequencing of

---

[41] To avoid the temporally later falsification of 8.12 by 8.19, 8.12 must already be undermined or read obliquely or ironized *vel sim.*

the affair in poems 1–14 are obvious and overwhelming; when next we meet her in poem 36, there is talk of a reconciliation, thus obviously presupposing the rupture of their love – just as the initial sequence left us with its rupture (poem 11). The temporal relation between the Lesbia of poem 36 and that of poem 37 is not obvious, but nothing prevents and much recommends taking the latter poem's invective to follow from the failure of the reconciliation (if ever it was to be taken as real) in the former. Then, with a book-final poem 51 and the bracketing of 52–60, we are relieved from needing to invent a motivation for the shift in Catullus' attitude toward Lesbia, from the loving longing of 51 to the bitter accusation of al fresco promiscuity in 58 (and possibly her inhuman hard-heartedness in 60, if she is its unnamed addressee). With that, then, all serious objections to taking the Lesbia plot in **A** as sequential dissolve,[42] while the indisputable grounds for taking at least most of it as sequential remain.

This particular result is anticipated here for its exemplary value. I find that temporal sequencing in fact obtains over the first-person and social poetry of **A** and **C** both internally and in relation to each other; that **B** is looked forward to in **A** and back on in **C**, that poems 65, 68a, and 68b further ratify the priority of **A** and **B** via their metapoetic assertion that future Catullan poems will now *always* be colored by grief for the brother (65) and by their backward glance (in 68a and 68b) at earlier erotic verse, along with the indication in poem 65 that poems 66 and 67 (which Catullus in his grief "should not be able to compose") had been composed earlier and for a purpose different from the gift-poems they now become. As in poem 51, the Lesbia drama of 68b also has a later temporal frame, uncontroversially so this time: the grief-stricken Catullus is "now" recalling his earlier lovemaking with Lesbia, on an occasion which will have preceded the brother's death (per 68.16–20). Catullus' resolution at the end of 68b then prepares the ground for the Lesbia story in **C2** – whose own sequentiality is, again, effortless to accept, laborious to deny.[43]

So too for other recurring characters. It is not always the case that textually later poems are verifiably later temporally, but where temporal ordering is indicated, it repeatedly tracks poem sequence. Retrojections are

---

[42] The objections I find trivial are worries about Lesbia's presence in poem 13, after the break-up of 11 (she need not be present for her *unguentum* to be given to Fabullus, and mention of this *unguentum* may well be unflattering, and so in keeping with one of the emotional registers of poem 11), and Catullus' mention of her beauty in poem 43 (that she is his *ex*-girlfriend does not negate the competitive social advantage her superior beauty affords him over Mamurra, vis-à-vis his girlfriend Ameana). These will of course be spelled out more fully in their turn.

[43] Dyson (2007) sees and shows this clearly.

few and easily explained,[44] again with the exception that the status of poem 116 remains an open question.

An important qualification: in claiming that the dramatic time of the corpus is sequential, I am making no claims for the sequentiality of the poems' historical composition, though some such correspondence is possible; still less, for any mapping of dramatic time onto an independently recoverable historical timeline. Indeed, on a rigorous and strictly literal reading, such a mapping appears to be flatly impossible.[45] If it is true that Fact-and-Fiction are collaborative co-authors of our Catullan storyline, however, this historical "impossibility" is downgraded to a mere internal "inconsistency" within an at least partially fictional narrative. It will then be a literary-historical question, whether there is any problem positing such an apparent inconsistency to a careful author like Catullus: would readers reject, or be unduly confused by, such a move? Learned readers will judge for themselves; I myself find no reason to suppose that ancient readers would even think to press the historical timeline so literally and so relentlessly.[46]

Prospectus

In principle and in brief, it is the book reconstruction aspect of this work which governs its organization. After a more detailed introductory look at

---

[44] Dedication poems are written after but textually precede the poems they dedicate. Otherwise, only the Bithynian-journey poems 31 and 46 violate sequence – but these have been preceded by three poems looking back on that journey (4, 10, 28), which superabundantly fix the retrojected dramatic times of 31 and 46 as precisely that. The variation is itself artful, and with the absence of any alternative way of taking them there is no danger of confusion.

[45] Poem 11 famously alludes to Caesar's invasion of Britain in the summer of 55 BCE; on a sequential reading, the Saturnalia mentioned in poem 14 must therefore be that of 55 at the earliest. Meanwhile, the sole clear date in the elegiac-metered poems is given by poem 113, which presents as present-tense fact Pompey's consulship . . . in 55. Even resisting the reasonable inference (per _facto consule nunc iterum_, with Thomson (1997) 350) that the dramatic date of 113 is _early_ in the year, it would be absurd for the narrated "events" of poems 15–116 to "take place" in the final days of the same December.

[46] The same assumption, namely that Catullus fictionalizes to suit his artistic ends, drives my rejection of the traditional, once-orthodox historical reconstruction of the corpus (dating from Schwabe (1862)), on which the beginning of the Lesbia affair, the death of the brother, and poem 68 at least must predate the death of Metellus Celer in 59 BCE, and therefore predate Catullus' represented Bithynian service and all of the clearly identifiable historical references, by several years at least. Even if the necessary historical assumptions had not been so thoroughly undermined by the work of Peter Wiseman in particular, readers starting from the expectation that Catullus partially fictionalizes his poetic world could never have credited the traditional reconstruction, built as it is precisely from strong assumptions about the accurate historicity of narrative events in the poems. For me, then, the dramatized "events" of the poems should all be assumed to take place in the tight mid-50s timeframe indicated by the clear evidence. Those who dissent from this conclusion, I readily concede, will take themselves to have strong grounds to resist my project _in toto_. See Skinner (2003) xix–xxii for a summary of the abundant further grounds for modern doubts on the Schwabian picture.

the Catullan arrangement problem (Prolegomenon), the matter of **Ax** is foregrounded (Chapter 1); afterwards, my exposition tracks the sequence of the corpus, beginning with **A** (Chapter 2), passing in turn through **B** and **C1** (Chapter 3), and ending with **C2** (Chapter 4). The more literary-critical and metapoetic arguments fall naturally into that structure, with the discussion of each question tied to the specific poem(s) and text(s) in which it arises. A summative look at the collection is naturally reserved for the end (Conclusion).

In greater detail: following this Introduction but preceding the first chapter is a preliminary critical glance at the Catullan corpus, the problem of its arrangement, and prevailing contemporary views thereon. Its purpose, first, is to set forth the principal formal and thematic groupings and disjunctions evident in our corpus and to indicate for each of them, with extensive bibliography but brief summaries of the relevant facts and arguments, the relative strength (and popularity) of the case for taking each to reflect authorial arrangement. Second, there are questions of method and the like to be addressed. Among these are the inference from the coherent artistic units we can directly observe to the historical books we must posit; the potential consequences of the possibility that some texts circulated in more than one authorized form; and the persuasive structure of the arguments for design which we will consider. I have kept this prolegomenon separate on behalf of readers in small need of another précis of the arrangement problem,[47] as well as those at home with a mainstream conceptual kit on questions of the poetry book. Such readers may pass quickly over this section with my compliments.

After this, and in accordance with the fundamental role which the bracketing of **Ax** plays in my global argument, Chapter 1 examines first these poems and then the remaining corpus, with these poems bracketed. The argument moves in the following stages. First, it shows the ways in which **Ax** is heterogeneous and distinct from **A**; then, it surveys various possibilities (not, for want of evidence, a single conclusive one) concerning the nature of these poems and their possible modes of circulation. Finally and most importantly, it brings to light the exuberant symmetries which the remainder of the tripartite corpus instantiates. The conclusion follows: the authorial design and arrangement of most of the corpus follows irresistibly from the exclusion of **Ax**,[48] while the separation-with-

---

[47] I refer those in need of a more intensive survey to Skinner's (2007) comprehensive account.

[48] To be precise, the claim is that the non-fortuitous global symmetry of **A** (1–51) and **C2** (69–116) follow directly from the exclusion of **Ax**, while the sequence and collective unities of **B** (61–64) and **C1** (65–68b) become highly attractive but not yet conclusive at this stage.

retention of **Ax** merely renders the acceptance of authorial design an overwhelmingly better option than its denial.

Chapter 2 turns to **A**, offering an account of its structure and metapoetics. Beginning with a discussion of the designs and principles of poem-arrangement found pervasively in the Catullan corpus, it sets out a pluralist and antireductionist account of the poems' sequence. Features such as formal and thematic alternation in consecutive poems have frequent and deep explanatory power over why *this* poem sits next to *this* one, but in general these do not conduce to a uniquely correct, hegemonic account of their placement.[49] There are usually multiple ways of persuasively bringing out the artistry behind a given instance of poem adjacency. By contrast, however, I understand my claims for internal articulation or division in Catullus' books in a much thicker, realist sense: a theorist who splits poems 1–26 in **A** between poems 11 and 12 rather than 14 and 14b is wrong on my view, as I am wrong on hers.

I then set out an account of poem-sequence for each of what I take as the three parts of **A**: poems 1–14, their jocular inversion 14b–26, and 27–51, forming a second half in respect to 1–26 taken collectively. This material is closely divided in quantity between the structural and metapoetic foci of this work, with the latter concentrated in the discussions of poems 14 and 50–51. Finally, the chapter concludes with an account of narrative time in these poems.

Chapter 3 turns to **B** and **C1**. Its first half puts the case that the poems of **B** are anticipated in **A** and recalled in **C1**, that their principal themes are coherent and develop in artistically satisfying ways, and that these units respond structurally to each other in ways analogous to the responsion between **A** and **C2**. Its second half turns its focus to **C1**. Here I argue for the dramatic belatedness of the unit relative to **A** and **B**, as signaled first by the death of the brother in poem 65; for its structural bipartition (65 introducing 66 and 67, 162 total lines; 68a *not* introducing 68b, 160 total lines); and for shifting metapoetic characterizations of its framing- and gift-poems. This long section concludes with an account of how poem 68b, the close of **C1**, ties the Lesbia plot and key textual moments in **A** together with the principal themes and textually marked passages of **B**, while also setting the scene for the poetic and narrative worlds which now follow in **C2**.

---

[49] "Hegemonic" is a tendentious term, but the position I am arguing against is no straw man: there are indeed Latin poetry books with structural principles of this sort. The standard model of the *Eclogues'* structure has it that annular patterns array poems 1 and 9, 2 and 8, 3 and 7, and 4 and 6 around the central 5th poem (as seen by Maury (1944); cf. Skutsch (1969b), Steenkamp (2011)). This model does indeed seem (to me) so clearly compelling as to crowd out and contradict alternative accounts.

A résumé of my claims about narrative or dramatic time for the ensemble of **B** and **C1** concludes the chapter.

Chapter 4 on **C2** is similarly designed. It begins with an account of how its opening manages the generic and thematic transition from **C1**, passing to a discussion of structure and narrative in the first half of **C2**, poems 69–92, followed by those of their second half, 93–116. Like the previous chapters, this one also ends with an account of narrative time in the poems in question.

Following Chapter 4, a Conclusion rounds out the work. Rather than attempting to give a systematic general account of ways in which Catullan poetry reads differently, if the core results of the work are sound, two studies are offered as (particularly far-reaching and consequential) examples thereof. The first of these argues that the Troy myth is more widely and meaningfully present in Catullus than has been understood, amounting to an Ariadnean thread for the three-book ensemble, guiding us from nearly its beginning to nearly its end and authorizing a pointedly particular universal view of the text, its poet, and their great love Lesbia. The second of the two, then, casts a final eye on Lesbia's initial textual moment, and with it on her relationship not just to Catullus' poetry, but to poetry itself.

Prolegomenon to the Catullus Problem

A Partisan Introduction

While this prolegomenon will introduce a traditional problem in Catullan scholarship, it will not be a comprehensive survey of the scholarship or a balanced account of all of its major trends and approaches.[1] Instead, it sets out what has proved to be the most fruitful way of searching for authorial design in the Catullan poems and explains the interpretive progress that has been achieved by application of this approach. Other approaches are certainly possible, and this one may, if taken alone, ultimately prove inadequate to the problem it confronts. But it has produced nearly all of the progress made to date in the area of Catullan arrangement. The argument here is that applying this approach in one further instance will produce a broadly convincing general account of the authorial design.

The method in question is as follows. One divides the poems in the transmitted sequence into groups of consecutive poems. Start with the broadest, most obvious criteria of form and content, then work one's way down. Find as many ways as possible of demonstrating that adjacent poems are similar to each other and different from the rest. Look for patterns within each group, especially at its liminal points: does the beginning "look like" a literary overture, the end like a literary closure? For any sequence of poems whose pattern is sufficiently rich, attribute to the author. Finally, once a given sequence is identified, there remains the question of the form(s) in which it circulated: as freestanding work occupying its own papyrus roll, or as a section of a larger work and roll?

To bring out what is at stake in speaking of "this approach," it will be useful to look at other ways of finding (or denying) artistic order in the poems. One alternative treats their transmitted sequence as entirely unreliable, proposing

---

[1] Skinner (2007) provides a thorough account of scholarship on the *Catullfrage*.

to reorder them on other criteria.[2] Also possible is that an authorial Catullan run of poems might have *some*, but only an imperfect or anomalous, correspondence with the set of poems established by one's formal criteria: one could in principle be right that a certain set of poems naturally "group" and show sufficient signs of authorial sequence, but wrongly conclude that its terminal points are those of a Catullan book or artistic unit.[3]

Allowing for such possibilities, there are two other ways to approach the transmitted sequence without first grouping the poems and then asking after their patterned arrangement: we may call the former of these alternatives "local" or "bottom-up," and the latter "global" or "top-down." On a fully local approach, one might closely interrogate each point in the transmitted sequence, seeking to prove in each case that the adjacency of *this* poem to *this* one to *this* one is artful: if each link is artful, the corpus will constitute an artful chain. At the opposite end of the spectrum, one would start from the hypothesis that the corpus is one ordered artistic design and look directly to some "pattern" which proves it, e.g. a superstructure of thematic ring-correspondences ranging from beginning to end.

To be clear, I mention these poles neither to dismiss them nor to set up "extreme" straw men to be defeated by my own sensibly "moderate" position. My point is, rather, that in spite of their significant persuasive force, they have failed to prove conclusive.[4] The course of my argument will indeed employ highly local considerations at many points. Its conclusion will endorse the reality of the apparent global pattern, explaining it as supervenient on the ensemble of Catullus' three related

---

[2] Fröhlich (1843), Brunér (1863), Herrmann (1957).

[3] As Jocelyn (1999) and Butrica (2007), in suggesting an authorial 1–61 based on a metrical principle of unity, hypothesize a collection whose final poem runs over a clear formal disjunction, with the 235 lines of poem 61 rivaling a maximum of 34 lines in the preceding 1–60. While this is a theoretical possibility, so little recommends it that I find nothing to argue against: the metrical affinity of 61 with the meters of 1–60 (and its near-identity with that of poem 34) motivates considering the possibility, but the proposals fail to advance any further reason to think it actually true.

[4] While the bottom-up approach easily produces strong indicators of the artful arrangement of many or most handfuls of consecutive Catullan poems, the weakest links prove too weak to ensure that the entire chain is *one* chain. This approach fails to rule out, for instance, the hypothesis that the corpus contains fragments of multiple artistic sequences, stitched together by recension or left in their current state by textual accident. The top-down approach, by contrast, begins from the observation that the corpus as undifferentiated whole has a plausibly pattern-like movement (a dedicatory opening; a basic short–long–short sweep; and its longest and most ambitious, highest-genre poem, 64, seemingly "nestled" by the rest, generically ascending to and descending from it). While this is easily enough symmetry to take plausibly as a design, it is not enough symmetry to rule out the possibility of accident: Hutchinson (2003) 210–11, for example, argues for the independent circulation of 61–64, followed by their eventual arrangement between the authorial collections 1–60 and 65–116 in codex form. Top-down theories must therefore attempt to elaborate upon the patterning that everyone can see until everyone will agree it could not be accidental; the problem has been that once the proposed pattern is sufficiently elaborate, not everyone can see it.

works.[5] To persuade readers not already committed, though, it has been necessary not only to divide and group poems but also to track down designs within those groups. The following section will investigate how Catullan scholarship has performed these tasks.

Formal and Content Disjunctions in the Corpus

This much is not in dispute: there are clear formal differentiae by which all of the poems sort into classes beginning at a certain point in their transmitted sequence and ending at a later one. To say so is not yet to say anything about how these classes came to be or what they may mean; in nearly any account of the corpus, there will be some differentiae that mean less than others. Some classes, moreover, overlap, and some fall into subclasses. Which ones, if any, matter, and why, and how much, begin as open questions – even if my shorthand may quite clearly foreshadow my own answers.

According to the two most obvious formal criteria, namely poem-length and meter,[6] the principal non-overlapping classes are as follows:

> "the *polymetra*" (my **A** *with* **Ax**): Poems 1–60 are shorter poems (3+ to 34 lines) in lyric meter, mostly Phalaecian hendecasyllables. 848+ lines in all.[7]
>
> **B**: Poems 61–64 or **B** are longer poems (66+ to 408 lines) in various non-elegiac meters. 802+ lines in all.
>
> **C1**: Poems 65–68/68b are longer elegies (24 to 120 or 160 lines). 326 lines in all.
>
> **C2**: Poems 69–116 or **C2** are epigrams and short elegies (2 to 26 lines).[8] 320+ lines in all.

---

[5] Claes' (2002) case for the ordered arrangement of the poems relies mostly on local arguments; at its best it puts beyond serious doubt that many consecutive poems throughout the corpus are artfully chained to each other. My debts to this case in Chapters 2 and 4 are extensive. Its structure, unfortunately, requires Claes to ask more of the least persuasive instances than they can give, in order to rule out, e.g., an editor's having stitched together two authorial collections at a given point of weakness. Though Dettmer (1997) also contains insightful local claims, the work as a whole is an argument for a grand global pattern which is flatly unconvincing.

[6] Along with the conspicuousness of these twin criteria, their presumptive relevance is grounded by the fact that they correspond to differences of genre: an ancient reader of a poetry book will quickly form corresponding expectations upon seeing a ten-line hendecasyllabic poem, a multi-column epithalamium, or a 24-line elegy as initial piece.

[7] The addition sign indicates the likely presence of lacuna(e) of uncertain length. Although "polymetra" and "polymetric" are in common use for 1–60, I avoid them on the grounds that "polymetric" descriptively picks out **B** as well as **A**, and because "lyric" is a fitting and more substantive characterization of **A** (but not **B**) as a whole.

[8] Poem 76 is the outlier, with twenty-six lines; the second longest, poem 99, has sixteen; others no more than twelve. As with "polymetra" above, "epigrams" is a commonly used but problematic characterization of 69–116, being clearly inapplicable to at least poems 76 and 99.

One of these classes, **C1**, clearly has a dual membership in that the criteria of "length" and "meter" pull in separate directions; it is affiliated by the criterion of length with the preceding and by the criterion of meter with the following poems. These are the overlapping classes:

"the *carmina maiora*" (**B** and **C1**): Poems 61–68/68b are longer poems (24 to 408 lines).[9] 1,128+ lines in all.
C: Poems 65–116 are in elegiac distichs. 646+ lines in all.

Prior to asking which, if any, of these six classes are artistically fundamental, and which most correspond to authorial design, it must be noted that they are hardly subjective realities in our corpus. They locate fundamental formal *breaks* or *disjunctions* at exactly three points: at 60|61, at 64|65, and at 68(b)|69. As we will see, the literature has surveyed additional breaks, identified by less sweeping criteria, most of these thematic rather than formal.

The numbered claims below identify those further groupings and disjunctions recognized by existing scholarship. They also note the principal considerations adduced in favor of authorial provenance. What follows is essentially, for each run of poems, a précis of the existing case that its order is authorial. It is intended to demonstrate which cases are more widely accepted and which less so, as well as by whom and for what reasons. Here it should be acknowledged that the skeptical case is everywhere underrepresented. To my knowledge, only one study has critically engaged the contemporary case for many of these groupings of poems.[10]

1) The dedicatory poem 1 is very likely to have introduced (some of) the poems immediately following it.

2) Poems 2–14 display extensive thematic coherence, with the poet's love and loss of Lesbia and foreign travel its most prominent continuities.[11]

---

[9] Although a handful of poems in 1–60 and a single poem in 69–116 exceed poem 65 in line-count, the proper place of 65 among the run of longer poems is not in serious question. That the poem plainly introduces poem 66 (containing ninety-four lines) is sufficient to show this.

[10] Bellandi (2007) 63–84. Gaisser (2008), though sympathetic to Bellandi's conclusions, criticizes his arguments as tendentious and overly subjective, notably his aesthetic evaluation of the juxtaposition of solemn with obscene poems (the hymn to Diana in 34 after prostitution in 32 and 33; the consolation to Calvus in 96 preceding the bodily invective of 97) and the reversal of poems 11 and 51 from their imputed temporal order (Bellandi (2007) 66–69). Against narrow self-interest, I must agree with Gaisser that the skeptical case is stronger than its recent expression would indicate. With Bellandi's work not yet available, Skinner (2007) 46 could write: "the last firm denials of Catullan arrangement in its entirety were those of Coppel (1973: 141–84) and Goold (1973: 8–10), both of whom mainly reiterated the arguments of Brunér [1863] and Wheeler [1934]."

[11] Lesbia: sparrow poems 2 and 3, kiss poems 5 and 7, break-up poems 8 and 11, probable mention of her in 13. Travel: the yacht in 4, Veranius' return from Spain in 9, Catullus' Bithynian service in 10,

3)   The sequence of these poems is broadly agreed to be especially artful.[12]

4)   Elements in poem 14, especially the gift of a poetic *libellus*, recall shared equivalents in poem 1, thus drawing for many a convincing frame around the unit.[13]

While the Lesbia plot is concentrated in poems 2–11, poems 12–14 plausibly belong to the same sequence. Veranius promptly reappears in poem 12, Lesbia is probably mentioned in the following poem (*meae puellae*, 13.12), both 12 and 13 are linked by addressee and occasion with 9, and 14 resonates with 1. Even if the more subjective (3) is resisted, these considerations amount to a strong and now widely accepted case for taking poems 1–14 as a unit and thus locating a disjunction at 14|14b.[14] This case is strengthened by the coherence of the unit that follows 1–14:

5)   Poem 14b is probably a fragment of a poem introducing the poems following it.[15]

6)   Poems 15–26 have a dominant theme in the Juventius-and-love-rivals plot, which is essentially coterminous with these poems.

7)   These poems and their sequence are widely thought to reprise and invert 1–14.[16]

Some caution is recommended by the fact that 14b seems to be fragmentary. Yet, by addressing its *readers* and foreseeing their possible reluctance

---

     Veranius and Fabullus in 12, Fabullus' (reunion?) dinner in 13. The two themes meet in the travelogue of poem 11 (lines 1–12, its first half); non-Lesbia poems present further recurrences: Bithynia in 4 and 10, male friends' girlfriends in 6 and 10, gifts in 12–14.

[12] 2 must dramatically precede 3, as 5 must precede 7; the break-up in 8 and 11 presupposes a relationship, which 2, 3, 5, and 7 handily provide; the three pairs of Lesbia poems are widely taken as sequentially before, during, and after the (initial) affair. The Lesbia poems' alternation with the others is widely understood as artful *uariatio*.

[13] Hubbard (1983) 226–27.

[14] Skinner (2007) 48 asserts that this view is now the consensus; compare Hubbard (2005) 259: "the sequence 1–14, on which everyone now seems to agree." Bellandi (2007) 70–71 argues the skeptical case: neither conceding nor contesting the sequentiality of the Lesbia poems in 2–11, he finds her presence in poem 13 incompatible with that claim, given its placement after the break-up in 11; pronounces the convergence of travel and Lesbia in poem 11 a "dubious" unifying feature; and notes that earlier studies had seen 1–13 (Heck (1951)) or 1–11 (Segal (1968b)) as constituting the initial unit, while each study arguing for 1–14 has described its structure differently. This last point misses the fact that accounts of poetic structure routinely disagree even for texts whose authorial arrangement is in no doubt at all.

[15] All modern editions print 14b as a separate poem from 14. Against Claes' (2002) recent defense of 14/14b unity, Skinner (2003) 226 n. 28 is decisive: assuming 14/14b unity, the "banishing" of the bad poets at the end of 14 would be made senselessly conditional on their reading Catullus' trifling verse. With the three surviving lines of 14b clearly separate, there is little reason to doubt that their mention of and address to readers (*lectores*) of Catullan foolery (*mearum ineptiarum*) touching the physical book (*manusque uestras . . . admouere nobis*) constitute a self-adverting poetic introduction.

[16] Stroh (1990), Beck (1996), Holzberg (2002).

to touch the book, it is easily interpreted as making reference to the obscenity and invective so widespread in the poems that follow it. Although Catullus' rivals Furius and Aurelius appear earlier (in poem 11, where the rivalry and Juventius are at most implicit) and Juventius appears later (in poem 48, with the rivals at most implicit), their collocation in six of the nine poems beginning with 15 and ending with 26 is a clear continuity.[17] This continuity is further supported by a detailed case for internal ordering and global response with 1–14; though doubts do remain,[18] many have been persuaded by this case.[19] Moreover, some kind of disjunction at 26|27 is further assured by a formal discontinuity falling there:

8) There is a metrical shift beginning with poem 27, with the Phalaecian hendecasyllable now frequently (in over 20 percent of cases) opening with iambs or trochees rather than spondees.[20]

9) Poem 27 is widely thought to be introductory.[21]

The metrical shift is complicated by the fact that poem 1 shares this feature in four of its ten verses, while poems 2, 3, and 7 contain it once each.[22] It is not clear what we are to make either of this fact or of the "exceptions" early in the corpus, but there is no plausible case that the phenomenon is random, and it clearly suggests a disjunction at 26|27.

These are the soundest results of more than one age's investigations into poems 1–60. Poem 1 makes for a good beginning; the poems following it

---

[17] On the arithmetic here, "poems 18–20," we recall, are non-Catullan poems whose placement in an early printed edition has disturbed our numeration. The three poems in 15–26 falling outside the Juventius/rivals plot (17 attacking an anonymous cuckold, 22 attacking the poet Suffenus, 25 attacking Thallus as *cinaedus* and thief) are the three non-hendecasyllabic poems in the unit.

[18] Bellandi (2007) 72–73. His grounds for skepticism are that poems 17 and 22 do not fit the postulated pederastic theme, poem 48 to Juventius falls outside these poems, and poem 26 is an inadequate end. Here he quotes Hubbard (2005) 259: "[the] view that either C. 1–26 or C. 14b–26 constitutes a *libellus* founders on the inadequacy of C. 26, a five-line squib . . . as any kind of epilogue." I note, however, that Hubbard's denial that 14b–26 are an independent *libellus* is not a denial of authorial ordering, which he in fact postulates in the same piece, taking 14b–51 as an authorial collection. By contrast, Bellandi seems to take the premise that 14b–26 are not an independent book as sufficient to claim that their ordering is not authorial.

Even granting, as we should not, that poems 17 and 22 are inert in respect to the other poems, Bellandi's case rests on two premises for which I find no warrant at all. First, that Catullus would not have arranged two poems unrelated to Juventius or pederasty in a sequence containing seven such poems, and second, that if Catullus did arrange a cluster of Juventius-related poems in one run of text, he would not have arranged a single Juventius poem elsewhere.

[19] Wiseman (1969), Skinner (1981), Stroh (1990), Beck (1996), Holzberg (2002).

[20] First seen by Skutsch (1969a), who understood the difference to bespeak a "change in technique" between the composition of the poems on either side of 26|27.

[21] Wiseman (1969); his analysis is picked up by Cairns (1975) and Van Sickle (1981).

[22] 2.4, 3.17, 7.2; possibly 3.12, if *illud* is read rather than *illuc*.

are coherent and widely considered to be artfully structured; poem 14 supplies a good ending. 14b is likewise a good beginning for the poems that follow it; those strike one as coherent and artfully structured as well. That poem 26 makes for a good ending is not beyond dispute, but the poems introduced by 14b have characteristics which certainly *terminate* there. For any critic who agrees on the global inversion of 1–14 by 14b–26, this relation itself classes the two units as 1–26, a presumably meaningful unit of its own. Next, we find at 26|27 a formal disjunction which, though it may be puzzled over, is undeniable. This amounts to a many-faceted, albeit qualified, argument for grouping 1–26 or 2–26;[23] at the least, it distinguishes 14b–26 from poems 27 and following without qualification. Finally, for most critics, poem 27 is yet another introductory poem: a third good beginning. The presence of subordinate textual articulation at 14|14b and 26|27 within the larger 1–60 is thus well supported, with enough redundancies to challenge doubts on some points – for instance, the overall specularity of 1–14 and 14b–26, and/or a programmatic reading of poem 27.

From poem 27, the terrain shifts, and doubts ramify. Consecutive and alternating poems are frequently related; to attribute to Catullus the ordering one encounters is a respectable posture. Yet no equivalent to the two previous thematic unities can be found.[24] No convincing *global* pattern of another kind has been detected. The last few poems (wherever, precisely, one draws the line) have been thought especially problematic. The apparent ending, poem 60, has widely (though not universally) been judged inadequate to the task.[25] I will argue that the formal break at 51|52 resolves this problem, separating **Ax** from **A** proper. The place for this argument, however, is yet to come.

We now come to the first principal break in the collection, at 60|61. As we have already seen, a formal continuity runs from poem 61 to the last principal break, at 68b|69: these poems are long. Within that range, however, there is the break at 64|65. As it is made up of "long non-elegiac" poems, 61–64 or **B** has a "negative" or external unity, one defined

---

[23] The metrical affiliation of poem 1 with the later poems is sometimes given as a reason to exclude it formally from the poems immediately following it (see Copley (1951)). The matter is discussed in its place; in hereafter omitting " . . . or 2–26" I am not attempting to ignore or beg the question. There are indeed substantive matters which turn on it.

[24] There have been proposals along these lines, such as Holzberg's (2002) thematic grouping of 27–34, 35–45, and 46–60. Dettmer (1997) accepts the standard 1–14; afterwards, her grouping runs 15–24, 25–33, 34–44, and 45–60. No such division of the later poems (excluding here the existing case against **Ax**) seems to have found endorsement in any subsequent study.

[25] Poem 60 has however attracted extensive attempts at rehabilitation, including Nappa (2003) and Hawkins (2014).

by contrast from 65–68(b) or **C1**. A rough sketch of the current case that **B** has a "positive" or internal unity is as follows:

10) These poems are thematically similar in that 61, 62, and 64 are *set* at weddings; 61–62 *are* wedding songs, and 64 *contains* one towards its end; 63 may pointedly invert or subvert nuptial themes.

11) Like poem 1, the beginning of 61 mentions a Muse and a prominent contemporary Roman for whom it is made.

12) The opening, with the god bidden to be present at a human wedding, **may** draw a ring with the conclusion of poem 64, which asserts that the gods no longer attend human weddings.[26]

As the case now stands, we can take or leave these points.[27] The thematic continuity is certainly "not nothing," but caution is recommended by the presence of a (partial?) exception-case in a set with only four members. The sequence has a good beginning, with elements persuasively similar to the good beginning of poem 1, and may have a matching end. These are suggestive facts, at least, but they fall short of supporting an irresistible case – not least because an opponent of 61–64 unity can explain the good beginning of 61 in exactly those terms, as the good beginning of a long and ambitious piece.[28]

Turning to the longer elegies 65–68(b):

13) Poem 65 is introductory (at least of poem 66, and possibly of the elegiac-metered poems as a whole).

14) Like poem 1 and the beginning of 61, poem 65 mentions the Muses and is dedicated to a prominent contemporary Roman.

15) If 68a and 68b are separate poems, they may well be related, the former introducing or anticipating the latter.

16) Nuptial themes are prominent in these poems, which are also framed by the death of the brother and the issue of Catullus' subsequent poetic (in)capacities.

While poem 67, the satirical dialogue between the poet and a Veronese door, is peculiar in this sequence in some ways, it is quite plain that the

---

[26] Wiseman (1979) 177.

[27] I mean this as both a generalization about current scholarly practice and as an endorsement of the same. It is reasonable that opinion should divide on this question; if you have external reasons to favor overarching artistic unities in the corpus, this will look like an instance, but if you have external reasons to deny the same, this will not be enough evidence to change your mind.

[28] Within 61–64, the first two poems are clearly grouped *qua* wedding songs. Whether the remaining two form a meaningful class need not detain us here.

(marriage-themed) content of these poems reinforces their grouping by meter and length. They also have a good beginning, once again helpfully similar to those of poems 1 and 61.

On the other hand, both nuptial theme and poem length range over the 64|65 break, just as the metrical continuity ranges over the 68(b)|69 break. What else can be said for each continuity? The case for deeper "long poem" affiliation, *in fine*, is as follows:

17) Poems 61–68(b) are long poems largely sharing a nuptial theme; for some critics, these poems are elaborately arrayed in concentric circles around the epic poem 64, the longest and most ambitious piece.

How sound these claims are is no small question; merely as observation of the literature, the case is often cited but has not been felt to compel agreement.

The case for elegiac affiliation, on the other hand, can be summarized as follows:

18) In addition to the common meter, shared mention of Callimachean translations as poetic gift tie the final poem 116 with the initial poem 65, drawing a presumptive ring around the poems in elegiac meter.[29] The brother in the initial poem 65 (and 68 or 68a and 68b) is picked up in one of the short poems 69–116 (101), just as Lesbia in 68(b) is picked up extensively in those poems.

Broadly speaking, the "long poem" (61–68(b)) unity was for quite some time the more strongly felt and more frequently mentioned of the two. After 116 received fresh and rehabilitating scrutiny – and the framing responses with poem 65 were brought to light – the elegiac (65–116) unity has become far more prominent. In particular, the "good beginning" of poem 65 shares elements with the putative good beginning of 61 (and the clear good beginning of 1), while 116 is not clearly a "good end" unless it is

---

[29] Noticed already by Süss (1877). On this, Hutchinson (2003) 212 speaks for many contemporaries: "this forms a ring so palpable and significant as to indicate both that 116 is the end of the book and 65 its beginning." Traditional dissatisfaction with poem 116 had earlier created such doubt about its appropriateness as concluding poem that Wiseman (1969) 29 argued for its expulsion in his first study in Catullan arrangement. In subsequent years the poem received extensive rehabilitation (MacLeod (1973a), Forsyth (1977), King (1988)), with its stylistic and metrical peculiarities now seen as pointed rather than careless. Wiseman (1979) 176 himself was persuaded, and came to accept the poem and the framing device for 65–116, just as Hubbard (1983) 219–21 once resisted the 65–116 frame and the authorial unity of these poems but later came to endorse them ((2005) 269–70). Bellandi (2007) 82, by contrast, sees no substantive framing between 65 and 116 beyond the repeated words *carmina Battiadae*, of which he asks *ma non è un po' poco?* The shared context of a poet pronouncing on his own poetic plans fails to rate his notice here.

the good end to what begins with 65. It is also unclear that poem 69 constitutes a good beginning, and it fails to resonate obviously with any of the other poems located at terminal points. Hence, the case for seeing the *carmina maiora* 61–68(b) not only as a fundamental artistic reality but also as a *more* fundamental one than 65–116 is probably now defunct.

Within the poems following the last principal break at 68(b)|69, a single proposal for internal disjunction, namely at 92|93, has won significant credence. A summary case for it is as follows:

19)   Poems 69–92 have a dominant theme in the poet's love and loss of Lesbia and a related love-rivalry plot, which are essentially coterminous with these poems.[30]

20)   Though poems 93–116 are clearly looser in organization, invective against Caesar and his associates is frequent throughout; such political abuse, depending on the identification of some of its targets, may be its dominant theme.

The predominance in 69–92 of poems on Lesbia and rivalry for her love is clear, as is the extended disappearance of the theme from poem 93 on, as well as the inflected mood of the final Lesbia poems (fair words in 104; reconciliation in 107 and 109). The final poem of 69–92 verbally references poem 70; that these are the first and last Lesbia poems counters the worry about an untidy "almost first to last" frame. Otherwise, the redundancies seen in the inner articulations of 1–60 are plainly less rich here. As opposed to the metrical disjunction coterminous with the content disjunction at 26|27, with clear internal coherences on *both* sides of 14|14b, the break at 92|93 has principally the thematic coherence of 69–92 to recommend it, while arguments for thematic coherence in 93–116 can reasonably be resisted.[31] Nonetheless, that poems 69–92 have a readily apparent unity of content is difficult to deny. At the very least, this unity locates a break after 92 and groups 93–116 by exclusion.

In summary, the most basic formal characteristics of the poems, their length and meter, establish principal disjunctions in our corpus at 60|61, 64|65, and 68(b)|69. Poems 1–60 form a clear class by themselves. Poems 61–64 can be classed on their own and with 65–68(b), just as 65–68(b) can be classed with 61–64 and with 69–116. Within 1–60, there are internal disjunctions at 14|14b and 26|27 and multiple grounds for grouping 1–14, 14b–26, and their conjunction, 1–26. The class 27–60 is set off negatively by exclusion from 1–26 and positively by its metrical difference, and it

---

[30]   Heck (1951), Wiseman (1969) 25–29, Schmidt (1973) 228–34, Skinner (2003) 60–61.
[31]   Hubbard (1983) 219, Bellandi (2007) 79 n. 171.

seems to have a good beginning; the extent and nature of its unifying elements otherwise remains an open question. More substantive unities have been proposed for 61–64 and 61–68(b); they have also been resisted. The class of longer elegiacs 65–68(b) is grouped together in multiple ways, just as it is grouped with the following short poems 69–116. These poems, finally, begin with a set of poems containing a content-unity which ends with poem 92. The disjunction at 92|93 thus formed may or may not be further confirmed by significant unifying features within 93–116. To schematize the picture, while the poems can be exhaustively classed as follows:

Short, various meters		Long poems		Short, elegiac meter	
1–60		61–68b		69–116	
1–26	27–60	61–64	65–68b	69–92	93–116
"tighter"	"looser"	not elegiac	elegiac	Lesbia and C.'s	political
Phalaecians	Phalaecians			rivals	invective?
1–14 14b–26					

Contemporary scholarship has come increasingly to class them in this form:

Short, lyric meters		Long, various meters	Elegiac meter	
1–60		61–64	65–116	
1–26	27–60		65b–68	69–116
"tighter"	"looser"		long	short
1–14 14b–26				69–92 93–116

Each unit presents its own case for careful patterning and artistic unity.

Arguing about Books

There remain a few preliminary points of method and assumption which a study of Catullan design might be expected to take up extensively. This one will not do so, but will treat them instead as cases of *praeteritio*.

First, I will say little about the positive case for a disturbed corpus with a generally non-authorial ordering.[32] My decision to pass over this case

---

[32] Fröhlich (1843), Brunér (1863), Ellis (1876), Schmidt (1914), Wheeler (1934), Coppel (1973), Goold (1973).

owes in part to the paucity of up-to-date work in support of it.[33] A more significant reason, however, has to do with the dialectical structure of my own case. My argument is that poems 52–60 should be excluded, and that the specularities then displayed by the rest could not be accidental. If my arguments fail to make that case, it will not help much if I succeed in undermining any *a priori* grounds for thinking the poems chaotic. If the readings I will offer of the corpus minus 52–60 are to inspire much conviction, readers will need positive grounds to believe that this is the corpus we are invited to read. Similarly, if the new arguments do persuasively show pattern and design, I do not *fear* any previous arguments for chaos. There are simply no grounds for denying Catullan arrangement such that a critic could ever agree that parts of it *look like* authorial books, but still reject the possibility that Catullus could have produced such things.[34]

Another concept from the scholarly literature that I will not be discussing hereafter is the once-beloved posthumous editor – "Anonymous Posthumous," as Wiseman satirically dubbed him – as a possible source of patterned but not authorial arrangement.[35] Mr. Posthumous is no longer in fashion as an explanatory principle;[36] he has rightly been supplanted by the growing sense that accidents of transmission offer a better model for the interplay between order and disorder in our poems.[37] It is nonetheless important for me to state my grounds for assuming that the artful patterning I claim for the poems must be authorial. Just as I find it utterly

---

[33] The lack of fresh arguments against a designed corpus does not mean that the view is no longer tenable. There is plainly an asymmetry in terms of one's incentive to think about the problem and add to the literature: a scholar impressed by a "new pattern" might well write it up, while those unimpressed by the last few are more likely to devote themselves to research topics they find more promising. Plainly, though, a good argument for design does deserve either an answer or assent.

[34] The closest approximation of a serious *a priori* argument against my thesis might be this: "Isn't it just extraordinarily neat that a young poet would plot out his entire body of work . . . and then have fate pay you the courtesy of bringing about his sudden death, but only when all and only these poems were ready?" I do think this worry could have some force, but only as directed to a single-role, grand-scheme theorist. The present arguments are not of that sort; I do not argue for a "closed" corpus or an impregnable, pre-determined unity. Catullus may have produced or intended to produce other works, and **Ax** might indeed be (a fragment of) one of them. In my view, Catullus represents himself as working on a future work, **B**, as his present work, **A**, is coming together. After these, he produces **C**, whose structure chiastically reprises those of his first two books. I do not say that this self-presentation reflects historical fact, but I do not see why it could not. My Catullus need not have started his *oeuvre* with a master plan; he need only have intended that any book he produced should have a nice structure, and then, with two books produced, hit upon the idea that his third should mirror the first two jointly.

[35] Wiseman (1979) 182. If the order of the poems is not authorial, of course, there will still have been some human agency by which it came to us; I am not dismissing the posthumous editor in that sense.

[36] Excepting Bellandi (2007) 85–96.   [37] See especially Hutchinson (2003) and Barchiesi (2005).

implausible that the specularities in our corpus could have fallen into place by chance, so too does it seem implausible that the particular specularities I will adduce could have *potentially* inhered in a small body of poems that was not *designed* to exhibit them.[38] A redactor could find two sparrow poems and two kiss poems and arrange them in alternation with other poems, but only the author could have crafted the complexities we find in the opening and closural poems' responsions. So I think, and I miss my guess badly if many or any readers find that my account leaves open much idea-space between "too good to be random" and "not so good that it must be authorial." As a grace to the weary reader, I will refrain from uselessly repeating this point at each step. Likewise, my notice of patterning will avoid tedious repetition of the phrase "this could hardly be accidental."

Another hypothesized item which will not be discussed hereafter is the *liber Catulli*, the authorial, single-volume *Gesamtausgabe*. The problem here is not, as was once believed, the putative impossibility of fitting all of our roughly 2,300-line corpus onto a single bookroll. As has now become clear, that would of course have been possible.[39] Nor do I think that the poet's characterization of his book as a *libellus* in poem 1 rules much out. The final line of *Satires* 1 characterizes its book in the same way, and although Horace's "little book" is only about half as long as the Catullan corpus, it is, at 1,030 lines, one of the longest Latin poetry books known to us.[40] The problem is rather that such a book of poetry, with the length and internal partitions it would display, would clearly be more discrepant from attested Latin poetry books than a plurality of Catullan books would be. The former would require us to reify a much more unusual entity than the latter, and is accordingly less attractive a proposal.[41] I will be arguing that

---

[38] An overdetermined example: if a collection of 26 poems for children began sequentially with *apple*, *ball* ... *zebra*, the poems were certainly composed around the pattern rather than subsequently alphabetized, not only because the pattern is "too good" to be chance (though it obviously is), but also because the likelihood of any poem in a small set beginning with e.g. *zebra* (not to mention the notorious *xylophone*) would otherwise be exiguous.

[39] Scherf (1996) 12–16.

[40] But of course the diminutive need not be understood in terms of physical size at all (Stroup (2010) 105–07). Self-characterized "trifles" (*nugas*) in poem 1 hardly worry either, since these can refer to *earlier* poetic efforts, which Nepos appreciated *then*. Then too, earlier discussions often overlooked the fact that almost half of the Catullan corpus (by line-count) consists of lines significantly shorter than the hexameter, which would require less horizontal space on the roll. And why have so many Catullans worried about the physical possibility of fitting these 13,000-odd words onto a papyrus roll, while so few Livians ever worried about the significantly higher word-counts of his books? "Ah, but that's historical prose, the conventions are different." Precisely: this question should have always been contested by asking what poets *tend* to do, not what papyrus rolls *can* do.

[41] My authorial **B** is formally *more* unusual than **A** or **C**, but much *less* unusual than the *Gesamtausgabe*. **A** is not unusual at all; for **C**, the generic shift in the middle is the sole formal peculiarity.

the corpus contains three stretches of consecutive Latin verse, each between six hundred and one thousand lines, and each artistically coherent and formally unified in various ways. We have dozens of examples of such things from antiquity which we take uncontroversially as books, and none which we do not. It is not a trivial step to infer that the three coherent poetic unities bespeak three books of poems, but it starts out as a highly plausible one.[42]

A competing view – which I will discuss at length – might take at least one of my Catullan books, **A**, as several short authorial books or *libelli*.[43] Here I see internal partitions rather than separate books, though still conceding that these *could* at one point have been separately circulating books, which then grew, as it were, into the full version.[44] Here again, I will claim, the comparative evidence favors my argument: my books are of normative length, while potential subdivided *libelli* (especially the 152+ lines of 14b–26) are short enough to raise reasonable doubts. In most respects, however, I prefer to stress the broad compatibility of most of my claims with a theory of this sort. Just as long as "my" parts are coterminous with "your" *libelli*, and as long as you see the sequence and interpretive connections between your *libelli* in a way isomorphic with those of my parts, we will substantially agree on most points that matter.

One final case of *praeteritio* remains. I will not take up the question of the titles of Catullus' works – whether inferences may be drawn about these from the ways in which he is cited by ancient authors. This is, first, because I agree with Scherf over Butrica that little can be inferred from later references to hendecasyllabic poems as *in hendecasyllabis*, to epithalamia as *epithalamia*, and the like.[45] A second reason is that, as Butrica himself notes, any widely known titulature might not be authorial. Did Imperial readers call my **A** the *Passer Catulli*? I would hesitate to base a Catullan argument on that premise, even if I did know it to be true. Finally, the

---

[42] By contrast, there is no tripartite work of similar length – nor anything even remotely analogous – which we *do* regard as a book. The explanatory economy of the one-book Catullan theory is therefore dominated by that of the three-book theory, given my arguments for tripartition.

[43] I mention the term *libellus* here because this is the term preferred by proponents of such a picture; I avoid using it myself outside references to poems 1 and 14. It seems possible but unproven to me that *libellus*, for Catullus and his readers, is a (near) technical term for poetry rolls with certain formal characteristics (though I am also uncertain to what extent Catullan "*libellus* theorists" assume this). Even if that is the case, then, what those characteristics are and where the boundaries of the concept lie seem hopelessly underdetermined.

[44] It is in fact crucial to my understanding of **A** that its parts invite us to imagine them as composed and circulated sequentially; while this could reflect the historical fact of the matter, I think it equally plausible that this is a literary device internal to the poems' self-dramatization.

[45] Scherf (1996) 30–46, Butrica (2007).

possibility (or likelihood) that scribes and readers in fact produced and consumed the Catullan poems in many different combinations tells against the relevance of later references. My arguments look directly to the text, seeing non-accidental patterns which imply that there *is* a tripartite design uniting the corpus minus **Ax**, that that design is intrinsic to the poems' artistry, and that it can be interpreted as such. These claims are not at all incompatible with the ancient citations; more importantly, they would not be *refuted* by the ancient witnesses even if these attested to different collections from the books claimed here.[46] If the most popular form of Catullan bookroll circulating in the Empire had somehow effaced the author's design, this would no more refute my claims than a textual error refutes an editor's correction thereof. I would, indeed, score my own thesis as true if Catullus died pen-in-hand, his editors mistakenly attached **Ax** to the end of **A**, and no physical roll containing only poems 1–51 ever actually existed.

Status Quaestionis

It is widely agreed that the beginning of the corpus reflects authorial order, either as one or two independently circulating rolls or as part of a larger work. It is unclear, for want of recent comment, how widely it is accepted that the ordered beginning is constituted *precisely* by 1–14 or 1–14 and 14b–26; what is clear is that these precise units are now the leading candidates. About poems 27–60 there is no consensus. Poems 61–64 may or may not have circulated as a book; if they did not, the four probably traveled individually. If they did circulate as a book, their independent circulation is *also* possible.[47] Poems 65–116 in elegiac meter have a good claim to be a book, but if so, we hardly understand and are troubled by the relative haphazardness of the later poems. Just so does the arrangement of the later lyric poems trouble us far more than that of the former – with the exception that the final transmitted poem of the elegiac book can confidently be seen as a literary closure, far more so than for the short lyrics.

---

[46] Scherf (1996). One inference from the ancient citations which does clearly matter is that Catullus' books were never known as "Books 1–3." This, however, poses no problem for a three-book theory: the books are formally and generically distinct, and it has been rightly observed that no one would call Horace's fourth book, the first book of the *Odes*, "Horace Book 4." While I do, of course, posit a tight supervenient unity to these three works, we have no reason to think that this tight unity would *require* these formally different works to be called "Books 1–3."

[47] If, as Skinner (2003) xxvii thinks, Catullus assembled the 61–64 book years after the poems' original composition, it is not likely that their unity and sequence as such will be artistically relevant, or a premise on which literary argument can be grounded.

Finally, given the realities of ancient book circulation and use, we must be sensitive to the possibility that any pristine authorial design has been disturbed, in possibly irremediable ways, by ad hoc omissions, suppletions, transpositions, and the like.

The problem is hardly the hopeless morass that it has been made out to be. Attention to the evident formal classes and points of formal disjunction in our corpus has paid off. It has provided us with compelling reasons to pronounce firmly and affirmatively on the poet's arrangement of some portions of his work, thus isolating the more doubtful parts. To be sure, extensive uncertainty about the more specific physical modalities remains. These are real problems, but tractable ones. As I hope presently to show, they are in large part *soluble* as well, and in one move: aligning the one clear formal break that remains, at 51|52, with the break in Catullus' design.

CHAPTER I

Ax (poems 52–60)

1 Introduction

This chapter consists of a long but simple argument for the authorial design of most of our corpus. I begin by recalling the points of articulation in this design, with my shorthand for its principal parts:

A: poems 1–51, consisting in a bipartite first half and unitary second half:
    1–14 and 14b–26
    27–51
    [**Ax:** poems 52–60]
B: 61–64
C: 65–116, consisting in two bipartite halves:
    C1: 65–68b:
        65–67 to Ortalus
        68a and 68b to Mallius
    C2: 69–116: 69–92 and 93–116

Poems 52–60 (**Ax**) are artistically incongruous with the poems preceding and following them; they either fall entirely outside the multi-work design of the remaining corpus, or else function as a self-segregating minor unit appended to **A**. As the preceding survey has argued, all of the plausibly authorial *artistic* sequences we have uncovered have begun and ended at the points of clear *formal* and thematic disjunction in the corpus. The disjunctions located at 14|14b and 26|27 (grouping 1–14 and 14b–26), and 64|65 (grouping **C**, 65–116) have been particularly successful, rendering the authorial unity and design of at least some parts of our corpus broadly persuasive. Minding the disjunction at 51|52, I will argue, should do the same for most of the corpus: given the textual separation of **Ax**, the unity and design of **A** and **C** follow promptly, while that of **B** is rendered highly likely.

The argument for detaching **Ax** runs as follows: looking at Catullus' short lyric poems 1–60 from within, we see that there are serious difficulties with taking these rougher and scrappier poems as the authorial continuation of the generically different and more ambitious 1–51, let alone as their consummation or denouement. The run of poems from 1–51 (**A**) is at least as good an initial candidate for "normative-length Catullan book of short lyric poems" as 1–60 (**A**+**Ax**), and is therefore at least as good a candidate to hold up for comparison with 61–64 (**B**) and 65–116 (**C**), the other plausible or likely candidates for normative-length Catullan books. Yet even if that were not the case, even if the formal disjunction at 51|52 were no more than suggestive, a clear and simple pattern emerges on comparing **A** with **B** and **C**. This patterning can be plausibly accounted for only by positing the authorial unity of **A** and **C** at least, as well as the joint design of their ensemble.

To be clear: I do *not* draw from this claim the conclusion that the patterning we get from hypothetically taking **Ax** as a textual intrusion is so "good" that it *proves* **Ax** is a textual intrusion. What I do claim is that the patterning is good enough to need explaining. A textual intrusion story indeed offers a plausible explanation: it fits the evidence, asking only that we believe that a transmission accident of the sort that certainly *might* happen really *did* happen. But I find that it is not the *only* plausible explanation for the neater specularity of the corpus-minus-**Ax**. If these poems are in fact a "sub-unit" of **A** they will not be the only such entity; nor, for that matter, will they be the only part of **A** to self-marginalize.[1] It is true that I cannot, as predecessors also could not, give a fully convincing account of these poems and how they fit. But textual corruption alone may well have rendered any such account permanently unrecoverable. To take only the most pressing problem, only nine lines into **Ax** we read, as poem 54, what is easily the most corrupt and least intelligible multi-line passage in the corpus.[2]

The literature on Catullan arrangement has long seen the argument for separating **Ax** from within the short lyric poems 1–60.[3] The argument from

---

[1] That is, "separation and inclusion" stories will need to confront the question, "why would the endpoints of **B** and **C** respond to a 'transitional point' towards the end of the lyric book, rather than its ending proper?" A partial answer here will be, "for reasons quite similar to those on view for the 14b–26 sub-unit, namely, in order for the poet to 'have it both ways' about some of his 'obscene' or 'less reputable' pieces: if you don't want smut everywhere and you also don't want to ban smut completely, you use the zoning laws."

[2] Trappes-Lomax (2007) 130–31.

[3] Segal (1968b) 307 n.1, Skinner (1981) 80–92, Hubbard (1983) 220–22 and (2005) 260–62, 269. Skinner has since partially retracted her view (2007) 50 n.12: "I am still not completely comfortable with either option [book-end after 51 or 60]." Hutchinson (2003) argues that poems 52, 59, and 60 are intrusions; by my lights, it is more economical to take the entire sequence as the intrusion, rather than posit two separate textual disturbances within an authorial sequence 50, 51, 53, 54 ... 58b.

without them is original to this work.[4] By my own assessment, each argument on its own is sufficient to claim that a textual discontinuity at 51|52 is the best explanation of the available evidence; that either argument independently converges on this same conclusion, I will argue, is compelling in the strict and literal sense. In turn, just such a discontinuity is all I think I *need* you to agree to, for you also to agree with the claim that ultimately matters for this work: the neatness and legibility of the remaining corpus are authorial and hence interpretable. In noticing that neatness and relying upon that legibility, you are not indulging the ingenuity of a middling modern Latinist, you are encountering the *ingenium* of a classic Latin poet. You are reading Catullus.

To anticipate, the shared patterning may be summarized as follows:

1) **A** and **C2** have in common both a global thematic movement and many individual thematic resonances: a tight first half of poems dominated by Lesbia's love lost and Catullan invective against his erotic rivals, followed by a looser and more widely ranging half, but again with various close parallels, including political invective at the beginning and the extended absence and return of Lesbia, with mention of a reconciliation.

2) The terminal points of **A**, **B**, and **C** conduct a deep and programmatically rich intratextual dialogue.

3) **A** and **C2** are formally specular: each has a basic internal articulation (26|27 and 92|93) at its middle by poem-count. By majority reckoning, this match is either precise (twenty-five for each half of **A** and each half of **C2**) or nearly so, depending on the contested credentials of poems 2b and 95b.

In the case of (1), the exclusion of **Ax** enhances an argument which could be made in any case, and many of my claims here will be familiar from existing discussions. Points (2) and (3), by contrast, are more deeply contingent on this textual move. For (3), the discontinuities at 26|27 and 92|93 are familiar and widely accepted, as we have seen; the arithmetical correspondence emerges, of course, only from bracketing 52–60. While not all readers will

---

Book-end after poem 50 was asserted as early as Richter (1881) 24–26, now by Clausen (1976) 37–41. Doubts about the final section of 1–60 also in Kroll (1924), Barwick (1928) 80, and Heck (1951) 56 n.1. Since the proposal for book-end is motivated not by the formal difference of 1–50 from 51 (which is not to be found) but by aesthetic dissatisfaction with the latter poem, it has no purchase on us who think poem 51 is brilliant. I do hope that is all of us now.

[4] Outside the literature on excluding 52–60 itself, Van Sickle (1981) is to my knowledge the only work which substantively explores possible consequences of assuming book-end at poem 51.

prefer the poem count on which there is a perfect century of Catullan short poems decanting into two groups of fifty, each divided into twenty-five-poem halves, few readers (and no editors to date) will prefer a count which effaces all of the arithmetical symmetries. Above all, the claim that the disjunctions at 26|27 and 92|93 are both *medial* breaks, and in a strong sense, requires the exclusion of **Ax** but is scarcely threatened by alternative poem counts.[5]

For (2), the crucial assertion that essentially all of the terminal points (1 and 50–51, opening of 61 and close of 64, 65 and 116) respond to each other, we are again partially dependent on excluding **Ax**. Some links have been brought to light already (1-116, 1-opening of 61-65, 65-116), but a clear view of Catullus' totalizing scheme requires revising the end of **A** from the (frankly embarrassing) sequence 58b–59–60 to the (splendid) 50–51. Above all, the close of **A** with a poetic epistle (50) commenting on gift-exchange of poetry, followed by a translation of a Greek poem (51), reflects both the opening of **C** (65–66) and its close (116, which mentions but then *refuses* a poetic translation to its addressee Gellius).

For organizational reasons, the full discussion of **B** and **C1** is reserved for Chapter 3. The case for global specularity between them, matching the one we will presently survey in **A** and **C2**, must wait until then as well. There is admittedly a cost to this delay, in that the end-point responses discussed here will be directly relevant there; I have paid this cost in order to collect and present, as forcefully as possible, the consequences which flow directly from the detachment of **Ax**.

If you accept the case for bracketing **Ax**, you will accept the tidy arrangement it uncovers. If you are merely *tempted* to bracket **Ax**, the signs of tidiness will likely seem too plural and too consilient to be mere accidents arising from the mistaken excision of this most heterogeneous run of the text. If you deny that many or all of the poems (or many or all of those after 14 or 26) indicate global authorial design, this chapter agrees with you on one run of text and has previously unseen considerations to offer you on the rest.

---

[5] Given the expulsion of **Ax**, the introductory poem 27 is precisely medial whether or not we accept 2/2b unification (25th of 49 or 26th of 50). The mediality of the break within **C2** (25 poems in 69–92, 25 or 24 in 93–116) is of course independent of removing **Ax**, and is helpful in its own right. On the numbers more broadly, I find it unnecessary and counterproductive to litigate every recorded alternative to the poem-divisions in Mynors' edition. Different views will countenance differing parallelisms which persuade to different degrees. For example, readers taking both 2/2b and 95/95b as unitary will count an alternative, but still precisely mirroring count: 24 and 25 poems in the halves of **A**, 25 and 24 in those of **C2**. Splitting 2/2b but uniting 95/95b results in asymmetry – but then again, the humorous point of poem 116 is that it denies a 117, so it seems plausible that the arithmetical correspondence is aware of this, and comes up one short for that reason.

Only if you are unshakeably committed to the total irrelevance of the formal break at 51|52 are you beyond my reasonable hope of persuading.

This dynamic is best of all: the strongest grounds for skepticism about Catullan arrangement are also the strongest grounds for sympathy with detaching 52–60. The more you believe that textual disturbances such as ad hoc private "suppletions" of an authorial book are common in ancient books, the more you will believe that **Ax** looks to be a perfect candidate.[6] If you think a posthumous editor stitched together the corpus, you can still think precisely that about the stitching at 51|52. And then, I think, I've got you: the rest of the short poems (1–51 and 69–116) are too closely parallel for coincidence to explain. Similarly, the less likely you are to countenance textual disturbance in the corpus, the more likely you are to see authorial design everywhere in that corpus already: I expect you will *agree* that "my" corpus-without-**Ax** has clearer signs of patterning than the ones that already convinced you, over the entire corpus. Better evidence for your own basic view should be welcome for you, too, and I think you will like the option of keeping **Ax** as a separate annex.

Stans pede in uno, thus the argument of this chapter. The rest, as they say, is commentary.

2   Appendix Catulliana (52–60)

First, I do not deny that these poems are Catullan. I seek neither to banish them from the corpus nor to discourage their study. It has often been thought, it is true, that 52–60 are ill-fitting and disappointing. Much of their content is obscure to us; most of it is slight; Catullus might well have excluded these, it has been thought, from a collection aspiring to last more than one age.[7] In this section, rather than restating the grounds for aesthetic dissatisfaction with these poems, I focus primarily on bringing to light the features which distinguish them from the preceding poems. It is true that a single instance of uniqueness does not itself prove anything: the

---

[6] So Barchiesi (2005) 336–37, who proposes a "fuzzier model" of arrangement for 1–60. On such a model, authorial patterning will be present and observable here and there, though disturbed in multiple and unknowable ways by the intervention of copyists, thus frustrating attempts to reconstruct a "perfect book" from the received text. Barchiesi's arguments have been justly influential; the view presented here is both indebted to it and corrective: fuzz has indeed descended onto the authorial book, but only a single, identifiable layer.

[7] By "slight" (so Hubbard (2005) 269) more is meant here than merely "short." The five-line poem 58 is universally conceded to be polished, effective, and important. Poem 57 largely escapes condemnation as well, and poem 53 is widely granted to be genuinely amusing. Opinion on 60 is polarized, and 55 enjoys a mixed repute. But 52, 54, 56, 58b, and 59 are surely among the least well loved Catullan poems.

greater Asclepiads of poem 30 are unique in Catullus, but one does not eject it on that account. A comparison of 1–51 to 52–60, however, yields enough discrepancies to supply an irrefutable case for difference and a strong one for questionable fit. Then, too, evaluative judgments are intrinsically vulnerable and tend to persuade neither widely nor deeply. This is so for two reasons: First, one is in principle rightly cautious about retrojecting one's own literary judgment. Second, many Latin texts – to say nothing of Latin literature itself – have been traditionally condemned, only to be rehabilitated once their poetics are more fully brought to light by changes in critical attitudes.[8] For that reason I will rely much more heavily on less subjective arguments, even as I admit that I too am susceptible to the traditional view of these poems as less compelling, on average, than the rest.

Conspectus

Poem	Opening	Meter	Lines
52	*quid est Catulle, quid moraris emori?*	iambic trimeters	4
53	*risi nescio quem modo e corona*	hendecasyllables	5
54	*Othonis caput oppido est pusillum*	hendecasyllables	7
55	*oramus, si forte non molestum est*	(hen)decasyllables	22
56	*o rem ridiculam, Cato et iocosam*	hendecasylables	7
57	*pulcre conuenit improbis cinaedis*	hendecasyllables	10
58	*Caeli, Lesbia nostra, Lesbia illa*	hendecasyllables	5
58b	*non custos si fingar ille Cretum*	(hen)decasyllables	10
59	*Bononiensis Rufa Rufulum fellat*	choliambs	5
60	*num te leaena montibus Libystinis*	choliambs	5

Anomalous Meter and Length

Poem 52 is metrically unique in Catullus, the sole poem in "standard" iambic trimeters, with long initial syllables permitted in the first two feet. After two metrically unremarkable poems, the poet's "search for Camerius" in 55 is anomalous in allowing ten-syllable lines, with the central choriamb of the hendecasyllable replaced by a molossus in fourteen of its twenty-two lines. Its companion piece, 58b, also exhibits this feature (though in different proportion, only twice in ten lines). The final two poems are metrically anomalous as consecutive poems in the same non-

---

[8] Of these poems in particular, I note Nappa's (2003) and now Hawkins' (2014) extensive rehabilitations of poem 60.

hendecasyllabic meter: such poems elsewhere are carefully separated and widely distributed. Poems 29–31 are also consecutive non-hendecasyllables, but these feature three *different* meters.[9] Poem 59.3 also contains a resolution, permitted elsewhere in 1–60 only at 22.19, where the "slip" looks mimetic of the content, and only arguably at 37.5.[10]

As Otto Skutsch first noticed, there is a marked difference within 1–60 in Catullus' treatment of the Aeolic base of the hendecasyllable, its first two syllables.[11] Only three hendecasyllabic lines in poems 2–26 have non-spondaic openings, whereas nearly a quarter of those in 27–60 begin with either a trochee or an iamb; poem 1, in turn, resembles the later poems, with non-spondaic openings in four of its ten lines. As a group, 52–60 is distinct from both the conservative, almost purely spondaic 2–26 and from the much freer 27–51. In 52–60, a maximum of eight hendecasyllables out of sixty-six are non-spondaic (about 12.1 percent); in 27–51, 59 of 233 such lines are so (about 26.5 percent). Four of the eight apparent non-spondaic openings in 52–60, however, are personal names; both because there is greater uncertainty about their orthography and scansion, and because proper names plausibly afford special grounds for metrical license, it might be more instructive to calculate the figures with these excluded. While only four of sixty-six (roughly 6.1 percent) such lines in 52–60 contain the less ambiguous type of metrical license, the tally of verses in 27–51 decreases only slightly, to 56/223 or about 25.1 percent. This is a clear difference, even if we might wish the sample-size in 52–60 were a bit larger.

The collective brevity of these pieces is another clear distinction. Within 1–51, only poem 26 contains five lines; the fragmentary 14b looks like it might have come in at four to six, but poem 2b, if I am correct that it is separate from poem 2, probably will have been somewhat longer originally. Only six poems of 50 would then be shorter than eight lines: 14b (four to six?); 26 (five); 48 (six); 27, 47, and 49 (seven). By contrast, seven of the ten pieces in **Ax** are that short.[12] Poem 52 is especially striking: at four lines, not

---

[9] I argue below for a structural explanation for the sequence 29–31; along with 59–60, the non-hendecasyllabic sequence 51–52 is of course removed on my proposal.

[10] At 22.19, for Catullus' metrical practice to slacken precisely where he says "everyone has unacknowledged flaws" seems not to be an accident; at 37.5, assuming a consonantal *u* in *confutuere* removes the alleged resolution.

[11] Skutsch (1969a).

[12] 57 and 58 have ten lines apiece; 15 poems in 1–51 are as short as nine of these ten. It is of course true that three of the shortest poems in 1–51 are found near the end, at 47–49; my account of this fact will be that the "backward glance" or "reprise" as closural motif unites all of these poems except 49, whose prominent placement just before the closural dyad (as I will call it) of 50–51 can be explained in several ways, as we will see.

only is it the shortest non-fragmentary poem in 1–60, but also it is rendered even shorter in content by the fact that its final line merely repeats its first one.[13]

It is particularly striking to contrast the non-hendecasyllabic poems in **Ax** (52, 59, and 60) with the fourteen such poems in 1–51. Simply put, they are utterly dissimilar. At four, five, and five lines respectively, their combined heft barely matches that of the shortest non-hendecasyllabic piece in 1–51 alone, whether we count poem 30 (twelve long lines) or poem 51 (sixteen shorter lines) as such.[14] Where in 1–51 even the shortest non-hendecasyllabic poem is longer than half of the hendecasyllabic ones, 52, 59, and 60 are the shortest complete poems in 1–60.[15] Beyond the purely arithmetical point, it is clear that the uses carefully signaled by the choice of meter in 1–51 are overturned in 52–60. As metrical minority (fourteen of fifty for 1–51), non-hendecasyllabic poems are already thereby *marked*; the majority of them are further marked by length (sixteen of fifty poems contain at least twenty lines: seven of the thirty-six hendecasyllables, as against nine of the fourteen non-hendecasyllables). These formal markers correspond to – and, for the attentive reader, come to indicate – equivalent markedness in content. Though the point is somewhat subjective, few will deny above-average significance to the Lesbia poems 8, 11, 37 (and thus to the companion piece 39), and 51; to the Bithynian journey-poems 4 and 31; to the literary criticism of 22 and 44; to the attack on Mamurra, Caesar, and Pompey in 29; or to the hymn to Diana, 34: obvious highlights! The three remaining poems 17, 25, and 30 are more problematic in this regard. Nonetheless, the general correlation between longer, particularly important, and non-hendecasyllabic poems in 1–51 is beyond serious question.

By contrast, no poems in 1–60 seem at greater risk of being dismissed as mere "squibs" than 52 and 59; 60 has historically been seen this way as well. If anything, 52–60 seem to *reverse* the metrical signaling established in 1–51, in that it is precisely the hendecasyllabic pieces we particularly notice here. Poem 55 is marked for its relative length (twenty-two out of eighty lines for

---

[13] The repeated frame makes a rather different effect in its other appearances (poems 16, 36, and 58), where the greater lengths (fourteen, twenty, and ten lines) give scope for us to have "forgotten" the opening and thus be struck by its recall at the end. For 52, noting that the framing line (52.1 = 52.4) in fact is a pure iambic trimeter (unlike the two framed lines 52.2–3 but as in poems 4 and 29), a truly invidious view of it would suspect that the poet simply found himself unable to fit his intended point in lines 2–3 with his intended meter.

[14] By syllable-count, poem 51 sums to 152, compared to 192 for poem 30; 53, 59, and 60 contain forty-eight, sixty-one, and sixty respectively.

[15] Eighteen of thirty-six hendecasyllabic poems in 1–51 (including 2b and 14b) contain eleven lines or fewer.

the entire sequence; with it come the ten lines of its companion piece, 58b); 57 and 58 are marked for their bracing comment on Caesar and Lesbia respectively.

Generic and Other Differences

Poems 53, 56, and 59 resemble many of Martial's epigrams in constituting what we would call jokes; poems 1–51 of course *contain* plays on words, amusing scenarios, and the like, but no poem in 1–51 just is a joke, that is, an anecdote with a setup/punchline structure.[16] Neither 53 nor 57 has an addressee; the only parallels in 1–51 are 10 and 45; these long, narrative poems are completely dissimilar in every other respect. Poem 59 is also unique for addressing itself to unnamed, unhinted-at parties (the subject of *uidistis* at 59.3; the closest parallel is *hospites* at 4.1, which, however, provides enough information to visualize the scene dramatically) – except for poem 60, which also does so (although most critics see Lesbia, others a male friend).[17] Poems 59 and 60 are also unusual in that they provide only the faintest indication as to the Catullan speaker's motivations for producing them. We usually know (or eventually find out) the root of his grudge against his invective targets.[18] The point of the two Camerius poems (55 and 58b) is likewise unclear.

While **Ax** does not, of course, contain the only instances of "obscenity" in 1–60, there are clear respects in which such material is either more extreme than in 1–51, put to different use, or both.[19] There is a world of difference between the threats of homosexual rape in poems 15, 16, and 21 and the narrated homosexual rape of 56. In 15 and 21, the rhetoric of bodily domination is used to warn Aurelius off the "crime" of seeking the affection of "Catullus' boy," Juventius; in poem 16, it is part of a cleverly self-performing and self-refuting literary game. In 56, on either of the going

---

[16] Poem 32 is probably the closest, but the outrageous humor of its final line (*pertundo tunicamque palliumque*) cannot count as a punchline a mere three lines after the smutty genius of 32.8: *nouem continuas fututiones*. Poem 42 does end with a punchline, but its length and dramatic/dialogic form also distinguish it sharply from these joking anecdotes.

[17] See Nappa (2003) for extensive discussion and 59 n.9 for bibliography.

[18] Alfenus' wrongdoing in poem 30 is unclear: his "abandonment" of Catullus perhaps consists in his failure to send poetry, as Cornificius has failed to do (38), and as Calvus is warned against doing (50), perhaps in failing to assist Catullus in seeking financial emolument from his stint in Bithynia. Otherwise, only at 33 (Vibennius father and son) and 42 (in which the motivation is clear, but the identity of the invective target mysterious) are we in doubt. Poems 34 and 45 are the only poems in 1–51 not recognizably delivered in the Catullan first person voice; their presence and placement will be explained in the final chapter.

[19] On Catullan obscenity, see Lateiner (1977), Richlin (1992), and Fitzgerald (1995) 59–86.

understandings of what the *pupulus* was found doing before his rape,[20] the poet's motivation to tell Cato the story *after the fact* is merely that it is amusing. The pose of retributive moralism in the early poems is replaced by a much more anarchic Priapism here. The frank accusation of pathic homosexuality by Caesar in 57 is harsher in several respects than anything in poem 29.[21]

The same is less obviously true of Lesbia in poem 58, compared to the accusations of promiscuity leveled at her in 1–51, but it is still the case that she is attacked with properly obscene diction in 58 (*glubit*, 58.5), as she is not in 1–51.[22] Poem 59 is also more obscene, it is probably safe to say, than anything in 1–51: *Rufa Rufulum fellat* is extremely frank invective against a respectable Roman lady.[23] The only woman other than Lesbia mentioned in a graphically sexual context in 1–51 is Ipsitilla in poem 32 (that Ameana is *defututa* is merely *said* at 41.1). In that she is a prostitute and a presumptively fictitious one at that, and that the sex implied is neither oral nor incestuous, and therefore not polluting, 32 counts as far milder. Note too that only 56 and 59 find laughter in *actual* sexual violence, as opposed to the threat thereof.

Next there is the bizarre pair, 55 and 58b. Though many have wanted to stitch the latter onto the former,[24] no concrete proposal has found much success. Neither do the two poems make much sense as they are; 58b is widely written off as an "unfinished draft."[25] It is also unparalleled for such companion-poems to be separated by three unrelated poems instead of by one or none, or else by many poems.[26]

Textual disturbance may be at fault here: the text of poem 54 is utterly hopeless; 55 and 58b are quite troubled, and 59 and 60 may be fragmentary. An opponent of a separate **Ax** can indeed appeal to problems of

---

[20] Either masturbating or (as is grammatically dubious) having sex with a *puella* (Lesbia?). For the grammatical difficulty, see Kroll (1968) *ad loc.*; for wider discussion, Tanner (1972).

[21] In 29 the primary target is Mamurra, and Caesar (and Pompey) by extension; in 58 the two are equally attacked. Caesar is not *named* in 29, and denying the identification of him as its *cinaedus Romulus* is thus at least thinkable; Catullus has given himself no "out" in 58.

[22] *trecentos ... ilia rumpens, hanc ... omnes amatis ... semitarii moechi*: not mild words to be sure.

[23] Contrast Postumia in poem 27, accused only of drunkenness. Besides Lesbia, the women rudely noticed in 1–51 are either unnamed (the young wife in 17, the *moecha putida* of 42), *scorta* or otherwise demimondaines (6, 10, 41, 43), or presumptively fictional (Ipsitilla in 32). Caecilius' *docta puella* in 35 and Acme in 45 are not, I think, targets of Catullan aggression.

[24] Trappes-Lomax (2007) 138–39 takes this view, and provides bibliography.

[25] So Thomson (1997) 344.

[26] One intervening poem: the *passer* in 2 and 3 (possibly), kisses in 5 and 7, Egnatius in 37 and 39, Ameana at 41 and 43; consecutive poems: Aurelius in 15 and 16, Furius in 23 and 24 (also at 26), rapacious provincial officials in 28 and 29. Many poems: Catullus' two estates at 31 and 44, the two Sapphic Lesbia poems 11 and 51.

transmission, but a proponent can do so as well. The increased frequency and severity of these disturbances relative to the preceding poems is at least consistent with different circumstances of transmission at the earliest stages of the tradition.

Finally, there is the issue of the dating of poem 52. Though most Catullans accept that the "consulship" by which Vatinius falsely swears at 52.2 is the *future* one which he, as Caesarian henchman and praetor in 55 BCE, confidently expects, the case for identifying it with his actual suffect consulship in December of 47 BCE cannot be dismissed out of hand.[27] Hutchinson points out that *per consulatum* can be taken temporally, thus punning on the brevity of Vatinius' tenure of office. The latter, that is, swears falsely not only "on his consulship" but also "throughout his (entire, days-long) consulship." If that is correct, it marks the only datable reference in the poems outside 56–54 BCE – another possible difference.

Objections

Two sorts of objections can now be anticipated. First, it might be objected that some of the differences between 1–51 and 52–60 are either byproducts of progressive tendencies in 1–60 (rather than owing to a sharp disjunction after 51), or that the actual discontinuity is to be located elsewhere. On the other sort of objection, one would seek to mitigate the evidence for discontinuity by pursuing the contrary case for positive continuity, arguing that 52–60 are connected to the preceding poems by, as it were, intratextual connective tissue.

An objector of the first kind would point to the three brief poems 47–49 (twenty lines total): why not begin the "mostly short" concluding section with poem 47? Similarly, the declining metrical freedom in the hendeca-syllabic base is also evident in poem 50 (one instance in twenty-one lines), and in 46–48 (one instance in twenty-four lines): why not begin the metrically tighter close with 46?

The argument fails. At most it could account for only two anomalous aspects, namely poem-length and the treatment of the hendecasyllabic base; the metrical uniqueness of 52 (followed by that of 55 and 58b) and its bodily invective, which the following poems pick up so extensively, mark clear differences for which this objection does not account. Even for

---

[27] Barrett (1972) and Hutchinson (2003) 208 argue for the later date; see Ryan (1995) for the opposing case. As Barrett 35–36 remarks, an oath sworn on an expected or future state of affairs would ordinarily be sworn *per spem* (*c. gen.*) or *per rem futuram* or the like; no clear parallel for the alleged use here has been shown.

poem-length, the case for gradation rather than disjunction is inconclusive: 52–60 contain a single "long" poem, 55, surrounded by three "short" ones on one side and six on the other. Hypothesizing a mostly short final section beginning at 46 or 47 adds two more lengthy exceptions: the consecutive twenty-one- and sixteen-line poems 50 and 51.[28] As a principle of unity, this is hardly irresistible. When the other features surveyed here are added, however, we see sharp distinctions beginning with 52 itself (unprecedented brevity, unprecedented meter) and continuing immediately with 53 (lack of addressee, anecdotal or joke structure, barely precedented brevity); 54 is hard to evaluate for its hopeless corruption, but 55 is likewise metrically and otherwise unprecedented.

Regarding proposals to locate the disjunction elsewhere, it is of course impossible to consider and refute each hypothetical suggestion. Apart from poem 46, I find no plausible cases.[29] Scherf argues that this poem marks a programmatic shift, with the *egelidos tepores* at 46.1 indicating that a warmer and gentler – that is, a less abusive – wind will blow for the rest of the book.[30] But beside the fact that this is a dubious characterization of 46–60 in any case (think of 47, 52, 54, 57, 58, 59, and 60), the suggestion is deeply compromised by the very next poem: why would a programmatic turn to mildness be followed *immediately* by invective? The case for poem 27 announcing an invective program would be ruined if it were followed by, say, the home-coming villa-poem 31 rather than poems 28 and 29 with their political invective. Likewise, it is scarcely credible that a programmatic turn *from* invective in 46 would be immediately contradicted by political invective against Piso and his associates, especially given that Piso had been one of the targets of poem 28.

Bracketing 52–60 yields alternative accounts both for programmaticity in poem 46 and for the brevity of poems 47–49. The final sentence of poem 46 (9–11) is a farewell, introduced by *o dulces comitum ualete coetus*. This indeed introduces impending closure, a five-poem closing sequence bidding *adieu* in turn to Catullus' most important associates: Veranius and Fabullus (47), Juventius (48), Calvus (50), and Lesbia (51). Cicero in poem 49 has of course not appeared previously in the book; the placement of the poem can still be

[28] A similar problem arises in the matter of the Aeolic base: poem 54 is the sole problem-case for claiming "stricter" treatment of the base in 52–60. If one's "stricter final section" is taken to begin earlier, it must also account for the very free poem 49 and possibly 45, 42, and so on.

[29] Clausen proposed ending the sequence with poem 50. So complete, however, has been the rehabilitaton of poem 51, and so indispensable the responsion between it and poem 11, *qua* Sapphic Lesbia-poem, that that proposal is now all but unthinkable.

[30] Scherf (1996) 84–85.

explained as a specular responsion with poem 1 (poems of "gratitude" to prominent Roman men of letters, with *patrona* at 1.9 and *patronus* at 49.7 unique responsions).[31] If that is accepted, we see that the placement of short poems in 1–51 is consistent and tight. Poems containing fewer than eight lines appear only in liminal moments: 14b and 26, framing that unit; 27, introducing the following one; and 47–49, just before the closural sequence 50–51.

Turning to the second objection, I now summarize the principal intratextual connections which have been alleged between 52–60 and previous poems: that the final stanza of poem 51 and poem 52 are each four-line soliloquies; that poem 51 ends with *otium*, while the political/forensic themes in 52–54 are united by *negotium*; that Calvus in poem 50 reappears in 53; that many of these poems, from 47 on, have a strongly Roman (as opposed to, e.g., Veronese) local coloring; and that the two Sapphic poems 11 and 51 are respectively the eleventh and eleventh-to-last poems.

Rather than expatiate at length against the persuasiveness of these connections, I am all but content to state them transparently and to leave their evaluation to the reader. My own sense is that the consecutive four-line soliloquies would constitute a clumsy, unlovely specularity if meant to be read consecutively (less so, if 52 begins a separate section, or a separate work entirely), and that the *otium/negotium* connection is a wispy confection, while the "Romanness" of these poems is only slightly more substantial.[32] The arguably specular arrangement of 11 and 51 might be more serious, though the claim rests on vulnerable assumptions, namely the unity of poems 2 and 54, as well as the integrity and authorial placement of 58b. This leaves Calvus, in my view the most serious matter. Indeed, I would score the recurrence of Catullus-and-Calvus in the first two poems in **Ax**, 52 and 53 – with these two poems clearly connected *to each other* (*Vatinius*, 52.3, *Vatiniana . . . crimina*, 53.2–3) by the figure of Calvus' political enemy – as the primary grounds to maintain that these poems *are* connected to poem 50, and meant to be read with it in mind.[33]

---

[31] Since only one poem can be strictly speaking the last, but Catullus' concluding "agenda" could well be too rich for any one poem to satisfy, I trust it does not stretch the concept of "ending" or "framing" to the point of vacuousness to see an antepenultimate poem 49 responding to poem 1. On the other hand, I submit, it would indeed flirt with vacuousness to explain each poem from 46–60 in those terms.

[32] I do not mean to mock this reading; the Roman setting would be a perfectly reasonable recurrence to *notice* here, if indeed there were not discontinuity at 51|52. My point is rather that this recurrence is not at all robust enough to count against the case for discontinuity.

[33] Further supporting such linkage between poem 50 and 52–53 is the suggestiveness of poem 49 to Cicero (directly referring to his work as legal advocate, arguably glancing at his less impressive poetic career) immediately preceding Calvus *qua* poet in 50, with 53 shortly returning to Calvus *qua* forensic orator.

I do not think this connection is dispositive or even close to it, and I would certainly insist that it is not necessarily a problem for my view at all: rather, this is just to say that if **Ax** is a separate but connected part of **A**, the presence of Catullus and Calvus at either end seems overwhelmingly likely to be the point of contact or interface.

Positive Characterization

These poems, then, are unlike 1–51. But what *are* they like? The existing literature in favor of their exclusion argues that they are a second-rate miscellany: isolated individual pieces, perhaps unfinished drafts, possibly swept up among the rest of the poet's *Nachlass* and assembled together with it, though it can plausibly be allowed that among this ephemeral (52–54, 56) and incomplete or experimental (55, 58b, 59, 60?) lot, two polished and important pieces (57 and 58) and one genuinely funny squib (53, though we remain unsure what *salaputium* means) fortuitously appear.[34] Many hypotheses could account for their exclusion; the simplest would be that they were composed after the collection had been circulated. In particular, the placement of 58b is extremely helpful in casting suspicion on the entire stretch between it and 55, wherein the two poems we would most hate to lose are found. Since few readers take 58b as a successful freestanding responsion to 55, and since the sum of three intervening poems goes against the poet's practice in any case, grounds for thinking the entire sequence authorial and consistent with the poet's practice in 1–51 are weak. The text fits easily with the hypothesis that a posthumous copyist, not wishing to make an aesthetic intervention in the text, mechanically tacked on the poems that he wished to preserve.

Since, as we have seen, a satisfying closural sequence can be shown to begin at poem 46 or thereabouts, one might suppose that poem 51, with its recall of the most memorable figure in the book, and especially given the emotional and (apparent) temporal reversal it effects in the Lesbia cycle, is an extraordinary surprise and makes for a haunting, unforgettable climax. For that poem, then, to be followed by so ectopic a squib as poem 52, by such a near nullity of a piece, followed by similar ones, would stand as a clear indicator of their distinct status. In tacking on these poems at the end of his roll, our hypothetical literary preservationist may have assumed that readers would not miss that point.

---

[34] Clausen (1976) 40: "Very little can be made of 54; 55 reads like a failed metrical experiment; 58b must be unfinished; and 60 is a scrap. Would Catullus end his pretty book of poems with such? No; but the editor, more concerned to preserve than to present, would."

I indicate my distance from this story not out of convinced dissent but rather, in part, out of strategic caution. Then too, there are positive indications that 52–60 do belong together, if not necessarily here. If one takes the widespread, gratuitous (as opposed to strategic) obscenity of 52–60 as a marker of their own internal unity, perhaps these poems gesture at a different sort of collection or sequence: they mark a clear escalation in the frequency and prominence of the "Priapic pose" on the poet's part. Poems 52, 53, and 54 are all linked by bodily invective or humor: Nonius' tumors, Calvus' short stature, Otho's proportions, and Libo's crepitations (if, in fact, we read that correctly). Poem 56 humorously narrates the speaker's rape of a boy; 57 and 58 are obscene, sexual invective; 59 makes a joke of another rape. Several of these pieces comically "reserve" their lexical obscenities to their final line: perhaps *salaputium* (54.5), but certainly *rigida mea cecidi* (56.7), *glubit* (58.5), and *tunderetur* (59.5). To contrast the "satiric dialogue" in poem 55 with that of poem 10, where the *scortum* in 10 is quick-witted (in fact, the only character in the poems who gets one over on the poet), the *scortum* in 55 opts for a different and lower register of humor, baring her breasts to Catullus to show that she is not hiding Camerius therein. These poems are also linked to each other by repeated diction and similarity of conceit: *Vatinius* in poem 52 and *Vatiniana* in 53, as we have seen; poem 55 ends with Catullus wishing to be *particeps amoris*, and poem 56 shows him, forcibly, doing just that; Caesar and Mamurra's sexual degradation in 57 is followed by Lesbia's in 58 and by Rufa's in 59. Though many of the prosopographical issues are unclear, finally, the frequency with which prominent political figures are named and, mostly, abused is certainly high.

Possibly framing these poems, 52 and 60 share a few features. Each assumes the pose of aggrieved party or victim (as does 58), and (uniquely) contains an intimation of the poet's mortality: where Catullus begins and ends 52 by asking himself *quid moraris emori?*, in 60 the unnamed addressee has abandoned Catullus *in nouissimo casu*. Could these similarities mark off this run of poems as a unity on its own or as a sub-unity within 1–60? Especially once it is conceded that the level of textual disturbance here is high, it is not at all impossible to see in these shared features recognizable principles of unity for the putative section they may constitute.

Possibilities

What, then, *should* we think of these poems? I now set out, with brief comment, options which I take to be representative of the range of plausible accounts:

1) They are a miscellany, united principally by their author's having rejected them from his artfully structured book. Shared features such as their brevity and obscenity might be explained as follows: Catullus, in winnowing down a larger body of lyric poems, omitted some of his shortest and roughest pieces for artistic reasons (say, in order to effect a sharper thematic distinction between the lyric collection and the epigrams). As to their shared slightness, one naturally would expect slighter pieces to be winnowed down, especially if a round-numbered total count of poems was expected or desired. Belated caution or good sense kept 57 out; 55 and 58b really are a metrical experiment. Such a model might appeal especially to scholars sympathetic to a performance model of the poems' composition, whereby poems well-received at convivia or the like would subsequently make it into later authorial collections; those who think Catullus must have died soon after the dramatic date of the poems can have this, too. The posthumous editor, then, will have put these poems in the place they best fit, the end of what was known or correctly guessed to be the authorized lyric book.

2) They are the remains of an additional unit in **A**, rejected or abandoned "pre-publication." The Catullo-Calvus connection with poem 50 and the address to Caesar in poem 54 could be used to argue for this possibility: just as 14b introduces a new poem and 16 includes comment on the kiss poems from 1–14, so 52 could have been intended as a third very short unit-introducing poem (like 14b and 27), with 54 alluding to Caesar's "reader response" to 29. The foreseen pattern would then be a reprise of the movement from 1–14 to 14b–26: fifteen sparingly obscene poems followed by ten mostly obscene ones there; for 27–51 and 52–60, twenty-five intermittently obscene poems, once more followed by ten mostly obscene ones. Reasons for their exclusion and explanation for their survival as in option (1) above.

3) They are fragments or selections of a separate, possibly later work. The Priapean fragment preserved by the indirect tradition (Mynors' Fragment 1) is here suggestive: wouldn't these poems fit? This approach should be particularly attractive for those who favor the late dating (47 BCE) of poem 52; Vatinius' brief tenure of the suffect consulship in 47 could then be taken as an intentional marker of these poems' belatedness relative to **A**. Also plausibly in its favor is 54.6–7: *irascere iterum meis iambis | immerentibus, unice imperator.* Since this could plausibly indicate Caesar's reaction not only to poem 29 but to

the elegiac collection as well, it might be later than both.[35] To explain their transmission, we would hypothesize a private reader or bookseller appending these additional poems onto the end of a copy of **A**.

4)   They are the remains of an additional body of short lyric poems, like those of **A** in many ways, but "deauthorized" or "suppressed" by an act of authorial recension subsequent to their initial circulation. On this option, the represented temporal sequencing within the internal units of **A** may reflect historical facts about the poems' composition: smaller collections did circulate among Catullus' friends, one of which is witnessed by our **Ax**, though we presumably will posit textual disturbance to explain the dubious overall coherence of the unit. With the poems of **B** and **C** coalescing, Catullus will have sought to assemble an authoritative, "monumental" presentation of the great body of his work. For the lyric collection, 1–14, 14b–26, and 27–51 make the cut, but 52–60 do not; this decision is taken early enough to permit the crafting of the global design seen in the **A-B-C** collection. This would still explain the appropriateness of their transmission: excluded from the monumental collection **A-B-C**, but poems that did circulate and hook thematically into the social world of the poems, they would always have retained a sort of "deuterocanonical" status vis-à-vis the others.

5)   52–60 are indeed the authorial culmination of **A**. Structural fitting is as in scenario (3): an introductory poem announcing, perhaps as pure poetic fiction, a new dramatic moment, followed shortly by a character from 27–51 depicted as having reacted to invective content in those poems. Any obscurities attributed to textual corruption and the loss of paratextual markers marking them off as a separate part or section.

Which one? My own answer is to recommend suspension of judgment, in that I find sufficient plausibility in each option that "some one of the other four" seems to me always to deserve more credence than any single one does. Nonetheless, I do tend to depreciate options (1) and (2) to some extent. Against (1), the internal resonances within poems 52–60 strike me as uncomfortably high;[36] against (1) and (2) alike, in our lack of any clear

---

[35]   Further, poem 116 closes **C2** with a promise of (low-register) invective against Gellius; this might point forward to anticipated poems which have not survived. **Ax** does contain characters from **C2** otherwise excluded from **A**: Caelius (poems 58 and 100) and possibly "Rufulus" = Rufus (poems 59, 69, and 77). The point would stand whether any, none, or all of these names pick out Marcus Caelius Rufus. If **Ax** is a fragment of a work, it could answer to the "preview" of poem 116, so long as Gellius were attacked elsewhere in it.

[36]   One must concede, however, the logical quicksand here: if Catullus *regularly* crafts intratextual resonances between his pieces, even ones residing in separate works, and if he winnowed down his

parallel for an editorial "preservationist" seeking to rescue from oblivion a few freestanding pieces or a rejected sequence of poems *as well as* multiple authorially arranged works, *Nachlass*-theories of **Ax** start out burdened by reasonable doubt as to whether that sort of account reflects ordinary or plausible poetic practice at Rome.

By contrast, I fail to see that any positive consideration tells against options (3) and (4), excepting only the initial presumption in favor of textual conservatism.[37] As Barchiesi's (2005) influential discussion of the physical book has emphasized, the kind of textual intervention that would explain the unauthorized presence of **Ax** at the end of (some copy or copies of) **A** would not be abnormal or unusual. As between these two options, I find much that recommends option (4) in particular, and accordingly regard it as the single best hypothesis, the leading candidate.

First, the poems of **A**, as we will see in greater detail in the next chapter, depict or "stage" the progressive textualization and circulation of its component parts; these are "events" in the social and literary world of the depicted Catullus and his circle of associates. There is no need here to raise the unanswerable question of whether each part *in fact* circulated among the poet's friends in a way that tracks the manner represented. What matters, rather, is the evident verisimilitude of the depiction of poetic practice. Just as poem 13 is not compelling historical evidence that Catullus once invited a man named Fabullus to dine with him, but the same poem *is* good historical evidence for elite Roman men inviting each other to dinner parties, so too do we have good reason to take it that the small-scale circulation of smaller runs of poetry "like" **Ax** reflects historical norms and practices. And if that is the case, the core hypothesis on which option (4) rests would constitute attractively normal poetic practice.

---

larger body of work by deciding to exclude ones with a *particular set* of features, a body of excluded Catullan work might exhibit a merely specious appearance of "fitting together."

[37] That is, if a few dozen lines of pseudepigrapha had followed *Aeneid* 12.952 *uitaque cum gemitu fugit indignata sub umbras* in our text of Vergil, the correct conclusion that they should be excised would need to prove its merits first; if the case for their suspicion were merely "no better than" the case for their defense, few or none would actually *believe* the truth.

I suppose it would be fitting here to explain why I do not offer the spuriousness or non-Catullan authorship of **Ax** among my leading options, especially since the hypothesis might indeed nicely account for certain features of these poems, for example their roughness and brevity. The reason is not that I am sure these poems are "inimitably Catullan" but the following: if one were trying to pass counterfeit poems off as Catullan, it would be foolish to affect the unparalleled (as far as we know) metrical peculiarity seen in the Camerius poem(s) 55 and 58b. Absent the Camerius piece(s) (which, again, contain nearly half of the line-count in **Ax**), one actually might be tempted to entertain their hypothetical spuriousness. As it is, however, the option requires its own unproven hypothesis (Camerius as textual intrusion into the fake bits, or Catullus' having written *other* lost poems with the (hen)decasyllablic peculiarity) to get off the ground as a plausible option.

Similarly, we also have good historical evidence for a later act of authorial recension amounting to the "deauthorizing" of earlier work and earlier authorial recensions. I am naturally thinking here of the epigram opening (our version of) Ovid's *Amores*. In these two couplets, the three-book work not only writes its own five-book backstory, but asserts the authorial supersession of that earlier, longer work; by asserting their poet's preference for the new, reduced version, the speaking books depreciate all of their now-excluded material. And while of course they call our attention and curiosity precisely *to* the empty space(s) left in our "improved" recension, as well as any traces of textual suturing, they also clearly dissuade us from (re)reading what has been omitted, opening up interpretive space between reading *amores*, erotic poetry written by Ovid (which the deleted material remains), and reading the *Amores* and Ovid, their author-editor-arranger (which now can only properly be done using the new version). If you already know and possess the old recension, you are now told you must disregard or mentally bracket at least some of it.

Here too, one can be as dubious or dismissive about the historicity of the "five-volume *Amores*" as one likes; the point, once again, is that it is hard to see how the epigram could work, if it were not recognizable practice at Rome, half a century after Catullus at any rate, for belated authorial recensions to intervene in the canonicity and interpretive status of already circulated work, and not necessarily by inclusion of additional work or alteration of previous work alone.[38] Furthermore, it is worth noting that the act of suppression-by-recension that Ovid either brings about or plausibly fictionalizes is far more extreme than the one Catullus would have pulled off, in declining to "rerelease" **Ax**: if one poet can plausibly place two full papyrus *rolls* under erasure, the other poet can plausibly do the same to (at most) two individual *sheets* of papyrus.

In sum, option (4) fits the evidence perfectly and is perfectly plausible. I do expect that very claim will disquiet here: isn't this somehow "too clever by half"? Does it not try to "have it both ways" on whether **Ax** hooks on to the end of **A**? Is this not a "just-so story"? To such worries – I do sympathize with them – it is hard to mount much defense, beyond recalling that I *agree* that the historical facts about these poems' composition and transmission are beyond conclusive recovery, and that my goal is

---

[38] It is, to be sure, clear that the epigram invites us to receive it as clever and surprising, a novelty. But I take it that the novelty is far less plausibly felt to lie in Ovid's *invention* of such "recensional authority," and far more likely to consist in the epigram's explicit *notice* of that phenomenon, as well as the self-subversions implicit in the advice, "don't think about the missing stuff, it's irrelevant now!"

rather to show that the bracketing of **Ax** is low in dialectical cost on most or all reasonable ways of seeing the poems. And then, if I aim a dart at a dartboard, dead center is probably the last place I would intuitively expect it to land – but I would still deny that there is any one other single place the dart is more likely to land. So, I admit it: option (4) is more likely false than true. I don't need it to be true. But an unprovable hypothesis might still be true, even though it is highly attractive and fits all available facts.

Finally, I come to option (5), the retention of **Ax** as final short-lyric "unit," a part of Catullan design at every time and without qualification. I do not fear this option, because few or no major claims of mine are incompatible with it; if I do not love it either, it is because it renders some issues messy and leaves important questions unanswerable. Worst of all, the shift in poetic register and genre at 51|52 seems to be (uniquely) illegible, given the text as we have it. Nonetheless, it might be true: it would not need much textual corruption for a short and sweet metapoetic marker to go irretrievably missing, and a short and sweet metapoetic marker would be all we would need, to bring to light a compelling account of 52–60 as (merely) "another short smutty bit, like 14b–26." Then too, just following Catullus and Calvus in 52–53, we do indeed come to a textual black hole with poem 54. The metapoetic legibility of **Ax** might well have lived and died precisely there.[39]

If I am right that that is plausible, there is a problem here that simply cannot be resolved definitively: the case neither for removing **Ax** nor for retaining it can be put beyond doubt. What we need, then, is a way to proceed. I hope I have now compellingly shown that we are overwhelmingly justified in examining the corpus with **Ax** bracketed. The remainder of this chapter will put the case that our corpus without **Ax** displays overwhelming evidence for its authorial design. Chapter 2 will then read **A** and its metapoetics as that evidence suggests, namely as a work of art, a poetry book. In an addendum to that chapter, I then return to **Ax**, offering a speculative proposal for how it might have fit in and been legible at (or as) the authorial ending of **A**. The dialectical end-game, I hope, will be not to settle any question so much as to *defuse our worries* about the historical, point-of-fact explanation for **Ax**. "It's plausible that it doesn't belong here; if it does belong here, it's plausible that it worked *like this*; even if it didn't work like this, the example shows, there is no particular

---

[39] Notice that the metapoetic legibility of **Ax** will be a legitimate question on options in which it is authorially abandoned or deauthorized as well; it will just be a less pressing one for our purposes.

reason to think that the way it really worked (whatever that might be) would change the view of much of anything outside these poems." This is the extent of my own firm convictions on the matter, and it is all the conviction that I wish to replicate in others.

3   Structural Consequences of Excluding Ax

Specularity of A and C2

This section seeks simply and quickly to set out the most prominent thematic correspondences between the respective halves of **A** and **C2**. A substantive tour of these poems will come in the following chapter. My aim here is to ground the claim that the respective halves do indeed substantively reflect the formula "P is to Q as P′ is to Q′." Accordingly, the correspondences are pointed out in the least interpretively committed way possible. Liberal use of question marks will indicate areas of textual uncertainty and/or disagreement in the literature.[40]

The first twenty-four or twenty-five poems in **A** and the first twenty-five in **C2** closely mirror each other in theme and arrangement. After the dedicatory opening of **A**, an initial run of Lesbia poems (2, 2b?, 3, 5, 7, 8, 11, 13?) is interspersed with others (2b?, 4, 6, 9, 10, 12, 13, 14) giving way to an invective campaign against Furius and Aurelius, rivals for the affections of Juventius (15, 16, 21, 23, 26; Juventius is addressed once, in 24), again with a few interspersed poems (the introductory 14b and non-hendecasyllabic 17, 22, and 25). The end of this unit is signaled at least by the thematic disjunction following it, if not also by internal closural gestures of its own.

So in **C2** do we find an initial run of Lesbia poems: 70, 72, 75, 76, 78b?, 79, 83, 85, 86, 87, 92. In 1–26, the affair between the poet and "his girl" seems not to have begun in poem 2, is only clearly ongoing in (after?) poems 5 and 7, and then has terminated abruptly at some point prior to the dramatic setting of 8. In **C2**, the affair is on again in the initial Lesbia poem 70 (though clearly all is not well), and then seems off again from poem 72. Both runs are notably dialogic, imputing words, attitudes, and motivations to Lesbia, to which Catullus responds (2, 2b?, 3, 7, 8 ~ 70, 72, 83, 85, 87, 92). There is one poem addressed to Juventius (81), again in the context of romantic rivalry. Lesbia poems often alternate with other poems, but are found consecutively as well in either sequence (2–3 or 2–2b–3 and 7–8 ~ 75–76, 78b–79?, 85–86–87).

---

[40] I do appeal to the familiar set of "Lesbia poems," which includes, as seems clearly warranted to me, those poems which present the poet obsessing over an unnamed woman.

The interspersed poems in **C2**, meanwhile, reflect the invective against Catullus' rivals in 14b–26, with the exception that most of these are now rivals for *Lesbia's* affection rather than Juventius' (Rufus in 69, 71, 73? and 77; Lesbius in 78b? and 79; Quintius? in 82;[41] Lesbia's husband in 83; Gellius in 74, 80, and 88–91). One of the two principal rivals in **C2**, in fact, is even onomastically specular with one of the two in **A**: RVF-us ~ FVR-ius.[42]

The correspondence between poems 8 and 76 (itself the eighth poem in its series) is particularly close: each finds the poet conducting a lengthy soliloquy, as he seeks to set aside his unhappy love. The first two Lesbia poems in **C2** (70 and 72) are separated by a single poem; they feature central themes (the reliability of lovers' speech, "marrying Jupiter") and dialogue between the lovers; the comparison with 5 and 7 is hard to resist.[43] Note especially the backward-glancing *dicebas* at 72.1 as reflex of *quaeris* in 7.1, as well as the Jovian presence at 7.5: *oraclum Iouis*. The other paired initial poems in **C2**, 69 and 71, are similarly linked by the shared presence of an animal, namely a goat, in erotic contexts; this, too, has a reflex in the paired sparrow poems at the beginning of **A**.[44]

The apparent finality of the rupture with Lesbia in 1–26 (11, but with 8.12–19 clearly implying irresolution) is, however, contrapuntal with that in 69–92. The latter's close represents the poet's fallacious proof that Lesbia loves him; self-deceit ties the two together. The great themes of foreign travel and provincial service in 1–26 (4, 9–13) are seen in one poem in 69–92 (84: Arrius' service in Syria). Six poems addressing Furius and/or Aurelius in 1–26 (11, 15, 16, 21, 23, 26) match the six Gellius poems; though the respective roles differ, three poems featuring Veranius and/or Fabullus (9, 12, 13) match the three featuring Rufus.[45]

As for the second halves, **A**'s begins with a probably programmatic introduction (27) warning of "bitterer cups" to come, followed by two

---

[41] Unless Quintius, placed after the Juventius poem, is a rival for *him*.

[42] Various attempts have been made to identify either target of Catullus' invective: for identification of Catullus' Furius with poets Furius Bibaculus and/or Furius "Alpinus," see Wheeler (1934) 78, Lyne (1978) 171 n. 13, Marsilio and Podlesney (2006); for Rufus as Caelius Rufus, see Schwabe (1862), Ellis (1876) lix n. 1, Lindsay (1948). Even if these characters are historical, nothing prevents Catullus from having noticed and played upon the specularity of their names.

[43] Though the marital theme recalls 2b.3: *quod zonam soluit diu ligatam*; a female garment is also read at 69.3 in the context of seduction. Note too that two poems in 69–92, 78b and 79, refer to Lesbia in connection with kisses. For a more in-depth study of 5 and 7 as a pair, see Segal (1968a).

[44] On the erotic goat, see Kutzko (2008).

[45] Both numerical correspondences are vulnerable to alternate counts, especially if 78 is considered a Gellius poem and 73 a Rufus poem, both of which possibilities are warranted (though 24 can also be considered a Furius/Aurelius poem, making seven apiece). There may well be authorially designed correspondences in count here, but my case hardly requires it.

scathing attacks on political figures (Piso and Memmius in 28, Mamurra, Caesar, and Pompey in 29). The second half of **C2** opens with the frank dismissal of Caesar in 93, followed by the barely disguised attack on Mamurra (*Mentula*) in 94. To explain the absence of an equivalent to 27 in **C2**, one might well think the frankness of 93 to be sufficiently bracing (in the late 50s BCE) as to mark a programmatic turn all by itself.[46] Lesbia recurs after an extended absence in both second halves (35?,[47] 36, 37, 43, 51 ~ 104, 107, 109), with the *surprise* of her reconciliation with Catullus in 36 refracted by their *inevitable* reconciliation in 107.[48]

There is one Juventius poem apiece (48 ~ 99), each on the theme of kisses: the former looks forward to future kisses; the latter announces that there will be no more.[49] Foreign travel in **A** (28, 29, 31, 45?, 46, 47) is once again cut down, very memorably so, to the brother's Asian grave in 101. Note especially Catullus' two Asian travel poems in 27–51: *aue atque uale* at 101.10 answers both the *salue* (31.12) of the homecoming poem and the *ualete* (46.9) of the departure poem. We may also compare the "travels" of Cinna's *Zmyrna* in 95 to the *papyrus* addressed by Catullus in 35.1, bound for Comum with a message for Caecilius. Further political poems are also found in both collections (politics: 41, 43, 47, 49 ~ 103?, 104?, 105, 106?, 108?, 113–15), as well as poems commenting on the work of other poets (35, 36, 38, 44, 50 ~ 95, 95b?, 96?, 105, 116). Particularly close are the references to Volusius' *Annales* in 36 and 95,[50] and the poetic consolation Catullus requests of Cornificius (38), as against the one he provides to Calvus (96), or alternatively Catullus' *dolor* in respect to Calvus (50), as against Catullus' comment on the grieving Calvus' *dolor* (96).

A few correspondences, it is true, fall in the "wrong" half: Commentary on a woman's beauty as compared to Lesbia's (43 ~ 84) appears in **A**'s second half and **C2**'s first half. The two poems attacking Mentula over his real estate holdings, 114–15, are all but final for **C2**, and recall Furius' pestilential villa in 26, the last poem in **A**'s first half.[51] The wayward

---

[46] Compare Wiseman (1969) 28. Chapter 4 will argue for a framing responsion with metapoetic significance for poems 93–116: *nil nimium* **studeo** (93.1) and *saepe tibi* **studioso** *animo* (116.1) begin the first and last poems of the sequence.

[47] On the possible reference to Lesbia in 35, see Kutzko (2006).

[48] So I read the latter reconciliation; others may of course take the correspondence straight.

[49] It is perhaps a studied contrast that poems 48 and 99 are respectively the shortest and longest poems in their halves.

[50] On the reference to Volusius in 36, see Clark (1968).

[51] Though Catullus' own real estate holdings in the second half of **A** (31 and 44) make a partial match. There is a nice opposition between 26 and 114–115: Furius' mortgaged *uillula* mocks his poverty; Mentula's vast estates, his avarice.

correspondence of 43–84 is too isolated to trouble us; that of 26–114/115 is, I think, less a miss in this way than it is a match in another way, *qua* final/ penultimate invective "villafication."[52]

There is further closural patterning within and between the halves of the two collections: both the final poem of the second half of **A** and the final poem of the first half of **C2** (51, 92) address Lesbia; both the final poem of the second half and the penultimate poem of the first half of **C2** (116, 91) address Gellius; Calvus is the addressee of 50, the penultimate poem in **A**, and of 14, the "other" internal close in the first half of **A**; both of Calvus' closes and Gellius' close (14, 51, 116) are, as the following chapters will explore further, dramas of composition.

Terminal Responsions in A, B, and C

With poem 51 the final poem of **A**, the following results obtain:

1) The opening and close of **A** reflect each other
2) The opening and close of **A** reflect the opening of **C**
3) The opening and close of **A** reflect the close of **C**[53]
4) The opening of **B** reflects the openings of **A** and **C**
5) The close of **B** reflects the close of **A** and opening of **C**

I take these points up in turn, first delineating the "opening" and "close" of each unit. For **A**, I take it that any reader coming to its end will remember not only poem 1 but also the *passer* poems as falling "in the beginning"; I thus count up to the end of poem 3 as such. I take the "closural dyad" 50–51 to be the end.[54] The endpoints of **C** are simple: the first (65) and last (116) poems only. For **B** the matter is trickier: it would be vacuous to count all of 61 and all of 64 as endpoints, since only 62 and 63 could count as falling between such a "beginning" and "end." We have, for the end, a fairly objective closing section in 64.382–408, in which the poet-narrator declares the end of the prophetic song of the Parcae and returns from the realm of myth to his contemporary world. The "beginning" cannot, however, be as clearly delineated. In light of this, I simply note that all of my correspondences in poem 61 are located within the first 65 lines, and that the amount of *content* in these eight- and seven-syllable lines is not much greater than that of the 27 hexameters of the final section of 64, or the 41+ hendecasyllables of 1–3.

---

[52] John Henderson's (2004) 67 happy pun.

[53] Tatum (1997) has laid some of the groundwork for this and later arguments relating to the opening of **A** (poem 1) and the opening and close of **C** (poems 65, 66, 116).

[54] This characterization of 50–51 will be defended in Chapter 2.

Readers will easily evaluate for themselves whether the last few parallels mentioned here unduly stretch the rubric "beginning of poems 61–64."

1)   1–3 and 50–51

The high-level parallels between 1–3 and 50–51 are obvious: the two dedicatory poems to literary friends (1 and 50) are followed by the first and final Lesbia poems in **A** (1 is followed by 2–3, 50 by 51). Separation from and longing for a beloved (poet for *puella* in 2; *puella* for *passer* in 3; poet for another poet and for Lesbia respectively in 50 and 51); a light parody of a hymn and of a dirge, with erotic longing clearly the deeper theme (2, 3); a light parody of erotic longing followed by an erotic longing to be taken seriously (50 and 51); the "third party" mediating between Catullus and Lesbia changes from pet bird in 2 and 3 to a man (*ille*, 51.1), about whom we are free to speculate: Lesbia's husband?

Verbal recollections and smaller points of similarity are too numerous to discuss individually. As these are overwhelmingly tied to poem 50 rather than 51, I print the former poem, noting below its clearer correspondences with poems 1–3.

> Hesterno, Licini, die **otiosi**
> multum **lusimus** in meis **tabellis**,
> ut conuenerat esse **delicatos**:
> scribens **uersiculos** uterque nostrum
> **ludebat** numero **modo hoc modo illoc**,   5
> reddens mutua per **iocum** atque uinum.
> atque illinc abii tuo **lepore**
> **incensus**, Licini, facetiisque,
> ut nec me miserum cibus iuuaret,
> nec somnus tegeret **quiete ocellos**,   10
> sed toto, indomitus furore, lecto
> uersarer cupiens uidere lucem,
> ut tecum loquerer, simulque ut essem.
> at defessa **labore** membra postquam
> semimortua lectulo iacebant,   15
> **hoc**, iucunde, **tibi poema feci**,
> ex quo perspiceres meum **dolorem**.
> nunc **audax** caue sis, precesque nostras,
> oramus, caue despuas, ocelle,
> ne poenas **Nemesis** reposcat a te.   20
> est uemens dea: laedere hanc caueto.

otiosi ~ nugas, 1.4; *lusimus, ludebat ~ ludere*, 2.2 and 2.9; *tabellis ~ libellum ...*
expolitum, 1.1–2; *delicatos ~ deliciae*, 2.1 and 3.4; *uersiculos ~ nugas*, 1.4; *modo hoc*

modo illoc ~ modo huc modo illuc, 3.9; *iocum ~ iocari*, 2.6; *lepore ~ lepidum*, 1.1; *incensus ~ ardor*, 2.8; *quiete ~ acquiescat*, 2.8; *ocellos, ocelle ~ ocelli*, 3.19; *labore ~ laboriosis*, 1.7; *hoc . . . tibi poema feci ~ habe tibi . . . hoc libelli*, 1.9; *dolorem ~ doloris*, 2.9; *audax ~ ausus es*, 1.5; *Nemesis ~ patrona uirgo*, 1.10

Besides the dedicatory words themselves, literary buzzwords and references to poetry and its physical media abound. The contrast is especially pointed between the "just now polished" *libellus*, marking a finished composition, and "yesterday's play" in *tabellae*, marking the *least* polished and *most* provisional composition possible. The *nugae* Cornelius valued in the past match the *uersiculi* Calvus and Catullus wrote "yesterday"; both are separate from the *current* gift, the *libellus* and *poema* respectively. Poems 2 and 3 are also activated in 50: *ludere* is read twice in both 2 and 50; *modo hoc modo illoc* at 50.5 are a pointed recollection of the verbal motif *modo huc modo illuc* at 3.9, in that *illoc* (but not *illuc*) is a nonstandard and archaizing form; the following correspondence strikes me as a presumptively *voulu* and particularly intricate self-revision:

> **tecum** lud **ere**, **si** c **ut** ipsa, **possem**
> ut **tecum** loquerer, simulque **ut** **essem**.

There are thematic ties between the opening and 51 as well. The poet-speakers in 2 and 51 both wish for the union the third parties enjoy; darkness as figuration of mortality in 3 is surely present in the poet's erotic loss of vision at 51.11–12.[55] Finally, a comparison between the sparrow's chirping (*pipiabat*, 3.10) and the poet's ringing ears in 51.10–12 (*sonitu suopte / tintinnant aures*) would not be compelling in and of itself, but it will be vindicated in what follows.

2)   *1–3/50–51 and 65*

Probably the most striking single result of separating poems 52–60 from 1–51 is the specularity thereby produced between the end of **A** (50–51) and beginning of **C** (65–66). Even critics who deny that poem 51 is the referent of *hoc . . . poema* at 50.16 will be struck by the correspondence: in either case, a poem dealing with poetic gift-exchange, the mental anguish produced by the separation between poet and beloved, and the relationship between that anguish and poetic creation, is followed by a translation of

---

[55] Between the appearance of *nox* in Catullus as figure for death early in the Lesbia cycle (5.6, *perpetua una dormienda*) and the fact that *teguntur . . . lumina nocte* is the closest poem 51 comes to the explicit death-reference of his source (τεθνάκην δ' ὀλίγω 'πιδεύης | φαίνομ' ἔμ' αὔται, Sappho 31.15–16), this point can hardly be denied.

a Greek poem. Both translations are of authors of obvious programmatic importance for the putative Catullan books in question. Both reflect the circumstances of the cover-letter introducing them (or of the preceding poem, for the skeptics). Indeed, they are the same circumstance: love and separation and thus *desiderium*. Both effect a provocative reversal of tone: humorous exaggeration in 50 introduces or precedes what may be the most poignant moment in **A**; grief and gloom in 65 introduce the frivolous, exaggerated Lock in 66. We see, in turn, the same plot in the opening of **A**: the gift of poetry in poem 1, love and separation in 2, and a winking display of grief over a frivolous and absurd loss in 3.

These thematic correspondences would be clear and compelling enough on their own; in fact, a remarkable quantity of verbal self-reference stitches poem 65 both to 1–3 (and environs) and 50–51 as well. To resort to brute arithmetic, no fewer than nine (out of 134) word-tokens in poem 65 recall the same lexeme or root found in **A** only in poems 1–3 and 50–51; another two have a unique responsion in poem 7. Five more words or roots in 65 (*cura, doctus, gremium, salio* and compounds, *rub-*) appear in those same poems, and once or twice besides in **A**. Still more are meaningfully echoed. I print 65 with the responsions unique to the terminal points of **A** in bold type, others in italics:

> Etsi me assiduo confectum *cura* **dolore**
>   seuocat a *doctis*, Ortale, **uirginibus**,
> nec potis est dulcis *Musarum* expromere fetus
>   mens *animi*, tantis fluctuat ipsa malis –
> namque mei nuper *Lethaeo gurgite* fratris   5
>   pallidulum **manans** alluit unda pedem,
> Troia Rhoeteo quem subter litore tellus
>   **ereptum** nostris obterit ex *oculis*.
>   . . .
> numquam ego te, uita frater amabilior,   10
> **aspiciam** posthac? at certe semper amabo,
>   semper *maesta* tua *carmina morte canam*,[56]
> qualia sub *densis* ramorum concinit umbris

---

[56] The consensus of manuscripts reads *morte* **tegam**; if genuine, this lexeme too responds uniquely in **A** to its close (the twinned 50.10 *nec somnus* **tegeret** *quiete ocellos* and 51.11–12 *gemina* **teguntur** | *lumina nocte*). Lenchantin de Gubernatis defends the reading, explaining "terrò [i carmi] nascosti, comporò in ritiro"; Kroll, by contrast, asserts that the reading is "nicht zu retten" in this way. The paradosis certainly does strike one as *lectio difficillima*. On my contention that poem 65 extensively recalls the diction of 1–3 and 50–51, however, it would be quite the coincidence for the tradition erroneously to have generated another such correspondence. I print editors' preferred emendation *canam* not from conviction but dialectically, since it is only after being convinced by the rest of the evidence that readers will be likely to reconsider this potential addition.

Daulias, absumpti fata gemens Ityli –
sed tamen in tantis maeroribus, Ortale, mitto   15
   haec expressa tibi *carmina* **Battiadae**,
ne tua dicta uagis nequiquam *credita* uentis
   effluxisse meo forte *putes animo*,
ut missum sponsi **furtiuo** munere **malum**
   procurrit casto **uirginis** e *gremio*,   20
quod miserae oblitae molli sub *ueste locatum*,
   dum aduentu *matris prosilit*, excutitur,
atque illud prono praeceps agitur decursu,
   huic **manat tristi** conscius *ore rubor*.

Working backward through **A**, we find ***eripit** sensus mihi nam simul te* |
*Lesbia **aspexi*** . . . (51.6–7) behind the description of the brother's death at
65.7–11. The numbing of the poet's sensations upon catching sight of his
beloved performs two functions. First, it mimes the loss of faculties
brought about by death, evoked both by the physical reality of the
"crushing" of the body in *obterit* and by the etymological implication
of *Lethaeo*. Second, that Catullus will never again catch sight of his
brother deepens the contrast between the two contexts. Here, too, we
may appeal to 51.11–22: *gemina teguntur lumina nocte*. Not only does *nox*
first appear in Catullus as a figure for death (5.6: *nox est perpetua una
dormienda*), but also the catalogue of physical symptoms in Catullus'
source-text ends with near-death (31.15–16): τεθνάκην δ' ὀλίγω 'πιδεύης |
φαίνομ' ἔμ' αὔτᾳ. The symptom *tenuis sub artus* | *flamma **demanat***
(51.9–10) is likewise picked up and reversed at 65.6, where instead of
flame spreading intense sensation down into the limbs, the spreading
(*manans*) wave of Lethe laps the brother's foot, anaesthetizing him. All
three words are unique to 51 in **A** (*mano* and its compounds only there,
aspicio likewise, *rapio* and compounds likewise if we accept the expulsion
of 59.3).

At 50.17 Catullus writes to Calvus that he made "this poem" *ex quo
perspiceres meum **dolorem***; at 65.1 Catullus' separation from the Muses
and his consequent poetic incapacity are explained by his *assiduo . . .
dolore*. This framing responsion is highly conspicuous, especially if we
accept, as I argue below, that the referent of *hoc . . . poema* is poem 51: one
book ends with a poem written to illustrate Catullus' *dolor*; the other
opens with his *dolor* now preventing composition. Poem 7 is less clearly
"at the beginning" of **A**, but it too is clearly recalled: ***Batti** ueteris sacrum
sepulchrum* and ***furtiuos** . . . amores*; not only Cyrene and hence
Callimachus, but a funereal presence as well; a secret love and gift appear

at 65.19–24.[57] The maiden's blushing red face recalls Lesbia's swollen red eyes in the final line of 3: *rubent ocelli ~ manat . . . ore rubor*; 65.5 doubly recalls 3.13–14: *malae tenebrae | Orci quae omnia bella deuoratis*: *Lethaeo ~ Orci, gurgite ~ deuoratis*. Both maidens are mentioned in relation to their mothers: 3.7 ~ 65.22–24; 65.20–22 (*gremio . . . matris . . . prosilit*) recall 3.7–9:

> . . . tam bene quam puella **matrem**,
> nec sese a **gremio** illius mouebat,
> sed **circumsiliens** modo huc modo illuc . . .

Both the sparrow in 2–3 and the apple in 65 are erotic proxies or substitutes (for *gremio* at 3.8 and 65.20 compare *sinu* at 2.2).[58] Poem 2b is also here, in the *malum* of course (2b.2, 65.19), uniquely in Catullus. The untying of the belt at 2b.3 **zonam** soluit diu **ligatam** is echoed in the reference to the maiden's clothing: *molli sub* **ueste** *locatum*. The final line of poem 2 appears as well: *et* **tristis** *animi leuare* **curas**. The intratext is distributed between the first and last lines of 65: cares of the mind open and the maiden's sad face closes the poem. *Doloris* at 2.7 is also present at 65.1; remarkably, all appearances of *dolor* in Catullus are thus closely linked: 2.7 and 50.17 framing **A**; 65.1 responding at the opening of **C**, and then twice in 96: Catullus' consolation to Calvus, the addressee of poem 50. Like 2 and 3, 65 also features a bird: *Daulias* at 65.14 is Procne the nightingale; mourning instead of mourned for.

Poems 1 and 65 interact most obviously as program- and dedication-poems and instances of gift-exchange. The inversions are clear: where poem 1 introduces a *lepidum nouum libellum*, at 65.12 the poet promises *semper maesta tua carmina morte canam*; the emotional contrast is, of course, apparent from the opening couplet, composed in the paradigmatically mournful meter and mentioning pain and anxiety; contrast the jaunty hendecasyllables of poem 1, *lepidum, expolitum*, and even the remarkable degree of rhyme at line-end (1–2, 3–4, 6–7, 9–10). Where Catullan poetry is referred to as *nugas* at 1.4, the poet has now become more serious in his grief: *carmina . . . canam*, an expression of higher poetic register, programmatically promising more of the same.[59] Where Cornelius is freely gifted with the little book *because* he thought well of Catullus' trifles, Hortalus is sent poem 66 *lest* he think Catullus unmindful of his poetic obligation. Where *lepidum* is widely thought to encode λεπτός,

---

[57] Perhaps not all readers will hear "life and love" (5.1) in Catullus' "love and death" (*semper amabo . . . carmina morte canam*), the "one perpetual night" of death (5.6) and "lights/eyes covered in twin night" (51.11–12) in the brother *ereptum nostris . . . ex oculis* and in *numquam . . . semper . . . semper*.

[58] Regardless of whether and how *passer* is a double entendre, the poet interprets the girl's play with it as *solaciolum* for an erotic longing.

[59] Compare also the internal *nugas ~uersiculos* (1.4~50.4).

"thin," and with it a Callimachean sensibility,[60] *Daulias*, especially just after *sub densis ramorum . . . umbris*, echoes δαυλός, "thick." The *doctis . . . uirginibus* at 65.2 and the *uirgo* at 65.19–24 recall the Muse, addressed at 1.9 as *patrona Virgo*, the noun a *hapax* in **A** (if the reading is correct). The form *doctis* also appears at 1.7, of Cornelius Nepos' three-roll history. Where Catullan memory is prominent in poem 1 (grateful recollection of Cornelius' support, prayer for poetic survival), 65 opens and closes with failure of memory: separation from the daughters of Mnemosyne, the brother's Lethaean oblivion, and the maiden's shame-provoking unmindfulness.

3) *1–3/50–51 and 116*

Where poem 116 had once been seen as a slight and unambitious piece, hardly capable of sustaining the role of final poem in an authorial collection, scholarship now recognizes that it is an "inverted dedication" to Gellius, the invective recipient of Catullan poetic "gifts."[61] Merely as such, it mirrors the dedicatory poems 1 and 65. The repetition of the phrase *carmina Battiadae* as object of *mitto* in poems 65 and 116 speaks strongly in favor of authorial choice underlying the transmitted position of these two poems, with the entirety of the elegiac corpus between them. So too does the gift of Greek poems link 116 with the closural dyad 50–51. Since the point of 116 is that Catullus will now *not* send the "soothing" (*lenirem*, 116.3) poems of Callimachus but rather his own invective to Gellius (whether these are the invective poems placed earlier or advance notice of a new collection of poems to come), it is entirely fitting for 116 not to be followed by a translation, or indeed by anything. And so we naturally look to poem 50, and specifically to its dedicatory conclusion, as the text to which poem 116 ought to respond. We duly find that the warning to Calvus with which poem 50 ends is now the reality Gellius in 116 faces – namely, poetic nemesis. Verbal recall is likewise conclusive:

50.14–21	116
at defessa **labore** membra postquam	Saepe tibi studioso animo uenante requirens
semimortua lectulo iacebant,	**carmina** uti possem mittere Battiadae,
hoc, iucunde, tibi, **poema** feci,	**qui** te lenirem nobis, **neu** conarere
ex quo perspiceres meum dolorem.	tela infesta <meum> mittere in usque caput,
nunc audax caue sis, **precesque nostras,**	**hunc** uideo mihi **nunc** frustra sumptum esse **laborem,**
oramus, caue despuas, ocelle.	Gelli, nec **nostras** hic ualuisse **preces**.
ne **poenas** Nemesis reposcat a te.	contra nos tela ista tua euitabimus acta
est uemens dea: laedere hanc caueto.	at fixus nostris tu dabi' **supplicium**.

---

[60] This orthodox understanding is revised by Volk (2010) 203–8 and rejected by Tsantsanoglou (2009) and Porter (2011), not convincingly to my view.

[61] MacLeod (1973a), Forsyth (1977), Tatum (1997).

In both dedications, relative clauses of purpose state the earlier motivation for the respective gift; each has to do with Catullan hurt in respect to
the addressee. Resumptive *nunc* then moves forward to the current state of
affairs, with punishment either potentially or actually in the offing.
Verbally, *preces* + *nostras* is particularly solid; that correspondence and
the shared syntactical and rhetorical progression of the two poems bespeak
careful compositional modeling.[62] Also helpful is the loaded *otiosi* of
Catullus and Calvus in 50.1, paralleled by opposition to Catullus' *studioso
animo* at 116.1.

Let us turn to links between 116 and the beginning of **A**. Besides the
general thematic correspondence between poems 1 and 116 *qua* dedications,
the most persuasive similarity, I think, resides partially in that same phrase
at 116.1: poem 1 presents the learning of Nepos' three rolls, (*doctis . . . et
laboriosis*) as a foil for Catullan verse (*lepidum nouum libellum . . . nugas*)
just as Catullus' contemplated high-minded Callimachean gift (*studioso
animo*; *hunc . . . laborem*) is a foil for the coarser invective he is "forced" by
a refractory Gellius to send in its stead. A similar role as foil, indeed, holds
also of poem 50, taking poem 51 as the high-genre, classic composition
(*hoc . . . poema*), set off against Catullo-Calvan play, light verse, and
provisory scribbling (*lusimus in meis tabellis / scribens uersiculos*). Add
now Catullus' focus, in poem 65, on poetic kinds: the "sweet" poetry he
cannot compose with his brother now dead, and the *maesta carmina* he will
now *always* sing. The message rings clear: all four terminal points in both of
Catullus' collections of first-person poetry focalize precisely the relation
between his "lower" and "higher genre" work which so exercises his
contemporary readers.

Further verbal links might or might not be pushed, for instance Dettmer's
linking of *dabi'* in the final line of 116 with *dono* in 1.1 – the second and
penultimate words of the corpus.[63] Rather more persuasive, I would say, is
Kathryn Gutzwiller's recent finding that a network of intertextual connections jointly links poems 1 and 116 with structurally equivalent (or inverted)
textual moments in the *Aetia* of Callimachus and the *Garland* of Meleager.[64]
Specifically, poem 1 imitates both the first and final poems of the *Garland*
and Callimachus' first *aition* proper, while 116 imitates both the opening

---

[62] The poems move from past to present to future, with studied similarities (temporal clause and
purpose clause concerning the gift of poetry > resumptive *nunc* introducing a two-clause "present"
concerning the recipient's ingratitude, with *preces nostras* in the second clause > future punishment)
but variation between indicative/realized and subjunctive/ideal action (50: realized, ideal, ideal; 116:
ideal, realized, realized).

[63] Dettmer (1997) 224–25.   [64] Gutzwiller (2012) 88–93.

words of the *Aetia* prologue and, once again, the final poem of the *Garland*.[65] Though one or another of these proposed intertexts might be resisted on its own, their cumulative force is significant, bringing the two poems together by drawing their readers to the same model texts, whose importance for Catullus' generic self-modeling is beyond dispute.[66]

4) Openings of A, B, and C

It has been noted that the opening of poem 61 invokes the wedding god Hymenaeus with the matronymic *Uraniae genus*; this reference to a named, particular Muse matches the reference to an unnamed Muse at poem 1.9, and the reference to the Muses collectively at 65.2. That the Muses are present at book-initial moments is, of course, a proemic trope. Moreover, all three references invoke the Muses in a surprisingly *parental* guise: the augmentative of *pater* at *patrona Virgo* in poem 1 is a bold enough *iunctura* that many editors seek to emend it away; the matronym of 61.2 is marked in respect to greater frequency of patronyms; the poet's separation from the Muses in 65 is part of a metaphor on which Catullan *union* with them would otherwise result in their sweet *offspring* (*dulces . . . fetus*) coming forth from Catullus' *mens animi* (65.2–3). All three initial references to the Muses are even more surprising, then: not just parental but *paternal*.

The invocation of Hymenaeus at the beginning of poem 61 recognizably reprises the human/divine "love triangle" motif of poem 51, but now cheerfully and without the hint of adultery and its dangers: poet/ beloved/beloved's godlike lover (husband?) become groom/bride/marriage god. Wilamowitz and a number of successors famously or notoriously argued that Sappho 31 actually *is* a wedding song. Though I need not endorse so rightly controversial a claim, any extent to which the god-likeness of the man recalls an epithalamic *makarismos* of the bridegroom would obviously connect 51 directly with 61, as Sappho's renown as an epithalamic poet does in any case.[67] Indeed, it is tempting to suppose that

---

[65] 1.1–2 ~ AP 4.1.1–3; 1.6–7 ~ AP 12.257.3–4 and 257.8; 1.10 ~ *Aet.* fr. 7.14; 116.1 ~ *Aet.* fr. 1.1; 116.5 ~ AP 12.257.3–5.

[66] More broadly, Gutzwiller (2012) brings out provocatively how deeply we can trace Greek precedent for poems at liminal or transitional moments in the Catullan corpus: not just poem 1 but 2 and 3 as well, 27 at the central break within **A**, poem 70 (the second in **C2**), 93 (the first in the second half of **C2**), and not only the book-final 116 but also the penultimate pair 114 and 115. To this can of course be added 51 (book-final for **A**), as well as 66 (all but initial for **C**); introductory poem 65 is also intertextually dense, as we will see. The value of these further links for demonstrating Catullan arrangement and points of articulation is likely to be considerable.

[67] Wilamowitz (1913) 58, followed by Snell (1931) 82 and Merkelbach (1957) 7. The classic rebuttal is Page (1955) 30–33, endorsed by many, including Most (1996) 26–27. It is important to stress that my point requires only a very weak version of this claim (that the poem is reminiscent of an epithalamic

Sappho's work is a Catullan model at precisely this point. Since it is probable that a book of her poetry circulated under the name of *epithalamia*,[68] it would be fitting if Catullus' non-epithalamic lyric book ends with homage to his most important lyric model, from a poem of hers outside of but pointing to her epithalamic work proper. Just this relation would obtain between Catullus' **A** and **B** as well.[69]

These points of contact are supported by verbal recall:

51		61	
Ille mi par esse deo uidetur		Collis o Heliconii	
ille, si fas est, superare diuos		cultor, Vraniae genus,	
qui sedens aduersus identidem te		*qui* **rapis** teneram ad uirum	
spectat et audit		uirginem, o Hymenaee Hymen,	
dulce ridentem, *misero* quod omnis	5	o Hymen Hymenaee;	5
eripit sensus mihi, nam simul te		cinge tempora floribus	
Lesbia, aspexi, nihil est super mi		suaue olentis amaraci	
. . .		**flammeum** cape *laetus*, huc	
lingua sed *torpet*, tenuis sub *artus*		huc ueni, niueo gerens	
flamma demanat, sonitu suopte	10	luteum pede soccum;	10
tintinant aures, gemina teguntur		excitusque *hilari* die,	
lumina *nocte*.		nuptialia concinens	
otium, Catulle, tibi molestum est,		uoce carmina **tinnula**,	
otio exsultas nimiumque gestis,		*pelle humum pedibus, manu*	
otium et reges prius et beatas	15	pineam quate *taedam*.	15
perdidit urbes.		namque Iunia Manlio	
		qualis Idalium colens	
		uenit ad Phrygium Venus	
		iudicem, bona cum bona	
		nubet alite uirgo.	20

All three words highlighted in bold in poem 51 above represent unique appearances of their respective roots in **A**. The most impressive, by virtue of the infrequency of the root and the location of either word in its poem's third strophe, is *tintinant/tinnula*. Other parallels are negative. The union

---

context), and is even compatible with the claim being false altogether (that is, if Catullus and/or his readers will have understood Sappho in this way). Such a reading as Segal's (1996), which "could be used to point in that direction" (69 n.19), would suffice.

[68] The going theory is that the Greek lyric poets' work was not compiled into books until the Alexandrians, who arranged their poems "according to formal criteria of occasion, subject, and meter" (Zetzel (1983) 89). As to the larger question of whether "standard editions" of particular poets circulated in the Hellenistic world, opinion is divided: Acosta-Hughes (2010), e.g., assumes one "standard Alexandrian edition" of Sappho, contradicting Harvey's (1955) reasonable argument against assuming "standard editions" in general. On Alexandrian Sappho, see also Yatromanolakis (1999, 2007).

[69] Page (1955) 112–26.

in 61 summons the happy god to the proceedings but robs the poor poet of his senses (either second strophe), leaving him with a speechless torpor, ringing ears, and in darkness, as against the singing, dancing, and torchlight of the marriage-god (either third strophe). I will discuss the centrality of the Troy-myth for Catullus later; for now, I will state that if Troy is already activated in 51, as the paradigm case of a rich city destroyed by *otium*,[70] then the fourth strophes map onto each other as well. The bride in 61.16–20 is as beautiful as Venus at the moment she took the greatest pains to display her beauty, namely upon the Judgment of Paris, the *aition* for both the destruction of Troy and the *otium* which destroyed it. The full version of that argument, however, must wait.

References to poem 51 occur in later portions of 61 as well. At 61.64–65, 69–70, and 74–75 the poet-speaker asks *quis huic deo* [sc. *Hymenaeo*] *compararier ausit*? It is not merely that Lesbia's lover, and implicitly Lesbia herself, are "compared to gods" in 51 (*par esse . . . uidetur ~ comparier*); since Catullus' *si fas est* at 51.2 is unparalleled in the Sappho poem that he is translating, his raising of the *propriety* of human/divine comparison is striking. The triple repetition of *quis huic deo* in 61 is no less so. Both raise the same question, thus clearly inviting us to examine the two poems together. Finally, the end of poem 61 explicitly recalls 51, when the poet expresses his wish for the marriage to produce a son in short order: *Torquatus uolo paruulus . . . dulce rideat ad patrem* (209–12). Then, once again, the Troy-myth is activated, as child and mother are likened to Telemachus and Penelope in the poem's penultimate strophe (219–23).

The opening of **C** resonates here as well. As we have seen, poem 65 opens (lines 1–4) with mention of the Muses, reflecting the matronymic *Uraniae genus* at 61.2. Next we find the *pale* postmortem *foot* of Catullus' departed brother (*pallidulum . . . pedem*, 65.6) reflected in the invocation to Hymenaeus, who wears brightly colored slippers on snow-white feet: *niueo gerens luteum pede soccum* (61.9–10); probably also meaningful is the contrast between the god who "steal[s]" the young bride to her husband (*rapis*, 61.3) and Catullus' "stolen" brother (*ereptum*, 65.8). The Troy-myth is activated at 61.16–20 (in an erotic context), as well as at 65.7–8 (in a deathly context).

Next comes a strikingly close correspondence of the highest importance:

excitusque **hilari** die		aspiciam posthac? at certe semper amabo,	
nuptialia concinens 61.12		semper **maesta** tua **carmina morte canam** 65.12	
uoce **carmina** tinnula		**qualia** sub densis ramorum **concinit** umbris	
		Daulias . . .	

[70] Claimed by Putnam (2006) 88 and D'Angour (2006).

On the hypothesis that 65 is the first poem of its book, the first-person future *canam* at 65.12 will surely be taken as programmatic; by that same token, the ease with which we can see the introductory program here itself *recommends* the hypothesis that 65 is book-initial. Similarly, the corresponding passage at 61.12–13 tells powerfully in favor of taking 61–64 as an artistic unity. If these poems did constitute an authorial roll, a competent reader will not have failed to notice this, the first mention of *song* in the book: the text announces itself as wedding poetry. Even granting that poem 63 is a problem case (if Attis' story is "nuptial," it is by inversion or negation), three-fourths of the putative book by poem-count clearly answers to this description, as does about nine-tenths of it by line-count. Add now the exact line-correspondence (lines 12–13) of the highly distinctive pair *carmina* + _concino_, and the case for program in *both* passages, with studied contrast between them, is made: cheerful ~ gloomy, nuptial ~ funereal.[71] If there is a problem here, it is a surfeit of evidence: Catullus makes it all too obvious.

We have already tied the poet's tinnitus at 51.11 to the wedding god's high-pitched voice, with passerine chirping (*pipiabat*, 3.10) behind it in **A**. Here in 65, Catullus' programmatic announcement of mournful song passes immediately to birdsong (13–14); like Procne, Catullus figuratively becomes a bird in his simile. And now see this:

> ... iudicem, bona cum bona
> nubet alite **(?)** uirgo.   61.20
> floridis **uelut** enitens
> myrtus Asia **ramulis** ...

The stanza of poem 61 containing the Troy myth ends with the usually dead metaphor of good bird for favorable omen. Readers may prefer it to stay dead here, in spite of the intratexts; no need to insist. But now the second simile at the opening of 61 (poem 65 likewise has two similes) likens the bride to a carefully tended myrtle; the fact that *ramulis* here and *ramorum* at 65.13 are unique Catullan occurrences of the lemma(ta) should be noted. Finally, there remains to tie together the motifs of apple, girl, lap, and mother. Poem 65 ends with all four (*malum, uirginis e gremio, matris*: 65.19, 20, 22); poems 2b–3 contain them all (*malum, puella matrem, a gremio*: 2b.2, 3.7, 8); poem 61 has three of them explicitly, slightly belated

---

[71] Further correspondences by line-count include the opening reference to the Muses (*Uraniae ~ doctis ... uirginibus*, 61.2 and 65.2), the poems' principal honorands (*namque Iunia Manlio ~ Ortale, mitto haec ... tibi carmina*, 61.16 and 65.15–16), and marrying or marriageable maidens (*bona ... nubet ... uirgo ~ sponsi ... casto uirginis e gremio*, 61.19–20 and 65.19–20).

(*puellulam, a gremio, matris*: 61.57, 58, 59). The apple is implicit, but heavily so: the first simile (61.16–19) likens the bride to Venus at the Judgment of Paris, the *aition* of the Troy myth. The *aition* of the Judgment, in turn, is the prize at stake: the mother of all mythological apples. The context of all three Catullan apples is nuptial.

5) Closes of A, B, and C

The context of the final section of poem 64 (382–408) is human/divine interaction: no longer, as in the mythic past, do gods appear before mortal eyes. If *perdidit urbes*, the final words of poem 51 and thus of **A**, recall Troy, they presage the myth's appearance at the opening of **B**, the turn to the mythic *past* in poem 64, the internal *prophecy* of the Trojan War towards the end of 64, and finally the return to the poet and reader's *hic et nunc* in the concluding lines. The strongest verbal parallel is between 51.12 and 64.408: *lumina nocte*, the close of the penultimate stanza of poem 51 and **A** (a god-like apparition covers the poet in darkness),[72] and *lumine claro*, the last words of poem 64 and **B** (the "clear light" in which gods no longer appear to mortals).

Here, too, we have a curious correspondence in line-count: 64.408 is the twelfth line of the final section of poem 64, after the turn from myth to the present at 64.397. Just so, of course, is 51.12 the twelfth line of the final poem. Two lines above either break, we find mention of Nemesis:

. . .		. . .	
ne poenas **Nemesis** reposcat a te	50.20	aut rapidi Tritonis era aut **Ramnusia uirgo**	64.395
est uemens dea: laedere hanc caueto.		armatas hominumst praesens hortata cateruas.	
Ille mi par esse deo uidetur,	51.1	sed postquam tellus scelerest imbuta nefando,	
ille, si fas est, superare diuos,		iustitiamque omnes cupida de mente fugarunt,	
qui sedens aduersus identidem te		perfudere manus fraterno sanguine fratres,	
spectat et audit		destitit exstinctos natus lugere parentes,	400
dulce ridentem, misero quod omnis	5	optauit genitor primaeui funera nati,	
eripit sensus mihi: nam simul te,		liber uti nuptae poteretur flore puellae,	
Lesbia, aspexi, nihil est super mi		ignaro mater substernens se improba nato	
. . .		impia non ueritast diuos scelerare penates:	
lingua sed torpet, tenuis sub artus		omnia fanda nefanda malo permixta furore	405
flamma demanat, sonitu suopte	10	iustificam nobis mentem auertere deorum.	
tintinant aures, gemina teguntur		quare nec tales dignantur uisere coetus,	
lumina nocte.		nec se contingi patiuntur **lumine claro**.	

Needless to say, the correspondence remains even if the line-count is considered merely coincidental. *Ramnusia* is read as early as the *editio princeps*, where our manuscripts have *ramunsia* (thus O) and *ranusia* (thus

---

[72] The verbal recall passes over the true close of poem 51 (ll. 13–16), but the final portion of poem 64 and these lines both have a traditionalist moralizing *cum* hell-in-a-handbasket theory of history in common; in both, the turn to this theme from what precedes is surprising and poses an interpretive challenge.

G and R). It is clearly, then, the least intrusive reconstruction; Baehrens'
emendation *Amarunsia* (that is, Artemis) hypostatizes an otherwise unattested adjective, motivated by the worry that Nemesis is not elsewhere
depicted in combat. For my purposes, it is beneficial that mention of
Nemesis here should be pointed; it makes the intratext more noticeable
and meaningful. Some of this meaning, in turn, is likely to reside in the
minority mythological tradition, according to which Nemesis, in her former
earth-dwelling days, conceived and bore one Helen of Troy.[73]

I conclude this discussion of end-point responsions by approaching
poem 65 and **C** directly from a reading of 64 and **B**. Though verbal
similarities here are limited in the main to single lemmata, one is worth
seeing:

talia praefantes quondam **felicia** Peleo
carmina diuino **cecinerunt** pectore Parcae.   semper **maesta** tua **carmina** morte **canam**
64.382–83   65.12

First we note matching "happiness" in the first and last references to
song in **B** (*hilari die . . . concinens,* 61.11–12), and the specular relationship
between the invocation of a god to a mortal wedding there and the claim
that gods no longer attend human weddings here (*tales . . . coetus* at 64.407,
the penultimate line of **B**); the case for **B** as an authorial unity is strengthened still further. The absent presence of the *Streitapfel* in 61 is likewise
cashed out by the setting of poem 64 itself, where it is again an absent
presence. Since *maesta . . . carmina . . . concinit* at 65.12–13 clearly recalls
hilari . . . concinens . . . carmina at 61.12–13, we now have a sturdy intratextual triad.

Other correspondences are thematic. Programmatic reference to song, we
have seen, moves from the nuptial in 61 to the funereal in 65; the Song of the
Parcae had just moved poem 64 from a Thessalian wedding to myriad Trojan
funerals (348–51); the marriage in poem 64 is *felix* for the terrifying quantity of
deaths it will produce. Poem 65, then, introduces death at Troy from its sixth
line; the return from myth to the poet-speaker's here-and-now at the end of 64
is answered by the same poet's here-and-now loss of his brother, dead and
buried in the most mythical of places.

Even more immediately, the final two lines of 64 proclaim human-
divine separation in general; the first two of poem 65 announce Catullus'
separation from the Muses in particular. The first simile in poem 65 recalls
the myth of Procne, whose sister Philomela reveals her rape and

---

[73] Skinner (1984) persuasively dismisses the case for emendation and discusses the significance of
Nemesis in relation to Helen.

glossectomy by Tereus by depicting them in weaving; the description of a woven object, needless to say, takes up the majority of poem 64. The vengeful murder of the child Itylus mentioned at 65.14 may remind us of the vengeful offering of the child Polyxena to Achilles' shade (64.362–70), or perhaps the fall of Polyxena's corpse and the blood that "wets" the tomb (368–70) is recalled by the closing simile of 65, the apple falling from the maiden's lap and the red blush on her face (64.368–70 and 65.19–24: *proiciet ... corpus; madefient caede sepulcra ~ malum ... procurrit; manat ... ore rubor*). Whether we take this as a competing option or as an additional resonance, the maiden's carelessness, which betrays her beloved's love-pledge, also recalls Theseus' carelessness with respect to his pledge to Ariadne.

Finally, Holzberg has shown how nicely the mention of contemporary wrongdoing in the conclusion of poem 64 prepares the reader for the irruption of similar crimes (particularly incest) in the elegiac-metered poems that follow.[74] The close, then, is resonant in this respect not with the opening of **C**, but with a crucial motif of **C** as a whole. For many readers, myself included, the horrifying and morally dubious content of the myths in poem 64 ironize – or at least complicate – the discourse of moral decline in its final section.[75] The choice of the Procne myth as comparandum for the here-and-now Catullus' songs of grief in poem 65 is provocative in light of the grieving Procne's responsibility for her own bereavement. Regardless, whether we jump boldly into this rabbit hole or peer timidly into it, the problematic contrast between virtue and vice in myth and reality which closes poem 64 immediately reappears in the (apparently) pious, fraternal grief of the poet, as compared with its morally troubling mythological correlate.

4 Conclusions

To return to the persuasive structure of the argument: **Ax** looks like it should be separated from the preceding poems, and if you examine the preceding (and following) poems omitting **Ax**, they look like ordered wholes. Many questions do remain; most importantly, I take it that the case for 61–62–63–64 as authorial sequence has been much strengthened, but not yet sufficiently demonstrated, by the end-point responsions discussed above. And even if these four poems are a unity, a physical book that

---

[74] Holzberg (2002) 148–50. On incest in Catullus see especially Rankin (1976a) and Watson (2006).
[75] Curran (1969), Skinner (1984), Gaisser (1995) 613.

circulated as such, it will require still further argument to show what, if any, "reading order" obtains over **A**, **B**, and **C** as wholes.[76] We are also yet to consider **C1** in detail; the argument that **C** consists of two halves, with **C1** responding at half-scale to **B**, just as **C2** does to **A**, remains to be made.

Nonetheless, the authorial sequence of **C1** is also overwhelmingly likely given the expulsion of 52–60. Both the internal (i.e. 65–116, long seen)[77] and external end-point responsions verify 65 as the opening and 116 as the closing poem. The analogous relationship between the halves of **A** and **C2** (1–26 : 27–51 :: 69–92 : 93–116) has been demonstrated, and with it the case against doubting their ordering is made. And since, of course, poem 65 clearly introduces poem 66, the only links in the sequence of **C** not directly covered by the preceding are now those from 66–69. Those links will be considered in Chapter 3; but already at this point, it is unclear whether any positive grounds to doubt them remains. Opponents now need to be unimpressed by the case for removing **Ax**, need to deny that the terminal points look nicely ordered if it is removed, need to find many or most lower-level indicia of ordering to be illusory, *and* they need as plausible a poem-count as any (25 + 25 poems, or thereabouts, per medially divided collection of short poems) not to be the right one. The idea-space from which Catullan design can be doubted has narrowed and taken on a conspicuously odd and willful shape.

---

[76] We recall that the three Catullan books will not have been called "Books 1–3"; if (represented) temporal ordering obtains between them it will have to be seen in the text.

[77] See e.g. Forsyth (1977); Skinner (2003) 1–5.

CHAPTER 2

A (poems 1–51)

1   Introduction

The previous chapter argued that **Ax** (poems 52–60) is to be bracketed from **A** (1–51), and that once this bracketing is made, the authorial arrangement of **A** and **C** (65–116) is vindicated: their terminal points are in such close dialogue, and **A** is mirrored so finely by **C2** (69–116), that authorial design is the only reasonable explanation. Meanwhile, the case for **B** (61–64) as an authorial unity is greatly enhanced, in that its terminal points participate fully in the intratextual dialogue of **A** and **C**.

Much work remains. Holding **A** and **C2** up to each other ruled out the thesis that either one's structure is fortuitous, but did not bring sufficiently to light their principles of poem arrangement. Neither **B** nor **C1** has been examined at all, save for the bookends of **B** and poem 65, the opening of **C1**. This chapter will first present the various kinds of Catullan patterning that it will examine, stressing especially the pluralism and antireductionism governing its approach (§2); it will then give an account of the structure and metapoetry of **A** (§3), followed by an account of narrative time therein (§4); these investigations will pave the way for the similar accounts of **B** and **C1** in Chapter 3 and **C2** in Chapter 4.

2   Patterns of Patterns in Catullus

This chapter will examine Catullan principles of arrangement under three general headings: local, terminal, and global. By local, I mean patterns that enhance our credence that the placement of one poem beside another is artistic or intentional. The most frequent (and, I think, most important) type of local pattern will be the placement of correspondences (or pointed contrasts) either in two adjacent poems or in two poems with one between;

I will term pairs of the latter kind "semi-adjacent."[1] By terminal, I mean devices marking beginning and end; in Catullus, verbal and thematic recall between the two is the most important but not the only such device. By global, I mean those that are apparent when the ensemble(s) are examined as such. Some of these have internal thematic and narrative coherences, others perhaps not; the careful distribution of non-hendecasyllabic poems is another sort of global pattern, found in each of the sub-units in **A**. Other global patterning is *external*, as we have already seen. The second halves of **A** and **C2** share the global pattern of having *less* global patterning than their respective first halves; all four halves and both wholes of **A** and **C2** have at least near identical poem-counts, and so on.

All three kinds of patterning are found in each part of the corpus. They will be presented here under the assumption that the evidence is additive, and with the intended result that the sum is superabundant: everything is designed; not every design is equally intricate. The second half of **C2** (93–116) has always struck readers as far less elaborately ordered than, say, the first half of **A** (1–26). So it clearly is, and no embarrassment need attach to this concession. Quite the contrary: with notable exceptions – above all the holy words of 101 – readers consistently find the artistry of these poems rougher in other respects as well.[2] If the sequence of the fussier poems is fussier, and that of the rougher poems is rougher, what exactly is the problem? The picture of Catullan arrangement offered here is not a scheme within which any one principle must be present over every patch of text, let alone as deeply present.

It is useful at this point to comment more specifically on the patterns of local correspondence to be surveyed. Poems 10–13 provide an example of adjacent or AABB patterning: foreign places, dispraised girlfriends, and a humiliated and angry Catullus in 10 and 11; dinner parties and gifts to and from Fabullus in 12 and 13. Semi-adjacent, ABAB patterning, appears in poems 37–40: choliambic meter, Egnatius, and Celtiberian dentifrice in 37 and 39; the request or threat of poetry, the contemplation of punishment, and forms of *quilibet* collocated with *meos amores* in lines 6–7 of the eight-line poems 38 and 40.

The heterogeneity of the examples chosen above is deliberate. It is exemplary of what we do, in fact, find in the corpus, and it brings to light a crucial

---

[1] Claes' (2002) 27–30 terms of art are "simple" and "disjunctive concatenation."

[2] As for **Ax** in the previous chapter, I will here use "rough" and "roughness" in a slightly loaded way: neither to presuppose nor to rule out the possibility that the cluster of features for which, e.g., poem 102 can be called "doggerel" (Fordyce 1961: 390) might be under full artistic control, and that the poems might be fully successful in being what they are and doing what they do (whatever that is).

point for this investigation, namely its antireductionism. Adjacent and semi-adjacent patterning amount to dense lily pads on the Catullan pond, especially in **A**; a readerly frog, able to leap between adjacent and semi-adjacent correspondences, will find one of many valid ways across, rather than a single right way. Critics largely agree that there is a tight coherence to, for instance, poems 1–14, but they disagree as to what it is. One reader will see a clear and perspicuous similarity (or pointed contrast) between two adjacent poems, perhaps involving a theme that she is pleased to emphasize; she will duly declare the similarity to be explanatory of the poems' adjacency. Another will do likewise, but with a different similarity or contrast. In some cases, on this pluralist reading, they will both be right, in the sense that each has identified a meaningful similarity. Yet they will both be wrong as well, in the sense that neither similarity is more privileged than the other. In other cases one will be *more* right, or more *interestingly* right, than the other.

Furthermore, in most cases, there is patterning to spare. If one or another connection is rejected as frail, others will succor or replace it. In 38 and 40 above, for instance, the shared eight-line length, taken alone, might not constitute a non-fortuitous correspondence; together with the collocation of *quilibet* and *meos amores* on either set of lines 6–7, however, there is a clear formalistic match. And then the shared thematic elements of anger and the traffic in poetry put the question beyond serious doubt: poems 38 and 40 have their eyes on each other.

But why does this bear notice? The Egnatius poems 37 and 39 make an unmistakable pair, while the pair 38 and 40 will likely be missed more often than not; I might draw no more result from their correspondences than the important conclusion that our authorial poem-arranger is still minding the store. This is my contention: any noticeable correspondence is one readers are invited to interrogate, if only briefly. Debating these matters – adjudicating which matches are merely present, which ones are interpretively suggestive, and which ones can be interpreted in determinate ways – is what these patterns are for; we readers *use* the arrangement of the Catullan poems in accordance with its design when we do so. The account of local correspondences given below, far from aspiring to comprehensiveness, is governed by considerations of economy. It strives to present as compelling a set of correspondences as possible in the smallest possible space. The correspondences selected thus aim for an optimal degree of apparent *discernibility* and *relevance*.[3]

---

[3] Thus the "merely" verbal is downplayed in what follows; readers are referred to Claes' (2002) 30–51 extensive account of "lexical concatenation," which includes lists of lemmata and synonyms repeated in adjacent poems (35–50).

There is, however, an important exception to this pluralism, namely the terminal points and the runs of text they delimit. By my own reckoning, the account of local correspondences given here for poems 1–14 is one good way to bring out their connective tissue, but not *the* correct way. The claim that 1–14, 14b–26, etc., are the correct units within which to find connective tissue is, by contrast, put forth in a strong and unequivocal sense. Reasons for this will emerge in their turn; for now, I will only state that their structural reality is deep, and that the arguments in their favor are in general more *like* the arguments for ejecting 52–60 than they are like the claim, e.g., that continuities between poems 35 and 36 explain their adjacency – hence the different status of the assertions made about them.

3   The Structure and Metapoetry of A: A Calvanist Reading

The view of **A** to be given here is as follows. The text consists of three distinct runs: 1–14, 14b–26, and 27–51. Of these, the first two are a thematic diptych, together forming the book's first half. The figure of Licinius Calvus is crucial for delimiting all three units and explaining the metapoetics not only of the final poem, 51, but also of the initial diptych, 1–26, as a whole. I take up each run in turn, passing for each one from local to terminal and global patterning.

1–14

After the dedicatory poem 1 comes the famous *passer* in poem 2. Depending on the credentials of 2b,[4] the sparrow hymn is either adjacent or semi-adjacent to its companion piece 3, the sparrow dirge. The sequence thus immediately establishes one of these two types of collocation, and strongly indicates that textual and temporal sequence will coincide in what follows: the living sparrow in 2 is a dead one in 3.

Skipping 4 for a moment: the poet's beloved in the kiss-poem 5 is now named as Lesbia, whose identity with the *puella* of poems 2–3 we may infer. Comparing the separation of poet and *puella* in 2 with the now-thriving love affair in 5, we might assign a "dramatic date" for poem 2 (and possibly 3) "before" the affair begins, with either 2b or 5 marking its beginning.[5] We

---

[4] In favor of 2/2b unification, see Adler (1981) 138ff, Dettmer (1984); against, see Quinn (1973) 95, Wiseman (1985) 12, Thomson (1997) *ad loc*, Johnson (2003). Pearcy (1980) places 2b between lines 8 and 9 of poem 2; Segal (1968b) argues for unification with a lacuna between 2 and 2b.

[5] Uncertainty about 2b urges caution here.

now skip 6; poem 7 is another kiss-poem to Lesbia, who asks the poet to quantify the kisses requested in 5; again the temporal and textual sequences match. The pairing of poems is now itself a pattern: 2–3–5–7 are four poems, two motivic pairs, one story. The internal link provided by the sparrow and kiss motifs is unmistakable, but what is often missed (because it is not looked for) is the correspondence that moves us from one pair to the other. Once sought, this correspondence conspicuously asserts itself: death. The dead sparrow in 3 is answered by Catullus' appeal to mortality as a motivating force in 5.[6]

Following these, poem 8 reveals that the affair with Lesbia (here *puella*) has ended, and by her agency (*nunc iam illa non uolt*, 8.9). Structural arguments are perennially in danger of seeming – and being – both trivial and reductive. In this case, the point is anything but trivial. One *must* see death already in the first Lesbia poems. The frivolous dead sparrow in poem 3 prefigures the not-so-frivolous relationship between eros and dust in 5, even as the self-interestedness of erotic persuasion tells superficially against the seriousness of poem 5. One does not read Catullan love poetry well if one believes that Catullan love is ever free or far from death. As for reductiveness, the danger here is scant. If one comes to the break-up announced in poem 8 with mortality in mind, the language of the announcement will mean more than otherwise (*quod uides perisse ... fulsere quondam candidi tibi soles*, 8.2–3; cf. 5.4–6: the recurrence of suns, against our brief light and eternal sleep). If one appreciates that the Catullan speaker is not only driven in eros by his mortality, but also regards the death of his love in precisely those terms, his question to Lesbia at 8.15 (*quae tibi manet uita?*) will be richer. For it is Catullus, there, who doubts that life truly will go on. The possibility that Lesbia has an all too easy answer to this – to whatever extent one wishes to speculate that she loves him less than he her – is likewise more painful, more powerful. To gain access to this enriched understanding, we need not claim that death is the sole relevant link, or even a uniquely privileged link, between 2–3 and 5–7.

Given the problem of 2b, best guesses for the arrangement of the initial Lesbia poems might be as follows (full-sized letters signify **L**esbia and **O**ther poems, superscript **S**parrows and **K**isses):

---

[6] *Mortuus est* at 3.3 – *uiuamus* at 5.1; *iter tenebricosum . . . unde negant redire quemquam* at 3.11–12 – *soles occidere et redire possunt, nobis . . . nox est perpetua* at 5.4–6; notice also the tomb of Battus at 7.6.

1	2	2b	3	4	5	6	7	8
O	L^S	...	L^S	O	L^K	O	L^K	L
or:								
O	L^S	L	L^S	O	L^K	O	L^K	L

Assuming the unity of 2, the introductory poem is followed by adjacent Lesbia–sparrow poems, pairs of semi-adjacent non-Lesbia poems and Lesbia–kiss poems, and an adjacent Lesbia poem. Both adjacent and semi-adjacent arrangements of Lesbia poems are found: sparrows together, kisses separated, and finally the unpaired Lesbia break-up poem. Poems 2 and 3 likely precede the affair, which flourishes over 5 and 7 (or is perhaps consummated by the success of 5) and ends before 8.[7]

2b presents us with two possibilities easily integrated into the scheme above. The likelihood that the poem is unrelated to Lesbia seems low; whatever is "welcome" at 2b.1 is likely to have brought the beloved into erotic union. Since *gratum* is neuter, this cannot grammatically be the *passer* itself; my own guess is that 2b will not have featured the sparrow. We would then have a Lesbia triptych after the introductory poem, with the rest as before.[8] Poem 2 would be before the affair, which now begins at 2b. Either option presents nice patterning and contrasting adjacent and semi-adjacent arrangement. The textual/dramatic match alone certainly seems authorial, telling so textured and compelling a story.

It is thus unclear that we need further to integrate or explain the non-Lesbia poems 1, 4, and 6. Poem 1 is sufficiently explained as introductory. The thematic differences of 4 and 6 from the rest might simply be a negative unity, rendering these poems similar just as two citizens of different countries are similarly considered "foreigners" in a third. There is no denying that this is a pattern, and we have no grounds to think it implausible that a Roman poet would employ a pattern of this sort.

In fact, however, the garrulous *phaselus* or yacht of poem 4 can be integrated with its neighbors in various ways: the poem's opening closely reflects a phrase from the semi-adjacent 2b: *ferunt . . . fuisse ~ ait fuisse* (2b.1–2, 4.2). As in the narrated voyage of the yacht, the dead sparrow of 3 is on a

---

[7] 8.3–8 precludes any doubt that there ever was an erotic consummation – if Catullus, speaking "to himself," lies to himself about *that*, all grounds for trusting or even taking seriously any content at all are removed, leaving us with the flattest and least interesting Catullus-character (and therefore Catullan text) possible.

[8] Johnson (2003).

journey (*iter*, 3.11); both are "final." The yacht, meanwhile, "flies" (*uolare*, 4.5). Merely on the sonic level, *phaselus* at 4.1 recalls *passer* in poems 2 and 3; noting especially Catullus' markedly stylized use of diminutives in **A**, it is relevant that $p^h as\bar{e}lus$ will sound almost identical with an imagined *passéllus*.[9] Looking forward in the poems now, the garrulous yacht is "getting old" in its penultimate line (*senet*, 4.26); garrulous old men feature in the second line of poem 5 (*rumoresque senum seueriorum*). Skipping forward to the semi-adjacent 6, we see that it contains another constructed artifact, a bed which both does and does not talk (*tacitum cubile clamat*, 6.7). What is most significant, I think, is the prominent series of non-human agents: the "walking" (*inambulatioque*, 6.11) and "yelling" bed in 6; the yacht in 4; the sparrow of 3 and 2; the apple of 2b, which is assigned agency in untying the girdle.[10] Walking this progression back, we ask whether poem 1 fits. Of course it does. The object in question there is the paradigmatic speaking thing: the book.

Again, scanning adjacent poems for correspondences will strike some as an uninteresting game, even if its results are significant. Perhaps that is even true for poem 4 and environs. But Poem 6 is different: the poet's friend Flavius is carrying on a secret love affair with a charmless *scortum*. His bed and physical condition attest to the sex; her want of *lepos* may be deduced from Flavius' silence about the affair to Catullus. The connection with the kiss-poems 5 and 7 is obvious. Both of these end with anxieties about the effects of third-party knowledge on the affair with Lesbia. The affair is threatened by moralistic (5.2), invidious (5.12), and merely nosy (7.11) outsiders – just as the poet's questions threaten his friend's purported affair. That the shaming inflicted by the poem might doom Flavius' affair seems quite possible, and quite possibly the speaker's intention.

To read poem 6 in light of its surrounding poems (and vice versa) is to notice core Catullan themes: erotic love in relation to male friendship, and the problem of the poet-lover's self-awareness (or lack thereof), expressed in moments of reflective interiority. Is the Catullus-character a hypocrite to be seen through? Or merely all too fully a part of the social world that he chronicles? Does the *mala lingua* feared at the end of 7 explain the break-up in 8? Or does Catullus' own *mala lingua* explain it? Does his own status as a *malus* with a hostile gaze (*inuidere possit*) towards a friend's love invoke the *lex talionis*? Or is the real explanation both together? These are good

---

[9] If *passer* encodes an erotic/anatomical allegory, this point is doubly relevant; indeed, Väisänen (1984) and Nuzzo (1994) argue for an erotic reading of poem 4. See also Kronenberg (2015) for the same claim about the close parody of poem 4, *Catalepton* 10.

[10] Many English speakers, including myself, will need positive effort to hear "the apple that untied the belt" as the highly figured phrase it is.

questions, rich questions, for all that we are unlikely and probably unwise to answer them determinately.

Although the exact poem-count depends on at least two open questions (the matter of 2b and whether to count poem 1 in the sequence 2–14 or as standing before it), the break-up with Lesbia clearly represents some kind of median in the sequence 1–14. Now the "second half" begins with the soliloquy of poem 8, and the relative prominence of Lesbia over Catullus' friends is reversed: no poems in 8–14 deign to address her directly,[11] and only in poem 11 is she the dominant thematic presence.

On the subject of correspondences that move us through 8–14, we may be brief. The welcome to Veranius (9) combines dominant themes from the two previous non-Lesbia poems: travel from the provinces (4) and a male friend (6). Catullus' self-characterization in a quasi-conjugal role (drawing his neck close and kissing his friend's mouth and eyes, 9.8–9) recalls the kissing and lip-biting at the end of 8; the male Veranius makes an obvious reversal from Lesbia, as does the greeting to him from the farewell to her. Readers will also note the kiss motif in 5, 7, 8, and again in 9. Next, poem 10 has a third male Catullan friend (after 6 and 9), a third return from the provinces (after 4 and 9), and a third female love interest (after Lesbia and Flavius' unseen *scortum*). Crucially, we now come to understand the circumstances of poem 4: the master of the yacht is indeed Catullus, and its journey was his return home from provincial service. Poem 8 had invited us to consider Catullus himself its sceptic target: written in choliambs, the paradigmatic meter of satirical comment and mockery, the poem is about Catullus much more than it is about Lesbia; it flaunts his irresolution, the obvious gap between the command *obdura* that he twice issues to himself and the dubious *iam Catullus obdurat* he asserts.[12] Here, in the semi-adjacent poem 10, the joke is once again on Catullus, as Varus' *scortillum* skewers Catullus' false claim that he has procured a team of slaves in Bithynia.

This moves us along to the masterpiece that is poem 11. Two more friends, Furius and Aurelius, match the two friends in the preceding 9 and 10; the travelogue in the first half (11.1–12) responds to the respective journeys in the same poems. More prominently, of course, the message of farewell to Lesbia implements Catullus' irresolute resolution in poem 8: be firm, Catullus. As male friends pose a threat to, or at least present problems for, love affairs in poems 5–7 and 10, they will serve well for reporting the end of an affair here.

---

[11] I take it that the address to her from *uale, puella* at 8.12 is not a true address, rather a dramatization of Catullus addressing her in a fantasy.

[12] See Skinner (1971) on this and other ironies in poem 8.

We recall Catullus' irresolution in 8, and the fact that his humiliation by a woman in 10 is his second such embarrassment, after Lesbia's rejection. The latter strengthens our sense of his dismissal of her as powerful revenge-fantasy (17–20, the penultimate stanza), while the former shows how deeply he needs to express his grief to her (21–24, the final lines).

With Lesbia dismissed, three more poems to friends conclude the unit. Foreign travel links poem 12 also to 9–11, in that the stolen napkin in 12 had been a gift from Spain; the same device connects 12 with 13 and 14, both of which feature gifts (*unguentum* in 13, poetic *libellus* in 14). Veranius in poem 9 is now paired with another friend, Fabullus, who is named in the final line of 12 and addressed in the first line of 13. Poem 12 also shares with 13 the theme of the *cena* (hinted at, perhaps, in 9 as well, the natural setting for Veranius' travel narration). Poems 12 and 14 similarly threaten to repay their recipients' wrongdoings with "harmful" invective and health-endangering verse. Poem 13 obliquely reprises poem 11 and Lesbia, with whose *unguentum* Fabullus will be gifted. Finally, the paired poems 12 and 13, with their respectively threatening and jocular tones, are answered in the entirely unserious "injustice" and "revenge" constituted by the gift of "bad" poetry in poem 14, addressed to the poet Licinius Calvus.

The chart below summarizes the local correspondences we have just seen:

```
1–2: introduction
  2–2b: Lesbia
  2————3: Lesbia, sparrow
       3–4: final journey
          4–5: garrulous old age
       3————5: Lesbia, death
          5–6–7: friends, girlfriends, secrets
1–2–2b–3–4————6: inanimate speakers and agents
          5————7: Lesbia, kisses
             7–8: Lesbia, current/past affair and kisses
                8–9: goodbye/hello, kisses
          5————7–8–9: kisses
                   9–10: male friends, return home, foreign travel
                8————10: Catullus' (self-) deceptions exposed
                   10–11: male friends, anger at women, foreign lands
                      11–12: male friends, foreign lands, love/hostility
                         12–13: dining, gifts, Fabullus
                      11————13: Lesbia
          9–10–11–12–13: foreign lands, male friends
                      12————14: retaliatory poetry, love/hostility
                         12–13–14: male friends and gifts
```

On the matter of global patterning, a few points are clear. First, non-hendecasyllabic poems (4, 8, and 11) are distributed as evenly as possible: [3–4 poems, 41+ lines] > **poem 4** > [3 poems, 42 lines] > **poem 8** > [2 poems, 45 lines] > **poem 11** > [3 poems, 54 lines]. Second, the rupture between Catullus and Lesbia – whether we place this at poem 8 or between 7 and 8[13] – is in some way medial, dividing the unit into respectively more and less Lesbia-themed halves. The second half, in turn, has two plausible candidates for *Leitmotif*, namely foreign travel (9–13) and the poet's male friends (9–14). That we should not be tempted to choose between these motifs is indicated by the presence of each in the first half: poem 4 is the travelogue in the first half, while 6 (and also 1, to the extent it counts) is the poem on male friendship.

One could present a finer-grained scheme. An important point is that the second-half correlate of the non-Lesbia poems 4 and 6 is poem 10. Like 4, 10 pertains not merely to travel but to the *poet's* travel, while 6 resembles 10 in that both comment on Catullus' friends' lovers. This unique responsion in 1–14 strikes me as far too prominent to omit. The simplest useful model of thematic overlap across the diptych, then, might go as follows: the Lesbia poems are concentrated in the first half of the diptych (2, 2b, 3, 5, 7), while poems on foreign travel (9, 10, 11, 12, 13) and male friends (9, 10, 11, 12, 13, 14) are concentrated in the second half. Poem 10, the only poem in the second half to comment on a male friend's lover, thus responds to two first-half poems: 4 (the only poem to concern Catullus' male friends) and 6 (the only poem to comment on a male friend's lover).

Much, of course, has been left out (poetry of objects, gifts, aggressive content). Most important, perhaps, is the terminal thematic responsion, the gift of poetry and the physical book, to which we now turn.

	Ni te **plus** oculis meis amarem, 14.1
	iucundissime Calue, munere isto
	odissem te odio Vatiniano:
	nam quid feci ego quidue sum locutus,
	cur me tot male perderes poetis? 5
	isti di mala multa dent **clienti**,
	qui tantum tibi misit impiorum.
Cui dono lepidum **nouum libellum** 1.1	quod si, ut suspicor, hoc **nouum** ac **repertum**
arido modo pumice **expolitum**?	munus dat tibi Sulla litterator,
Corneli, tibi: namque tu solebas	non est mi male, sed bene ac beate, 10
meas esse aliquid putare nugas	quod non dispereunt tui **labores**.
iam tum, cum ausus es unus Italorum 5	**di magni**, horribilem et sacrum **libellum**!

---

[13] I tend to see the middle falling in the interstice, to the extent this matters.

omne aeuum tribus explicare chartis,   quem tu scilicet ad tuum Catullum
doctis, **Iuppiter**, et **laboriosis**.   misti, continuo ut die **periret**,
quare habe tibi quidquid hoc libelli,   Saturnalibus, optimo dierum!   15
qualecumque quod o, **patrona** uirgo,   non non hoc tibi, false, sic abibit:
plus uno **maneat** perenne **saeclo**.   10   nam, si luxerit, ad librariorum
                                           curram scrinia; Caesios, Aquinos,
                                           Suffenum, **omnia** colligam uenena,
                                           ac te his suppliciis remunerabor.   20
                                           uos hinc interea ualete **abite**
                                           illuc, unde malum pedem attulistis,
                                           saecli incommoda, pessimi poetae!

nouum 1.1 ⁓ 14.8; *(lepidum nouum) libellum* 1.1 ⁓ *(horribilem et sacrum) libellum* 14.12; *expolitum* 1.2 ⁓ *repertum* 14.8; *omne* 1.6 ⁓ *omnia* 14.19; *Iuppiter* 1.7 ⁓ *di magni* 14.12; *laboriosis* 1.7 ⁓ *labores* 14.11; *patrona* 1.9 ⁓ *clienti* 14.6; *plus* 1.10 ⁓ 14.1; *maneat* 1.10 ⁓ *abite* 14.21; *saeclo* 1.10 ⁓ *saecli* 14.23

Poem 14 inverts the drama of gift exchange depicted in poem 1.[14] In that poem, in gratitude to Cornelius for the favorable opinion of his poetry, Catullus gives him the charming, novel book, remarking favorably on Cornelius' own comprehensive work, and praying for its long endurance. In poem 14, Catullus asks for Calvus' grounds for sending a horrid, accursed book as Saturnalia gift, opining on the source of the book and Calvus' malicious motivations; in return, Catullus promises to purchase a comprehensive collection of poets he views unfavorably, and to repay Calvus with this punishment; he then commands the poets given to him by Calvus to depart. Neither thematic matches nor verbal recollections are in any doubt; keeping to the most impressive of the latter, note that these are (probably)[15] the sole appearances of *libellus* in Catullus, as well as the highly mannered "redistribution" of *plus . . . saeclo* in 1.10 (the first and final word of the final line) in the first and final lines of poem 14.

The case that 1–14 is an internal unity consists in its abundance of all three (local, terminal, and global) kinds of patterning, along with several factors which will be examined presently: the disjunctions between 1–14 and the poems that follow; the internal unity of 14b–26 and its specular relation to 1–14; and the clear indication that the leading "characters" of 14b–26 have *read* (at least some of) 1–14.[16]

---

[14] Hubbard (1983) 226–27.
[15] The transmitted reading *in omnibus libellis* at 55.4 has been defended by suggesting that *libellis* means "bookshops," but this is dubious.
[16] At least some of 1–14 are "words on papyrus" in the dramatized temporal frame of 14b–26.

Before pursuing these matters, however, we must turn to the drama of composition in poem 14. It is my contention, that is, that poem 14 has been misunderstood on a crucial point, and that setting the matter right reveals a metapoetic frame through which to see 14b–26. Namely, it has been the consensus understanding that Calvus' gift to Catullus was of *bad* poems and poets, in the sense that they were low-quality or unskilled; Catullus' threatened retribution will consist in purchased copies of the incompetent poetasters' rolls. I argue instead that the badness of the poems in Calvus' Saturnalia gift inheres more in their hostility; that what nearly kills Catullus is invective; that Catullus does not intend to buy books as immediate revenge-gift, but rather to collect these poets' invective venom in order to infuse his next set of compositions, 14b–26, with it. These poems, inspired by Calvus' Saturnalian gag gift and conceived on the night of the Saturnalia, are a carnivalesque inversion of 1–14:[17] a metapoetic, genre-crossing *tour de force*.

We begin with the transparent falsehood of the poem's conceit: on most valences of "bad" (4x in the poem: *male* at 14.5 and 10, *malum* 14.22, *pessimi*, 14.23), reading bad poetry will not actually kill you. Whichever sense of "bad" applies to Calvus' gift, it is through wordplay on the sense of "sick" that Catullus' deduction of Calvus' "homicidal" intent makes sense (*non est mi male* at 14.10 and *incommoda* at 14.23 are both easily taken of health).[18] That the "sickening agent" might be the poor quality of the poetry may not be initially implausible, but neither does it enjoy any initial presumption. And the evidence points overwhelmingly in a different direction. The next morning, Catullus threatens (14.17–20), he will "collect all the venom"; *uenenum* of speech means "hostile speech," and nowhere does it seem to mean "incompetent speech."[19] That the grammatical referent of *his suppliciis remunerabor* is *uenena* is at least as plausible as referring it to *Caesios, Aquinos, Suffenum*, to the extent that these might be different. The venom of hostile speech is at the point of semantic contact between "hostility" and "illness," and thus explains "(wrongfully) kill" and "die" (*male perderes … periret*, 14.5, 14). That the poets on Calvus' roll are "impious" (*impiorum*, 14.7) and the roll itself "accursed" (*sacrum*, 14.12) also fits better with this reading: both of these adjectives may be associated with the administering of poison. The poetic texture of 14 is thus denser, the poem more resonant, on this reading.

This reading also has later comparanda in **A** in its favor. In poem 36 we are told that Lesbia had vowed to consign the "worst poet's choicest

---

[17] See Döpp (1993a) on Saturnalia and its carnivalesque features in Roman literature.
[18] OLD *malum* 7b, *incommodum* 3.   [19] OLD s.v. 3b.

writings" to the flames, that is, Catullus' invective against her. From her perspective, of course, the *hostility* of these poems is the problem, and the *quality* of its invective is irrelevant – or indeed, the invective will be *worse* for her inasmuch as it is of higher quality, with the public laughing louder and longer at her expense.[20] It is Catullus, then, who invokes *malus* in the sense of *poor in quality*, substituting the *Annales* of Volusius for his own verse as he appropriates and fulfills Lesbia's learned vow.

Then we come to poem 44, where once again we find a pun upon *malus*. Catullus contracted a "nasty cough" (*malam tussim*, 44.7) from reading a "bad/sick book" (*malum librum*, 44.21). Bad in what sense? "Hostile" or "harmful" is directly supported by "poisons" and "plagues": *orationem in Antium petitorem | plenam ueneni et pestilentiae legi* (44.12–13).[21] Once again, the poisonous writings are "evil" (*nefaria scripta*, 44.18).

Catullus, whose ox is gored by name neither in Calvus' gift (we assume) nor by Sestius' speech, will not have been in sympathy with the attack on Antius; if he had, he would speak of its *acerrima uerba*, *dicacitas*, or the like. What one judges harsh but fair criticism one does not call *uenenum*.[22] But then, being out of sympathy with the invective content, he will have also found the speech wanting in invective form.[23] Few conclusions are this predictable. Thus, on my reading, we positively expect to find the hostile literary criticism implied by *frigida* and *frigus* (44.7, 20), and likewise the literary criticisms of poem 22. For readers who see only or primarily literary judgment here and in poem 14, the repetition of *uenenum* is difficult to explain. Again: applied to speech, the word means hostility; otherwise, it means venom. Venom sickens and kills; Catullus is sickened by verbal venom in one poem and is the victim of attempted homicide by verbal venom in another. This is his conceit, in both cases.

At this point, an obvious but weak objection is that Catullus is an invective poet himself, and that he gives reasonable people abundant grounds to detect *uenenum* in his verse. The pseudo-principle "it's not

[20] An Anglophone Lesbia could refer to poems 8 and 11 as "those dreadful poems" without pausing to form a defensible negative verdict on their literary qualities. Of course, she will likely agree, if asked, that the poems are poor in quality; we infer hostility as the real cause of her judgment, and perhaps wickedness as her avowed analysis, but again with " . . . because [unjustly?] hostile [to me]" readily inferable.

[21] Thomson (1997) *ad loc.* asserts that *pestilentiae* refers to the book's literary quality, not its aggression; I fail to see how he has determined this.

[22] Compare Cicero on *contumelia* (*Pro Caelio* 6): *quae si petulantius iactatur, convicium, si facetius, urbanitas nominatur.*

[23] Two sentiments which Catullus the partisan could never bespeak himself of in verse: "this attack on Mamurra is mediocre in quality" and "dear friend of mine though Calvus is, this jeremiad against him has a lively wit and makes some interesting points."

wrong when I do it" is, whether naively or winkingly so, intensely relevant to the following run of poems, 14b–26.

Poems 14 and 14b–26: The Horror, the Programmatic Horror

The temporal indicators in the poetic threat near the close of 14 should be closely observed (14.17–20). Catullus must be composing by lamplight, for he promises to run to the booksellers' stalls *si luxerit,* "when daylight comes" (14.17). He will collect "the Caesii, the Aquini, and Suffenus, all the venom(s)" and "repay [Calvus] with these punishments." Meanwhile (14.21), he performatively "banishes" the *pessimi poetae* who inhabit Calvus' roll.

This raises a minor but valid question: if, as is the traditional understanding, the immediate threat is to send Calvus these books, why does Catullus' letter specify its temporal priority to the purchase? The imagined epistle of poem 14 is unlikely to be sent at night; and why, in any case, bother sending it separately from the "gifts" that he will purchase first thing in the morning? If they are, in fact, sent together, it would be confusing from Calvus' standpoint for the cover letter to say "I *will* purchase and send you copies of Suffenus etc.," rather than, "These gift-punishments are for you." But if the "gifts" are not to be sent with the epistle but later, how can we understand the rush to purchase them as soon as possible?[24]

These questions were unlikely to be posed by readers who took themselves to understand poem 14 already. They are, however, directly relevant now. On this reading, Catullus probably does send poem 14 to Calvus "first thing in the morning" (possibly wrapped around the gag gift itself, with the "banishment" in the final lines "performed" for Calvus immediately, as he recognizes his gift),[25] at the same time that he "runs" to the booksellers. The point of his anticipatory *si luxerit* is to express his enthusiasm for his next poetic project, which has just, thanks to Calvus, fallen into his lap: trying his hand at invective. For this does not come naturally to him: he must study Suffenus *et al.* to drain off all the literary poison that he can and concentrate it into his verse. Since the hinge between the now-completed and upcoming runs of poetry is a poem set on the Saturnalia, the

---

[24] A speciously appealing answer would appeal to *colligam,* taking it in the sense of "put together a literary work" (OLD s.v. 8), and suppose that Catullus will anthologize the bad poetry, repaying Calvus with a collection homologous to the original gift. This will not work: Catullus explicitly specifies that he will collect "all" the venom(s) from at least three and almost certainly more poets. It would undercut his rhetoric to allow that some poetry on these rolls might not count as venom, thus allowing a selection of these multiple rolls to be made, which would still count as containing "all" their venom.

[25] The return of the gift roll is suggested by 14.20–21: *uos hinc ... abite* | *illuc, unde malum pedem attulistis.* I recall here that I am still imagining the drama on the literary, not the historical, level.

subsequent run might as well be a humorous inversion of the preceding. This temporal framing – an enthusiastic poet composing quickly – answers to both poetic and narrative needs within 1–51. We must imagine enough time for Furius and Aurelius to read and react to 1–14, now reduced by its completion to words on papyrus, before 14b–26 are complete. Yet we must not imagine so much time as to interrupt our sense of the poems' tight spatiotemporal world.

Turning now to the text of 14b–26 itself, we see that it contains strong verbal indications of its relationship to 14. The fragmentary introduction 14b anticipates a reader "shuddering" to touch the physical book or "shrinking" from it; the central line of 14, the central line of the central poem in 14b–26 (which comments on Suffenus, as seen in poem 14), and the final line of the final poem all contain the root *horr-*, which I now propose is offered as metapoetic characterization for this sequence, just as *lepidum* is at 1.1:[26]

14.12 (of 23 lines)	di magni, **horribilem** et sacrum libellum
14b.3 (of >3)	non **horrebitis** admouere nobis
22.11 (of 21)	rursus uidetur [Suffenus], tantum ab**horret** ac mutat
26.5 (of 5)	o uentum **horribilem** atque pestilentem![27]

Hubbard, arguing against the status of 14b–26 as independent *libellus*, notes its apparent lack of a clear close to balance its apparently clear prologue, 14b.[28] While I cannot in any case see reasons to deny that a small piece like poem 26 could close an internal part within a poetry book, *horrebitis* and *horribilem* in 14b and 26 do make for a framing motif. Add to this the presence of the same root at the precise arithmetic middle both of the middle poem in the sequence and of poem 14 anticipating the sequence:[29] this cannot be written off as fortuitous.[30] Note, too, the existence of a second, external framing motif for 14b–26:

---

[26] The root appears in **A** also at 4.8 (*horridamque Thraciam*) and, if Haupt's (1853) emendation is correct, 11.11 (*horribile aequor*). If *horribilis* at 14.12 and 26.5 evokes the verbal force of *horreo* in the sense of "bristle," the "shagginess" of these poems contrasts metapoetically with the smooth "polish" of 1–14 (*libellum . . . pumice expolitum*). Though admittedly *horridus* rather than *horribilis* is regular for this sense of *horreo*, there are parallels (Cic. *Mur.* 74 and Mart. 11.15.2, and indeed possibly Catullus 11.11, the "rough sea"), and the counterpoint with the markedly physical *libellus* in poem 1 encourages the corresponding reading for the *libellus* in 14. Note, too, that the cut edges of a *liber* do in fact "bristle" before they are rubbed smooth.

[27] Notice the correspondence between this ending and *plenam ueneni et pestilentiae* at 44.12.

[28] Hubbard (2005) 259; he does not separately consider the case for 14b–26 as an "internal unit."

[29] The key words *horribilem* and *abhorret* are even medial within their lines, respectively the third and fourth of six words.

[30] We can be utterly confident: Catullus counts lines. Poem 61 has lacunae after lines 78 and 107, whose lengths (four and three lines) can be deduced from its stanzaic nature. Our line 111 (*nocte, quae medio die*) was thus originally the 118th of 235 lines: 117.5 lines into a 235-line poem we read its sole

14.21 (3 lines before 14b)   **uos hinc** interea ualete **abite**
27.5 (5 lines after 26)   at **uos** quo lubet **hinc abite**, lymphae

Also clear and also crucial is the foreshadowing of poem 22 at 14.18–
19: *Caesios, Aquinos, Suffenum, omnia colligam uenena.* The poets
Caesius and Aquinus are merely representative types of the poets
Catullus will buy; Suffenus, for whatever reason, merits individual
notice. Understanding 14b–26 as the retaliatory gift to Calvus explains
the choice of subject in 22: Catullus has already told us that he is reading
Suffenus, and told us why. Incongruity between author and text is, as in
poem 16, the dominant theme of 22. Where this incongruity defends
Catullus in 16, it vilifies Suffenus in 22: the latter is "charming, sharp-
tongued, and sophisticated" (*uenustus et dicax et urbanus*, 22.2) in life
but "more boorish than the boorish countryside" (*infaceto ... infacetior
rure*, 22.14) in his verse.[31] Catullus, meanwhile, is *castus* and *pius* himself;
his verses have a "witty" charm (*salem ac leporem*, 16.7) even if they are
somewhat "effeminate" (*molliculi* 16.4, 8), and they are highly effective
in their prurience (*et quod pruriat ...*, 16.8–11). The real contrast is
underappreciated: Suffenus tries but fails to reproduce genuine and
praiseworthy personal traits in his verse; Catullus succeeds at simulating
alien and culpable ones. This is in his defense? Yes, in the joke. The
outrageousness of this defense is what makes it a good joke; the fact that
the joke *is* a joke is what ultimately defends Catullus. Horrible jocular
punishment, Catullus teases in poem 16, awaits those who miss this
point.

A crucial interpretive point may now be drawn. Most of the content of
15–26 (the threatened rape of Furius and Aurelius; the corporal punishment of the *municeps* in 17 and Thallus in 25; Catullus' protective, "conjugal" posture in respect to Juventius) is revealed as a literary joke. The case
for such a reading, to be sure, has long been persuasive, even absent these
metapoetic arguments. On aesthetic grounds, the rhetoric and tone of the

---

appearance of *medius*. For the ways in which Catullan poetry belies its own authorial pose of
arithmetical indifference, or rather hostility (in particular and especially the number of kisses in
poem 5: *conturbabimus illa ne sciamus* the sum whereof), see Henderson (1999) 69–86.

[31] Suffenus' characterization at 22.2 presents not three related qualities but a single one: he has (the
right kind of) verbal sharpness. It is instructive to see how the different metaphorical fields in this
poem come together: *infacetior* and *rure* oppose *uenustus et dicax et urbanus*, while both the expensive
finery of his books (22.4–8) and Suffenus' urbanity oppose *caprimulgus aut fossor*, the impoverished,
presumably servile rustic he becomes in his verse. On "Suffenus" as invective poet (or pseudonym
thereof) see Adamik (1995); Watson (1990) and Shapiro (2011) view him rather as an inferior poet
aspiring to a superior genre, a reading that is clearly inconsistent with this book's understanding of
Suffenus' *uenena* in poem 14.

poems are hard to take at anything like face value;[32] on Roman cultural or legal grounds, the same sort of argument can also be made.[33] But even if it is already clear from within 15–26 that the Juventius plot and the like are unserious, it is crucial to see that poem 14 – and probably 14b as well – provides external warrant for such a reading. What is serious here is literary.[34] The literary joke itself is, certainly, fully part of Catullan art. That these poems occupy 150 or so lines is definitive proof of that. But the material with which this joke is made – the pederastic love rectangle of Catullus–Juventius–Furius–Aurelius and related content – is a Late Republican analogue of the twentieth-century Aristocrats joke. The audience gets it and enjoys it both ways: it works; the fact that it works is ridiculous and shameful; the joke and the shame are on *us*, and we know it; yet instead of shame we feel self-flattery at our knowledge. Catullan hypocrisy is the lifeblood of all of this; it is the tribute which artistic virtue pays to moral vice.

What, then, of Juventius himself? He might well be a fiction, the *gentilicium* offering a handy *redender Name* for a young ἐρώμενος, especially if Catullus held a grudge against the *gens*.[35] The same consideration, of course, could indicate that "Juventius" is a pseudonym for some other contemporary youth. It is possible, however, that he and his name are real. In this case, rather than assume that he could be no more than a freedman of the noble *Iuuentii* – since a freeborn aristocrat would be disgraced by pedication[36] – we might assume that he is a young adult son of the *gens*, the target of Catullus' patently absurd but effective humorous conceit.[37]

The unit now begins with 14b, a programmatic address to readers. Though it is fragmentary, enough survives to enable comprehension.

---

[32] Holzberg (2002) 24–28 and Stroh (1990) *passim* and 143, *bene*: "dies ist der Ton eines jugendlichen Männerstammtischs."

[33] For a freeborn Roman citizen to allow himself to be penetrated constitutes *stuprum*, which is both a prosecutable offense and a source of lifelong disgrace: Stroh (1990) 137–38, Fantham (1991), Williams (1999) 103–36. If a real member of the *gens Iuuentia* was identifiable to contemporary readers, these poems are a potential danger to his reputation and standing – unless, that is, they were understood as mere lampoons; see MacLeod (1973b), Ingleheart (2014).

[34] One poem, namely 22, is pointedly exempted from the metapoetic disclaimer. Here it makes sense to take Catullus at his word: poem 14 signals that Suffenus will be one of his generic models for 14b–26; poem 22 comments on a poet we "already know" to be on his mind.

[35] See Ingleheart (2014) 65–67, with bibliography.   [36] So Stroh (1990) 137 n.30.

[37] The cumulative weight of the possible evidence that he is one M. Iuuentius Thalna (Claes (2002) 79–80) is considerable: he is addressed as *flosculus Iuuentiorum* at 24.1, while 25.1 addresses one "*Thallus*," which, in addition to the resonance, looks like an apparent bilingual gloss on *flosculus*; the verbal motif *quot . . . aliis erunt in annis* links 24.2–3 to Juventius with 49.2–3 to Cicero, which poem is preceded by the only other poem in **A** addressing Juventius; Thalna's father was a friend of Cicero (*Att.* 13.28 with Shackleton Bailey (1966) 345).

The poetry is now more strongly self-deprecating than in poem 1 ("foolish," *ineptiarum*, rather than "trifling," *nugas*); it contemplates, surely in light of the obscene content that follows, that readers may "shudder" to touch it; the speaker is the book itself. Nine poems follow. The six in hendecasyllables (15, 16, 21, 23, 24, and 26) are all addressed to and concern the (jocular) love interest Juventius, Furius, and/or Aurelius from poem 11, who are now represented as rivals for the lad's affection. The three remaining poems (17, 22, and 25) deal with, respectively, an unnamed Transpadane cuckold, the self-regarding bad poet Suffenus, and a thief of Catullan property, Thallus. Signs of studied specularity between 1–14 and 14b–26 as wholes are evident. The erotic plot changes from heterosexual to pederastic; the three non-hendecasyllabic poems in each group mirror each other in metrical type and sequence; and many poems have clear thematic correspondences:

1	14b	prologue: polished ~ rough verse
4, 8, 11	17, 22, 25	iambic>choliambic>Aeolic ~ Aeolic>choliambic>iambic non-hendecasyllabic poems
4	17	speaking boat ~ bridge spoken to
8	22	psychological incoherence of Catullus ~ Suffenus
5, 7, 8, 9	15, 16, 21	kisses ~ pedication and irrumation
9	23	self-*makarismos* ~ sarcastic invective *makarismos*
10, 13	23, 24, 26	poverty
11	15, 21, 23, 24, 26	"divorce" ~ "marriage"
12	25	witty ~ aggressive *reflagitatio*
14	23	"sickness" ~ "good health"
1, 14	22	physical book, literary criticism, and Suffenus
11	17	female infidelity; Catullus' dismissal ~ *municeps'* lack of diligence
1	16	Cornelius' ~ Furius and Aurelius' literary judgments of Catullus

Of these, the divorce/marriage inversion most requires comment. I appeal here to Mayer's justly influential demonstration that the dismissal of Lesbia in poem 11 has the form of a *diuortium per nuntios*, the formulaic repudiation of a wife by agents of her husband.[38] Where the urbane poet in 1–14 bids his unfaithful "spouse" farewell, not without harsh words, it is true, but also with his own love and suffering on display, the hypermasculine poet-speaker of 14b–26 is fully self-assured and fully vigilant over "his" pederastic "spouse." This, I propose, is the best explanation for why Furius

[38] Mayer (1983).

and Aurelius carry over between the two units: Catullus' agents in his "divorce" become rivals threatening his "marriage." Once again, a network of local correspondences helps us to move from one poem to the next. Aurelius is threatened with rape should he make erotic overtures to Juventius in 15; he and Furius are threatened with rape for a biographical reading of the kiss-poems in 16. Catullus performs his manliness with the threat of rape in 16, and likewise by his exposure of the foolish husband in 17 for his want of marital vigilance. The next poem, 21, now asserts that Aurelius has designs on Juventius' love and repeats the threat of rape. Four consecutive threat-poems: the delinquency is erotic conduct in two (15, 21) and *about* erotic conduct in the other two (16, 17); the threatened penalty is bodily in all four and sexual in three (15, 16, 21). This brings us halfway through the sequence.

We now move to poem 22, whose arrangement in local terms can be explained metrically: its non-hendecasyllabic meter ties it to the semi-adjacent 17. As in 1–14, the choliambic poem of 14b–26 is medial for its unit; poems 8 and 22 also share the theme of self-examination, which the poet attempts in the former and comments upon in the latter. Mention of Suffenus connects it, as we have seen, to the final poem of 1–14; the motif of the luxurious physical book ties it to poem 1 as well. The placement of poem 22 in the middle of its own unit is thus structurally overdetermined: its meter and its theme of self-examination pull it to the middle, while the polished book/poor content themes pull equally toward either pole, leaving the middle as a point of equilibrium.

The second half of the pederastic love rectangle follows, now with Furius as target. Poem 23 felicitates him and his kin for their "blessed" life of poverty, punning on *beatus* in the sense of "rich." The poverty theme is a continuation from the semi-adjacent 21, and is set in opposition to the extravagance of Suffenus' physical books in 22. It also refracts Catullus' jocular poverty in 1–14 (10, 13). Poem 24, the sole address to Juventius, follows. It reveals Catullus' motivation for attacking Furius in 23 (he is a rival for Juventius), and also makes humorously blatant the insincerity of 23's pseudo-philosophical pose: where the blessedness of poverty is a pretext for both attacking Furius and denying him a loan, the shamefulness of Furius' poverty is a strategy of mockery to Juventius in 24. Likewise, the fact that Furius is ashamed of his poverty in 23, while Catullus' poverty in poems 10 and 13 is light-hearted, further performs Catullan jocular hypocrisy. The non-hendecasyllabic *reflagitatio* of poem 25, addressed to Thallus, intervenes; to the extent that we need a local correspondence, the gift of "Midas' riches" (*diuitias Midae*) in 24 contrasts with Thallus' theft of Catullus' goods. Finally, poem 26 ends the sequence with Furius' poverty, as in 23 and 24: his diminutive *uillula* is punningly "exposed" to 15,200 pestilent winds and "mortgaged" for that number of sesterces.

The following chart summarizes local correspondences:

14b–15: introduction, promised *horror*. Aurelius and Juventius
    15–16: Aurelius, threatened rape
       16–17: wrongly inferred/not inferred sexual crimes
    15———17: punishment by vigilant lover, punished nonvigilant lover
    15–16 ——21; Aurelius threatened with rape
    15–16–17–21: sex and punishment
          21–22: poverty/riches
      17 ——22: non-hendecasyllabic meter, foolish ignorance
          21–22–23: poverty/riches/poverty
             23–24: Furius' poverty; Furius and Juventius
             24–25: gift and theft
             24———26: Furius' poverty
                25–26: storm raging at close

In sum: local patterning is abundant in 14b–26, and the presence of global patterning, including the responsion with 1–14 and tight thematic unity, is beyond dispute. Terminal responsions have at least mitigated the sense that some have felt of a weak ending. Above all, the metapoetic tie we have seen between poem 14 and this sequence transforms the way 14b–26 read; by making sense of the diptych effect of 1–26, it explains the larger unity of 1–26 as well.

Poems 27–51

The belated discovery of the internal unities 1–14 and 14b–26 has had its disadvantages. The tightness of their thematic coherences has widely been taken as the way Catullan design works. Scholars have looked for, and some have convinced themselves of, the existence of further such unitary stretches within 27–60. None has taken. On the case that will emerge in these pages, there is no such further unit: 1–26 acts as a tight, coherent story (or two stories: I prefer to say one story retold, with a tragedy-to-farce movement in the retelling); 27–51, by contrast, is partially defined by its relative looseness. While poems 27–51 are also structured by the overlapping correspondences in adjacent and semi-adjacent poems, as well as by the careful placement of non-hendecasyllabic poems, these poems are relatively lacking in overall thematic or narrative patterning. The problem here lies not in that fact but in the mistaken, if implicit, scholarly expectation that authorial patterning will always turn out to be *that* sort of patterning.

I will now make a cursory run through 27–51, to demonstrate how obvious and obviously authorial its local patterning is. The very brevity of this run is essential to my rhetoric here: one need only point out a handful of bare, readily observable facts to show where the links are and how far from doctored they are.

Poem 27 is introductory, at least for 28 and 29: Catullus needs a stiff drink for the courage to attack Piso, Memmius, and Mamurra by name, and Caesar and Pompey by implication.[39] Poem 28 hooks back up with the travel poems and Veranius/Fabullus poems in 1–14; looking closely, we realize that Catullus had yet to see these returned friends, as he now does, welcoming them in 28. Poem 29 is linked with 30 and 31 by their non-hendecasyllabic meter; as with 1–14 and 14b–26, we here have one of each metrical kind (iambic, Aeolic, choliambic), this time strung consecutively. Poem 31 is Catullus' homecoming to his villa at Sirmio; in 32, he inverts the genre of "invitation poem" by requesting that the prostitute Ipsitilla invite him to *her* home. Poems 32 and 33 both address prostitutes. One plausible explanation of poem 30 is that it evokes the rhetoric of a *propempticon*, virtually constituting the send-off speech by a poet "abandoned" by his "departing" addressee, Alfenus.[40] If this is true, the theme of travel (specifically, of social reception and leave-taking) ties together the entire run from 28 to 33: welcome home to friends (28); comment on the behavior of the newly returned Mamurra (29); send-off (30); speech on arrival home (31); invitation to home (or demand that Ipsitilla *stay* at home, 32); banishment into exile (33).

The next poem is the hymn to Diana, 34. It is admittedly a surprising change, and not all will be satisfied by the thought of it as daring inversion from 32–33, the filthiest poems in 27–51 followed by the purest one. But even if poem 34 were deemed a pure isolate in respect to its immediate predecessors, it is deeply integrated with those following it: the hymn to a goddess is followed by a poem about a poem about a goddess, the *Magna Mater* of poem 35. This poem also features a poet and his learned girlfriend; just so does poem 36 concern Catullus and *his* learned girlfriend, as Lesbia makes her return. One-upping her learned vow, Catullus in 36 hymnically invokes a third consecutive goddess, Venus (36.11–17). Now poem 37, like 36, features Lesbia. Additionally, 35–36–37 are all united by their addressees, all of which are inanimate, all of which are *written on*: epistolary papyrus, Volusius' *cacata charta*, the vandalized *taberna*.

---

[39] This is the minimalist version of the programmaticity of poem 27; a fuller version will be discussed and defended below.

[40] Claes (2002) 71; the reading is supported by the well-noticed intratexts with Ariadne's speech at 64.132–201.

We may concede some grounds for doubt regarding local explanations for 38 from the left (request for good verse after destruction of bad verse in the semi-adjacent 36; Catullus in need of consolation after the unhappy Lesbia poem 37); on the right, we have already seen the ABAB correspondences tying 37–39 (Egnatius, etc.) and 38–40 (request/threat of poetry, etc.). Ravidus (or whatever his name is) in 40 is insane; so is Ameana in 41.[41] Ameana is also the addressee of 43, and taken collectively, the clues that she is the unnamed *moecha* of 42 are persuasive. Ameana's inelegant speech in 43 is recalled in the pestilential speech of Sestius, which causes Catullus' *tussis* in 44; the two poems also share contrast between town and country.[42] The *tussis* in 44 meets the *sternuit* in 45. Poem 45 also recalls provincial service (Septimius prefers his Acme to service in Britain and Syria), which theme continues in 46 (Catullus' departure from Bithynia) and 47 (Piso and henchmen's post-provincial riches, Veranius and Fabullus' poverty).

With **Ax** removed, it is attractive to take *comitum ualete coetus* at 46.9 as marking the start of a farewell sequence for the book, with all of the major themes and the great majority of the important characters reprised: Bithynia and the provinces (46); rapacious provincial administration and Veranius and Fabullus (47); Juventius (48); Calvus (50), and, of course, Lesbia (51). Only Cicero in 49 is a problem here. We may say that his political and literary prominence grants him valuable "(ante)penultimate" poetic real estate before the paired close 50–51 – or we may take up the various verbal hints connecting 49 with 48 and the earlier Juventius poems, and find an explanation for the 48–49 sequence (and for Catullus' thanksgiving to Cicero) in that connection.[43] If the "farewell sequence" is rejected, 48 and 49 are still tied to each other in this way, as are 50 and 51; 49 and 50 are also tied by the forensic rivalry and poetic non-rivalry, respectively, of Cicero and Calvus.[44]

The table below summarizes these links:

27–28–29: wine-fueled political invective
27–28: wine, strong and weak
    28–29: provincial service (return from, poor and rich)
        29–30–31: non-hendecasyllables
            31–32: Catullus enters a house (and bed)
            32–33: prostitution

---

[41] *mala mens* (40.1), *uecordem ... rixam* (40.4) ~ *medicosque conuocate | non est sana puella* (41.6–7).
[42] *Prouincia* (43.6) ~ *funde ... seu Sabine seu Tiburs ... suburbana* (44.1, 6).   [43] Claes (2002) 80.
[44] Claes (2002) 81.

28–29–30–31–32–33: coming and going, speeches of
   33–34: most obscene to purest
     34–35–36: goddesses
      35–36–37: object addressees, poets' girlfriends
       36–37: Lesbia

37——39: Egnatius
  38——40: poems requested/threatened
    40–41: madness, the loves of others
     41–42–43: Ameana (or unattractive women, if Ameana not in 42)
    40——42: retaliatory poetry
      43–44: town/country, inelegant speech
     42——44: invective as punishment or crime
       44–45: coughing and sneezing
        45–46–47: provincial service
         46–47–48——50–51: farewell sequence
         47–48: hunger and satiety
          48–49: Juventius linked to Cicero
           49–50: rival orators
            50–51: diptych

Again, it is not the purpose of this table to assert that these connections are uniquely privileged but rather to show that in almost every case relevant and useful connections can clearly and quickly be found.[45] It is true that one or two of them can be doubted wholesale. I myself am hardly certain about 33–34: it is indeed surprising to read the Diana hymn after the prostitution in 32 and 33, and it may be that either I have failed to uncover the "real" justification for the sequence, or that there is no such justification, and Catullus has simply broken form here.[46]

The metrical patterning of non-hendacasyllables is also careful. The first seven poems (27–33) have the pattern **H-H-N-N-N-H-H**, with the distribution of metrical types in the **N**on-hendecasyllabic poems (versus **H**endecasyllabic ones) seen earlier. The next poem, 34, is in Aeolic meter, which will recur only in the final poem, 51. The three remaining non-hendecasyllabic poems are the choliambic 37, 39, and 44: the first two of

---

[45] Additional connections are also readily available; the outline makes almost nothing, for instance, of lexical repetition, which in many cases is hard to cavil at.

[46] While these twenty-five linkages will take you through every link in the sequence if you so desire, each reader may decide for herself which correspondences to accept. I have, however, kept contested readings to a minimum and added redundancies so that the chain doesn't break if you don't think, e.g., that the *moecha* of 42 is Ameana. My point about the farewell sequence, of course, rests on arguments given elsewhere.

these are the Egnatius poems, which the short hendecasyllables of 38 duly separate; the last is placed close to the midpoint between 39 and 51, breaking up the metrical monotony of poems 40–50 as effectively as possible.

Looking beyond local patterning, the first problem which must be confronted is the introductory and programmatic reading of 27, as was first claimed by Wiseman (1969) 7–8.[47] Aside from the case for this reading on its own, there is the highly probative fact that the shift in Catullus' metrical practice begins here. It is true, however, that there is also a positive problem with this reading: coming directly from 14b–26, a programmatic turn to "bitterer cups [of invective]" arguably rings false. A chronological reader has just read the bitterest poems in **A**; how can poem 28 and those following it be bitterer than these?

On the programmaticity of poem 27, the problem is that there are too many plausible (but not necessarily compatible) ways to understand its introductory function. It seems to me that there are two general interpretations, with distinct versions possible on each and significant possible overlap. That at least one of these works seems clear to me. Which one is better or more correct, however, I leave to individual tastes.[48]

First, the requested cups in poem 27 might be stronger in alcohol by volume, facilitating authorial courage in the bolder invective that follows. The invective, then, might be bolder primarily in that its targets are more powerful. At least the two immediately following poems, 28 and 29, are introduced by 27. These attack Piso, Memmius, and Mamurra by name and only minimally disguise their attack on the two most powerful of Catullus' contemporaries, Caesar and Pompey.[49] The stronger version of this claim will see this sympotic courage also in effect in poems 41, 43, 47, and arguably 49, attacking (respectively) Mamurra again twice, Piso again once, and Cicero.[50]

---

[47] See also Cairns (1975), Batstone (2007), and Gutzwiller (2012) 99–100.

[48] I doubt that we can take the programmatic announcement made by poem 27 to be the looser metrical practice itself (Skinner (1981) 27), on the grounds that a reader would have no confirmation of such a programmatic indicator for quite some time: the following poem, 28, is devoid of non-spondaic openings, and the three subsequent poems 29–31 are in non-hendecasyllabic meters.

[49] Catullus refers to his *irrumator praetor* at 10.11–12, but Memmius is unnamed, and in whose cohort Catullus served may not be immediately obvious to "everyone." Even if that is wrong, and even acknowledging the likelihood that Lesbia "is" a *mulier potens*, there is no question that more powerful people are attacked more often in 27–51.

[50] Sarcasm is widely suspected in the thanksgiving to Cicero; the strongest grounds for this are twofold. First, the ambivalence of *optimus omnium patronus* (49.7): "best of all patrons," but possibly also "best patron of *everybody*" (see Quinn (1973) 234–35 and the excellent discussion of Selden (1992) 464–66); then, the pointedness of the contrast between Catullus as facetiously "worst" *poeta* and Cicero (the notorious poetaster) as *patronus*. (Favoring this reading, Stroup (2010) 227 glosses poem 49 happily: "Marcus, don't quit your day job.") I would also add that my interpretation of the

Another possibility is that bitterer cups prefigure the increased harshness of the invective to come. The invective is harsher, perhaps, because 27–51 compares itself to 1–26 as a whole (thus diluting the harshness of 14b–26), but more plausibly in that the invective of 14b–26 – in keeping with the arguments just seen – is not to be taken seriously. To the extent that the invective content of these poems is metapoetically undercut, there is no question that 27–51 counts as harsher, given how much of 1–14 is not invective at all (1–5, 7, 9); is self-satirical (much of 8, 10, and 13); or is insincerely (14) or mildly (12) insulting. Then too, Caesar (and possibly Crassus or Pompey)[51] are apparently praised in poem 11.

A further possibility is that the invective content of 1–26 comes off gentler because its targets are suspected or known to be more often fictional. The *scorta* in poems 6 and 10 may surely be total fictions, as may Flavius in 6, the *municeps* in 17, Suffenus in 14 and 22 (the name is suspicious), Thallus in 25, and even Juventius, Furius, and Aurelius.[52] Poems 27–51 certainly contain more and harsher invective against figures whose historicity (and public identity) are undeniable than do poems 1–26 (at least 28, 29, 41, 43, 44, and 47). Ipsitilla in 32 seems obviously fictional, and, e.g., poems 33 and 42 may likewise attack fictional addressees. Yet only a few poems in 27–51 are clearly not sincere attacks on real people.[53] Though these cases are problematized by historical and interpretive uncertainties, it is fair to say that only on a maximizing interpretation for 1–26 and a minimizing interpretation for 27–51 will the former have given greater and wider offense, or been thought to do so by its earliest readers, than the latter.

To sum up, I see no positive difficulty with the former reading ("stronger" cups), but I believe that the latter sort of reading ("bitterer" cups) might be better. The problem with it lies in the uncertainty of the evidence from our perspective, for what appear to be contingent reasons. Wherever one comes down, this picture of poem 27 (namely, how it functions as an introduction, and to what) suits my overall view of **A** perfectly. For if the

---

"worst poets" at 14.23 as hostile ones adds another possible layer of dispraise to Catullus' self-characterization as *pessimus* to Cicero.

[51] Wiseman (1985) 144–45 and others think poem 11 alludes to Crassus; Krebs (2008) sees Pompey in *magni* (i.e. *Magni*) at 11.10.

[52] Holzberg (2002) suggests they are *redende Namen*.

[53] These would be 31 (which may satirize Catullus himself), 34, 46, 50, and 51. I tend not to take any criticism in 30 and 38 seriously, am unsure whether 35 is critical of Caecilius, and am hostile to seeing subversive criticism of Acme and Septimius in 45 but sympathetic to seeing the same in 48 and 49. The point here is that the relevant variables are far too many for tallying up to be a plausible or persuasive strategy on this question.

poem were as clearly introductory as poem 1 is, and as 14b will have been on standard assumptions about its lacuna, a rival view would be hard to dismiss, namely that these three units are fully independent of each other. The unit 1–14 wants for nothing with respect to its artistic unity, and 14 makes a good ending for the beginning made by poem 1. The unit 14b–26 is that good or nearly that good as well, and now we have what I hope is a satisfying account of the relationship between the two parts. It is not clear that poems 1–26 need any suppletion, save that their roughly 400-line bulk makes them a bit short for the normative length of Latin poetry books. By my own claim that 27–51 need not have thematic unity to be complete and authorially arranged, it would be hard to insist that 27–51 continues 1–26, if it, like 1–26, could also stand reasonably on its own.

But, in fact, it hardly does. Though we might imagine a roll beginning with poem 27, we can hardly imagine ourselves not finding the introduction abrupt and the content obscure, unless we read into it the expectations and understandings provided by (at least) 1–14. The terminal responsion which 50–51 represents is, as we have seen, a responsion to the beginning of 1–14 much more than to poem 27 and following; there, the only ring-compositional device of any substance is that the thematic pairing of wine and poetry in 27 is not found again until the beginning of the closural dyad, at 50.1–6.[54]

Poems 27–51 have more than enough local patterning to rule out their representing a posthumous anthology. They have a clear enough beginning to make sense as an internal unit within a book. The content of this unit makes sense with 1–26 fresh in one's mind, less so otherwise, while 1–26 makes sense without 27–51. The end of 27–51, then, brings our attention far more to 1–14 (to 14 via Calvus in 50; to 11 *qua* Sapphic-metered Lesbia poem; to 1 *qua* poem of poetic gift-exchange; to 2 and 3 via a third party with the beloved absent Lesbia, as well as the apparent beginning of her narrative, all of which are common to 51), than to anything within 27–51. All of this makes sense of and is explained by taking Catullus' book as 1–51. This is especially so given that poem 1 shares the metrical practice of 27–51, but also shares the specular terminal responsion with poem 14; it is thus integral with and inseparable from the first unit, 1–14. Characters in 14b–26 and 27–51 are aware of poems from 1–14 as *written* text; the end of 27–51

---

[54] There is a helpful parallel for "second-half framing via wine" in Horace's first book of *Odes*: 1.20 introduces the second half of the book – which divides thus into halves of 19 poems apiece – with a second address (after 1.1 of course) to Maecenas, inviting him to drink Horace's Sabine wine (Santirocco (1986) 54–55). The final poem of the book is then the wine-themed 1.38, *Persicos odi*. Like Catullus 27, *Odes* 1.20 is a "proem in the middle" by poem-count.

bids serial *adieu* to nearly every major theme preceding. Textual disturbance alone probably ensures that **Ax** will never be fully understood; everything else is explained by putting the rest of **A** together on a roll; more questions go unanswered by every other proposal. We have found Catullus' lyric book.

Before turning to **B** and **C**, however, one question remains: why does the ending of **A**, and the second closural drama of composition in **A**, coincide with the second appearance of Calvus?

The Closural Dyad: Poems 50–51

The claim that poems 50 and 51 form a closural dyad is more substantive than the claim that 50 is merely the penultimate and 51 the final poem of **A**. It is not, however, identical to the claim that poem 50 is a cover letter for 51, that 51 is the referent of *hoc . . . poema feci* at 50.16. There are three separate contentions at stake: that 52–60 are not the continuation of 1–51; that 50 and 51 invite our joint attention; that at 50.16, Catullus dedicates poem 51 to his addressee, Calvus.

Before running through the particular thematic and verbal correspondences marked here, I give a conspectus of high-level thematic responsions; given the thoroughness and familiarity of previous discussions, both of these will be brief. Either poem opens

1) with a figure enjoying the company of a charming beloved (50.1–6, 51.1–5),
2) followed by Catullus, separated from his beloved (from 50.7 and 51.5)
3) and suffering from eroticized distress (same lines),
4) whose severe physical symptoms are catalogued (50.9–13, 51.6–12).

The following section of poem 50 (lines 14–17, narrating Catullus' composition of "this poem" for Calvus) is not directly paralleled in 51; passing over this difference, either poem concludes

5) with a gnomic warning about surprisingly drastic dangers (50.18–21, 51.13–16).

In all of these we find direct correspondences mixed with ones arising from opposition: the beloved is the male Calvus, then the female Lesbia; the figure initially "with" the beloved is Catullus in 50 and the unnamed *ille* in 51; the desire to repeat the social contact in 50 becomes the inability to endure such contact in 51; the nocturnal Catullus wishing for day in 50 becomes the diurnal Catullus plunged into night in 51. Along the same lines, the entire complex of

thematic similarities cohabitates with an opposition in emotional tone: poem
50 offers a jocular sketch of fictitious erotic desire and a wildly exaggerated
pain of absence; poem 51 is arguably the most poignant moment in Catullus,
and the poet's erotic desire for and painful absence from Lesbia seem as serious
and real as anything in the poems.

In this we see another parallel, but now with poem 50 as emblem for 50
and 51 together. The sequence 50–51 progresses from a lighter to a darker
tone, from comic longing to serious loss, and from comic to serious
composition. This is exactly the self-narrated arc of poem 50: yesterday
the two poets cheerfully wrote (and must have erased) *uersiculi* on wax; last
night Catullus suffered; today, after managing at last to sleep, he commits
his grief to a fair sheet of epistolary papyrus.

Now we turn closely to the text, where the most important verbal
parallels are marked in bold type:

Hesterno, Licini, die **otiosi**
multum lusimus in meis tabellis,
ut conuenerat esse delicatos:
scribens uersiculos uterque nostrum
ludebat numero modo hoc modo illoc,   5
reddens mutua per iocum atque uinum.
atque illinc abii tuo lepore
incensus, Licini, facetiisque,
ut nec **me miserum** cibus iuuaret,
nec somnus **tegeret** quiete **ocellos**,   10
sed toto, indomitus furore, lecto
uersarer cupiens uidere lucem,
ut tecum loquerer, simulque ut essem.
at defessa labore membra postquam
semimortua lectulo iacebant,   15
hoc, iucunde, tibi poema feci,
ex quo perspiceres meum dolorem.
nunc audax **caue** sis, precesque nostras,
oramus, **caue** despuas, ocelle,
ne poenas Nemesis reposcat a te.   20
est uemens **dea**: laedere hanc **caueto**.

Ille mi par esse **deo** uidetur,
ille, si fas est, superare diuos,
qui sedens aduersus identidem te
    spectat et audit
dulce ridentem, **misero** quod omnes   5
eripit sensus **mihi**: nam simul te,
Lesbia, aspexi, nihil est super mi
. . .
lingua sed torpet, tenuis sub artus
flamma demanat, sonitu suopte   10
tintinant aures, gemina **teguntur**
    lumina nocte.
otium, Catulle, tibi molestum est:
otio exsultas nimiumque gestis:
otium et reges prius et beatas   15
    perdidit urbes.

otiosi 50.1 ~ *otium/o* 51.13, 14, 15; *per iocum* 50.6 ~ *ridentem* 51.5; *lepore incensus* 50.7–8
~ *tenuis . . . flamma* 51.9–10;[55] *me miserum* 50.9 ~ *misero . . . mihi* 51.5–6; *tegeret . . .*
ocellos 50.10 ~ *teguntur lumina* 51.11–12; *quiete* 50.10 ~ *sonitu suopte* 51.10; *lucem* 50.12 ~
nocte 51.12; *tecum loquerer* 50.13 ~ *lingua . . . torpet* 51.9; *simul* 50.13 ~ 51.6; *membra*
50.14 ~ *artus* 51.9; *perspiceres* 50.17 ~ *aspexi* 51.7; *caue(to)* 50.18, 19, 21 ~ *otium/o* 51.13,
14, 15; *poenas Nemesis* 50.20 ~ *si fas . . . diuos* 51.2, *perdidit* 51.16; *dea* 50.21 ~ *deo* 51.1

[55] *incensus ~ flamma* is clear, but *lepore ~ tenuis* is more venturesome, requiring the etymological
connection of λέπτον . . . πῦρ (underlying *tenuis . . . flamma*) with *lepidus* and thence *lepos*.

Again, little comment or elaboration seems necessary. More emphasis, perhaps, should be placed on the end-point correspondences than the literature has done. Not only is the framing device of *otiosi / otium* persuasive, but so are the shared motifs of the gods and danger: the apotropaic verbal gesture *si fas est* at 51.2, considering its absence in the Sapphic source text, pointedly recalls the closing warning about divine punishment in 50; the destructive power of *otium* ending 51 compares also to that of Nemesis in 50.[56] Tripled "caution" at the end of 50 is nicely opposed to tripled "leisure" at the end of 51, again in light of its destructive power.[57] The correspondence between *dea* and *deo* is bolstered by their respective final and initial placement, and also by the various gender inversions relevant to the two Catullan poems and the Sapphic model.[58] The same point is also of signal importance in respect to *misero . . . mihi* at 51.5–6: the masculine adjective is the only indication before the self-address *Catulle* at 51.13 that the female speaker in Sappho has become male in Catullus; this element is marked both by its lack of responsion in Sappho and by the telltale *me miserum* at 50.9. With *si fas . . . superare diuos* again recalling divine retribution at 50.20–21, two of the clearest liberties taken with Sappho in 51.1–12 are explained by the poem's concurrent agenda of reflecting poem 50 as well. The case is clear: if verbal and thematic responsions constitute reason enough to "read poems together," then these two poems should be read together.

The claim that *hoc . . . poema* at 50.16 refers to poem 51 remains. Though it was first proposed in 1965, the contemporary prominence of this view is owed to Wray's seminal 2001 study.[59] His case rests on responsions as presented above, with two further considerations. First, the etymological wordplay at 50.16:

> at defessa labore membra postquam
> semimortua lectulo iacebant   15
> **hoc**, iucunde, tibi **poema feci**
> ex quo perspiceres meum dolorem.

Catullus' *poema* transliterates ποίημα, which is of course a verbal noun from ποιέω, rendered by *feci*. This is, evidently, an etymological Greek-to-Latin

---

[56] Németh (1974) 48 also notes that *reposcat a te*, just following *Nemesis*, sounds pointedly identical to *reposcat* Ἄτη. We will see further Greek in poem 50; this instance, if accepted, is possibly redolent of the "ruin" with which 51 ends.

[57] The fact that each concluding warning contains four lines is helpful.

[58] Skinner (1997), Clark (2008).

[59] Wray (2001). Reactions have ranged from outright rejection (Bellandi (2007), Feeney (2012)) to provisional support to full endorsement (Dettmer (1997) 107–08 and Skinner (1981) 91 accept and develop upon the earlier case). No detailed rebuttal has yet been written; the skeptical point of view in the following pages is ventriloquized.

gloss, a Latin act performed on a Greek poem: "I composed [*feci*] this composition [ποίημα]." Second, there is the parallel provided by 65.15–16 and 66: the sole other known translation in Catullus is preceded by a cover letter to its dedicatee, in which the phrase *haec . . . carmina* looks forward to the following translated poem, rather than constituting a self-reference to the present poem.[60]

In addition to the already acute difficulty of conceding that 50 and 51 invite joint attention but denying that 50 points to 51, there is an as-yet unnoticed link that makes it unthinkable that the two of them should not be sent together: Catullus' translation of Sappho 31 is not limited to poem 51, but distributed between it and 50.

As is well known, poem 51 is in the main a close translation, but some correspondences are looser, and a few outright liberties are taken. I print the two poems with literal correspondences in bold type:

φαίνεταί μοι κῆνος ἴσος θέοισιν	**Ille mi par esse deo uidetur,**
ἔμμεν' ὤνηρ, **ὄττις ἐνάντιός τοι**	ille, si fas est, superare diuos,
ἰσδάνει καὶ πλάσιον **ἆδυ φωνεί-**	**qui sedens aduersus** identidem te
σας ὑπακούει	spectat **et audit**
καὶ γελαίσας ἰμέροεν, τό μ' ἦ μὰν 5	**dulce ridentem,** misero **quod** omnes 5
καρδίαν ἐν στήθεσιν ἐπτόαισεν,	eripit sensus **mihi: nam simul te,**
ὡς γὰρ ἔς σ' ἴδω βρόχε' ὣς με φώναι-	Lesbia, **aspexi, nihil est** super **mi**
σ' οὐδ' ἓν ἔτ' εἴκει,	. . .
ἀλλ' ἄκαν μὲν **γλῶσσα** †ἔαγε **λέπτον**	**lingua sed** torpet, **tenuis** sub **artus**
δ' αὔτικα **χρῶι πῦρ** ὑπαδεδρόμηκεν, 10	**flamma** demanat, **sonitu** suopte 10
ὀππάτεσσι δ' οὐδ' ἓν ὄρημμ', **ἐπιρρόμ-**	**tintinant** aures, gemina teguntur
βεισι δ' ἄκουαι,	**lumina** nocte.
κὰδ δέ μ' ἴδρως κακχέεται, τρόμος δὲ	otium, Catulle, tibi molestum est:
παῖσαν ἄγρει, χλωροτέρα δὲ ποίας	otio exsultas nimiumque gestis:
ἔμμι, τεθνάκην δ' ὀλίγω 'πιδεύης 15	otium et reges prius et beatas 15
φαίνομ' ἔμ' αὔται·	perdidit urbes.
ἀλλὰ πὰν τόλματον ἐπεὶ †καὶ πένητα†	

φαίνεταί μοι κῆνος ἴσος θέοισιν 31.1 ~ *ille mi par esse deo uidetur* 51.1; ὄττις ἐνάντιός τοι ἰσδάνει . . . ὑπακούει 31.2–4 ~ *qui sedens aduersus . . . te . . . et audit* 51.3–4; ἆδυ φωνείσας 31.3–4 ~ *dulce ridentem* 51.5; τό μ' ἦ μὰν 31.5 ~ *quod . . . mihi* 51.5–6; ὡς γὰρ ἔς σ' ἴδω 31.7 ~ *nam simul te . . . aspexi* 51.6–7; με 31.7 ~ *mi* 51.7; οὐδ' ἓν 31.8 ~ *nihil est* 51.7; ἀλλ' . . . γλῶσσα 31.9 ~ *lingua sed* 51.9; λέπτον . . . πῦρ 31.9–10 ~ *tenuis . . . flamma* 51.9–10; χρῶι 31.10 ~ *artus* 51.9;[61] ὀππάτεσσι 31.11 ~ *lumina* 51.12; ἐπιρρόμβεισι δ' ἄκουαι 31.11–12 ~ *sonitu . . . tintinant* 31.10–11

---

[60] Note also that the demonstrative in *habe tibi quidquid hoc libelli* points beyond the words of poem 1 itself to the physical book containing it and also to the poems following poem 1, understood as content as well as physical *realia*.

[61] I follow Vine (1992) on the identification of *artus* with Sappho's χρῶι, although I see a more straightforward intertext with poem 50 below.

Two obvious and much-discussed patches of non-correspondence are immediately visible. Sappho's fourth stanza is not translated, and Catullus' fourth and final stanza does not appear to correspond to the surviving line of Sappho's fifth.[62] Why might this be so? The reason, I now show, is that poem 51 demands to be read not only with Sappho 31, and not only with poem 50, but with both simultaneously. This is Catullus' adaptive art at its densest and most brilliant.

φαίνεταί μοι κῆνος ἴσος θέοισι
νέμμεν' ὤνηρ, ὄττις ἐνάντιός τοι
ἰσδάνει καὶ πλάσιον ἆδυ φωνείσας ὐπακούει
καὶ **γελαίσας ἰμέροεν**, τό μ' ἦ μὰν   31.5
καρδίαν ἐν στήθεσιν ἐπτόαισεν,
ὠς γὰρ ἔς σ' ἴδω βρόχε' **ὠς** με **φώναι-**
σ' οὐδ' ἒν ἔτ' εἴκει,
ἀλλ' ἄκαν μὲν γλῶσσα †ἔαγε **λέπτον**
δ' **αὔτικα** χρῶι **πῦρ** ὐπαδεδρόμηκεν,   10
ὀππάτεσσι δ' οὐδ' ἒν ὄρημμ', ἐπιρρόμβεισι δ' ἄκουαι,
κὰδ δέ μ' **ἴδρως κακχέεται**, **τρόμος** δὲ
παῖσαν ἄγρει, χλωροτέρα δὲ ποίας
ἔμμι, **τεθνάκην** δ' **ὀλίγω** 'πιδεύης   15
φαίνομ' ἔμ' αὔται·
ἀλλὰ πᾶν **τόλματον** ἐπεὶ †καὶ πένητα†

Hesterno, Licini, die otiosi
multum lusimus in meis tabellis,
ut conuenerat esse **delicatos**:
scribens uersiculos uterque nostrum
ludebat numero modo hoc modo illoc,   50.5
reddens mutua per **iocum** atque uinum.
atque illinc abii tuo **lepore**
incensus, Licini, facetiisque,
ut nec me miserum cibus iuuaret,
nec somnus tegeret quiete **ocellos**,   10
sed toto, **indomitus** furore, lecto
uersarer cupiens **uidere** lucem,
ut tecum loquerer, **simul**que **ut** essem.
at defessa labore membra postquam
semimortua lectulo iacebant,   15
hoc, iucunde, tibi poema feci,
ex quo perspiceres meum dolorem.
nunc **audax** caue sis, precesque nostras,
oramus, caue **despuas**, ocelle,
ne poenas Nemesis reposcat a te.   20
est uemens dea: laedere hanc caueto.

γελαίσας 31.5 ~ *iocum* 50.6; *ἰμέροεν* 31.5 ~ *delicatos* 50.3; *ὠς ... ὠς* 31.7 ~ *ut ... ut* 50.13; *ἴδω* 31.7 ~ *uidere* 50.12; *φώναισ'* 31.7–8 ~ *loquerer* 50.13; *ἀλλ'* 31.9 ~ *sed* 50.11; *λέπτον* 31.9 ~ *lepore* 51.7; *αὔτικα* 31.10 ~ *simul* 50.13; *πῦρ* 31.10 ~ *incensus* 50.8; *ὀππάτεσσι* 31.11 ~ *ocellos* 50.10; *ἴδρως κακχέεται* 31.13 ~ *despuas* 50.19; *τρόμος* 31.13 ~ *uersarer* 50.12; *παῖσαν* 31.14 ~ *toto* 50.11; *ἄγρει* 31.14 ~ *indomitus* 50.11; *τεθνάκην δ' ὀλίγω* 'πιδεύης 31.15 ~ *semimortua* 50.15; *τόλματον* 31.17 ~ *audax* 50.18.

Catullus' symptoms are Sapphic in poem 50 as well. It is true that many items here, notably "seeing," "eyes," and "speech," are sufficiently explained at one remove: Sappho 31 is translated in poem 51, and poem 50 is crafted to respond to it. Others, however, reflect Sappho as directly (*lepore*) or more so

---

[62] Fredricksmeyer (1965) argues that the final stanza is a dig at Lesbia and her otiose *ille*; Frank (1968) supports this argument. Alternative explanations have been suggested by Itzkowitz (1983: that Catullus' deviation from Sappho is a display of affected spontaneity), Newman (1983: that the fourth stanza is a comic turn), Vine (1992: that Catullus' fourth stanza may be adapted from a lost later stanza of Sappho's poem).

than they do poem 51 *(ut . . . ut, despuas, uersarer, toto, indomitus)*. Crucially, these correspondences account for the missing Sapphic lines: readers wondering where they went can find them here.

Most conspicuous are τεθνάκην δ' ὀλίγω 'πιδεύης ("little short of death") ~ *semimortua* and τόλματον ("to be endured") ~ *audax*.[63] Both look to be exact structural equivalents: both poets' "near death" ends the catalogue of symptoms and falls on the fifteenth line to boot; *nunc audax caue sis* effects a transition to a moralizing conclusion homologous with ἀλλὰ πὰν τόλματον, and each of these phrases likely begins the four-line conclusion of its poem.[64] If we accept that *lepidus* in Catullus recalls a metapoetic λέπτος, then λέπτον ... πῦρ ~ *lepore incensus* is equally clear, and the *double* translation of the phrase (i.e. this and *tenuis ... flamma* at 51.9–10) nicely distributes its respective literal and etymological/poetic valences.

The symptoms missing from poem 51 are sweating, trembling, turning green, and feeling deathly; the last of these we have already found in poem 50, while the third is clearly unexampled there, and admittedly does not appear in 50 either. In poem 50, the symptoms proper I count as loss of appetite, insomnia, and wild tossing and turning. This last one compares well with Sapphic trembling: τρόμος δὲ παῖσαν ἄγρει ~ **toto, indomitus** *furore, lecto* | **uersarer**. "Trembling" and "tossing," of course, resemble each other as involuntary motions caused by distress; the other two elements in Catullus are syntactical reworkings (as *uersarer* itself also is) of Sappho: *toto* is a wayward match for παῖσαν, *indomitus* perhaps an oblique gloss on ἄγρει (properly the Aeolic equivalent of αἱρεῖ, but similar in sound to – and perhaps easy to momentarily misread as cognate with – ἄγριος, "wild"). What of the remaining Sapphic symptom, "sweating"? Extraordinary, even bizarre: the sweat pouring down Sappho's body (**κὰδ** δέ μ' ἵδρως **κακχέεται**) is reflected in the downward motion of another bodily effluvium: ***despuas*** at 50.19 is contextually "reject" but literally "spit down." The missing stanza is, for the most part, found.

The verbal correspondences and our comparative symptomatology clinch the case: poem 50 itself casts its gaze on Sappho 31.[65] That being evident, two important results follow: the remaining correspondences all

---

[63] It may also be craft that the opening of either fifteenth line is sonically similar: *semimortua* ~ ἔμμι, τεθνάκην. The introduction of initial *s* corresponds to semi- / ἡμι-, and the sonic similarity gives way, at precisely the equivalent spot, to the semantic correspondence *mortua* ~ τεθνάκην.

[64] The semantic shift from the likely contextual meaning of τόλματον ("to be endured") hardly negates the fact that *audeo* is the closest Latin equivalent to τολμάω.

[65] If this is admitted, *lepore incensus* will itself count as evidence in favor of meaningful correspondence between *lepos* and λέπτος, since *incensus* would then by itself suffice to recall πῦρ.

enjoy a heavy presumption that they are "real," that none of them is a "mere epiphenomenon" of the pairing of 50 with 51. The mediation of poem 51 now loses explanatory priority for Sapphic correspondences in 50. Though 50 is certainly a looser adaptation in most respects, it, too, is an adaptation of Sappho 31, and the three poems are a triptych.[66]

What are the most general, highest-level results of the conclusion that both 50 and 51 must be read with Sappho 31? I began with the matter of the referent of *hoc . . . poema* at 50.16, claiming that the evidence points decisively to 51. One key result of this is to elevate the relative importance of poem 50, and with it the metapoetic nature of the triptych. Catullus' dedication of 51 to Calvus creates an (authorized and idealized, *qua* learned poet) internal reader; Catullus' stated purpose "that you might perceive [or: 'look carefully at'] my *dolor*" (*perspiceres meum dolorem*, 50.17) is then metapoetically mimed by our inspection of both poems under this rubric.

The inferable temporal sequence in 50 is: sleepless night, the composition of 51, and then the composition of 50 as cover letter; poem 50 literally has the last word. The most important element unique to 50 is composition: Catullus and Calvus (ll. 1–6), the composition of 51 (16–17), and the request for a reciprocal poem (18–21). I will offer a more determinate reading of this metapoetry presently; for now, I note that any such reading should see how appositely the dramatic narrative of poem 50 in general and the composing mentioned at 50.16–17 in particular fit into the context of Sappho 31 and Catullus 51. The temporal separation of the experience from the composition is arguably essential to these poems: *as soon as I catch sight of you*, each speaker says, *I lose my faculties*. Could the two lyrics take shape during the throes of such experience? On this level, the temporal sequence of 50 reads as a dramatic embellishment of what Catullus already found in Sappho: were we to imagine the drafting of the poem, the preparation of its fair copy, and the physical delivery of same to the beloved, we should not think that it took place with "that man" and the beloved

---

[66] Whether and how far to push readerly "looking" at this lovely poetic triad as metapoetic correlate for the love triangle in the Sapphic source text is a good question for a later discussion. This view of Sappho 31 as referent for Catullus 50 *as well as* 51 also lends itself to further questions for the reconstruction of the Sappho poem's (presumably final) fifth stanza, though these I find to be less answerable than the former. In brief: the generalizing and moralizing turn in the two Catullan poems seems likely to triangulate with the same sort of content in the model text, as ἀλλὰ πᾶν τόλματον already suggests: Does *beatas* ("wealthy") at 51.15 negatively echo πένητα ("poor man") at Σ 31.17? And might the tripled *otium* and *caueo* be vestiges of an equivalent Sapphic anaphora (perhaps of τολμ-)?

present, as it were, in the same room.[67] This, at any rate, is the argument which the compositional drama of 50–51 poses. The difference in poetic register between 51 and 50 is essential: *I wrote you this poem – after my tinnitus stopped!* is an unthinkable thing for Sappho 31 to say, and an appropriately amusing thing for 50 to say.

A second key interpretive layer, plainly, is gender. The simplest way to put this is just to notice how perfect Catullus' dual adaptation is: Sappho, female/female; poem 51, male/female; poem 50, male/male. A female speaker's words to a female beloved become a male speaker's words to beloveds of now one, now the other sex. Catullus finds two ways to play the woman in his metapoetic *schema*: as Sappho the composing poet in 51, and as dramatized speaker pining for a man in 50.

In any case, these issues of gender will almost certainly end up linked with the metapoetic questions surveyed above. Whatever it means for the address to Lesbia in 51 to be reframed as a subject for discussion between men, Wray definitively showed us that the motif is *echt* Catullan: after the initial run, every mention of her in 1–51 has this in common.[68]

It may seem to some to trivialize poem 51, and perhaps the Lesbia poems as a whole, if we reframe Catullus' (serious) love for her and pain at their separation as a metonym for his (comic, exaggerated) *dolor* for Calvus. For supporters, however, this reframing enriches poem 51 while subtracting nothing from it: poem 51 is closely paired not only with 50 but also with 11, the other Lesbia poem in Sapphic meter; behind poem 11 follow the other Lesbia poems. There is no question of effacing the perspective of poem 51 as seen from poem 11 and company: that view is too compelling to be deauthorized. My contention is that other views of the poem are also authorized: one pointedly between two men, and another pointedly between poets – between *three* poets, one of whom is a woman. Poem 51 is one sort of poem and another sort of meta-poem. It is not impossible for

---

[67] I am not here claiming that Sappho 31 itself is best taken as text rather than performance, epistle rather than drama. Rather, it is the Catullan triptych which takes it as textual, or even more modestly than that, as simply not created at the moment of performance. Compare the opening of poem 62, where the performing choruses discuss the "rehearsal" of the occurrently performed wedding song.

[68] Poems 51 and 11 are "notes passed, quite behind [Lesbia's] back" (Wray (2001) 109) respectively to Calvus and to Furius and Aurelius; 13 promises the gift of her *unguentum* to Fabullus; 36 addresses Volusius by way of his poem, with the gift-motif modified to the *uotum* to Venus and Cupid on [Lesbia's] behalf; 37 is the metapoetic irrumation of Catullus' rivals for Lesbia, especially Egnatius; 42 mentions Lesbia to disparage Mamurra by disparaging his *puella*, Ameana. And of course poems 2, 2b?, 3, 5, 7, and 8 are "gifts to a man" *qua* components of the *libellus* dedicated to Cornelius Nepos in poem 1.

a poem to authorize contradictory views of itself. Is this a flaw? Not by my lights.

On, then, to a more totalizing reading. Calvus, the internal Catullan reader through whose eyes we see the text, reads poem 50. If we disbelieve, as we must, the single-day composition and dedication of poems 50 and 51, our Calvus first notes the conceit, then plays along in order to see where Catullus' rhetorical point leads. Next, our attention is drawn to what we do *not* know: did Calvus ever play in Catullus' tablets? How much credence should we give to their depicted play? How fictional is it? The presence of the inner reader makes it the poem's question: Calvus knows, and Catullus knows that we know that Calvus knows, exactly how fictional the opening conceit of poem 50 is.

We then wonder what Calvus makes of Catullus' erotic "suffering" upon parting. Not literal, he knows. Fiction or exaggeration – is Catullus' *dolor* just a classic pose, or a pose that is classic for a reason? This he has to think about. The only easy answer comes if the earlier "play" was entirely fictional: if there was no underlying reality there, Calvus takes it that there is none *here*. This can hardly be the best reading: the solution trivializes the problem, renders it unworthy of having been put in the first place. It is the least interesting thing to say; we reject it. Now Calvus' ignorance is isomorphic with ours, as are his interpretive options: he is one of us in this respect, wondering what really happened and how much is a pose.

If Calvus understands *hoc ... poema* as poem 51, the content of that poem further focalizes the relation between art and experience. Catullus chooses a classic representation of overwhelming emotion: as soon as the poet looks at the beloved, s/he loses control of language – as this curiously-wrought literary catalogue of symptoms suggests. Our Calvus hears Catullus pointing out that the only way to *say* this is for the emotion *not* to be so overwhelming, at least when you write it up. The gap between art and experience is a necessary condition for their correspondence.

Two further points emerge. First, our reading cannot downplay, and in fact must explain, the programmaticity of the purpose clause at 50.17: "[I made this poem] so you could examine my pain." Opponents have a good question: why should Catullus send poem 51, in particular, to Calvus? Comes my answer: because his poet friend will have the eyes to see his *dolor*: "I made it for you [*tibi*], so you could see ... " Calvus is especially well placed to see it, once we reject the view that their poetic play is pure fiction. Calvus knows that his own presence in Catullus' poetry falls somewhere between fiction and reality; he either knows or surmises the same about Lesbia. This is the poet's *dolor*: if Lesbia were pure fiction, writing her need not hurt at all; if he could write up his Sapphic love-symptoms while experiencing them, they wouldn't hurt so much, if only because he would not need to revisit them again and again. This poetic *dolor* will not have been entirely unpleasant – some of it would be intensely pleasant – but *dolor* is certainly the right word.

Calvus was a real person, a contemporary of Catullus, an artist working in the same medium and living in the same city. Many or all of the inferences made just now about "Catullus' Calvus" or "Calvus as readerly heuristic" are attractive inferences to make about the historical Calvus as well. The following historical suppositions seem reasonably likely, at least:

1) It would have humiliated Catullus if Calvus publicly ridiculed either Catullus' "longing" for him or the notion of their writing together.
2) Knowing this, Catullus would only have written 50 if he were confident that Calvus would not do so.
3) Catullus would be unlikely to have such confidence without extensive personal familiarity with Calvus.
4) On social occasions, Catullus and Calvus would be likely to discuss poetry, if not actually to compose in each other's company.
5) Catullus would have written poem 50 expecting that Calvus would read it, and that he would think of their social/literary interactions as the reality underlying "yesterday's play" in the poem.
6) As a learned poet, Calvus was a maximally competent reader of learned poetry; Catullus would have expected Calvus to recognize any artistry that he expected his best readers to recognize.

If I am correct that Catullus' *dolor* is the painful congruence and incongruity between his art and his experience, then there is every chance that he made these compositions for Calvus because Calvus was, in fact, the perfect recipient: he both understood the artistic problem as well as anyone, and shared with Catullus the experience out of which this partial congruence was constructed.

4　Narrative Time in A

There is only one way to make a coherent story out of poems 1–8, and that coherent story is in fact so coherent and attractive that refusing to make the (modest) assumptions upon which it works is absurd. There are only a handful of assumptions one must make – and they are the only ones one must make in the corpus. These are:

1) dedicatory poems are placed earlier but composed later;
2) for recurring characters, the temporal "plot" matches the poem sequence;
3) the poems often have temporal frames: a "now" unfolding (at least roughly) in the sequential order of the poems, and other, recalled or anticipated times;
4) for non-recurring (and non-introductory) themes and figures, temporality can be presumed irrelevant;
5) important events can occur "between" poems, which readers must infer.

The necessity of inferring (1) is immediately obvious. No one imagines Catullus writing, "I give you this charming, novel book," and then setting about the task of producing a charming, novel book. Likewise (2): the temporal order of the sparrow poems 2 and 3 follows from the way of all flesh and the second law of thermodynamics; that the poem sequence tracks dramatic time is confirmed by the recoverable dialogue on kiss quantities in poems 5 and 7. Inference (3) is already present in poem 1 (the dedication of this *libellus* now is explained by an earlier time, when Cornelius Nepos composed his *Chronica* and thought well of Catullus' trifles, 1.2–7). Inference (4) is the best way to handle poem 6. Of course we may consider the relation between Catullus' jocular/malicious *curiositas* about Flavius' secret love and the poet's own anxieties about onlookers to his own secret love; we do not know, however, that Catullus addressed Flavius after requesting thousands of kisses but before answering Lesbia's question about the desired quantity. That would be silly, and is beyond what we have warrant to assume. Finally, (5) is the only way to make poems 7 and 8 work together: Lesbia has rejected Catullus, and Catullus is "now" advising himself to reject her back.

Every conceivable way out of these inferences is pointless.[69] Now in the second half of 1–14, we first find Catullus having heard of – this point will be important – his friend Veranius' return from Spain; Catullus looks forward to a reunion (poem 9). In the following poem, Catullus' own return is recent news: Varus, a close friend (close enough to ask the poet to accompany him from the forum to meet his new girlfriend) now sees Catullus for the first time since his return. This marks the second installment of the Catullan journey plot, after poem 4: both the dramatic present

---

[69] Two different sparrow-tending women dubbed "my girl"; the separate identities of the "[poet's] girl" in 2 and 3, "Lesbia" in 5 and 7, and "the girl" in 8; the precedence of 5 and 7 relative to 2 and 3: none of this works, there is no warrant for anything like it.

of the two poems ("shortly after") and the narrated past (Catullus' return from/stay in Bithynia) cohere nicely.

This now raises the question of the relative dramatic times of poems 9 and 10, whose plots are separate but parallel. Did Catullus' return precede Veranius' by enough time for the Lesbia-related events of poems 2–8 to occur, but not so long that Varus can plausibly not have seen him yet? This is plausible, and fits: we cannot prove that the temporal correspondence works this way, but all the evidence with which we are presented counts in its favor, nothing counts against it, and it works.

Poem 11 follows. Clearly this makes a second break-up poem with Lesbia, matching the sparrow- and kiss-poem pairs. Once again, assuming the temporal priority of the prior-in-poem-sequence 8 makes good sense: Catullus' irresolute resolution to reject Lesbia back in poem 8 is carried out appropriately: the penultimate stanza (17–20) implements his resolution; the final stanza (21–24) betrays its irresolution. We may or may not want to infer an intervening event – such as Lesbia sending a message suggesting her willingness to patch things up – provoking the dismissal. This is reasonable, on the one hand, and would alleviate any worry about Catullus effectively saying "you can't fire me, I quit"; on the other hand, readers may well feel that this goes beyond what the text encourages.

The napkins stolen by Asinius Marrucinus in poem 12, we are now told, were gifts sent from Spain by the Veranius we recently met, but also by another figure, Fabullus. The second mention of Spain confirms the temporal continuity between 9 and 12; Catullus' concern for this *mnemosynum* is compatible with regarding the dramatic time of poem 12 as following Veranius' return in 9. It is fine to suppose that the keepsake will be somewhat less important to Catullus after he is reunited with his friend – but note that the reunion has not yet occurred in 9, and nothing encourages us to think that it must have happened by 12.

Now Fabullus, the new character introduced in 12 and tied to Spain, Veranius, and napkin-giving, is addressed in 13; with him, too, Catullus foresees a *future* encounter. This poem also intersects with the Lesbia plot: Catullus the impoverished dinner host must ask Fabullus to supply the dinner, but the latter will receive the *unguentum* of "[Catullus'] girl." Neither the characterization (*meae puellae*), I think, nor the gift contradicts the close temporal priority of poem 11 to 13: Lesbia was referred to this way in poem 2, before the affair proper began; the presence of her *unguentum* at Catullus' house does not imply her presence; if there is some sort of bawdy sexual reference here, it is in keeping with Catullus' attitude toward her in poem 11 for him to wish to embarrass her.[70] Finally, the poem-sequence of 1–14 comes to an end with the epistle to Calvus; dramatically, the vignette is an isolate, unconnected to anything in poems 2–13. We can well imagine poem 1 being drafted now, duly arranged at the head of the *charta* which its specular piece, poem 14, ends: the ink dries, the pumice is applied, and Cornelius gets his charming novel *libellus*.

The argument that poem 14 promises the immediate future composition of invective poetry, as realized by 14b–26, was stated earlier in this chapter. Here, too, the indications of temporal progression in the poem-sequence are abundant. Poem 14b, as introduction, can be harmlessly exempted; poems 22 and 25 do not appear to interact with the other characters in **A**, and so may also be passed over. The recurring figures, though, do show temporal sequentiality. The two warnings to Aurelius, poems 15 and 21, appear in temporal order: "don't get any ideas about seducing Juventius" (15) must precede "stop trying to seduce Juventius" (21). Poem 16 looks back on the kiss-poems of 1–14, as we saw; poem 22 has Catullus' commentary on Suffenus, whose poetry he explicitly planned to read (14.17–20). While the three Furius poems (23, 24, and 26) do not present a progression of events, the drama of their reception by their target(s) is easily richer when taken in temporal sequence. Juventius, addressed in 24, might not even know that Furius is the party in question if he has not already heard or read poem 23,[71] while Catullus' clear intention in 24 to embarrass Juventius over Furius' poverty is rhetorically more effective if its repeated phrase "has neither slave nor coffer" (24.5, and 10) reminds Juventius of 23.1.[72] The same goes for the five-line parting shot, poem 26.

We now come to 27–51. Its programmatic introduction, unlike those of 1–14 and 14b–26, is neither a dedication nor a textualized introduction but rather a dramatic scene. Especially since it works so nicely for Catullus to fortify himself with wine "just before" openly attacking Memmius, Piso, Mamurra, Caesar, and Pompey, we should not assume temporal inversion but sequence for 27–28–29.

---

[70] Littman (1977) and Hallett (1978) read *unguentum* as bodily secretions; Witke (1980) and Hubbard (1983) 225 oppose this.

[71] I take it that our confusion about an earlier poem carries no weight. Poem 10 greatly clarifies poem 4, but that fact cannot be used to establish relative chronology within the represented world of the poems.

[72] And possibly Furius' social humiliation, to the extent that we care to imagine convivial belly-laughter as Catullus recites and Furius sits shame-faced and alone, like Catiline.

We skip now to the end, where we have already seen that the vignette of 50–51 assumes temporal–sequential inversion: poetic jam session > sleepless night > poem 51 composed to show Calvus Catullus' pain > 50 as cover letter. As a Lesbia poem, 51 of course fits into the equivalent plot, but poem 50 serves as its temporal frame, setting its composition "now" and reframing its backward glance toward Lesbia in just those terms. As a Lesbia poem, the narrative time of poem 51 is indeed initial: the Sapphic/Catullan speaker in the drama cannot previously have consummated his relationship with the addressee. The book ends with the end, but with the beginning inset.[73]

Poems 27–51 are richer than the first half in dramatic isolates. The only poems in 1–14 in which no character besides Catullus recurs elsewhere are 1, 4, and 6 (the dedication to Cornelius, the *phaselus*, and Flavius' secret love); in 14b–26, only the introductory 14b, and 17 and 25 (the Transpadane husband and Thallus), contain non-recurring characters. In 27–51, there are at least 12 such poems: 27 itself, 30–35, 38, 40, 44, 45, and 49.[74] By our earlier arguments for the internal divisions in **A**, 27–51 ought collectively to be belated in respect to 1–26.[75] Investigating the recurring characters within 27–51, we find only three story-lines: Veranius, Fabullus, and their praetor Piso and his cohort (28 and 47); Mamurra and Ameana (29, 41, probably 42, and 43); Lesbia and Egnatius (Lesbia in 36, 37, 43, and 51; Egnatius in 37 and 39). To these a fourth story, that of Catullus' Bithynian journey, should be added (28, 31, and 46).[76]

The problem case is Lesbia, specifically poems 36 and 37; I discuss the problem last, when the rest of the comparative evidence is in. Both Bithynian poems after 28 are retrojected: unlike poem 4, neither has a frame set in the poetic present. My claim is that the reader so readily spots this temporal inversion – in fact, she has no other plausible option for understanding poems 31 and 46 – that it hardly troubles the thesis that

---

[73] Compare the intertext with the *Aetia* prologue at book-end in **C2**, poem 116.

[74] Problem cases are 40 (*meos amores* = Juventius? Lesbia?), 42, and 46 (a border case: the Bithynian *comitum ... coetus* appear collectively as *cohortem*, 10.13, and ought to include *Cinna ... Gaius*, 10.30).

[75] Since 14b–26 echo only faintly in 27–51, it is in fact possible to take both 14b and 27–51 as belated in respect to 1–14, but not clearly ordered relative to each other. The most important question which turns on this is whether the "kisses" read by Furius and Aurelius refer back to 1–14, especially 5 and 7, forward to 48, or both. I take it that both the verbal recall of poem 5 in 16 and the overall thematic inversion of 1–14 in 14b–26 (which poem 16 is crucial for helping us understand) settle this question.

[76] The fact that the recurring plots in 27–51 are all grounded either by the first two poems after the introduction (Bithynia and Piso/Veranius/Fabullus in 28, Mamurra in 29) or the last one (Lesbia in 51) is itself a further mark of their patterned arrangement.

the post-Bithynian poems proceed dramatically in accordance with the sequence of the poems. What helps this case is that the other two recurring plots do proceed in temporal order.

I begin with Veranius and Fabullus in 28. The crucial point here is the dramatic scene: Catullus greets the two upon their return, seeing them for the first time.[77] For the entire Veranius/Fabullus drama, compare the reunion in poem 28 with the anticipated ones in poems 9 and 12: the circumstances render it far less gleeful than poem 9 expected, and the impoverished Catullus could not have expected Fabullus to bring dinner in poem 12, if he had known that the latter was also impoverished, and for the same reason.

Poem 28 also addresses Piso's impoverished *cohors inanis* (28.1) collectively; they too are greeted upon their return. Two apparent members of this cohort – and perhaps the only exceptions, besides Piso himself – are Porcius and Socration, Piso's "two left hands," in 47. Now we are close to the end of 27–51. Catullus has temporally later information about their habits back in Rome, as well as those of Veranius and Fabullus: Piso's favorites (habitually, the plural indicates) hold lavish *conuiuia* during daylight hours, while Veranius and Fabullus, like comic parasites,[78] "seek out invitations on street corners."

Poem 29 introducing Mamurra follows, and his story replicates the same temporal dynamic. Mamurra is just back from campaigning with Caesar in Gaul and Britain.[79] Catullus *sees* Mamurra loaded with Gallic and British wealth, asking who else can see and endure this (29.1–4). He now predicts Mamurra's behavior on return: the man will apply himself to satisfying his sexual appetites (*ille nunc superbus . . . perambulabit omnium cubilia*, 6–7). Though he is now rich, he has already run through three fortunes; he is now expected to squander the wealth of Gaul and Britain (*nunc Galliae timetur et Britanniae*, 20).

In the second half of 27–51, poem 41 first picks up the thread of Mamurra's story. Here we meet Ameana, his girlfriend. Both predictions are answered: she is indeed sexually exhausted by his attentions (*defututa,*

---

[77] Some commentators have understood the poem as a poetic epistle written during their service (e.g. Quinn (1973) 172, Godwin (1999) 143), but this is plainly false: an epistle-writing Catullus would not see that his friends' bags are light (*aptis sarcinulis et expeditis*, 28.2), nor could he see – even jocularly and nonliterally, as here – that they have been "stuffed" (28.11–13; *quantum uideo*, line 11). If a report had come his way, he would instead speak of *hearing* the news (cf. 9.5, of Veranius' return: *o mihi nuntii beati!*). It would also be premature to complain of their lack of profit, if their service were ongoing.

[78] Compare also Catullus himself (44.9–13).

[79] It is possible that the place he is "back" to is Transpadane Italy rather than Rome.

41.1); he, meanwhile, is bankrupt (*decoctoris* . . . *Formiani*, 4). The belatedness of 41 is explanatory: all the plunder in Gaul lasted Mamurra fewer than
eleven Catullan poems. The inference to be drawn with respect to
Ameana's proposal to Catullus here (sex for 10,000 sesterces, 41.2) is also
plain: having squandered the money, Mamurra is now reduced to pimping
out his girlfriend.[80]

Aside from the characters recurring within 27–51, there are a handful of
figures who appeared in 1–26 and now recur, once each, in 27–51. These
are of little evident value for determining relative dramatic chronology:
Caesar is flattered at 11.10 and then attacked in poem 29 (he cannot really
count as a "character," however, given his physical absence from
Catullus' dramatized company); Catullus' *irrumator praetor* (10.13–14)
in Bithynia is named as Memmius, with Catullus himself depicted as the
irrumated party (28.9–10); Calvus is present at the close of 1–14 and 27–51;
Juventius takes a bow in poem 48. The references to Caesar are temporally static: he has presumably crossed the Rhine and invaded Britain in
poem 11, and has clearly done so in 29; no explanation is given for the
apparent change in Catullus' attitude toward him. Memmius' name is
merely revealed in the latter poem mentioning him; no plot emerges. For
Calvus, the future-tense threat at the end of 14 is crucial in post-dating
14b–26.[81] As to my denial that 48 is the kiss-poem read by Furius and
Aurelius in poem 16, there is no clear temporal marker for 48 relative to
Juventius' appearances in 15, 21, and 24. As we have seen, play with verbal
motifs suggests a link with Cicero; whether or not that is so, I would say
with high confidence that there is a riddle of some sort here, whose
solution I cannot see.

To sum up what we have seen so far, the following table lists all recurring
characters in **A**, save Catullus and Lesbia. It illustrates which poems in
which of the book's three units mention them, listing all instances in which
narrative details internal to the poems containing them imply relative
temporal order. Where multiple poems are collectively prior or posterior
to another poem or poems, but their individual order is unknowable, I
group these in parentheses:

---

[80] I see no evidence for temporal sequence between 41 and 43, the other overt Ameana/Mamurra poem,
     nor for 42, which I think refers to her as well. Any order would work. Most important is that the first
     of the consecutive poems marking the return of the Mamurra plot, 41, is the one that hooks up
     temporally with its beginning, 29.

[81] The Calvus character in poem 50 is somewhat better placed to understand that Catullus' *precesque
     nostras* refers to the expectation of future poetic gift-exchange if the exchange dramatized in 14 has
     already happened.

Character	1–14	14b–26	27–51	Sequence
Veranius/Fabullus	9, 12, 13		28, 47	(9, 12, 13) > 28 > 47
Memmius	10		28	unclear
Varus	10	22		unclear
"Suffenus"	14	22		14 > 22
Furius/Aurelius	11	15, 16, 21, 23, 24, 26		(5, 7) > 16; 15 > 21; 23 > 24; 23 > 26
Caesar	11		29	unclear
Calvus	14		50	14 > (14b–26)
Juventius		15, 21, 24	40?, 48	15 > 21; 23 > 24
Piso(nis comites)			28, 47	28 > 47
Mamurra			29, 41, 43	29 > (41, 43)
Egnatius			37, 39	unclear
Ameana			41, 42?, 43	unclear

My rhetorical point is obvious: evidence for narrative sequentiality is not universal but abundant, and all of it points in the same direction. Meanwhile, the handful of exceptions are easily explained. The introductory poems 1 and 50 both dramatize their own composition, presumably after the poems they introduce (as is the case for 14b, though its narrative vignette is of the roll's future handling by intrepid readers). Bithynian poems 31 and 46 are temporal retrojections (and are also out of sequence relative to each other, homecoming to Sirmio preceding departure from Bithynia). These two poems, though, are preceded by *three* previous narrations about the journey (4, 10, and 28), each anchored within the ongoing, presumptively post-Bithynian poetic present. The journey is already "past" just after the sparrow's deathly journey begins. There is simply no way to understand poems 31 and 46 other than as artful retrojections.[82]

This brings us to Lesbia. Poem 2 is trivially and obviously prior to 3, as 5 is to 7, and as 2, 3, 5, and 7 collectively are to 8. It makes more sense to take poem 8 as before 11 than vice versa; poem 13 is at least not problematic after 8 and 11. Poem 51 has a temporal and dramatic frame that explains its earlier dramatic moment, and poem 43 does not constitute evidence.[83] The only problem case is 36–37 – the return of Lesbia.

[82] This retrojection can be explained either by the dramatized (and poem-arranging) author placing them out of sequence, or the sequentially poem-drafting and arranging dramatized poet retrojecting the dramatic date of two of his poems.

[83] That Lesbia is more beautiful than Ameana does not imply Catullus' positive disposition towards her at the time of his saying so. Compare poem 86.

I print poem 36:

> Annales Volusi, cacata carta,
> votum soluite pro mea puella.
> nam sanctae Veneri Cupidinique
> vovit, si sibi restitutus essem
> desissemque truces vibrare iambos,   5
> electissima pessimi poetae
> scripta tardipedi deo daturam
> infelicibus ustulanda lignis.
> et hoc pessima se puella vidit
> iocose lepide vovere divis.   10
> nunc o caeruleo creata ponto,
> quae sanctum Idalium Vriosque apertos
> quaeque Ancona Cnidumque harundinosam
> colis quaeque Amathunta quaeque Golgos
> quaeque Durrachium Hadriae tabernam,   15
> acceptum face redditumque votum,
> si non illepidum neque invenustum est.
> at vos interea venite in ignem,
> pleni ruris et inficetiarum.
> annales Volusi, cacata carta.   20

Lesbia has made the following vow to Venus and Cupid (36.4–8): "If Catullus is restored to me and stops brandishing his fierce iambs, I will give the choicest writings of the worst poet to the slow-footed god to be burned by accursed logs." Now that the two conditional clauses have been fulfilled, Venus is asked to register the fulfillment of the vow, with Volusius' *Annals* understood as the true referent of "the choicest writings of the worst poet."[84] Several narrative points are thus made clear:

1) Catullus has been "restored" to Lesbia.
2) Catullus has put aside invective against Lesbia.
3) Lesbia was aware of, and either possessed or could obtain, Catullus' written invective against her.

Note first that the temporal order of this poem is necessarily consistent with its place in the sequence of Lesbia poems thus far – a restoration requires an earlier fall. Next, what verses could these be? Scholars disagree about *iambos*, whether it should be read strictly as "poems in iambic meter," or whether, given the close association of iambic verse with

---

[84] This is both sincere and facetious: the former because Catullus no doubt believes that the *Annales* fit this description, the latter because that clearly is not what Lesbia meant.

aggressive sentiment, it merely means invective. Unless – limply, I think – we take Lesbia to be artistically or politically dissatisfied with Catullus' recent invective turn, the latter must be correct: *iambos* is represented, no less than *electissima . . . scripta*, as Lesbia's word. The entire wit of poem 36 turns on the twisting or reinterpretation of these precise words. We thus have no option of denying or dismissing the focalization of the vow through Lesbia's character. It is simply obvious that she cannot have requested divine assistance in stopping "invective in iambic meter" against her; she will obviously have wished for *all* invective against her to cease. Nor does the problem disappear if we take it as read that the particular invective verses she knew happened to be iambic: the substance of her condition would not only be that Catullus suppress previous invective against her (that is, poems 8 and 11), but also that he not produce any more, regardless of its metrical form.

To be sure, poems 36 and 37 still pose a serious problem. These two facts must be reconciled:

1) At poem 36's dramatic moment, Catullus must, in some sense, be "restored" to Lesbia and resolved not to level invective against her.
2) At poem 37's dramatic moment, Catullus is estranged from Lesbia and levels invective at her.

The solution must be that the two poems are composed at different times and under different circumstances. On a sequential/temporal reading, we must assume that the reconciliation marked by 36 has ended already by poem 37; if the order is inverted, we assume instead a reconciliation without any evidence of a second rupture.

The sequential reading is clearly superior. Once again, the earlier Lesbia poems establish precedent for assuming interstitial narrative events. A love affair clearly alive in one poem must have perished offstage at some time between it and the next poem: poem 36 is to 37 as 7 is to 8. That either party might desire the resumption of the affair is implicit in both 8 and 11. In the former, the poet's irresolution is on display, as his soliloquy oscillates between self-counsel to put Lesbia aside and expression of the erotic obsession which makes it so difficult for him to heed that counsel. In the latter, the poet's enlisting of Furius and Aurelius to report his farewell is at least consistent with the assumption that his attitude toward Lesbia was unknown and relevant to Lesbia. While in poem 8 the situation is clearly presented as one in which Lesbia has rejected Catullus, much of the power of poem 11 is undermined if we assume the same dramatic background as for poem 8. While there is, indeed, good reason to infer that the affair is emotionally more important to Catullus than it is to Lesbia, it would be rather extreme to imagine that Lesbia, who had blithely dropped Catullus just before poem 8, is rejected three poems later in a belated attempt to save face. On that reading, the only satisfaction Catullus can take in contemplating the delivery of the message is Lesbia's discomfort at the invective against her; if, rather, she had hoped for (and sent third-party enquiries about) Catullus' return, she will feel two different stings, namely the rejection itself and the invective in which it is given expression. This reading also accounts better for the rhetoric of the final stanza: *nec meum respectet ut ante amorem* then means "and tell her not to [do what she has just done, namely] look back on my love for her."[85] Poem 11, then, suggests a Lesbia who might still want Catullus back; poem 8 depicts a Catullus who is, in fact, susceptible to such an appeal.

According to the temporal/sequential reading, the dramatic situation progresses as follows: Lesbia and Catullus are reconciled; Lesbia tells the poet of her vow; poem 36 then performs the poet's learned one-upping of his lover's wit. Their affair then ruptures again; in anger, Catullus composes poem 37. In order to deepen his vengeance, in light of his recent promise to "stop brandishing invective" against her, he now brandishes against her an invective poem which closely recalls both previous invective poems: poem 37 verbally reprises the motif of superlative love from 8, and thematically reprises Lesbia's "hundreds" of simultaneous lovers from 11. Poem 36 had been a palinode *manqué* of poems 8 and 11 (with the axe falling on the *Annales* rather than on Catullus' own brilliant verses); poem 37 is now a palinode of 36. If there are indications already in poem 36 that the reconciliation is less than whole-hearted, this too mirrors the less than whole-hearted resolve of the two break-up poems 8 and 11.

Though readers are challenged by the need to make dramatic inferences, they are also guided by the close fit between these inferences and ones they had previously made in order to understand poems 7, 8, and 11. By contrast, assuming that the events of poem 37 occur before 36 creates obscurity rather than sheds light. Why a temporal inversion, when the previous Lesbia poems had been so clearly sequential? The reconciliation need not take root to explain the positive reference to Lesbia's beauty in poem 43. To ask it to explain the positive reference to her in 51 is ruinous:

---

[85] *Ante* and *respectet* are in my favor here; they assert that Lesbia did already "look back" on Catullus' love. If the situation is merely that Lesbia has rejected Catullus, who now returns the favor, this does not obtain. On my reading, the *ante* looks back on Lesbia's second thoughts or mediated suggestions of reconciliation, which are indeed "past" in relation to the anticipated moment when Catullus' rejection is delivered.

poem 51 as comment on a flourishing love affair is an absurdity. In terms of explanatory economy or Occam's razor considerations, the only gain offered by this reading is that it drops the need to hypothesize an abrupt break-up immediately after the reconciliation. I submit that this gain does not offset the significant costs of this reading.

In any case, a sequential reading also suggests (but does not compel) a nice explanation for the failure of the reconciliation: the speech-act of poem 36 itself, Catullus' reinterpretation of the vow. This, too, fits our Catullus, who could never suppress or disavow 1–14, even for Lesbia's sake; his pride had only barely allowed the partial palinode of poem 36. Lesbia's verdict on 36 will then be: "no, not good enough."[86] Catullus now warns her of the poetic consequences that her rejection will occasion. Lesbia shrugs. Catullus turns to leave. Lesbia adds: "And anyway, I've got Egnatius now."

Addendum: A Longer Drama of Composition?

As promised in Chapter 1, I now return to **Ax**, poems 52–60. There the case had been made that these poems are either a non-authorial presence, a textual intrusion following **A** and its closural dyad 50–51, or that they are (what remains of) a superadded unit, a kind of self-marginalizing postscript for the book. Alternatively, one can put the point negatively: these poems are *not* simply the uninterrupted continuation of the unit or part beginning with poem 27. Anyone finding that claim compelling, I trust, will have thought it a well-motivated proposal to examine 1–51 or **A** closely as a putative artistic whole, and to hold it up for close examination against **C2** (69–116), **C** in its entirety (65–116), and **B** (61–64). Doing so, I attempted to demonstrate that these units mirror each other so closely that only their joint authorial design could explain. Now, in the body of Chapter 2, I have examined **A** as the artistic whole Chapter 1 concluded it to be, finding it rich, coherent, and metapoetically legible.

But of course, as was conceded from the beginning, this result falls short of proving that poem 51 in fact is the final poem in a Catullan book starting with poem 1. Consider this premise: "It is inconceivable that Roman poets would craft books with elaborate symmetries, but then allow the final, public versions of those books to appear in such a way that those symmetries are sub-optimally evident." We plainly have no warrant to make so

---

[86] There is still another option: poem 36 is designed to be an offer Lesbia cannot not refuse. An acerbic retort then sets off poems 37 and 39.

sweeping and categorical a claim; yet we would plainly *need* some such premise, if we wished categorically to infer "**A** is Catullus' short lyric book" from "**A** is the neatest and most legible and 'perfect' possible presentation of Catullus' short lyric poems." It cannot be excluded that **Ax** *both* "goes after 51" *and* "spoils the pattern," to some extent.

On the other hand, it seems unlikely that **Ax** would follow **A**, and by authorial design, but that the metapoetic legibility built into that design should not continue into or include its final section. If 1–14, 14b–26, and 27–51 are each coherent and legible internal units, and if 52–60 follows them as book-final unit, it should also have been coherent and legible – in its pristine textual form, that is, if not necessarily as we have it. The proposal that follows, accordingly, offers itself not as a positive thesis whose truth I am asserting, but rather to fill out idea-space with the best and richest account now possible, both of how **Ax** might have fitted itself and been understood at the close of **A**, and of what might have gone textually wrong to conceal as much. This is not to say that I am slightly embarrassed by my own wild speculation here; in fact, I take this to be judicious speculation appositely applied. Rather – and for the last time – the point of framing this as only a *plausible* metapoetic account of **Ax** is the conviction that a plausible account is all I need, in order to defuse any lingering worries about these poems "ruining" the coherence and legibility we have now brought to light in **A**. It is plausible that **Ax** should go but also plausible that it should stay; if it stays, it will have originally made sense and fit. If there is a plausible and determinate proposal on which **Ax** does make sense, fits, and leaves our view of **A** and the rest of the corpus intact, there is no prior reason to suppose that its retention *should* threaten that view in the first place. Again, this is all the conviction I myself bear: either **Ax** goes, or it fits like this, or it fits some other way. We can live with this limited and localized uncertainty.

The proposal is this: the poems of **Ax** present themselves, within their dramatic conceit, as instances of the Catullo-Calvan exchange of verses described in poem 50. On the principal version of this I will now consider, they will themselves simply be (depicted as) the improvised verses Catullus and Calvus wrote together "yesterday," that is the day before the dramatized composition of 50. If Catullus' short-lyric book omits **Ax**, the epistolary papyrus which we imagine the day-after Catullus sending to Calvus would be imagined to contain poems 50 and 51; on this thesis, it would contain 52–60 as well. Alternatively, Catullus could be envisaged sending a letter to Calvus containing 50–51; in light of the jocular threat in 50, should Calvus fail to reciprocate, it might be the case that these poems present themselves as *subsequent* stages of the poet-friends' exchange of quickly composed verses.

I will now briefly pursue the former option, my preference of the two. First, we recall that the site for the poets' play was Catullus' tablets (*in meis tabellis*, 50.2) rather than Calvus'. These will have been carried back from *chez* Calvus (by a slave, presumably) to Catullus' house, and would obviously still be in his possession. We might have assumed that these scribblings in wax were erased, but the poem does not say so, and Catullus might easily have wanted to keep them. Why not furnish Calvus with a transcript of their session as well? Next, *uersiculos* (50.3): 52–60 do indeed answer to the description "verselets"; this is the undeniable point that so much scholarship has puzzled over, and the objection that these are mere squibs loses its force, if *uersiculi* just is the Latin for "squib." Likewise, *numero modo hoc modo illoc* (50.5): 52–60 are indeed in multiple meters: iambic trimeters in 53 (the freer kind than in 4 and 29, and hence easier to whip up on the spot), choliambs in 59 and 60, and hendecasyllables in the rest, but with 55 and 58b being that different sort of (hen)decasyllable, with the optional molossus in the middle. Again, the extra metrical option allows for extemporaneous ease, which would also explain the resolution at 59.3. Furthermore, such features as the wholesale repetition of earlier lines (52.1 = 52.4, 57.1 = 57.10), as well as the frequent recurrence of lines and phrases with minor alterations, make perfect sense on the assumption that these poems are meant to come off as improvisations.[87] The verses were written *per iocum atque uinum* (50.6): their overwhelmingly jocular mode is obvious (and poem 56 describes its own anecdote, twice, as a *res iocosa*), and if *uinum* in poem 27 had been needed to fuel the political *ueritas* of 28–29, it could easily catalyze the frank references to the powerful throughout 52–60, and would surely be needed to fuel the shocking sexual invective against Caesar in poem 57.

Two further "facts" provided in poem 50 about these Catullo-Calvan verselets remain. First, both poets composed (*uterque nostrum*, 50.4), and there was some form of interplay (*reddens mutua*, 50.6): the poets each played off each other's compositions.[88] Is it plausible that a Catullan poetry book should have ended with verses that Catullus in fact authored, but

---

[87] Clear examples are 55.3–5 *te campo . . . te in circo, te in . . . te in templo*; 56.1–4 *o rem ridiculam, Cato, et iocosam . . . ride, quidquid amas, Cato, Catullum: res est ridicula et nimis iocosa*; 58.1–2 *Lesbia nostra, Lesbia illa, illa Lesbia*; and 58b.1–4 *non custos si . . . non si . . . non . . . non.*

[88] Kroll (1968) *ad loc.* speaks of *Erwiderung*, adducing Vergilian and Ovidian verbal parallels (*Aen.* 6.672, *Met.* 8.717) and the contextual parallel of the poetic contest proposed in Horace *Satires* 1.4; *Eclogues* 3 and 7 are also obvious instances of represented improvised call-and-response.

with some of them composed by "Calvus," that is, dramatically ascribed to him? Vergil's first poetry book ends precisely that way: half of *Eclogues* 10 is represented as the work of the book's poet-speaker, half of it as the words of a contemporary poet and friend, Gallus – and a poet-friend the principal poet-speaker elaborately "loves," to boot.[89] It has always been imagined that the first of these poems, 52, begins and ends with Catullus addressing himself: *quid est, Catulle?* But what if these are Calvus' words? The following poem would indeed respond to this call: Calvus' address of Catullus (52.1, 4) would be answered by Catullus' mention of Calvus (*meus ... Caluos*, 53.3);[90] Calvus' reference to Vatinius (52.3) would be answered by Catullus' reference to Calvus' prosecution of the same Vatinius (*Vatiniana ... crimina*, 53.2–3); whatever gentle tease Catullus found in Calvus' suggestion that Catullus' "just die" would be answered by his recalling the anonymous spectator who called Calvus a *salaputium disertum* (53.5), whatever that means. The two poems are metrically different, and there is a difference of a single line in their lengths; but just so long as Catullus can plausibly respond to four lines of Calvus' iambic trimeter concerning himself and Vatinius with five hendecasyllables of his own concerning Calvus and Vatinius, poems 52 and 53 can plausibly count as one call and one response.

Like the first two poems, the final two poems of **Ax** also make for a highly plausible call-and-response pair. Poems 59 and 60 consist of five choliambs apiece addressed to unnamed addressees: a perfect formal match. In content, there is the shared evocation of death (grave theft in 59, anguished accusation of hard-heartedness *in nouissimo casu* in 60), common references to genitalia in each (*fellat* in 59, Scylla's *infima unguinum parte* in 60), and, if the hard-hearted party in 60 is Lesbia or another female beloved, a degraded and sexually deviant Roman lady in each.

What of the remaining six pieces, 54–58b? Their line-counts as printed in modern editions are too close to ignore, but nonconsecutive and too imperfect merely to accept: 7, 22, 7, 10, 5, 10.[91] The second and last of these (55 and 58b) are indeed a pair, the Camerius poems with the uniquely anomalous (hen)decasyllables, but they are nonconsecutive and of

---

[89] Precisely half, that is: 38½ lines are "by Vergil," and 38½ lines "Vergil doing Gallus." Gallus' song in *Eclogues* 10 is widely assumed to be deeply intertextual with the historical Gallus' actual poetry. So could Calvus' verse in **Ax** have been.

[90] While either poet could write the vocative *Catulle*, only Catullus could write the nominative *meus Calvos*; 53 would have to be Catullus' composition. We would then take *meus* as cleverly pointed: the Calvus who is relevant here is quite obviously *Catullus'* Calvus.

[91] The parallels in Vergilian pastoral certainly encourage us to expect that responses should follow calls sequentially and be of similar length.

different length (22 and 10 lines respectively; the obscurity of the latter, 58b, remains troubling in any case). The remaining pair by line-count and meter is 54 and 56; these are interrupted by 55, and their content does not appear to match, but the hopelessly corrupt text of 54 and the possibility that it is not a single poem anyway undermine all confidence in that appearance. In terms of content, one could plausibly see calls and responses between 56 and 57 (on the shared basis of degrading sex between two males), 57 and 58 (Caesar and Mamurra's vs. Lesbia's sexual degradation), 58 and 59 (invective against women said to have sex in public; both *fellatrices*, on one reading of *glubit*), 56 and 58 (sexual stimulation by hand, on the other reading of *glubit* and the solitary reading of *trusantem*), 56 and 59 (rape as punishment). One would be able, but might prefer not, to continue.

In sum, these poems as transmitted can be analyzed as formally responsive pairs, thematically responsive pairs, and consecutive pairs – but as transmitted, you only get two of the three together. Could these just have been the loose rules of the casual Catullo-Calvan engagement? Could Catullus' *tabelli* themselves have been shuffled? Rather than "assigning" each poem and each line determinately to one or the other poet, could (some or all of) these poems be represented as the joint productions of two poetically like-minded friends from the same poetic circles? I do not see how we could reasonably deny such possibilities, in particular in light of what we know about Calvus' poetic output. That is, the extant and metrically identifiable fragments reveal: poems in hendecasyllables (fragments 1–2 Blänsdorf), one in choliambs (fr. 3), an epithalamium in glyconics (4) and another in hexameters (5–8), a short epic on a mythological heroine (Io, 9–14), an elegiac dirge over a personal loss (his Quintilia, 15–16), and epigrammatic abuse of Caesar and Pompey (17–18). This of course matches Catullus' output perfectly, and indeed so closely that either putatively "imitated poet" might easily be imagined as bemused or angered by the choices of his contemporary "imitator," were it not the case that *both* of them agreed to coordinate their choices of genres, themes, and the construction of their overall poetic voices. In turn, two poets who co-modeled themselves so extensively might well have each made room for the other to make "guest appearances" in his own work, as I am proposing here. They might well have even seen it as a positive *desideratum*, that readers should never feel entirely sure where one stops and the other begins.

Turning now to the other option mentioned earlier, that we take **Ax** as *subsequent* round(s) of Calvan or Catullo-Calvan response poetry (picking up the "threat" that concludes poem 50), in general I find this less motivated than the temporally inset "dating" of these compositions to "yesterday's" poetic jam session, the "day before" the composition of poems 50 and 51.[92] There is, however, a striking textual reason to mention it as a separate option. That is, the lost archetype of our extant Catullan manuscripts read 50.16–17 between our 54.1 and 54.2. I print a composite orthography of the readings of the principal manuscript witnesses OGR:

Otonis caput oppido pusillum	54.1
hoc iucunde tibi poema feci	50.16
ex quo perspiceres meum dolorem	50.17
et heri rustice semilauta crura	54.2

With no apparent sense to be made of this and the original location of the repeated verses nearby, possibly visible on the same page of the exemplar, editors universally and reasonably assume a simple scribal error.[93] While I do not wish to assert otherwise, the following is indeed the case and can hardly go unreported here: if the now unrecoverable text of poem 54 contained "Calvus" adverting and responding to Catullus' mention of gift-exchange, the transmission has preserved the very two lines whose "quotation" or "adaptation" would instantly signal as much.

A brief enumeration of remaining questions might include the following:

Why would Catullus (as the all-directing artist, not as the represented "day-after" character) have done this?

As with 14b–26, a possible answer is that his art includes rougher and lower work, and it is part of the meta-artistry of the poems' arrangement to frame, contextualize, even apologize for those parts. If this works for us, **Ax** would go from mere doggerel to brilliant meta-doggerel. It will also presumably have been brilliantly intertextual meta-doggerel, in respect to the historical Calvus' poetry. And the "poetics of hypocrisy" explored in respect to 14b–26 would have a just perfect reflex in poem 57, if Catullus and Calvus are reclining on a *lectus* and composing the self-knowing accusation that Caesar and Mamurra engage in eroticized

---

[92] A pressing problem on this option would be, how to understand what would seem to us as the narratively unmotivated turn from the poignant (so 51) to abusive (58) recollection of Lesbia. By contrast, if poems 52–60 are dashed-off, jocular compositions dramatized as *earlier* creations, 58 is pointedly corrected by 51: "yes, Calvus, but her effect on me is in fact so intense and so painful."

[93] Such apparently senseless repetitions occur twice besides in the transmission: 67.21 appears after 64.386, and 68a.16 after 68b.49. In G, 50.16–17 and its reappearance after 54.1 are the initial lines of consecutive pages.

mutual poem composition on the same *lectulus*. "When *we* do it we're *delicati*, when those two do, they're *cinaedi*."

But did he adequately signal all of this?

We don't know: his pristine rolls could have paratextually indicated changes of speaker in the margins or interstitially ("CAT" and "CAL," perhaps). These would plausibly or inevitably have been lost in transmission.

But what about hoc poema feci, *singular, at 50.16, pointing forward only to 51?*

Assuming an imaginary epistolary *charta* with poems 50–60, Calvus would instantly remember and recognize 52–60 as "yesterday's" poems; from his point of view, only the initial poems 50–51 need their own comment, as 50 in fact provides.

But didn't I argue that we shouldn't in any case believe in the "day after" story of 50–51? Those poems aren't rough, not the way 52–60 are.

Poems 50 and 51, on the dramatized conceit, are merely written quickly, with at least some time for revision, possibly even all morning and afternoon; 52–60 are said to have been on-the-spot improvisations.

But doesn't this proposal, after all, saddle A with what I have insisted is an implausibly weak and poorly representative ending?

In temporal terms, 50 and 51 still have the last word. My proposal from the beginning is to take **Ax** as the *Appendix Catulliana*. By framing them like this, as meta-doggerel, Catullus himself would have marginalized them, appendicized them; by then having the terminal points of **B** and **C** interact with 50–51 rather than 60, Catullus would have emphatically made this point himself. Even if 52–60 are an inflamed and damaged organ, it is only their appendicization that my thesis urgently requires; their appendectomy, in the end, is an elective procedure.

CHAPTER 3

B (poems 61–64) and C1 (65–68b)

1 Introduction

I begin with a concession: the case that **B** is an authorial book confronts an objection with which **A** and **C** are not faced. An authorial **B** would be formally unique: there is no extant parallel for a Latin poetry book consisting of "a handful of longer poems in various meters." Moreover, there is a plausible alternative model of their physical realization and circulation: namely, each on its own. If, as I argued in the Prolegomenon, the single-roll *Gesamtausgabe* hypothesis is rendered implausible by the vast difference between such a poetry book and all extant ones, why does the same not obtain of 61–64?

I attempt to answer this challenge in two ways. On one hand, I concede the relative oddness of **B** as a book but find that various considerations mitigate the case against it. On the other, I hope to aggravate the demerits of denial: the indications of patterned sequentiality are too many and too good. Although the independent circulation of these poems can account for the presence of intratextual responses with the elegiac poems of **C1**, only their combined circulation in their transmitted sequence plausibly accounts for *this* network of responses, with all its structural specularity and artistic coherence. In terms of explanatory economy, the cost of hypothesizing a book like this one is payable, while the cost of denying *this* book is rather more extravagant.

Once again the dialectical terrain is complex, and once again I will take pains to stress compatibility where others have seen the contrary. To take the most obvious example, I fully assert the right to "have it both ways" about the two historical candidates for middle third of the Catullan corpus, 61–64 and 61–68(b). Studies arguing for the structural coherence of the so-called *carmina maiora* 61–68(b) are on my view not wrong,[1] and their

---

[1] Lieberg (1962), Most (1981).

results can in general be repackaged and preserved, now as responsions between two corpora rather than continuities within one. Similarly – and just as I argued for the sub-units of **A** – I do not regard one appealing modality of circulation as necessarily ruling out another. It makes sense that the monumental achievement of poem 64 could perhaps call for independent realization on its own roll. But it also makes sense for four long poems with deep thematic resonances to offer themselves to readers synoptically, implicitly offering themselves as a whole greater than the sum of its parts. And we do not know – nor do I think it makes sense – that the hypothetical individual circulation of 64 rules out its later appearance with poems composed, in part, to resonate with it.[2]

Another parallel with my structural claims for **A** is the disavowal of a single correct account of it. There are indeed patterns of correspondence across the poems such that meaningful structural schemata can be drawn up, but no such account seems so clearly richer than its competitors as to be uniquely correct. A benefit of this is that it frees us from the need to make our claims entirely contingent on controversial answers to multiple hard questions: (1) Is 68a a separate poem from 68b? (2) If so, is it part of the structural progression? (3) Does poem 65 so count, or is it merely a preface to 66? While I will indeed defend taking 68a as separate from but closely related to 68b – and though this naturally has consequences – I do not think that there is a simple answer to whether they count. The fact of the matter seems to be that if you do not count them, the correspondences with 61–64 will indeed be tidier. But this does not license ignoring the less systematic ways in which they too form correspondences.

I begin by recalling that much of the case has already been set down. The opening of **B** reprises motifs prominent at the beginning of **A**; book-end for **A** at poem 51 effects a transition from Sappho's celebrated poem there to Sappho's celebrated genre, the epithalamium, at the beginning of **B**.[3] Further correspondences are well worth toying with and might be worth pushing: the poet spectating an erotic scene in 51 and 61, the bridal couple and the wedding god Hymenaeus in 61 as a reflex of the couple and the man "surpassing the gods" in 51. The opening of **C**, meanwhile, picks up

---

[2] I find it sufficient to argue that 61–64 display a unity of design that vindicates their "book-ness"; I need not *also* show that the poems were never realized individually. As to dating, I take it there is no prospect of recovering the relative dating of 61–64, and I reject as baseless the traditional assumption under which 65 and 68 have been dated, namely that the affair with Lesbia and the brother's death precede Catullus' Bithynian service (Wiseman (1974) 104–18).

[3] See Fedeli (1972) for in-depth discussion of Catullus 61's relationship to epithalamic tradition, and Connely (1925) for Sappho in particular.

the programmatic promise of a "happy wedding song" at 61.11–13 with "songs made sad by death" at 65.12, while the end of **B** resonates with its beginning (a god called to a human wedding, set off by the claim that gods no longer attend human weddings), and prepares the reader for the return from the mythical past to the poet's social world in **C**, while mythological references at the beginning of **C** look back on **B**. And of course the beginning of **C1** is conspicuously tied to the end of **C2** by the framing references to Callimachus (65.15–16 ~ 116.2),[4] and **A** and **C2** are global structural responsions of each other. For readers persuaded by these earlier arguments, the present arguments will be pushing on an open door; it should not be hard to accept a set of global structural responsions when it is the second such set.

2　The Poet's Voice and B

One of the most pressing problems in respect to poems 61–64 and their place in Catullus' work is the fact that their generic forms threaten to deprive Catullus of what otherwise is his consistent indicator of literary aperture and closure, the first-person drama of composition. The dramas of poems 1 and 14, we recall, physically frame 1–14 and provide temporal and generic frames for both it and 14b–26; answering these dramas, 27–51 ends with the drama of 50–51, with its backward glance at the most prominent storyline in **A**. Meanwhile, **C** both begins (65) and ends (116) with dramas of composition, and specifically of Callimachean composition. Poems 61–64, by contrast, are less free in this respect.

Poem 61 is delivered by a single speaker who narrates and partially directs the drama unfolding around him. He addresses the bride and groom and other participants, in addition to invoking the marriage god; occasional glimpses of his subjectivity are present (189–93, 209–23), but in general his sentiments are largely constrained by the public nature and function of his role. Poem 62 is a dialogue between two choruses: Catullus does not speak. Poem 63 is split almost evenly between narration and the direct speech of Attis and Cybele; crucially, perhaps, the poet-speaker intervenes at the end (91–93), praying to Cybele that her cup pass him by. About three-eighths of poem 64 consists of character speech; in the rest, the speaker is notably subjective and interventionist by the standards of epic. He is emotionally moved by his own contemplation of heroes and the heroic age, promising them frequent song and apostrophizing Peleus in

---

[4] King (1988) 385.

particular (22–30); he cries out sympathetically over Ariadne's subjection to Venus' power (*a! misera . . .*, 71–72); he hymnically addresses Venus and Cupid himself, exclaiming again over Ariadne's erotic cares (94–102); he stages a narrative *praeteritio* to pass quickly over Ariadne's passage from Crete to Dia (116–23); his epilogue (382–408), though not formally first person, recalls the poem from the mythic world to that of his audience or readers and himself.[5]

I am not here addressing the longstanding question of whether and how we can take the represented subjectivity of short-poem Catullus, especially in respect to Lesbia, to underlie and explain the content of poems 61–64, above all the subjectivity of Attis in poem 63 and Ariadne in 64.[6] While my own sense is that the poems allow us to consider rather than compel us to accept that these characters are vehicles for their creator's sentiments, any global case for doing so must wait until the results of this work as a whole have been reached.[7] The much more tractable initial question before us is whether to take the *narrator's* moments of first-person subjectivity within these poems as belonging to the same speaker and consciousness that pronounces the poetry of **A** and **C**.

Asking this question in this way eliminates the purely dialogic poem 62. It also renders poem 61 a special case, since we can scarcely tell how much freedom to attribute to Catullus in composing an occasional poem that is not principally about or for him, and whose ritual setting was no doubt attended by a fair number of *senes seueriores*. To what extent the values and idealistic sentiments of this poem are his own, as opposed to mere platitudes appropriate to a wedding, must remain indeterminate.[8]

In reading the subjective moments of poems 63 and 64, however, we do not seem to be constrained in this way.[9] And if we overlay these moments on Catullan subjectivity elsewhere, the results do not fail to match: the poet of these two poems reveals his fascination at the possibility of marriage between gods and humans (64.22–30; also his fascination with heroes as

---

[5] There are also three less emotionally involved apostrophes to characters: Theseus (69), Ariadne (253), and Apollo (299).

[6] Harkins (1959) and Forsyth (1976) provide very different studies of 63 and 64 in relation to the persona Catullus develops elsewhere in his corpus. See also Stevens (2013) 206–56.

[7] I am not convinced that these questions are as interpretively useful as one might think.

[8] I do, however, insist that the frankness and self-possession of the Catullan voice tell strongly against writing off these sentiments as purely conventional. A poem composed by that speaker could, for instance, tactfully refrain from expressing his darker sentiments, but it is far less plausible to imagine him expressing cheerful (or moralizing) sentiments which he did not endorse.

[9] Unless, that is, one accepts Wiseman's (1985) argument that poem 63 is composed for a ritual context. I myself am unconvinced; see Lefèvre (1998).

transitional figures between the two realms), and is deeply anxious about relations between gods and humans (their displeasure with and separation from us, 64.382–408; the quasi-erotic madness provoked by Cybele and required of her attendants, 63.91–93; the merciless effects of *Amor* and *Venus* in our lives, 64.71–75 and 94–102). Poems 36, 51, 65, 68a, 68b, 70, 72, 76, and 109, and with them the core themes of Lesbia and Catullus' brother, resonate deeply here.

It is true that Catullus' pledge that he will "often" address the heroes in verse (64.22–24) looks like it ought to be a poetological prospectus on this reading, and it is not obvious that this promise is kept. Poems 65 and 101 allude to mythological heroes, and the royal couple in 66 were worshiped as mortal gods, but only 68b contains a sustained engagement with mythological material. Even then, one's first expectation would be for future poems more like 64 itself than like 68b. It is of course possible to invoke Catullus' early death to explain the failure of our poems to keep this apparent promise. On the other hand, we do not need such an explanation, viewing Catullus' represented story from within: the death of the brother effects a crisis in Catullus' career and explains the elegiac turn. As to the remaining subjective intervention in poem 64 (116–23), this too has a gently humorous resonance with **A**, considering poems 46, 31, and especially 4: why should Catullus digress from his subject to lay out the details of a sea voyage?[10]

3   Forward Glances to B in A

We have already seen the claim for a metapoetic understanding of 46.9–11, on which Catullus' farewell to his comrades on departure from Bithynia inaugurates the closing sequence of **A**, most of whose principal characters now take their sequential bows (Veranius and Fabullus in 47, Juventius in 48, Calvus in 50, Lesbia in 51). I now suggest that this metapoetic farewell contains a poetic forward glance as well. I print the poem:

> Iam **uer** egelidos refert tepores,
> iam caeli furor aequinoctialis
> iucundis Zephyri silescit auris.
> linquantur Phrygii, Catulle, campi
> Nicaeaeque ager uber aestuosae: 46.5

---

[10] Compare also the yacht's grandiose self-characterization of its transformation from tree to ship (4.13–16), redolent of the *Argo* in the *incipit* of Ennius' *Medea*, which is closely emulated also by the *incipit* of poem 64 (Khan (1967) 167). Cf. Thomas (1982).

ad claras Asiae uolemus urbes.
iam **mens** praetrepidans auet **uagari,**
iam laeti studio pedes uigescunt.
o dulces comitum ualete coetus,
longe quos simul a domo profectos 10
diuersae uarie uiae reportant!

Placed near the end of **A**, this appears to be its *first* moment in dramatic time. The generic form of the *Frühlingsgedicht* and the jaunty emotional tone are appropriate to this position in Catullus' story; postponed to this late position in the book, this earlier glance at youthful enthusiasm is set off in counterpoint to the harder and more cynical poetic world he now inhabits.

It is possible, however, to press this poem further metapoetically, as one of two moments in **A** that amount to yet another Catullan drama of composition: the composition, that is, of **B**. On this reading, the young poet in line 8 is exulting (*laeti*) in the growing vigor of his verse (*pedes uigescunt*); his apprenticeship or training (*studio*) is now paying off. He is accordingly eager to "cover new ground" (*mens . . . auet uagari,* 7). The poetic valences of *pes, studium,* and *mens* are of course highly familiar, and the figuration of one's poetry "traveling" to new subject matter is ubiquitous.[11] The farewell to Catullus' companions (*comitum ualete coetus*) could then cohere nicely with his growing poetic ambition: the social fiction of **A** has had its day.

The point of embarkation in poem 46 is the shore overlooking the countryside of Nicaea. This is on the Propontis; between here and Italy, the "famous cities of Asia" await. The site of the *most* famous Asian city – whose famous destruction will be alluded to shortly, in the closing words of **A** (51.13–16), is on the route, on the mouth of the Dardanelles. There are at least three senses in which the poetry of **B** "goes to" Troy: generically, in that its summative poem 64 is an epic; narratively, in that the song of the Parcae at the end of the poem prophesies Achilles' military career and death there; and etiologically, by way of the subject of the poem, the wedding of Peleus and Thetis. Catullus' ship will sail down the Ionian littoral before crossing the Aegean. There are further cities on this route that have archaic literary/generic resonances: Mytilene for Sappho, lyric, and epithalamium, and Smyrna – or Chios, or the other local pretenders – for Homer and epic.[12]

---

[11] Cf. Callimachus *Aetia* 1. fr. 1.25–27 Pf., Lucretius 1.926–27, Vergil *Georgics* 3.291–93. See Ferriss (2009) for "foot puns" elsewhere in Catullus.

[12] Cicero *Pro Archia* 19.

The crucial complication here is the issue of dramatic time. No meta-poetic reading of 46 can cancel out its place in the Catullus story, and within that temporal frame, the social poetry of **A** has yet to take place. On the other hand, the poem's position in the book, the regular temporal sequentiality we have seen in the other poems, and the parallel poems dramatizing Catullan composition together make it possible to understand the poem not as a poem written earlier but placed later, but rather as a poem written "now," but with an earlier dramatic date. The fact that the specular poems 31 and 46 are the sole unsignaled temporal inversions in **A** leaves the question indeterminate: either way of imagining the poem is authorized, but neither is conclusive.

Imagining the composition of poem 46 as "just before" the final poems of **A**, we would infer that Catullus, at this late moment in its dramatic world, is "just now" coming to outline his future work. By contrast, if we take poem 46 to have been composed at the dramatic moment it sets forth, he will have begun to outline that work while still in Bithynia, before all of the events dramatized in **A** have occurred. And indeed we find an intriguing case for the embedded drama of **B**'s composition elsewhere in **A**, namely in poem 35. Reading the metapoetry of poem 46 as issued at the moment of its drama-tization would "date" 46 as the beginning of Catullus' higher-genre ambi-tions, with poem 35 dated during the composition of **B**: throughout the dramatic time of **A**, when Catullus is not engaged with Lesbia or comment-ing on provincial administration, he is in his study writing longer poems.

Before examining poem 35 in detail, a curious feature of the sequence 34–36 should be brought to light. Poem 34, the hymn to Diana, is written in a stanzaic meter composed of glyconics followed by a pherecratean. The only other Catullan poem matching that description is poem 61. In 34, the poet's voice is absent, as the poem is performed by a chorus of girls and boys; for these features, poem 62 is the sole Catullan parallel. Poem 35 concerns the goddess Cybele, the Great Mother; poem 63 uniquely corre-sponds to this. Finally, poems 36 and 64 prominently cross-reference each other's hymnic address to Venus (and Cupid, in the latter poem):[13]

> nunc o caeruleo creata ponto
> quae **sanctum Idalium** Uriosque apertos
> quaeque Ancona Cnidumque harundinosam

[13] Wray (2001) 76–79 explores how the poem self-actualizes its own critique of Volusius' *Annales*, demonstrating that Catullus can "compose learned hexameters" – even ones that are in fact hendecasyllables! On this feature he remarks (76): "Catullus ... acquits himself of an astonishing mock-sacrificial prayer to Venus whose diction and line length swell the hendecasyllable's slender sails to unparalleled epic-hymnic proportions."

colis **quaeque** Amathunta **quaeque Golgos**
quaeque Durrachium Hadriae tabernam   36.15

sancte puer, curis hominum qui gaudia misces   64.95
quaeque regis **Golgos quaeque Idalium** frondosum

It is clear, then, that these three consecutive poems in **A** cross-check the four poems of **B** in sequence.[14] What conclusions, if any, can be drawn from this?

On my view, of course, this could hardly be accidental; the poetry of **A** will have embedded a cryptic prospectus of Catullus' work in progress. Yet I would not want to lean too heavily on this sequence in order to persuade someone not yet convinced that these are authorially ordered corpora. What I will say is that the observation is highly suggestive on its own, and hard to resist when combined with Giuseppe Biondi's (1998) reading of poem 35, on which the poem is a comment on the unfinished poem 63 itself.

On the surface, the situation in poem 35 is as follows: a poet named Caecilius is working on a poem on the Magna Mater (13–18); Catullus deems this to have been "elegantly begun" (17–18) and wishes to discuss the poem with its author (1–6). This fellow should therefore come to Verona immediately, disregarding the blandishments of the learned girlfriend whose love for him, Catullus hears, has been kindled by the poem (7–15). Traditional interpretive questions have centered on the identity of the "friend" of Catullus and Caecilius, whose "thoughts" (*cogitationes*) on the poem Catullus will convey (5–6), and on whether praise or blame is implied.[15]

The assumption that the poem in question is a draft of poem 63 itself solves numerous problems and is highly attractive on its own. The identity of the "friend" now has a ready solution: he is the party who told Catullus that Caecilius has passed the poem off as his own work, to great erotic effect.[16] We have never heard of this Caecilius or his learned poetry

---

[14] Poems 34 and 35 are unique correspondents within **A** to 61, 62, and 63; poem 64 is cross-checked elsewhere in **A** as well, notably in poem 30 (30.3–5 ~ 64.132–34, 30.10 ~ 64.142, 30.3–5); cf. 60.1–3 ~ 64.153–56.

[15] See Biondi (1998) and Hunink (2000) for discussion of the identity of the *amicus* and relevant bibliography.

[16] Hunink (2000), following up on Biondi's (1998) reading, proposes that the "friend" is rather the Attis of poem 63, whose regret in the second half of the poem – which Caecilius' *inchoate* draft may not include – will deter Caecilius from entanglements with Cybele (and/or the girlfriend, figured as Cybele). Although I rather like this, my immediate goal is limited to showing the reference to poem 63 in 35.

otherwise;[17] Catullus' other poet-friends are the celebrated Cinna and Calvus and the well-attested Q. Cornificius.[18] 35.14 refers to the poem as the *Dindymi dominam*; this phrase appears twice in poem 63 (*Dindymenae dominae*, 14, and *domina Dindymi*, 91; the latter is Catullus' address to the goddess in his own voice)[19] and is highly distinctive, otherwise unattested as form of address to Cybele. As Biondi convincingly puts it, for Catullus to comment on an unknown poet's work by this name comes off like imagining T.S. Eliot referring to some other poet's use of the phrase "cruellest month."[20]

A signal attraction of this reading is the delightful and funny point it gives to the conclusion. Catullus' flattery of the girl's learning and magnanimous "pardon" of her uncontrollable love for Caecilius are revealed as outrageous self-flattery, with Catullus revealed as the poem's true author; meanwhile, a syntactical ambiguity in the final line instantly jumps out (16–18):

> ignosco tibi, Sapphica puella
> musa doctior, est enim uenuste
> Magna Caecilio incohata Mater.

"I pardon you, girl more learned than the Sapphic muse: a charmingly begun Magna Mater *is indeed in Caecilius' possession*."

Leah Kronenberg rejects this reading, on the grounds that Catullus does not deal so gently with thieves of his property elsewhere (poems 12, 25, 33, and 42).[21] But Caecilius need not have stolen the draft; we may easily imagine him as a genuine literary associate of Catullus', to whom Catullus loans his work in progress, either as courtesy or with a view to receiving critique.[22] Then too, the principal explanation for the obliqueness of poem 35 is that Catullus does not wish to disabuse the girlfriend – he assumes that she will read 35 over Caecilius' shoulder; hence the direct address to her at its end – but rather wants to extricate Caecilius from her dangerous obsession with him. Staging a double drama of readership, Catullus builds the poem entirely around the conceit of two embedded readers: the intended one, who has access to the poem's deeper truth, as well as an over-

---

[17] Neudling (1955) 24–25.   [18] Neudling (1955) 52–57.

[19] That the poet addresses her thus, I would contend, gives *Dindymi Domina* its claim to name the poem, rather than the otherwise expected *Attis*.

[20] Biondi (1998) 43.

[21] Kronenberg (2014) argues that "Caecilius" is an alter ego for "Catullus." On this reading, too, the poem referred to in poem 35 is indeed 63.

[22] It is not clear that Catullus would be affronted rather than amused by Caecilius' private claim of authorship to his *puella*, if, as is reasonable to suspect, he could not have plausibly claimed this publicly.

the-shoulder one, for whom it is meant to stay a riddle.[23] Speculation as to how Caecilius came to possess the draft can and should be subordinated to the more pressing reality of Catullus' pointed vagueness.[24]

It is also worth pointing out the further speculation this reading authorizes: the *puella* hangs from the neck, and is expected to impede the departure, of the man in possession of a draft of poem 63. Catullus will shortly (poem 42) demand the return of his *codicilli* from an unwilling woman. While the surrounding poems 41 and 43 hint that Ameana might be the *moecha putida* of 42, that solution still leaves her *possession* of the *codicilli* as an entirely unexplained datum. This reading of poem 35, by contrast, explains how a woman could come to possess the item in question; that she is viciously attacked there but not here would be explained by her subsequent unwillingness to return the draft – which, rather than Caecilius, is her *real* love.

4   Backward Glances to A in C

Now that we have seen the marks of design in **A** and **C** and the symmetry between **A** and **C2**, it remains to discuss the relative order of the two collections. I should be clear that by "order" I do not mean the historical sequence in which the poems were composed or circulated: these facts are unrecoverable. Rather, I mean the artistic order: the order, if any, in which the two collections suggest that they are to be read. These are separate issues. The most economical, and perhaps most likely, assumption is that the artistic order tracks, or at least does not contradict, the order of circulation. But the poet who ends his lyric collection with the temporally initial moment of the Lesbia plot, and who alternates vertiginously from flashback to flash-forward in poem 64, might even have written a later collection of poems with an earlier or concurrent dramatic date: here is yet another question that we must approach without prejudice.[25]

In point of fact, however, I take it that **C** is clearly posterior to **A**. A comparison of the two initial poems, especially on the assumption that first poems should be interrogated for programmaticity, makes that clear.

---

[23] When Catullus turns to address the girl in closing lines 16–18, we may hear it like a filmic gangster on a wiretapped telephone, directly addressing the police.

[24] I would also venture that the poem's formal address to the papyrus which bears the epistolary poem to Caecilius (35.1–2), rather than to Caecilius himself, is consistent with such a reading. Catullus, that is, dramatizes himself wrestling with a compositional problem: he asks the text how best to convey a message to reader A, but only a riddle to reader B.

[25] The 'Vergil' poem in *Odes* 4.12 constitutes (for some) a parallel; see Thomas (2011) *ad loc.*

Let us first consider the varying representation of the poet's relationship with his dedicatee in these two poems.[26] In 1, Catullus depicts his choice of dedicatee as freely made: Cornelius Nepos is addressed because of the latter's earlier appreciation for Catullus' *nugae* (1.1–3). In 65, by contrast, Hortensius Hortalus has previously requested a poem from Catullus. These data fit perfectly with the assumption of the priority of **A**, which appropriately opens by thanking the influential author who "discovered" him. "Thinking [Catullus'] trifles were something" in 1.4 presumptively cashes out as taking an interest in him, commending him to others, introducing him socially to the right people, and the like. In 65, by contrast, a now-successful poet is replying to the notice of a pillar of the establishment: he must still treat the man with careful politesse, but the poet is now in a position to request forebearance and understanding. If his songs had never played on the radio, could he so presume? Should we not rather take the hint that the author of "something" at 1.4 is now Someone in poem 65? If so, the appearance of **A** and possibly also **B** will explain this transformation.

Next, we consider the content of the two poems and their programmaticity. Which comes first, *lepidum nouum* or *carmina maesta*? Starting only a decade or so later, Vergil will make canonical the meta-poetic career, the plot of generic ascent, in his case within the hexameter genres (bucolic > didactic > epic), and with respect to his principal Greek models (Theocritus > Hesiod > Homer).[27] To the extent one lends credence to the proposition that this dynamic was already conventional in the late Republic, one should initially expect the Phalaecian hendecasyllable to precede the elegies of **C1** (though not necessarily the epigrams of **C2**), *nugae* to precede *carmina* (1.3; 65.12), mock grief for a bird to precede real grief for a brother (3; 65), and short poems to precede long ones.

Yet even if Catullus did not find this convention already at hand, poem 65 can very plausibly be taken to invent it. First, because reading **C** after **A** creates a dramatically rich plot for the Catullus-character: the young man does a stint in the provinces; comes home, has erotic and poetic adventures in the big city; then, alas, is struck by tragedy. This story not only fits the biographical "facts" we are given, but also has considerable explanatory power over the poems. Reading **A** after **C**, by contrast, tells no good story, elucidates nothing. Rather, it creates a problem which itself must be solved.

---

[26] Tatum (1997) considers the nature of the relationships between Catullus and his dedicatees in 1, 65, 68, and 116.

[27] Theodorakopoulos (1997).

Let us hypothetically take **A** to follow **C**; already familiar with **C**, we turn for the first time to **A**, and then read poems 1–4. What would we say? That Catullus' grief has passed, as grief is wont to do? Of course: earlier generations of scholars operating with strong biographical assumptions had no trouble dating 65 before Catullus' Bithynian journey-poems.[28] But now we read **A** all the way through, uncovering how elaborately it mirrors **C**: we take it we were *meant* to notice this, to discover it. This, in turn, means holding the specular parts of the two collections up to each other. Both collections begin with grief and a bird; why would the poet revisit the figure he had used to express his eternal grief for his brother, now that, presumably some years later, he has cheered up enough for light, playful verses?

I submit that this looks very much like the wrong question, an interpretive dead end. If we interrogate the two birds, however, on the assumption of the priority of **A**, it all makes sense. The similarity between them makes us think now of the carefree Catullus, now of the grief-stricken one; it makes us feel the contrast, intensifies our mimetic experience of the grieving Catullus' pain. As poems do. As the poet of poem 50 *tells* us that poems do (*ex quo perspiceres meum dolorem*).

Then, too, poems 65 and 68a are very plausibly read as simply asserting their poetic belatedness, simply by closing off the priority of **C** over **A** as an interpretive option. First, let us consider 65.12: *semper morte tua carmina maesta canam*. At issue are how to construe this statement and whether to believe it. This statement is underdetermined, between at least these options: "every future song of mine will be a song made sad by your death" and "at every future stage of my career, at least some of my poems will be poems of grief for you." Reading through **C**, we find this last, weakest construal clearly substantiated: three more brother passages are to come. Do the non-brother poems in **C** answer to the description "songs made sad by the brother's death"? If so, to what extent? To me, that question looks like a very good question, and a very authorized one as well. Once again, though, if we read **A** after **C**, Catullus has simply broken his word, and then elaborately pointed this out to boot. Does he want us to interrogate his broken faith to his brother as we read through **A**? As we have seen, I am indeed in favor of finding interpretive space between what the poet at certain points says and what the poems mean – but not here. This particular irony looks weird, unattractive, another dead end.

Many more points can be offered as well; I will be summary. The second brother passage (68a.14–26) looks back on an earlier period when Catullus

[28] See e.g. Rothstein (1923).

enjoyed ample erotic "play." Some readers, of course, make a strong distinction in 68a between "the gifts of Venus" and "the gifts of the Muses"; on this distinction, Catullus is referring here only to his amatory pursuits, not to his amatory poetry. Any reader willing to resist this claim *pro tanto* has grounds to take Catullus' "playtime" to refer to **A**. And in fact Catullus' reference to a ludic past is unmistakably intratextual with poem 46, whose status as metapoetry has just been claimed:

> tempore quo primum uestis mihi tradita pura est   68.15
>   **iucundum** cum aetas florida **uer** ageret
>   . . .
> sed totum hoc **studium** luctu fraterna mihi mors
>   abstulit.   20
>
> Iam **uer** egelidos refert tepores,   46.1
> iam caeli furor aequinoctialis
> **iucundis** Zephyri silescit auris.
>   . . .
> iam mens praetrepidans auet uagari,   7
> iam laeti **studio** pedes uigescunt.

The young poet's "pursuit" has brought about his metrical vigor in 46, and he is emboldened to set sail by the "pleasant" breeze of the "spring" Zephyr; he now belatedly recalls the "pursuit" in which his flourishing age enjoyed its "pleasant spring," stolen now by the death of the brother.[29] Note too the "smooth sailing" of **A** (poems 4 and 46), contrasted with the images of shipwreck in 68a, now that disaster has struck.[30]

The similar reference to a poetic past in 68b is no less clear:

> sed dicam uobis, uos porro dicite multis   45
>   milibus et facite haec carta loquatur anus
>   . . .
> nam, mihi quam dederit duplex Amathusia curam,   51
>   scitis, et in quo me torruerit genere,

Catullus is addressing the Muses; the Muses *know* about the poet's earlier erotic troubles. The inference is more than plausible: they know this from the assistance they provided to their poet's expression of it, as witnessed by **A**. This would be compelling even without the recollection of Catullus' prayer to the *patrona uirgo*,[31] again in the context of the survival of the physical book

---

[29] These are unique appearances of *uer* in Catullus and the first two of six appearances of *stud-*.
[30] *Naufragum* and following at 68.3–4, *merser fortunae fluctibus* at 68.13; cf. also *fluctuat* at 65.4.
[31] The reading is of course uncertain.

(68.46 ~ 1.9–10), let alone the phrase *in quo . . . genere* (68.52), which hints that the muse knows which genre of poetry Catullus worked in.

Lesbia is Catullus' *puella* throughout A; in the first Lesbia epigram she is *mulier mea* (70.1; cf. 68b.128 and 87.1–2). Which will Lesbia be first, "girl" or "woman"? And the love affair Catullus wishes to be free of at 76.13 is now of long standing: *longum . . . amorem.*

Similarly, when last we hear of Juventius in **A** (poem 48), Catullus' desire for his kisses is insatiable. By contrast, after his protestations in poem 99, an offended Catullus will never "steal his kisses" again. Poem 99 looks like the end of that storyline.

Nor is Catullus the only once-carefree character in **C** to undergo a reversal: Calvus too (poem 96) has gone from fellow jocular poet-prankster (14), and facetious love interest (50), to grief-stricken lover and sorrowing poet (96).

One particularly strong indication of the corpus' artistic order is poetic rather than narrative. The last poem of **C** responds to the first: Catullus' refusal to send *carmina Battiadae* in 116 after doing so in 65. This closural gesture becomes particularly splendid if we also assume the belatedness of **C** in respect to **A**. On an idealized first reading of **C**, readers with **A** fresh in mind (or open for comparison) will have seen how close the structural parallels are. Now reaching the end of **C**, they might well expect a closural cover-letter-cum-translation. In point of fact, they find only the former, which amounts to a closural *recusatio* of the latter. Relative to **A**, the ending of **C** is catalectic, a pherecratean to **A**'s glyconic. It thus must be posterior to **A**.

5   Structural Responsions in B and C1

Pluralities of Response

Indeed, a conspicuous feature of the **A** ~ **C2** responsion is also found in **B** ~ **C1**, namely their matching "halves." First, by line count: poems 61–63 closely match the dimensions of 64, just as 65–67 closely match that of (the poem or dyad) 68.[32] And then, poems 64 and 68(b) share obvious similarities: the longest and most ambitious poems in **B** and **C**, each has an elaborate ring structure, each concerns a divine ("divine") woman's entrance into a house and her erotic union with a mortal (Thetis and Peleus ~ Lesbia and

---

[32] The stanzaic form of 61 allows us confidently to reconstruct the length of its lacunae, yielding an original line count of 235, while the most orthodox guess about poem 62 might put it at 72 lines. The "halves" of **B** might then respectively contain 400 and 408 lines, while those of **C1** could not be far from 166 and 160 lines.

Catullus), with this narrative element set off pointedly against an inset myth that occupies more textual space (Ariadne ~ Laodamia), and with the various narratives converging at Troy, the common tomb of Asia and Europe (68.89): Thetis will bear Achilles and lose him at Troy, where Laodamia loses Protesilaus and Catullus his brother.

The two "first halves" may have unities of their own;[33] I do not, however, wish to claim that they map onto each other closely as such, as 64 and 68(b) do. It is easy enough to map 63 onto 67 and 62 onto 66; the problem is that in spite of the programmatic mirroring between 61 and 65, we can hardly see these two poems as responses to each other as a whole.[34] But it is better that we are not tempted by this move, for otherwise we would think we had found *the* structural scheme, and thus be tempted to downplay or deny the other poem with which 68(b) invites a one-to-one comparison: namely 61. And this move, in turn, frees us from the need to choose between correspondents for the internal poems 62 and 63. The benefit here is that it is also well motivated to swap correspondents for these, pairing 67 with 63 and 66 with 62.

I now turn to substantiate this; first, however, I will visualize the point, stating clearly what I do and do not mean by it. My claim is that the tidiest useful model for the response between **B** and **C2** would either "fold" poem 65 into 66 and 68a into 68b or else omit them *qua* introductions,[35] leaving the three remaining pieces with two meaningful correspondents apiece, as follows:

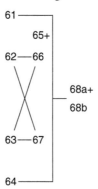

[33] For **B**, if Most (1981) 114 is right, the hexameters of poem 62 count as lyric *qua* stanzaic, as opposed to epic hexameters *kata stichon*. This understanding would divide **B** metrically into a lyric 61–63 and epic 64 (on the characterization of the Galliambic meter of 63 as lyric, note that this is a form of Ionic meter, attested by Sappho fr. 135, Alcaeus fr. A 10, and Alcman 34D).
[34] That the line count of 61 is almost ten times that of 65 (235 vs. 24) rules that out: these poems plainly *have* correspondences rather than *are* correspondents.
[35] Without, that is, thereby claiming that their content is inert in terms of demonstrating parallels between the two corpora.

At beginning, middle, and end of the Catullan long poems are three long narrative poems whose primary narratives are the same simple story: a woman enters a house and makes love to a man.[36] Wiseman long ago saw, and we will presently expand upon, the primary artistic function of this, namely building the contrast between the adulterous lovemaking of Catullus and Lesbia and the conjugal lovemaking in 61 and 64.[37]

Turning now to the two pairs of "internal" poems (62 and 63 within **B**, and 66 and 67 within **C1**), we see that each pair shares extensive formal and thematic resonances with the other. Poem 62 has a "star" (*Vesper/Hesperus*, the Evening Star, planet Venus) as its partial subject and partial addressee, the core conceit into which the intercalary invocation of the wedding god is fitted; the catasterized Lock is the partial subject of poem 66, as well as its speaker.[38] On the other hand, 62 is tied closely and conspicuously to poem 67 by its strictly dialogic form, uniquely in Catullus;[39] assuming (as most readers do) that the poet is the door's interlocutor in 67, the two poems are both male/female dialogues. Likewise, poem 63 shares with 66 the conspicuous themes of bodily cutting and separation (Attis' self-castration as religious devotion and Berenice's votive lock), as well as permanent and regretted spatial separation (Attis from his home and identity, the Lock from her mistress); yet it also shares a highly conspicuous theme with 67, namely impotence – and the related perversion of the marital relationship, as we will see.

Thematic Continuities

Poems 61, 62, and 64 all take place at weddings; the first two are wedding songs, while the latter *contains* a wedding song (64.323–81). If we again bracket 65 and 68a as introductory, we see that 66 and 68b are closely linked. The former tells of the consummation of a marriage (66.11–14), the husband's subsequent departure to war in "Asia" (19–20, 35–36), and his happy return vouchsafed by religious observance (34–36), while in the

---

[36] Others will judge for themselves, but I am not troubled by the fact that Thetis' imminent arrival and lovemaking to Peleus in poem 64 are predicted (329, 372–80) rather than narrated.

[37] Wiseman (1969) 22–25.

[38] Her transformation, in turn, is brought about by Venus, whose "star" Vesper/Hesperus is. Perhaps it would not be too outrageous to point to the bilingual (Latin/transliterated Greek) names for this star in 62 as echo of the Greek-to-Latin translation which poem 66 is.

[39] Like poem 62, the hymn to Diana 34 is spoken by boys and girls, but that poem is not formally dialogic in that the boys and girls form a single chorus speaking in unison. Poems in which Catullus clearly does not speak are 14b (where the book is speaker), 34, 62, and 66 (spoken entirely by the Lock).

latter that same plot is unhappily reprised, with the mythological husband dying on campaign for want of proper religious observance (68.73–86).[40] Poem 67 is easily the odd poem out next to these two, not only for its generically "low" content and the shocking central obscenity of 67.23–24, otherwise unparalleled in **C1**, but also by its not being directly preceded by a poetic epistle.[41] 63, similarly, is the odd poem out in **B**. Though not absurdly vacuous, it would not be one's first choice to claim that the common appearance of a single dubiously fitting piece in **B** and **C2** *just is* the thematic pattern in respect to 63 and 67. Assuming, however, that the sequence is authorial and meaningful, this claim will be at least partially true: there will need to be more to it than that fact, but that fact will be unavoidable.

It seems, however, possible to make a virtue of it. If there is one thing all of these poems are about, critics widely agree, it is marriage; the most obvious strategy for demonstrating the cohesiveness of 61–68 is to argue that 63, the sole poem overtly lacking the theme, contains it in a covert way. To be sure, I think this strategy has been fruitful. But even if we agree that poem 63 is relevantly "antinuptial" (in the sense of being about something the *opposite* of marriage, rather than being *against* marriage), the fact will hardly disappear that only in the case of 63 do we have to look to see the marriage theme.

Moreover, there is another plausible candidate for Ariadnean *Leitfaden* in these poems: the gods, and their relationships with humans, especially their presence and absence.[42] And if poem 63 is the only poem in **B** and **C1** that does not clearly instantiate the marriage theme, its fellow misfit 67 is the only one where the same is true of the human/divine theme.[43] If the throughline in **B** and **C1** is *both* themes together (marriage and divine/human interaction), each sequence of poems contains but a single problem case, and that problem case is at most half a problem.

---

[40] A further continuity runs through these poems: the offended divinity in the mythical backstory of 68b is Venus, who is also the agent of the Lock's catasterism in 66 (55–64), the divinity whom Attis' "hatred" for (i.e. rejection of, 63.17) motivates his self-castration, and the divinity associated with the celestial addressee of 62. The same divinity had previously given the poet cares in 68b (51–56), fails to relieve the addressee of 68a of *his* cares (5), torments Ariadne in 64 (71–75, 96–98), and is the referent of the first simile of 61 (the bride is as beautiful as she, 61.16–20).

[41] At 48 lines, poem 67 also stands out as far shorter than the other two non-introductory poems (poem 66 at 94 lines, 68b at 120).

[42] Wiseman (1979) 177: "if 61–4 do form a *volumen* on their own, then the gods' relationship with men might be seen as one of its unifying themes."

[43] The human speaker calls Jupiter's blessing upon the door (67.2); this is, of course, superficial. The gods do not otherwise appear in the poem.

Initial support for seeing these themes as jointly central to **B** at least can be taken both from its frame (the invocation of the wedding-god to a human wedding opening 61 and the denial that the gods visit *talis . . . coetus*, human gatherings of *this* sort,[44] in its penultimate line) and from the forward-pointing *envoi* of **A**: the man, woman, and "god" of poem 51,[45] along with any epithalamic resonance Roman readers would take from the Sapphic context, and any hint that *ille* is Lesbia's husband.

But it is of course the content of these poems as a whole that must be shown to answer to this characterization. The first 75 lines of poem 61 fit perfectly: the opening hymn (lines 1–45) prays for the divine presence of the wedding god, while the following encomium (46–75) insists on the power and necessity of his blessings for human society. He is worshiped above all gods (46–60), invoked by aging parents hoping for grandchildren (51–52), and listened for eagerly by new husbands (54–55); maidens disrobe by his agency and are given over to "wild" young men (52–53, 56–60). Each of the final three stanzas of the encomium, then, enunciates a crucial social function of the god, capped off by the pregnant question, *quis huic deo compararier ausit?* Without the god's offices, there can be no socially condoned sex (61–65), no legitimate offspring to perpetuate the *domus* (66–70), and no citizen youths to defend the land (71–75). The sequence runs from individual to familial and finally political concerns; all of these levels will resonate with later poems.

The first third of poem 61, then, is maximally consistent with taking gods/humans and marriage as the dual *Leitmotive* of **B** (and **C1**), and the recurrence of the refrain *io Hymen Hymenaee io,/io Hymen Hymenaee* in the second half (eleven times) ensures that the god is not forgotten throughout the poem.[46] Next, poem 62 is patently a wedding poem. As to the gods, both its hymnic refrain praying for the wedding god's presence (eight times) and the two choruses' conceit by which Vesper/Hesperus is the agent who brings about marriage keep the divine deeply present throughout the poem.[47]

In poem 63, then, we have an indisputable case of a poem on human/ divine relations, and a more than suggestive case for a poem reminiscent of

---

[44] Surely one cannot fail to think of weddings as the sort of gathering relevant here.

[45] This is emphasized, once again, by Catullus' expansion of his source material at 51.2: *ille, si fas est, superare diuos.*

[46] Venus, to whom the bride is likened at the opening (16–20), also putatively intervenes (189–98) to enhance the groom's handsome looks and conjugal desire.

[47] If Hesperus *qua* star is conceptually distinct from divinity (even when exerting its powers on mortal affairs), the catasterized Lock who expects sacrificial honors (66.79–86) draws the two concepts together.

marital themes. To summarize that case:[48] though Catullus' Attis is a Greek rather than the Phrygian shepherd whose cult is celebrated with Cybele's, the homonymy activates the versions of the myth in which the relationship between Attis and Cybele is marital or at least erotic. In addition, the diction in 63 is reminiscent of erotic language: Attis' *furor* (63.38, 78, 79, 92, cf. *furenti rabie* 4, *furibunda* 31); that he arrives in Phrygia *citato cupide pede* (2); that his arrival at *domum Cybebes* (20, 35) recalls the *deductio* of the bride to her husband's house (and cf. Attis' lost *domus* 58, 66, and Catullus' prayer that the madness of Cybele's cult be kept far from his *domus*, 92), while the word *domus* evokes not solely the married couple's home but marriage itself; and finally that Attis' permanent separation from his home and the transformation of his social identity map onto the transformation of *uirgines* into *nuptae*. Besides these there are intratextual considerations which are striking, but admittedly also raise a circularity problem.[49] Attis standing on the shore and delivering a regretful soliloquy cannot but prefigure Ariadne in 64, taken advantage of and jilted by Theseus, but soon to be wed to Bacchus, whose retinue of Maenads (64.254–64) look and sound so much like the troop of *Gallae* led by Attis (63.6–38). Nor do we miss the correspondences between Attis' situation and the case against marriage put by the girls' chorus in poem 62. Furthermore, the language of slavery proper to the lifelong religious service Attis will now assume (*famula*, 68, 90) is redolent of Ariadne again (*famularer serua*, 64.161), and of the language of erotic *seruitium* in 68b, by which Catullus' lover is his *era* (68.136).

Finally, we come to poem 64. Like 61–64 as a whole, 64 itself is framed not only by the divine in respect to marriage, but by a *modern* speaker's comment on the same: the epic narrator apostrophizes heroes in general (22–25) and Peleus in particular, amazed at his procuring divine assent to marry Thetis (25–30), while the epilogue glumly notes the absence of such unions and the withdrawal of divine presence from the modern world (397–408). Besides this we have a welter of human/divine engagements: Athena's construction of the *Argo*, the Argonauts' unprecedented voyeurship of naked Nereids, the wedding feast, Venus and Cupid's assault on Ariadne, her prayer to Jupiter and the Eumenides, Jupiter's assent and the

---

[48] Schäfer (1966), Forsyth (1970), Sandy (1971). Nauta (2004) 597 observes that "Attis' condition is one which stands in radical opposition to marriage."

[49] That is, one can argue that the poems are authorially arranged because they share the thematic unity of the marriage motif, and one can argue that poem 63 shares the thematic unity of the marriage motif because diction in the poems (authorially) adjacent to it recalls that motif. Arguing both points raises the problem of circularity.

subsequent death of Aegeus, Bacchus' marriage to Ariadne, the Parcae's song.

This joint characterization of the overriding theme of poems 61–64 is well supported: the two longer poems 61 and 64 answer perfectly to it, and in fact the shared theme makes for a useful bridging mechanism between the contemporary Roman world of 61 and the mythological epic 64. The ritually invoked wedding god mirrors the immortal wedding guests of the epic. It also limits the extent to which poem 63 seems to pose a problem to the unity: it is as fully a poem about divinity and humanity as one could wish, and the cumulative recollections of nuptial themes inverted make a good case.[50] We should have little problem accepting the thematic unity: two human weddings to which gods are called, and two narratives of divine intervention in human affairs, wrapped round no fewer than three myths involving sex and marriage between gods and mortals: Attis and Cybele, Peleus and Thetis, Ariadne and Bacchus.

Turning to **C1**, we see immediately that two of its three non-introductory pieces map perfectly onto the joint theme of **B**. In 66 a catasterized/divinized Lock looks back on the consummation of a human marriage, the couple's vow to the gods to vouchsafe the husband's return from battle, and the discharge of that vow upon the fulfillment of its condition. All of this would be enough, even if it were not the case that the divinity responsible for the catasterism is Arsinoe-Aphrodite, the late Ptolemaic queen now deified and identified with Catullus' Venus, and even if the human subjects of the poem, Berenice and Ptolemy III, were not worshiped in their lifetime as the θεοὶ Εὐεργέται.[51] Similarly, in 68b the mythological *comparanda* for Catullus and Lesbia are Protesilaus and Laodamia, whose story matches that of Berenice and Ptolemy, except that Protesilaus' return from war is denied by Venus, offended by the couple's failure to make sacrifice. Playing smaller roles in the same poem are a notoriously troubled divine marriage (that of Juno and Jupiter) and a human–divine marriage that becomes a fully divine one (Hebe and Hercules). And, of course, Catullus' Lesbia is his *diua*, and her entrance into his embrace at the end of **C2** is attended by Cupid, in language obviously reminiscent of the invocation that begins **B**.

This leaves only the absence of a substantial divine presence in poem 67 – the marital theme is a given, present in the Door's gossip about a woman's prior marriages, tainted by incest, impotence, and adultery. We will discuss the matter of poem 67, and its important connections with 66, shortly.

---

[50] For a further structural and mythological link between 63 and 64, see Traill (1981) 212–14.
[51] Du Quesnay (2012) 164.

To conclude this section, I am content simply to dismiss the alleged threat: only on the most unreasonable of assumptions would we have to deny the substantial continuities throughout these seven poems, just because one half of its claimed thematic unity is implicit in one poem (marriage in 63), and the other half is superficial in another poem (the gods in 67).

Dynamics of Development

Since there is some extent to which the thematic unity of 61–64 and 65–68b is compatible also with the independent circulation of 61–64, the question of how these two putative collections read, given *this* sequence, is particularly crucial for my argument. Reading 61–64 in order makes a clear progression in terms of poetic content, namely from the social world of **A** to the fully mythical/epic world of poem 64. Poem 61 is set at the wedding of a named – and probably readily identifiable – Roman gentleman, Manlius Torquatus; his presence here is unremarkable for readers coming from **A**. The next wedding poem is, however, more abstract: probably more Greek than Roman, this wedding takes place at no indicated time or place, and no details about the bridal couple are given. Poem 63 then moves us to a *mostly* mythological world, but the Attis-character himself belongs more to the world of history than of myth. And poem 64 is of course thoroughly epic, though its frame departs from and returns to a historical here and now.

By this same measure, **C2** inhabits a shifting, transitional zone: the introductory 65 and 68a return us to Catullus' familiar first-person world, but a world now darkened by his brother's death. The inset poems 66, 67, and 68b blend realism with fantasy; their thematic movement is opposite to that of **B** (from myth to reality) and prepares the reader for the full return to Catullus' social world in **C2**. Poem 66 concerns real historical personages – from two centuries past – but also wondrous divine interventions, apotheosis, a talking constellation. Poem 67 retains the core fantastic element of 66 with another inanimate object turned speaker, but moves decisively toward realism in its sordid glimpses of Transpadane hijinks. Finally, 68b's use of myth is at bottom realistic: the mythological content is expressed in similes that illustrate Catullus' reality. When toward the end of 68b Catullus has Cupid in a saffron tunic, darting here and there around Lesbia, we hardly take him literally; when he calls for Themis to bless his honorand with long life, the gesture is fully in line with conventional real-life religiosity.

So too do the two corpora share an emotional directionality. Poem 61, it can hardly be denied, is highly idealizing: its picture of nuptial bliss is overwhelmingly positive, exuberantly joyful. Poem 62 is balanced: the chorus of boys wins, but the girls' case against marriage receives equal time. Poem 63 is naturally horrifying. But what to say about 64?

Similarly for 66, 67, and 68b: our options for 66 are to find it "positive" like poem 61 or "balanced" like 62; the less weight one gives to the Lock's protestations of regret, the more 66 will match 61 rather than 62. Poem 67 is clearly "darker," though the comic tone keeps it far lighter than its dark counterpart in **B**, poem 63. But what to say about 68b?

It would be absurd at this point to identify definitively the mood of these two poems: no two critics are likely to agree on any fully realized reading of these poems. The point, rather, is that both poems invite the same basic question in the same basic way: light or dark, optimism or pessimism, comedy or tragedy? The speaker in 64 is moved with wonder to apostrophize the pantheon of heroes (22–30) and declares the Parcae's song *felicia* (382) – but the reader may well be horrified by Theseus and by Aegeus' fate, amazed at Achilles' future prowess, or again appalled at the tomb "wet" with a child's blood. So also for 68b: Laodamia's painful "lesson" and unbearable grief; Lesbia's entrance and embrace of Catullus. The poet interprets his own text positively: Lesbia's embrace, rare as it is, adulterous as it is, is worth it. But do we agree?

This is what the sequence of the two groups of long poems does, and it does it so well that it can hardly be an accident: reading the poems in this order leads us to the same question posed at the same point in the same way. **B** does this after progressively leading us to the point of maximum generic distance from the personal poetry of **A**, while **C1** culminates in our return – sadder but wiser, as the poet is, or thinks he is – to the point of embarkation: *lumina nocte* to *lumine claro* and back again as *lux mea, qua uiua.*

6 Narrative Time and Metapoetry in C1

Every transition point is vexed: how 65 frames 66, whether 67 fits at all, what to make of the forty lines of 68a, the common tomb of Catullan exegesis. The view I will now defend is as follows: the poetic gift to Ortalus which poem 65 introduces consists of both 66 and 67, which are anyway closely connected; these poems were composed before Catullus' brother's death, and are *faute de mieux* what Catullus is capable of sending to discharge his obligation. Poem 68a is indeed separate from 68b, but the two are addressed to the same recipient: *Allius* in the latter is a pseudonym for *Mallius* in the former.[52] Unlike 65, however, 68a is fully a *recusatio*, with Catullus in fact incapable of composing: to resolve the inconsistency, we posit the (dramatized) composition of 68b "after" the refusal of 68a, as Catullus regains his poetic voice.

Poems 65–67: The Ortalus Drama

I begin with the pairing of poems 66 and 67, then move back to the framing of the poems as a gift to Ortalus in 65. Fantuzzi and Hunter (2004) 476 have shown the likelihood that the first distich of poem 67 is a displaced translation of the final distich of Callimachus' Lock poem, which Catullus pointedly excludes from his own translation.[53] This point is of course appealing for my reading, in that it recalls Catullus' distribution of his Sapphic model-text between poems 50 and 51, as we have seen. Other connections between 66 and 67 have been recognized, in particular the resonance of the Door with the Lock (both inanimate speakers) and the pointed contrast between the "high" social world of the Alexandrian court and the "low" world of naughty Transpadane adulterers. It is, however, a recent piece by Regina Höschele (2009) which to my thinking seals the case: the most conspicuous and shocking wrongdoing in poem 67 is a perfect match – with wonted Catullan gender-inversion – for a key event in the backstory of poem 66, alluded to at 66.27–28. Berenice, the daughter of the king of Cyrene, was first married to Demetrius the Fair. Demetrius, however, carried on an affair with Apame, Berenice's mother, until Berenice, with the support of the city, had Demetrius killed. This is the "good crime" (*bonum . . . facinus*, 27) mentioned by the Lock, apostrophizing her mistress, "by which you obtained the royal marriage" (*quo regium adepta es | coniugium*, 27–28) – that is, the marriage to Ptolemy celebrated in Callimachus' and Catullus' poems. Similarly, the Veronese door has overheard her former *domina* telling of her earlier marriage in Brixia to an impotent husband, whose father's adultery with her "made

---

[52] Skinner (2003) 143 argues that Allius (possibly a play on *alius*/ἄλλος) is "a fictive construct endowed with a *redender Name* that changes with his literary function." This, however, is based upon a particular literary interpretation of 68a/68b that this book does not share. Many critics favor the unity of Mallius and Allius, though from the debate's inception scholars have arrived at this conclusion in different ways: Prescott (1940), e.g., argues for *Mali* as elision of *mi Alli*; he regards Palmer's (1879) argument that *Allius* is a pseudonym for *Mallius/Manlius*, required because 68b was meant for public consumption while 68a was not, as ridiculous. For lengthier discussion, see Tuplin (1981).

[53] Agnesini (2011) and DuQuesnay (2012) 181–83, however, excise 67.1–2 from 67 and attach them to the end of 66.

wicked his house" (*conscelerasse domum*, 24). Just as the dissolution of Berenice's marriage to Demetrius made her available for a royal marriage in Alexandria, so did the failure of the woman's marriage to an impotent husband make her available for a second marriage in Verona.

The North African cities, Cyrene and Alexandria are thus neatly doubled – not without a certain comic absurdity – by the Transpadane settlements Brixia and Verona. Prior adultery and incest between a son- and mother-in-law in Cyrene meets daughter- and father-in-law adultery/ incest in Brixia, but the blameless wife translated to Alexandria becomes the *guilty* wife translated to Verona. Where the Lock in poem 66 makes only a passing allusion to the earlier marital wrongdoing, focusing rather on pious and lawful conjugality in Alexandria, the Door in 67 is forthcoming about the earlier Brixian wrongdoing and reticent on the inferable conjugal scandals that took place in the Veronese house, behind her back and within her province.

In fine, these connections are easily sufficient to draw poem 67 close to 66, and they nicely parallel and build upon the adaptive artistry of poems 50 and 51. Both of Catullus' translation poems invert the gender of the speaker (Sappho to Catullus, masculine πλόκαμος to feminine *coma*); both speakers bemoan their separation from a female beloved brought about by her erotic union with a man; both poems are adjacent to another poem that adapts, Romanizes, and burlesques the conceit of the Greek translation, again with gender inversion (male/male longing in poem 50, role-reversed in-law adultery in 67); both poems "reassign" parts of their translation from the obvious correspondent to the less identifiable one; both poem-pairs are at liminal moments in their books (final for 50–51, virtually initial for 66–67).[54] Add now that Callimachus' original is known to have been the final poem in the *Aetia*, where the end of **C2** recalls the preface to the *Aetia*, and the final distich of Callimachus' model-text becomes the first distich of the Romanized adaptation. The case for non-fortuitousness is a good one.

Turning now to poem 65, the first point to notice is that the dedicatory words prima facie indicate the gift of multiple poems to Ortalus (65.16): *haec expressa tibi carmina Battiadae*. Since poem 67 is not straightforwardly a translation, and since *carmina* can also simply mean "verses" (as at 64.383, of the song of the *Parcae*), that marked valence has always been reasonably

---

[54] Naturally, the difference here is that the correspondence between the paired cover letter and the adaptation/translation in 50–51 is expanded to a triad of cover letter, translation, *and* adaptation in 65–66–67.

understood here. Now, however, we see that poem 67 is partially translated from Callimachus, and that it makes a pair with and asks to be read with and against poem 66: the unmarked valence of *carmina* recommends itself better. Admittedly, we must then adjust our understanding of *expressa*: "translated" is less fully true of 66–67 as a whole than of 66, but (OLD s. v. 6) "reproduced" or "modeled on" will work, and we will also shortly consider "pressed out" of the mode of their production by Catullus. *Battiadae* will also need to be understood in a wider sense: no longer solely "poems of (i.e. authored by) Callimachus," the second poem may need to be "Callimachean" in a broader sense.[55]

All of this, I trust, does in fact work. But it bears noticing that any account of C1 as authorial sequence all but requires some such explanation, if the sequence is to be fully comprehensible. Poems 65 and 68a make clear that Catullus is grappling with some form of poetic incapacity; on the traditional understanding, this incapacity must be reconciled with the existence of poems 66 and 68b, a hard enough task.[56] But poem 67, apparently separating these two epistle–gift poem sequences, poses yet another problem: why are its circumstances of composition uniquely unaddressed, how did (the dramatized) Catullus manage to create it, and why would he do so, even if he could? Including the poem on the *charta* sent to Ortalus usefully relieves us of this problem.

Now that we have seen the reasons for including 66 and 67 and shown that the language of 65 is compatible with doing so, it remains to examine the way in which poem 65 characterizes the poetic gift. First we note again the comparison with poem 50: after his night of longing for Calvus, Catullus composed "this composition," with the clear purpose of enabling Calvus to see his *dolor*. Here, Catullus' *dolor* is read in the poem's first line, and is responsible for Catullus' inability to compose – let alone to dash off

---

[55] The wider valence for *expressa* allows us to take both poems as "expressions" of Callimachus' Lock. The other, unfortunately unprovable, possibility is that there is some thicker, lost Callimachean co-model for 67, such that the poem simultaneously "expresses" both it and the Lock. Fantuzzi and Hunter (2004) 476 n. 133 suggest that the sequence of 66 and 67 (an "aggressive satire" following Callimachus' "last *aition*") mimes Callimachus' transition from *Aetia* to *Iambi*; this too is of course highly attractive for me.

A few words must be said on the apple simile of 67.19–24 as well: the possibility that the simile is a translation or adaptation from Callimachus' story of Acontius and Cydippe (frr. 67–75) has been discussed by Johnston (1983), King (1988) 384–85, and Hunter (1993). On my view, the common elements of apple, suitor, and maiden are plainly real, even if the Catullan simile is otherwise too poor a match with the Acontius story to take the latter as interpretively central for the former (on this point see Woodman (2012) 150–51).

[56] The air of the paradoxical here is strong enough that one thinkable option will surely be to interpret him as self-contradicting. Compare, of course, what has been argued for 14b–26: the poetics of self-contradiction would not be the same there and here, but the *fact* of self-contradiction could be so.

a masterpiece diptych like 50–51 in a single day! And yet, in spite of this pain (now "grief," *maeroribus*), Catullus sends *carmina Battiadae* (15–16). Here too a purpose clause follows; by contrast with poem 50, this is now followed by a simile. If sense is to be made of the represented situation, it must be from these lines, which pose one of the most pressing interpretive problems in the Catullan corpus. I print the poem:

> Etsi me assiduo confectum cura dolore   65.1
>   seuocat a doctis, Ortale, uirginibus,
> nec potis est dulcis Musarum expromere fetus
>   mens animi, tantis fluctuat ipsa malis –
> namque mei nuper Lethaeo gurgite fratris   5
>   pallidulum manans alluit unda pedem,
> Troia Rhoeteo quem subter litore tellus
>   ereptum nostris obterit ex oculis.
>   . . .
>
>   numquam ego te, uita frater amabilior,   10
> aspiciam posthac? at certe semper amabo,
>   semper maesta tua carmina morte canam,
> qualia sub densis ramorum concinit umbris
>   Daulias, absumpti fata gemens Ityli –
> sed tamen in tantis maeroribus, Ortale, mitto   15
>   haec expressa tibi carmina Battiadae,
> ne tua dicta uagis nequiquam credita uentis
>   effluxisse meo forte putes animo,
> ut missum sponsi furtiuo munere malum
>   procurrit casto uirginis e gremio,   20
> quod miserae oblitae molli sub ueste locatum,
>   dum aduentu matris prosilit, excutitur,
> atque illud prono praeceps agitur decursu,
>   huic manat tristi conscius ore rubor.

Catullus' emotional state keeps him separate from the learned maidens and Muses, and under some form of poetic incapacity (1–4); the cause of this is his brother's recent death and burial "at Troy" (5–8). Moved, the poet now apostrophizes the brother, lamenting their permanent separation and promising that he will "always sing songs made sad by [his] death," just as Procne-turned-nightingale sang for her son Itylus (9–14). Nonetheless, Catullus sends these *carmina Battiadae* (15–16), lest Ortalus think his words had been disregarded by Catullus (17–18).

So as not to beg any of the questions we are about to raise, I scruple to gloss the rest of the poem here. First, though, I will briefly examine the apparent self-contradiction in its simplest form: this is a poem (partially) about the death of Catullus' brother, which seems to say that that death renders Catullus unable to write poetry. How does this square? The options are to say (1) that it doesn't, (2) that poem 65 – perhaps as a brief introductory epistle – does not count as poetry, and (3) to interrogate closely the terms of his inability in lines 3–4, arguing that it is not *verse* per se which he cannot produce, but that the inability of his *mens animi* to "bring forth the sweet offspring of the Muses" indicates something more limited.

Option (1) strikes me as a last resort, unless (as with 14b–26) it were apparent that there is something positively attractive in a self-contradicting reading. Option (2) is not at all impossible; we might reflect, for instance, that it is a generic given that every word of Catullus' must scan. For the poetry to represent a situation in which the poet cannot compose, then, readers might simply understand that they are to forget that the words in which he states his inability themselves scan.[57] Nonetheless, option (3) can also work, and seems the most economical solution: the "offspring of the Muses" will be poems *simpliciter*, but the ones Catullus can compose are not *dulces* or sweet in their content, but rather gloomy. This understanding also squares Catullus' inability in lines 3–4 with his promise to the brother in 11–12, by which he will *always* sing *maesta ... carmina*: poem 65 is a "gloomy" poem promising more of the same, denying only that its author can write "sweet" poems.

We now confront the closing simile. The central difficulty is syntactical: on what does the *ut* clause beginning at line 19 depend? On *mitto* in line 15, or *effluxisse* in 18? What is at stake here is brought to light in the adaptive translations I offer, modifying the order of the clauses and rendering the content of Ortalus' imputed thought in direct speech in order to highlight the difference:

> A) In spite of my intense grief, Ortalus, I send you these translated verses of Callimachus, to prevent you by chance from thinking, "my words were vainly entrusted to the wandering winds and have flowed out of Catullus' mind" [which situation would be] like an apple, sent as a suitor's secret gift, runs forward from a maiden's chaste lap; the poor girl forgot she had placed it under her soft dress, and when she jumps up at her mother's arrival it is shaken out; it falls straight down, vertically; on her sad face, a guilty blush spreads.

---

[57] Could a character in an opera first sing of her inability to sing, regain her confidence, then turn performatively to the audience and (really) sing? In our case the equivalent seems plausible, though it would help to have a clear parallel.

B) In spite of my intense grief, Ortalus, to prevent you by chance from thinking, "my words were vainly entrusted to the wandering winds and have flowed out of Catullus' mind," I send you these translated verses of Callimachus, like an apple, sent as a suitor's secret gift, runs forward …

What is at stake between construals A and B is whether the simile reflects a potential state of affairs in which the verses of Callimachus are not sent (so A), or the actual state of affairs in question, in which they are indeed sent (so B). We have here a genuine ambiguity: neither reading is grammatically strained, both tell a coherent and plausible story; neither reading collapses on inspection. This is not to say there is no fact of the matter or that one reading is not better than the other; rather, it is to say that we must think the problem through.[58] Even if there is a univocally correct construal, a reader who quickly reads through the Latin and instantly assumes it, failing to notice the rejected possibility and what it *would* mean, has not read the poem well.

This point would be sufficiently made with a breezy appeal to the level of craft evident in this poem and this poet: an interpretive dilemma this pressing cannot be mistaken or accidental. The fact that the dilemma is found in the context of a simile, however, settles the point. That is, it would be absurd to deny in advance that a simile in an ancient poem might map closely onto its external context; and clearly we have no grounds to deny that it does until we have a look. Having a look, in turn, brings us directly to this dilemma.

I will consider horn A of the dilemma, which we may also call the "hypothetical" interpretation, in that it locates the simile within an unrealized, averted state of affairs. On this reading, the external correlates of the words in the simile cannot be the distich at 15–16: from within the hypothetical state of affairs, those words are unreal. What *is* real under this hypothesis is instead the indirect statement in 17–18. We then find that 19–20, the first distich of the simile, maps precisely onto it:

---

[58] On a first reading, even native speakers of Latin would constantly face evanescent alternative construals which *do* collapse on closer inspection, especially in reading relatively under-punctuated texts. When this happens, we merely forget our initial hesitation, and we certainly do not attribute it to the poet. Borderline cases of this phenomenon will surely be difficult; the point is that this case is nowhere close to the line.

> [ne] tua dicta uagis nequiquam credita uentis
> effluxisse meo [forte putes] animo,
> [ut] missum sponsi furtiuo munere malum
> procurrit casto uirginis e gremio,

giver	gift	p.p.p.	circumstance	verb	recipient	place
tua	dicta	credita	uagis uentis	effluxisse	meo	animo
sponsi	malum	missum	furtiuo munere	procurrit	uirginis	gremio

The linguistic mapping is perfect and easy, and the interpretation that produces it therefore cannot be easily dismissed: if this is not simply the solution, we will have to explain why not. The conceptual mapping fits as well: Ortalus parallels the suitor and Catullus the maiden; the request for a poem establishes a reciprocal relationship with Catullus in the way that the love-token does with the maiden; in either case, the request or gift is future-directed and uncertain of fulfillment; in either case, the recipient's forgetfulness amounts to or brings about the frustration of the other party's intention, constituting a breach of his trust.[59]

Where the mapping breaks down, even in advance of discussing the final two distichs, is first the misalignment between the suitor's secret action and Ortalus' request: the threat of familial and social disapproval that animates the simile has no correlate in Ortalus' respectable request. Next, there is an evident disanalogy between the *dicta* and the *malum*: where Ortalus' words have not been preserved and are now gone, the apple has been kept, and is only momentarily forgotten by the maiden, whereas Catullus' unmindfulness is at least of long standing.[60]

The two final distichs, then, introduce further problematic correspondences:

> quod miserae oblitae molli sub ueste locatum,
> dum aduentu matris prosilit, excutitur,
> atque illud prono praeceps agitur decursu,
> huic manat tristi conscius ore rubor.

Catullus' forgetting in line 18 is picked up again by *oblitae*, and the "flowing out" of the *dicta* by the "shaking out" (*excutitur*) of the *malum*. The maiden leaping forward to greet her mother has no correlate, unless we

---

[59] Given the maiden's shame and blush, the *sponsus* should not be taken as the maiden's parentally-sanctioned fiancé, as Skinner (2003) 17 and Stevens (2013) 168 argue.

[60] That is, if he has not forgotten his obligation once and for all, he has been remiss in it long enough to count as defaulting on it.

read *forte* in line 18 with *effluxisse* rather than *putes*; in that case, the mother's arrival is the particularization of the unspecified chance event Ortalus suspects. But again, though *molli sub ueste locatum* picks up the maiden's lap in line 20, it does not match the latter's correlate, Catullus' *animus*: the placement of Ortalus' *dicta* in Catullus' mind failed to take.

Or did it? The entire argument of poem 65 is that a chance event *has* prevented the fulfillment of Ortalus' *dicta*; the correlate to the mother's arrival would then be an irrational one, that is, a correlate outside the strictly logical/grammatical external correlate of the simile, which as we have seen is lines 17–18. The mother's arrival would then map onto the brother's departure in death (lines 5–14), which has dislodged Ortalus' words from the poet's now grief-stricken and incapacitated soul (1–4). Of course Ortalus himself has no access to this thought, but as we have seen this presents no serious objection, since in any case it is the grieving Catullus who is here constructing Ortalus' reaction.

This is an attractive (and beautiful) correspondence: we would not be troubled by the disanalogy between a maiden's "leaping forward" to greet her mother and the poet's wavering of mind at his brother's death (*mens animi, tantis fluctuat... malis*, line 4). The similarity between the two kinds of familial and socially appropriate reactions is quite satisfying. The problem is rather that the maiden's blushing shame is left without a good correlate: the maiden is ashamed before her mother not at her failure to fulfill the bond signaled by the love-token, but by the revelation that she has contracted it in the first place. In this she has violated expected norms; unless a go-between is imagined, she has met him in secret and possibly (from the mother's point of view) already lost her virginity to him.

If Ortalus' *dicta* still parallel the apple, then to correlate the maiden's shame at its exposure, Ortalus must now change roles from suitor to mother. This is because, though the maiden may also be ashamed at her failure to keep the suitor's secret, we cannot simply interpret out of existence her shame before her mother.[61] The maiden is now in a deadly serious situation in respect to her parents; even if she in entirely in love with and committed to the suitor, she cannot be indifferent to them. But, once again, Ortalus does not make sense

---

[61] Nor can the brother map onto the mother – he cannot be the person before whom Catullus is ashamed – if the brother's death prevents him fulfilling a promise to *Ortalus*.

as the mother. While Catullus would indeed be ashamed to see him in the forum, and the revelation of the apple could indeed figure the shared knowledge that Ortalus' *dicta* remained unfulfilled, the maiden has engaged in too much reciprocal exchange by the mother's lights, too little by the suitor's; Catullus and Ortalus reflect only the latter sense.

At this point, proponents of construal A have abundant resources with which to mount a defense. They may say that the grammatical and conceptual correspondence between lines 17–18 and 19–20 is so perfect and undeniable as to satisfy readers insisting on one-to-one correspondences; that there are still partial correspondences in what follows, which further enrich the simile; that the points of disanalogy merely reflect what is always the case with similes, just that they all have a terminal point, a final level of similarity after which the likeness breaks down. They will then say that this terminal point is deep enough on their reading. Especially if they point, as Woodman does, to the apparently proverbial untrustworthiness of a maiden's lap, they may understand the point of Catullus' simile as the expression of the deep shame he would feel were he to fall short of Ortalus' reasonable expectations of him.[62] The maiden's shame need not match Catullus' averted shame in its etiology; what is essential is that they would match in their extent. The poet particularizes extreme shame by way of an extremely powerful example of the phenomenon. Finally, they will say that the simile gains further force from its irrational correspondences: we feel the poet's grief in his choice of simile, in the focalized sympathy for the maiden (*miserae*, line 21) and in the shared sense of loss. These need not map one-to-one.

As is already clear from the distance I am keeping from this otherwise sympathetic exposition, I think that this argument is neither wrong on the one hand nor, on the other, sufficient. It would be superfluous for almost half of the poem to be devoted to expressing how deep Catullus' purely hypothetical shame would be. This would be true on its own terms: the sympathy we feel for the maiden is undercut – I would say, betrayed – by the thought that her predicament is merely something Catullus *would* mirror, if he did not have poem 66 lying around. (What a relief!) But the matter is worse: this deep – but fortunately averted – hypothetical shame is just intolerable, I would say, after we have learned how badly Catullus is actually suffering grief. We can understand why someone in the poet's

---

[62] Woodman (2012).

position might protest too much his devotion to Ortalus, but we owe no sympathy to a reading that would suggest, as this one does, any commensurability between the emotional suffering Catullus safely averts and the one he must endure.

Nor should we be satisfied with the mapping of the simile with which this construal leaves us. The suitor's secret gift, the couple's risky and fraught behavior, and the maiden's shame before her mother are not low-level details within the simile, such that their failure to correspond to the external situation is pardonable or expected. Rather, they substantially constitute the state of affairs in the simile, and certainly account for the pathos we feel for the maiden. Nor does the *dicta/malum* correspondence fit adequately. The revelation of the apple contrasts with what *should be* the disappearance or dissolution of the words. The physical description of the apple's fall (21–24) plainly emphasizes its physical presence in the simile; why would the poem do this, if the apple merely represents the (no longer extant) *dicta*? Why pleonastically (*prono praeceps ... decursu*) emphasize its vertically downward trajectory?[63] Another misfit: vain words in Catullus do not "go down," but are diffused in the wind.[64] These difficulties give us more than adequate cause to be dissatisfied with construal A.

Where construal A moves from a close apparent fit (in lines 19–20) to increasing difficulties thereafter, B moves from an initial implausibility to an increased richness on close inspection. As to the former, let us admit the difficulty: even if Catullus does send the verses in the way that a maiden forgetfully allows an apple to emerge, why should he say so? Why tell Ortalus? My answer will also serve as an explanation for the ways in which construal A *does* work: namely, Ortalus is meant to accept A; the deeper resonances afforded by B are for us. The simile is thus a genuine case of dramatic irony.

I reprint the relevant lines:

> sed tamen in tantis maeroribus, Ortale, mitto   15
>   haec expressa tibi carmina Battiadae,
> ne tua dicta uagis nequiquam credita uentis
>   effluxisse meo forte putes animo,

---

[63] On the possibility that the simile is a translation or adaptation from Callimachus' story of Acontius and Cydippe (frr. 67–75), see Johnston (1983), King (1988) 384–85, and Hunter (1993). On my view, the common elements of apple, suitor, and maiden are plainly real, but the Catullan simile is otherwise too poor a match with the Acontius story to take the latter as interpretively central for the former (on this point see Woodman (2012) 150–51). For the referent of the Catullan apple as Catullan poetry, Acontius' *inscribing* of a marital oath on the apple Cydippe *reads* is also helpful.

[64] 30.9–10, 64.139–42, 70.3–4.

ut missum sponsi furtiuo munere malum
    procurrit casto uirginis e gremio,   20
quod miserae oblitae molli sub ueste locatum,
    dum aduentu matris prosilit, excutitur,
atque illud prono praeceps agitur decursu,
    huic manat tristi conscius ore rubor.

On construal B, if the simile at 19–24 has a close and grammatical correlate to the external situation in 15–16, we should find it in the main clause of the simile, 19–20. The remaining distichs might map closely on each other, but need not: the negative purpose clause in 17–18, for instance, is neither the correlate of the simile nor part of the simile itself, but its own third entity. We immediately see that the syntactical correspondences, which we found so isomorphic on A, must be looser on B: the main verb is *procurrit* inside the simile, *mitto* outside of it. Where the poet is the grammatical subject and the verses the direct object in 15–16, the apple is the subject of an intransitive verb of motion in 19–20. On the safe assumption that Catullus cannot map onto the apple and must once again play the maiden (as the person from whom the item comes), the correspondences between the two distichs go as follows:

giver	circumstance	recipient	verb	gift	p.p.p.
[ego]	in tantis maeroribus	Ortale/tibi	mitto	carmina	expressa
uirginis	furtiuo munere?	?	procurrit	malum	missum

Locating the real correlates now in the direct object, now in the intransitive subject leaves the further linguistic correspondences frankly messy, especially by comparison with the perfect matches the rival construal gives. Nonetheless, we once again find a two-part predicate, with a temporally prior perfect participle subordinate to a finite verb implying motion. The recipient, though, is missing at the equivalent point in the simile. The circumstantial phrases also do not match, belonging to the (later) finite verb in the external situation and the (earlier) participial phrase in the simile. And *expressa* in its overt valence ("translated") is far from *mitto* ("send").[65]

What of the conceptual correspondences? The apple maps easily onto the verses, since both are conventional gifts. The switch between Catullus' active "sending" of the poems and the passive and accidental way the apple "runs forward" from the maiden might in fact be the point

---

[65] Note that on either construal the *missum ∼ mitto* correspondence is specious, amounting to misdirection.

of the simile: poem 66 is an accidental gift, one forced by circumstance. This, in turn, makes Ortalus the mother. With what results? The maiden's shame before her mother now can indeed map onto Catullus' shame before Ortalus: Catullus has an obligation to him which he has not met. Poem 66 is not the poem he expected; possibly it is not up to standards *qua* mere translation. But the mother in the simile is not overtly the recipient of a gift; here we would explain that, just as the "running forward" of the apple signals the unintended, accidental nature of the gift, the mother's inevitable confiscation of the love-token figures the manner of Ortalus' (also dissatisfied) receipt of the verses. The mother's arrival would then be some reminder of Catullus' unmet obligation: a letter from Ortalus, politely enquiring how things were coming along, would fit: poem 65 is then a letter of reply. Poems 66–67 would be something Catullus allegedly forgot he had, something brought to light by the arrival of Ortalus' letter. They are nothing to be proud of, but rather something that falls ignominiously to the ground.

As for the suitor, there is indeed another person in the external situation of 15–16, namely Callimachus. How does *he* fit into this drama?

The metaphor of pregnancy, as has been particularly well explored by Fitzgerald, pervades poem 65.[66] The poem begins with it:

> Etsi me assiduo confectum cura dolore
> seuocat a doctis, Ortale, uirginibus,
> nec potis est dulcis Musarum expromere fetus
> mens animi, tantis fluctuat ipsa malis –

Catullus is kept separate from intercourse with the Muses, and his *mens animi* is incapable of bringing forth poetry, their sweet offspring.[67] The metaphor of pregnancy and birth for intellectual "offspring" is a well-established one in Greek culture, as Leitao's recent study has explored.[68] In Plato, to take the most famous example, Socrates' *maieutic* exertions facilitate in the *birthing* of philosophical ideas;[69] here, lack of intercourse with the Muses rules out poetic conception in the poet's mind. Further supporting this reading is Fitzgerald's point that *fluctuat* can be taken as a

---

[66] Fitzgerald (1995) 189–95.
[67] Thomson's (1997) 445 claim that, after mention of *uirgines*, the word *fetus* "has of course practically ceased to be recognizable as a metaphor" is wrong: it is precisely only in the literal sense of *fetus* that *uirgines* do not produce them.
[68] Leitao (2012).   [69] *Theaetetus* 150b–c.

calque on Greek κυεῖ: Catullus' mind "is pregnant" with ills (*tantis ... malis*). The metaphor now moves from parthenogenesis to superfetation: Catullus, separated from intercourse with the Muses, cannot produce their "sweet" offspring, for his mind is already "swelling," namely with ills.[70] Understanding the claim to poetic incapacity as an incapacity to produce *sweet* poems, and recalling the promise always to sing poems made sad by grief, we see that Catullus' situation is perfectly isomorphic with his conceit.

Further strengthening the maternal figuration of Catullus' poetic craft is the fact that the grief-stricken poems he will henceforth sing are illustrated by means of a simile in which the sorrowing songbird is a mother, Procne, mourning her son:

> qualia sub densis ramorum concinit umbris
> Daulias, absumpti fata gemens Ityli –

We then observe that each of the next four distichs can be read through the metaphorical fields of sex, conception, pregnancy, and its possible outcomes:

> sed tamen in tantis maeroribus, Ortale, mitto   15
>   haec expressa tibi carmina Battiadae,
> ne tua dicta uagis nequiquam credita uentis
>   effluxisse meo forte putes animo,
> ut missum sponsi furtiuo munere malum
>   procurrit casto uirginis e gremio,   20
> quod miserae oblitae molli sub ueste locatum,
>   dum aduentu matris prosilit, excutitur,

Each distich implies (at least) two temporal stages: In the first distich, centuries-old verses *have been* translated – pressed out – by Catullus, and are *now* sent to Ortalus. Ortalus' averted thought would be that his *dicta*, intended to produce poetic creation in Catullus' soul, were not retained there but subsequently flowed out. The gift of the apple in the second distich comes from the suitor, and *was* placed in the maiden's lap some time *before* its emergence therefrom; and of course *gremium* also means "womb."[71] The gift under her dress *now*, upon her leaping forth, is dislodged and rolls to the ground.

---

[70] It might also be possible to take *malis*, contrasted with *dulces fetus*, as elliptical for *malis fetibus*: the poems taking shape in the poetic womb are distressed, painful ones.

[71] Adams (1982) 92.

Thus, on construal B, the point of the simile is this: poems 66–67 are a kind of miscarriage.

Ortalus, who is imagined as understanding construal A, in lines 17–18 takes it that his seminal words have been expelled from the Catullan womb: conception did not occur. In fact ἐκροή (from ἐκρέω, calqued by *effluuium* and *effluo*) is medical Greek for the expulsion of sperm from an atonic uterus; Soranus, distinguishing this phenomenon from ἔκτρωσις (early-term miscarriage) and ὠμοτοκία (late-term miscarriage or stillbirth), specifies that the former takes place within three days of intercourse.[72] We also find *effluo* used either in this sense or of miscarriage in Pliny (*Nat.* 20.76).

But in fact what has occurred is slightly different. Taking 19–20 to illustrate 15–16, as construal B requires, correlates the earlier sending of the apple with Catullus' pressing out of the verses of Callimachus; the running forth of the apple matches the sending of the verses. The following distich (21–22) then runs back over the same ground: the apple's earlier placement under the dress provides a further spatial specification of its sending; now, as the girl leaps forward, it is dislodged.

The notion that vigorous physical motion can induce miscarriage, whether by accident or intentionally, may well be universal or nearly so in human cultures; in antiquity, it is famously attested in the Hippocratic corpus (*Nat. Puer.* 13). In this passage a physician advises a pregnant woman to jump repeatedly, striking her heel against her buttocks while in the air; the fetus is then expelled, to the woman's wonder, and subsequently examined by the physician. A further helpful parallel is that *excutio* is attested several times in precisely the context of abortion, notably in Ovid; it may even be a *uox propria*.[73]

The final distich then contrasts the consequences of the dislodging for the "fetus" and the maiden: the former is driven straight down; the latter, her secret discovered, blushes. The "irrational" correspondence of the Lethe's "spreading wave" lapping the "pale foot" of the brother (5–8) is undeniable: the blush/blood spreading to/through the girl's face betokens life, and both it and *conscius* betoken remembrance, while the waters of

---

[72] Soranus, *Gyn.* 3.47.2: ἐκρεῖ γὰρ μετὰ τὴν συνουσίαν αἷς μὲν εὐθύς, αἷς δὲ μετὰ ἡμέρας τινὰς ὀλίγως | βράδιον, αἷς δὲ καὶ διατυπωθέν, ἄλλαις δὲ καὶ νεκρωθὲν ἢ παντελῶς ἄτροφον καὶ τοῖς χρόνοις ἐλλιπές, ὥστε γίνεσθαι ποτὲ μὲν ἔκροιαν, ποτὲ δὲ ἔκτρωσιν, ποτὲ δὲ ὠμοτοκίαν. 'ἔκροια' μὲν οὖν ἐστιν ἀπόπτυσμὸς τοῦ σπέρματος μετὰ τὴν συνουσίαν μετὰ πρώτην ἢ δευτέραν ⟨ἢ τρίτην⟩ ἡμέραν, 'ἔκτρωσις' δὲ ἡ μετὰ δεύτερον ἢ τρίτον μῆνα φθορὰ τοῦ ἐμβρύου, 'ὠμοτοκία' δὲ ἡ σύνεγγυς τῆς τελειώσεως πρὸ ὥρας ἀπότεξις ...

[73] Ovid, *Fasti* 1.624 and *Heroides* 11.42. Scribonius Largus' term for abortifacient (*Comp. praef.* 5) is *medicamentum quo conceptum excutitur*.

Lethe and the pale foot betoken death and oblivion. Within the metaphor, we note, there is also the demise of kin.

Answers now suggest themselves. How does Callimachus map onto the suitor in the simile, and the father in the metaphorical conceit it contains? He is suitor in that Catullus' translations/adaptations are not truly poetic offspring, but a proxy or simulacrum of the same, just as the suitor's gift to his absent and closely supervised beloved is an erotic proxy, and just as the sparrow in poem 2 had been a proxy for the way in which erotic *desiderium* is remedied. Callimachus is a "father" in that Catullus' ersatz gestation of his verses brings forth Latinate likenesses of them. So too had the maiden placed the erotic proxy in her *gremium*, an ersatz but homonymous womb. The adjective *casto* in line 20 now pointedly indicates the proxy: either "her *gremium*, in the innocent sense" or "her untouched *gremium*, which cannot really conceive and foster." The intended "fruit" of the suitor's gift was marriage; upon its dislodging, that expectation or hope has now miscarried.

Catullus tells us that he had previously translated/adapted these verses, pressing them out in pseudo-parturition. The verses were not a secret gift from Callimachus, but Catullus' translation of them had been a *furtiuum munus* just the same: a secret "act" or "performance" or "work," a private exercise. He had forgotten he had them; now a reminder of his obligation arrives; Ortalus maps onto the mother in this respect. Catullus' "leap forward" is his instant recognition of his need to fulfill his obligation to Ortalus; the inadequate, shameful, untimely, and counterfeit creation now comes to light, to neither party's satisfaction.

Finally, it is crucial to see that on construal B as well, the brother suggests himself as an irrational correspondence, providing a further, and deeply moving, resonance. For he too is a family member before whom the emergence of the gift constitutes a breach of obligation. Catullus owes the brother, and duly promises him, "songs made sad by [his] death." The inadequate fulfillment of obligation to Ortalus constitutes a positive violation of obligation to the brother; these poems and their frivolous fictions are a source of the poet's shame before the memory of a brother whose death is a hard reality.

Two further points are now essential. First, for Catullus to frame 66–67 as untimely juvenilia deserves no more claim on our belief than the equivalent claim that he wrote poem 51, and then 50 to cover it, the day after playing in his tablets with Calvus. In this case, indeed, there is probably a greater degree of insincerity or artifice: where we should indeed inspect poem 51 as a poem made to show Catullus' "pain" to Calvus, in respect to 66–67 it is a live interpretive option to reject the characterization entirely, as no more credible than a reciting poet's protestation that his verses have not yet received their *ultima manus*.[74] These are not Catullus' first insincere self-depreciating verses, nor is this his first insincere self-depreciating book-initial poem. Yet where we *can* take the simile literally is on the matter of relative depicted chronology: the poet composing poem 65 cannot now produce such poetry as this, because his brother has died; but he had already produced 66–67.

Finally, any reader confronting a simile this rich and challenging in the opening poem of a book will be well advised to consider its programmatic implications for the book as a whole. I will indeed claim that the entire elegiac book is colored by this dynamic: the poetry of 65–116 is, in a surprisingly robust sense, almost entirely constituted by the conflicting recompense (of gratitude or of retribution) it contemplates. As many readers have thought, the more anguished tone of the epigrams, for instance, is indeed indebted to the brother; but these poems violate the promise of 65.11–12 as well. We will also see, looking back at the end, that Catullus' moral standing in respect to his brother may well be even worse; it is not entirely inert that the first simile of poem 65 makes of Catullus a sorrowing songbird mourning over a death of which she is not innocent.

Poems 68a and 68b: The Gifts of the Muses and of Venus

It would be foolish to deny that 68a is a difficult text; if Syme's character-ization of Catullan studies as "that imbroglio of problems ... where argument moves in circles, and no new passage in or out" is anywhere apt, it is here.[75] It is nonetheless my contention that some of its notorious problems are idiopathic: as with the Sapphic–Catullan speakers gazing at their beloveds, some of the obscurity and pain inhere in the scholarly gaze rather than the poem. To take the clearest example: against the identity of the addressees of 68a and 68b it is often claimed that the former has no beloved, while the latter enjoys untroubled bliss with his beloved. But this claim is so obviously without merit that its persistence is hard to explain. In

---

[74] Since poem-recipients are also familiar with this sort of rhetoric, we may also imagine that Ortalus is himself prepared for the careful reading which leads to construal B. In that case, rather than dramatic irony, such that Ortalus goes for A but *we* understand B, a better characterization might be plausible deniability: if Ortalus is too foolish to appreciate the deeper beauty of B, he can have A. Or, indeed, if he does see B, the represented Catullus might have thought, he is probably the sort of reader who will appreciate its beauty.

[75] Syme (1956) 131.

fact the addressee in 68b and his love interest are merely *wished* felicity, not said to enjoy it: *sitis felices et tu simul et tua uita* (155). The addressee in 68a does not enjoy felicity with a beloved; rather, his love interest has left him: he does not merely lie "in a bachelor's bed," but "*abandoned* in a bachelor's bed" (*desertum*, 6). Nor is it possible to claim that Catullus could not refer to the lover who has abandoned his friend as his friend's *uita*: poem 104 addresses itself to an unnamed party who presumed that Catullus would "curse" Lesbia. The sole reasonable grounds for this presumption is obviously her estrangement from Catullus, yet 104.1 runs: *credis me potuisse meae maledicere uitae?* The matter is quite clear: at the end of 68b, Catullus' benediction of Mallius/Allius and his beloved is perfectly congruent with the assumption of their current estrangement, which the beginning of 68a indicates. There is not the slightest case against the identification to be found here.

But the principal difficulty is this: for what does Mallius ask Catullus? Are "the gift(s) of Venus and the Muses" one sort of thing, namely love poetry, or two sorts of things, namely love *and* poetry (or love poetry and "learned" poetry)? And if "love" is requested separately, how does this cash out? Is Catullus asked to arrange a relationship for his friend, or is he asked to *be* the love interest, to gratify his friend personally? I take it to be an ineliminable and interpretively controlling fact about this poem that it is hard to say what is going on: a solution to this problem will not – must not – make us forget that it was won only with difficulty.

The solution(s) I will offer take guidance from two points: first, the corresponding situation in poem 50,[76] and second, the extraordinary amount of data the poem provides. We are meant to use this data to reconstruct the content of the epistle to which 68a is the dramatized reply.

Except for *id gratumst mihi* on line 9, the first ten lines of the poem are entirely expository, conveying the content of Mallius' epistle, which I reconstruct here as Catullus' text allows or even encourages its reader to. I will then offer Catullus' reply, likewise with its rhetoric laid bare.

The letter Mallius writes to Catullus is, Catullus tells us, tear-stained and miserable. Mallius writes that he is suffering terrible fortune (68.1–2); a shipwreck has washed him up on the shore at the point of death, and he begs Catullus to rescue him (3–4). Mallius can't get to sleep (he shows himself a learned reader of poem 50), deprived of sex [=*Venus*, Mallius' word] since his lover abandoned their bed (5–6), and poetry [=*Musae*, also

---

[76] I will go so far as to say that Mallius flatters his correspondent by showing that he has read and deeply understood the rhetoric of **A**.

his word], or at least the available poetry on hand, does not help, such is his nocturnal anxiety (7–8; this anticipates the obvious possible reply from Catullus: Mallius wants *new* poetry). He calls upon Catullus as his friend and as someone obliged to him by the bond of *hospitium* (9, 12; with tasteful obliqueness: "you owe me"). In fact, it is shameful for Catullus to be in Verona when (never mind Mallius' personal distress) all of the best gentlemen these days are sleeping in empty beds themselves (27–29). Catullus can help (perhaps by returning in person and thus providing the gifts of Venus? – or if not, he can help from *afar*) by bestowing the gifts of (Venus and) the Muses, that is, by sending poetry (10).

That chronic insomnia is Mallius' sustained figure for his distress is indicated by the repetition of the theme in lines 5 (*molli requiescere somno*) and 8 (*cum mens anxia peruigilat*). This figure ties in to the themes of sex (or "Venus") and poetry (or "Muses"), and also provides a medical correlate cashing out the rhetoric of mortal danger and the shipwreck figure of the first four lines. Poetry is here understood in a medicinal sense: lack of satisfying sex is the cause of Mallius' condition, and his attempted palliative treatment of it with the old poetry on hand has failed. The words *amicum* and *hospitis* invite us to see the polite reminder of social obligation in Mallius' letter; presumably this will have been quite oblique (even if Catullus is not at all polite in poem 38). My reconstruction of the information given at 27–29 locates the simplest possible link between Mallius' request proper and his appeal to "all the best people"; his chance of persuading Catullus is greater the more he can show that many people (rhetorically, *all* people) Catullus is socially tied to are also in need.[77] My interpretation of line 29 is controversial; others understand "warming their cold limbs [erotically] in a bed [namely Lesbia's] abandoned [by you]," but I take this to be tactless, poorly motivated, and to raise more problems than it solves.[78] The phrase rather means "warming their cold limbs [as one does in a bed, even when alone] in a bed abandoned [by the respective love interest of each]."

The question of Catullus' *location* is clearly important, and clearly relates to "gifts of Venus" more closely than "gifts of the Muses"; it is possible but underdetermined that the request for "love" either requires or simply *is* the request for his presence; my disjunctive reconstruction hedges on this. Finally, the request itself will have flattered Catullus by emphasizing how

[77] So we take *turpe* as presumably marking a fairly breathless hyperbole, intended to be taken as such.
[78] This construal is favored, though hesitantly, by Quinn (1973) 378; its implausible tactlessness is pointed out by Skinner (2003) 147.

well positioned he is in respect to it (as in a hymnic *namque potes*): "you are particularly loved by Venus and the Muses" at once calls him a talented poet and storied lover (and possibly also "charming," as in *uenustus*). This expansion is admittedly not explicit, but the last two lines of the poem make clear that Mallius thinks Catullus to have a "line of credit" with Venus and the Muses; it would fit nicely for him to have said so.

Naturally, different readers would fill out Mallius' letter and its rhetoric in different ways; most important for me here is the claim that an account with this much detail is easily and plausibly extracted from the poem, as well as the claim that the differentiation of "Venus" and "the Muses" – whatever exactly it means – is owed to Mallius.

Now we see the reply. Catullus responds that he appreciates Mallius' situation and has not forgotten his request; unfortunately, he is in the same sorry state, only worse – surely Mallius would not have made this request if he had known (9–14). As to the gifts of the goddesses, he goes on to say, Venus did bless him abundantly in his youth (15–18), but the death of his brother has put an end to that, and to every other pleasure in his life (19–26). Mallius' claim that it is "shameful" for Catullus to be in Verona under the circumstances is therefore wrong; it's a "wretched" coincidence; Catullus trusts that Mallius will understand if he is unable to give the requested gifts (27–30). Neither can the Muses be much help: Catullus barely has any library in Verona, since he lives in Rome, and he currently has only one box of rolls at his disposal (33–36). Therefore he asks Mallius not to think him ill-disposed or dishonest because he falls short of the request (which Mallius had assumed him capable of carrying out); if he could help, he would (37–40).

If Mallius' reconstructed letter can leave underdetermined what is meant by the differentiation of "Venus" and the "Muses," so can Catullus' reply; he is picking up on his correspondent's distinction and dealing with each part in turn. Mallius' letter may have requested love poetry by way of the hendiadys "gifts of Venus and the Muses," which the letter itself unpacks into its constituent parts: the evidence is consistent with the assumption that he is rhetorically/poetically competent to craft so sophisticated a conceit.[79] Catullus' answer would then meet his rhetoric on its own terms: "I have no access now to Venus [= the 'love' and 'charm' (*uenustas*) in charming love poetry], and anyway I'm at a loss in terms of the 'poetry' part itself: my library isn't with me here." The standard objection to the reading of "the

---

[79] It is also prima facie more plausible to assume that Catullus invites us to think hard about a competent and interesting epistle to him than a pedestrian and boring one.

gifts of Venus and of the Muses" as hendiadys is that Catullus pointedly separates his refusal into two parts, corresponding to either genitive. This reconstruction, I submit, meets this objection by showing that the differentiation is Mallius', and that he might plausibly have differentiated the two in a rhetorical rather than substantive way; Catullus will have merely followed his lead.

This reading is helpful in respect to the language suggesting literary activity in Catullus' account of his estrangement from Venus;[80] it might be problematic in its relative difficulty in explaining lines 27–29, the "wickedness" of Catullus' absence from Rome. This point makes clear sense if we strongly differentiate Venus and the Muses. If Mallius' request for "gifts of Venus" requires or just is the request for Catullus' social presence in Rome, the rhetoric of Catullus' refusal is to deny the inference: of course Catullus could come to Rome, but in his grief he has lost his access to Venus (whatever that means: he is incapable or uninterested in sex? his company has lost its charm?), and so his presence would not in fact amount to "bestowing the gifts of Venus." If, however, the gift is really *one* gift, that of love poetry, it will require more ingenuity to reconstruct the rhetoric of Mallius' reference to Catullus' absence from Rome. I therefore understand that Mallius' letter called Catullus' absence wicked on the grounds that everyone who was anyone was at Rome, bereft of love and in need of Catullus' presence. But, Mallius would have stipulated, if fortune or duty must keep Catullus so far from his ailing friends, then Catullus must do what he still could, namely relieve their suffering with the gifts of Venus and the Muses.

The problem is not in any implausibility, but rather the suspicion – as a plausible hermeneutic rule of thumb – that the glimpses of Mallius' letter ought to be interpretively sufficient for our purposes. This reconstruction might well multiply entities beyond what is suggested by our textual indications.

I will now explore the implications of the contrary reading, namely that the differentiation of the goddesses is a more substantive one. On this reading we assume that Catullus' return to Rome is a necessary condition for his giving the "gifts of Venus"; the other request will of course be a request for poetry. Now, reading 68a against 65 encourages the view, as the consensus of the literature reflects, that Catullus treats Ortalus with far

---

[80] Skinner (2003): *studia, lusi*; if Catullus only means that he pursued many bedmates in his youth, and not at all that he wrote erotic poetry, the consistency of *studia* especially with literary pursuits amounts to positive misdirection on the poet's part.

more deference: he seems to be Catullus' social superior, where Mallius is rather his equal. This raises a problem for the two-request theory: "please do these two things for me: come back to Rome [and possibly more], *and* write me a learned poem." Neither is a small request to make of a Roman gentleman; is there anyone who can ask Catullus to make two large interventions in his life at the same time?

I think not; but even if *someone* could, Mallius does not seem to fit the bill. To rescue the two-request theory, then, we should either make the two requests formally disjunctive (either Catullus' presence or a poem), or at least make the former, which might not be fulfilled for some time, a kind of flattering foil for the more immediate latter request ("Catullus, please, as soon as you can, come back, *tout le monde* is dying for your return! And in the meantime, if there's any way you could write me a small piece . . . ").

Both this consideration and, in a different way, the crucial example of poem 50 tell against a strong version of the two-request theory. Because Mallius can hardly order Catullus around like this, the two requests ought to be literally or virtually disjunctive; further, Catullus' own rhetoric of erotic pining after a poet's presence has the tendency of folding the poet's erotic appeal into his *poetic* appeal – not to mention that it tends to render the erotic pining itself poetic, and as such decidedly nonliteral. All of these considerations point in the same direction: we cannot rule out a sophisticated, self-problematized hendiadys on Mallius' part; Mallius cannot reasonably ask Catullus to scurry right back to Rome, gift-poem in hand; and Mallius-the-reader's self-accrediting and addressee-flattering appropriation of Catullus' book-final conceit in poem 50 shows precisely his literary awareness and orientation. Besides these, the medical figure in lines 5–8 points to a disjunctive request: Mallius the erotic insomniac needs sleep, and though he may imagine two Catullan remedies, he only needs one of them: either Catullus' return will gratify him,[81] or the receipt of new love poetry will serve as the sleeping pill he needs, since the old stuff no longer works for him. One way or another, the independent "gifts of Venus" in 68a look less and less substantive and more and more assimilated into the poetry, the "gifts of the Muses."

There is a further gain to be made from this reading. If we see Catullus mechanically and unimaginatively picking up on his correspondent's (sophisticated) poetic figure, answering him *literally* in an all-too-businesslike, point-

---

[81] I take it that a literal understanding, by which an adult Catullus is requested to return to Rome and sexually gratify another adult male, is deeply incompatible with contemporary understanding of sexuality in Roman culture. See Most (1981) and Skinner (2003).

by-point rebuttal, we have a fascinating self-demonstration of the predicament 68a asserts its author to be in. This is internally resonant for Catullus: like the outrageous self-refutation of poem 16 and environs, this one too focalizes the problem of the relation between a poet's life and art. And then, it accounts for the highly prosaic texture of 68a, which is well known and much remarked on.[82] Supposing that the poet here, as in 14b–26, is interested in pursuing a poetics at variance with his usual practice, with his speaker's voice *in propria persona*. This needs proper metapoetic signaling (there, the Saturnalian inversion of 1–14, revenge for Calvus' invective gift; here, obviously, the death of the brother), but it also needs a positive artistic payoff. For 14b–26, we located this payoff in the sophisticated commentary on the poetics of self-contradiction; what is it here? I submit that the richness of the reconstructed dialogue is at least an important component: this prosy epistle allows us surprisingly rich access to a highly poetic fan-letter; then too, once we see the congruence between Catullus' rhetorical goals in 68a and his artistically hobbled persona, we have a further layer of poeticity in the following question: should we attribute the leadenness of 68a to the brother's death, or to (the represented) Catullus' knowledge that the competent reader Mallius would spot the good poetry of a self-contradicting *recusatio*?[83]

But the most important achievement of 68a must still be the metapoetic framing of 68b. Before turning to my reading of this, on which the composition of 68b is later than the sending of 68a, another hard choice on a difficult problem is required. The final distich runs:

> quod tibi non utriusque petenti copia postast:
> ultro ego deferrem, copia siqua foret.   40

I take it that Catullus is refusing both requests: "though you seek either [kind of gift], a supply of them has not been put at your disposal." If this means, "though you seek both, it is not a supply of *both* that is put at your disposal," then 68b must follow immediately. Objections to this are various and serious.[84]

---

[82] E.g. Kinsey (1967), Tuplin (1981).

[83] To the question of why poem 65 is not just as leaden, we may answer that Ortalus does indeed get his poems along with the introductory epistle (self-deprecating framing notwithstanding).

[84] Catullus has already assured himself that Mallius will pardon his inability to produce gifts of Venus (31–32); he need not now apologize again, if he is providing the other gift (of the Muses). By contrast, the stronger reaction he fears from Mallius, namely imputing active hostility or mendacity to Catullus (*mente maligna . . . aut animo non satis ingenuo*, 37–38) is better motivated if Catullus finds himself having to say no twice. The contrast between the prosaicness of 68a and the (hyper) poeticism of 68b is also solved on my reading and left obscure on this one.

These are the logical possibilities on the relationship between 68a and 68b and their addressees: (1) they are unrelated, two poems sent to two separate men; (2) the addressees are different, but Catullus sends Mallius a poem addressed to Allius; (3) the addressees are the same. I will now argue that 68b picks up 68a so thoroughly that (1) is scarcely thinkable and (2) would be utterly strange, leaving (3) easily the best option. Within this option, the textual proposal on which the corrupt manuscript readings conceal *mi Alli* at 68.11 and 30 is indeed implausible, as is the hypothetical "Mallius Allius" with two *gentilicia*; the best solution will be *Allius* as pseudonym (explained by the ill repute of his service to Catullus), with the elision in the first line (*qua m'Allius in re*, 41) giving the game away.

Given how numerous, extensive, and familiar these points of contact are, they seem to me best presented as list rather than connected exposition.[85] Aside from the similarity of the name itself, we find:

1) The *recusatio* of 68a is picked up in the framing lines of 68b. In its first line, the impossibility of Catullan composition in 68a has become the impossibility of his *not* composing (*non possum reticere, deae . . .*, 41), while at its end, the cause of that same incapacity in 68a is now the explanation for why 68b is the sort of poem it is (*hoc tibi, quod potui*, 149).

2) The conceit of "Venus and the Muses" in 68a is picked up immediately, with the Muses the initial addressees of 68b (*deae*), explicitly reminded of the *cura* previously given to Catullus by Venus (*quam dederit duplex Amathusia curam | scitis* 51–52). This prior *cura* in turn recalls Catullus' reference to the same in 68a (17–18).

3) Mallius/Allius is wished the felicity with his *uita* (155) that he does not currently enjoy (5–6), as argued above.

4) The cryptic reference of *hospitis officium* (12) is revealed: Mallius provided the *domus* in which Catullus and Lesbia made love.

5) The brother's death reappears as a central explanatory fact (19–26, 91–100). As is well known and puzzling, this reappearance is partially *verbatim* (22–24 = 94–96). Here too I think the later composition of 68b provides a good explanation: the verbatim repetition underscores the message that Catullus' persistent grief continues to inflect his poetry, where earlier it precluded it.[86] Taking 68a as the cover letter for an already composed 68b, by contrast, leaves us with an author composing

---

[85] I omit what appear to be less structurally crucial correspondences, such as the metaphor of shipwreck (2–3 ~ 63–66).

[86] Note that Catullus' ability to compose is not in question in the repeated lines.

stilted prosy verse as introduction to figuratively extravagant verse, who must also, for some reason, borrow from the latter to fill out the former.

6)   The *una … capsula* at Catullus' disposal in Verona (36) is almost certainly a hint about the generic model for 68b.[87] The point makes for such an oddly specific detail: nicely appropriate for the grief-dulled unpoetic mind of the represented Catullus in 68a, and hardly thinkable otherwise, it makes for a brilliantly ludic challenge to the reader. Note too the further responsion with poems 50/51: an introductory piece focusing on poetic "pining" between men, followed by a poignant Catullus/Lesbia poem (complete with moralizing epilogue).

7)   Mallius' figuratively medical complaint in 68a (5–8) and the similarity in circumstance between him and Catullus (both estranged from love, 5–6 ~ 19–26; both "tossed" on the waves, 3–4 ~ 11–14), are useful to think with in terms of the gift that poem 68b is. If I am right that the conclusion of 68b dramatizes the occurrent reawakening of the composing poet's desire for Lesbia, with his *amor* guiding his reasoning through his own bevy/covey of exemplary images, several results follow. For one, the later poem then dramatizes Catullus' return to love in 68b, after the depth of his grief in 68a has abated. And then, Mallius' complaint had foreseen poetry as a medical proxy for the literal sex that might cure his insomnia; given his own response to his own poetic creation, Catullus has good grounds to think his gift will help. Poem 68b might well be different from what Mallius had envisioned, but it is credibly taken as what the patient ordered.[88]

Poems 68a and 68b: All Together Now

I have now presented the case and believe I am entitled to conclude that the non-elegiac and elegiac Catullan long poems form two complementary pairs. We have seen that **C1** consists in two dramas of poetic gift-exchange, one to Ortalus (65–67), the other to Mallius (68a–b). The length of these is almost identical, and each has in its addressee an internal principle of unity.

---

[87] Lefèvre (1991).

[88] Recall also that literary poisons in poems 14 and 44 "sicken" and "kill"; 16.9–11 explicitly claims (though the Catullan speaker, as I have argued, is particularly untrustworthy there) that his verses provoke sexual arousal. I am not claiming that Mallius solely believes that his sympathetic reaction to the erotic verse will help him: *mens anxia peruigilat* (8) is compatible with supposing that the exercise of thinking through learned poetry will settle his troubled mind. But I think he means this part too. The widespread contemporary presumption that "respectable" and "titillating" art (or merely "pornography") are logically exclusive categories cannot be assumed valid for Catullus.

There are two verbal recollections unmistakably tying the beginning and end of this sequence:

> ut missum sponsi **furtiuo munere** malum   65.19
>   procurrit casto uirginis e **gremio,**

> sed **furtiua** dedit mira **munuscula** nocte,   68.145
>   ipsius ex ipso dempta uiri **gremio.**

and

> etsi me assiduo **confectum** cura dolore   65.1
>   seuocat a doctis, Ortale, uirginibus
> **nec potis est** dulcis **Musarum** expromere **fetus**

> Hoc tibi, quod **potui, confectum carmine** munus   68.149
>   pro multis, Alli, redditur officiis.

The two reminiscences effect dissonant emotional movements: the circumstances of Lesbia's "secret gifts" are troubling where the maiden's in poem 65 are far more innocent. With the completion of 68b, however, Catullus has poetically prevailed over the incapacity imposed by his grief – though even here, the persistent effects of that grief are stressed (*quod potui*).

Though this is surely sufficient, the far richer set of reminiscences at this point are to the terminal points of **B**. The epilogue of poem 64 is formally similar to that of 68b, whose beginning was just quoted (149–60); in addition to the poem-final *lumine claro* (64.408) matching *lux mea* in the final line of 68b (160), there is this matching reference to the gods and the blessings they formerly bestowed on the pious:

> praesentes namque ante **domos** inuisere castas   64.384
> heroum, et sese mortali ostendere coetu,
> **caelicolae** nondum spreta **pietate solebant.**

> huc addent diui quam plurima, quae **Themis** olim   68.153
>   antiquis **solita est** munera ferre **piis.**
> sitis felices et tu simul et tua uita
>   et **domus** <ipsa> in qua lusimus et domina,

Themis at 68.153 is also closely recalled by *Ramnusia uirgo*, Nemesis, a few lines later, at 64.395. Yet the richest set of reminiscences at the end of 68b looks even farther back: to poem 61, and to the opening and final Lesbia poems of **A**.

It is not hard to see why this should be so. Those reading **A**, **B**, and now **C1** in sequence come to this passage loaded with the sum of all the marriage and Lesbia contexts they have seen; just as **A** returned our focus to Lesbia with its final poem, so does the complementary dyad of **B/C1**. And that dyad had also presented multiple iterations of the same basic pattern, inflected one final time here in 68b. We first read of the wedding of Manlius Torquatus and his bride, her entry to his house, the cutting away of the narrative scene just before the couple's consummation, as the poet-speaker commands the maidens to close the door of the bridal chamber (61.224). In poem 62 another wedding, *deductio*, and consummation await. Skipping the problem case of 63 for brevity, in poem 64 there are three such scenes: the wedding of Peleus and Thetis, the premarital consummation between Ariadne and Theseus just before her abandonment by the gallant hero (implied at 147–48), and her imminent rescue by and consummation with Bacchus (251–65). Turning to 65, the fall of the apple from the maiden's lap now threatens to preempt the consummation of her love (unless it betokens an earlier, illicit consummation); the Lock in 66 recalls the marriage and consummation of her mistress and Ptolemy (13–18), and indeed boldly demands cultic offerings by brides before their own marital consummations (79–83), while the Brixian marriage in 67 was perversely consummated not by the husband but by the father-in-law.

And so we come to Catullus and Mallius. Poem 68a now recalls Catullus' initiation into sexual life, upon taking up the *toga uirilis* (68.15–18). This is followed by 68b: another woman enters another house and makes love to another man – to Catullus, finally. We are entitled now to presume on the sequence for hints; put another way, there are questions the sequence raises so often and so consistently that we cannot reasonably fail to pose them to ourselves.

Comment on poem 68(b) rarely fails to be embarrassed by Allius' favor: is this not sordid, and is it not actually a fairly trivial favor, unworthy of the elaborate thanks the poem renders? This problem has a solution; we find it by heeding the hints posed by the sequence. Catullus has now lost his brother; the moment of eros he commemorates in 68b can only be pluperfect in relation to the brother's death. As his grief ebbs enough to permit his return to love and to poetry, his thoughts naturally return to the object of his greatest love and his greatest poetry. After composing all of these scenes of consummation, not all of them strictly marital, what moment with Lesbia would come so naturally to his mind? What memory would return him so effectively from grief (which is a form of love, as 65.11–14 insists, but love defined by death) to erotic love, likened in its first appearance in **A** (poem 5) to life itself? What memory could flood his mind with such *amor* as to match the mythological *exemplum* he thinks with, that of Laodamia, who, having experienced her husband sexually – *once* – could never overcome her loss? Catullus' gift to Mallius/Allius is the memory of his adulterous consummation with Lesbia, which his friend made possible.

Moreover, it is highly likely that Catullus had already given MALlius a gift commemorating his – MANlius' – joyful consummation, with social and divine sanction, in poem 61.[89] And the two consummations take place *in the same house*. The implications are serious, if not shockingly maudlin. Catullus' long poems return to where they began; in a sense they go nowhere, except from other people's marriages to his own adultery. If the temporal order of **A** and **B** tracks the sequence, (the represented) Catullus himself performed the real-time narrative of the moments just before his friend's marital consummation (poem 61), in the same place he had already consummated his affair with his great love. Poem 68b brings readers back to this house for the second time, and brings Catullus back for a third time.

All this is complicated by Mallius' erotic troubles in 68a, after his marriage in 61. Recall that he is sleepless, deserted, in a bachelor's bed: *desertum in lecto caelibe*. Has he divorced or been widowed? Or is the marriage troubled? A suspiciously close parallel encourages us not to suppose the marriage celebrated in 61 is over:

> et tu non **orbum** luxti **deserta cubile,**   66.21
> sed fratris cari flebile discidium?

The speaker is the Lock, apostrophizing Berenice about her grief upon separation from her newlywed husband Ptolemy. If Berenice can be "abandoned" by a legal husband who is merely temporarily abroad, and if her bed in such a circumstance can be *orbum* – which might prima facie imply the death of her spouse – then Mallius can also be "abandoned" in a "bachelor bed" *qua* one temporarily emptied of his spouse. Mallius is temporarily bachelorized by marital discord, the possibility of which is repeatedly mentioned in Catullus: denied toward the end of poem 64, ordered not to occur in 66, clearly instantiated in 67, and recurring *passim* in 61 itself.[90] This in turn gives extraordinary point to Mallius' complaint:

---

[89] Feeney's (2010) 214 lucid and concise argument for this identification deserves to be quoted here: "Catullus addresses an epithalamium to a member of the Manlii Torquati ('Mallius' or 'Manlius', 61.16, 215; 'Torquatus', 61.209) ... The frequent spelling of 'Manlius' as 'Mallius' in the manuscripts of 61 reflects the common pronunciation of 'Manlius' as far back as Republican times, and 'Mallius' is also the name behind the tangle of manuscript attestations for the addressee of 68a. 68a, then, will be addressed to the same man. The pronunciation of his name as 'Mallius' is needed to effect the trick whereby the 'Mallius/Manlius' of 68a becomes the 'Allius' of 68b: in the first line of 68b, *non possum reticere, deae, qua me Allius in re | iuuerit* (68.41–2), the elision of *me* and *Allius* produces, precisely, *Mallius.*"

[90] 64.37–80, 66.87–88, 61.97–101, 134–48, cf. 214–28.

> quem neque sancta Venus molli requiescere somno   68.5
>   desertum in lecto caelibe perpetitur,
> nec ueterum dulci scriptorum carmine Musae
>   oblectant, cum mens anxia peruigilat:

For we know of a "sweet poem of old writing" in Mallius' possession, a love poem, the only sustained sexual narrative in Catullus, and arguably the only sexual scene at all that is at once *lepidus* and *uenustus*, non-abusive and non-invective, yet still frank and descriptive. And this poem is and always was his; in his anxiety, though, he understandably cannot turn to it for relief.[91]

Mallius will, however, recognize the older poem in the new one, in ways that go beyond the adaptation of the common plot in the common place. Lesbia's arrival and embrace is attended by a god whom Mallius will recall:

> aut nihil aut paulo qui tum concedere digna   68.131
>   lux mea se nostrum contulit in gremium,
> quam circumcursans hinc illinc saepe **Cupido**
>   **fulgebat crocina candidus** in **tunica**.

> **flammeum** cape laetus [*sc. Hymen*] huc   61.8
> huc ueni, **niueo** gerens
>   **luteum** pede **soccum**;

The god of love is resplendent, "white in a yellow tunic," the same contrast in skin and garment color displayed by the god of marriage in 61. Just after this distich, though, Catullus begins to think through his situation, resolving to endure Lesbia's infidelities patiently. This, of course, poses a problem:

> atqui nec **diuis homines componier** aequumst,   68.141
>   ingratum **tremuli** tolle **parentis** onus.

The archaizing passive infinitive ending in *componier* is paralleled in Catullus only in poem 61: *se citarier* (42, the god summoned to the wedding) and the refrain *quis huic deo | compararier ausit?* (64–65, 69–70, 74–75). Poem 61 also says of Hymen that *homines* (48) pay more honor to no other god's cult, and

---

[91] 68.68–69 (*isque domum nobis, isque dedit dominae | ad quam communes exerceremus amores*) is a recognized problem. It is objected, perhaps not persuasively, that *communes* cannot mean "common to my *domina* and to me." But with 68b written for the same person and set in the same house as 61, we may well hear: "He [M/Allius] provided a house to me and my mistress, for us to practice in it the amatory activities shared [by him as well]." Supporting this would be that *exercete iuuentam* are the closing words of 61, where this means "have frequent sex," and that poem 61 (which will have been set after the dramatic time of the consummation with Lesbia recalled in 68b) mentions Manlius' premarital sexual experiences, pronouncing them acceptable then but now to be set aside (139–41).

the *tremulus parens* invokes him in prayer on behalf of his children (51). The god's powers are enumerated in each of the stanzas ending in the refrain above, in ways that can only sting in Catullus' rehearing: without *Hymen*, *Venus* is of ill repute, the *domus* cannot produce legitimate children, the *parens* cannot rely on the continuity of his bloodline, and the *terra* cannot defend its borders. Catullus now acknowledges, and draws a remarkable conclusion from, the distance between his reality and that of poem 61:

> nec tamen illa mihi dextra deducta paterna
> fragrantem Assyrio uenit odore domum,
> sed furtiua **dedit** mira **munuscula** nocte,   145
> ipsius ex ipso **dempta** uiri **gremio**.
> quare **illud satis** est, si nobis is datur unis,
> quem lapide illa diem candidiore notat.

After reading the acknowledgment that Lesbia is not Catullus' wife (143–44), Mallius recognizes another of the marriage god's functions from 61, bitterly inverted:

> tu fero iuueni in manus
> floridam ipse puellulam
> **dedis** a **gremio** suae
> **matris**, o Hymenaee Hymen,
> o Hymen Hymenaee.   60

Catullus' conclusion, finally, reprises the leave-taking of Manlius and his bride in 61, turning likewise from the immediate scene to the future:

> claudite ostia, uirgines:
> **lusimus satis**. at boni   225
> coniuges, bene uiuite et
> **munere assiduo** ualentem
> exercete iuuentam.

The epithalamic song announces its closure with "we have played enough" picking up the earlier *ludite ut lubet* (204): poetic erotic play gives way to literal erotic play, with the final leave-taking (with artful variation of the formulaic *uiue uale*) bidding, once again, the spouses' constant employment of youthful conjugality.[92] Catullus' reality is otherwise: his dangerous enjoyment of stolen

---

[92] Note too that the blessings in the epilogue specify the house as *domus ipsa, in qua lusimus, et domina*. This can be the inclusive first-person plural: Catullus "played" the love song of poem 61 there, and both he and Manlius have "played" with their beloveds there. Note further that 68.17 (*multa satis lusi*) pings off this line, as does 61.225 (*lusimus satis*) and 50.2 to Calvus (*multum lusimus*).

eros will be infrequent, a special occasion at most.[93] He accepts this, immediately turning to thank M/Allius for his role in bringing this reality about.

How will Mallius have received this? The ways in which Catullus' fraught condition compare unfavorably to Mallius' might have offered consolation to the latter, except that he is not in fact enjoying the untroubled life of conjugal abundance wished upon him in his earlier poem. Two avenues suggest themselves; though they superficially point in opposite directions, it is not clear that they are mutually incompatible. On the one hand, Catullus might be marking a continuity between his tone towards Mallius in 68a and that here: "You think *you* have troubles?" The choice of this house as setting, and this reprisal of a now painful moment of Mallius' former happiness, can be taken as an all-too brilliant infliction of exemplary suffering: we might say that Catullus made this poem for Mallius so that Mallius could see and suffer his pain. *Hoc tibi quod potui*: "This might in fact hurt, too." Even this, to be sure, need not be "hostile or insincere" (68.37–38): the Catullus who really does accept his need for Lesbia, on any terms, also believes that her love – and this pain – are worth it.

On the other possibility, we will think of Catullus' crafting of this letter closely in terms of the pseudo-medical role it was requested to fill. Mallius finds himself not in fact enjoying the untroubled marital bliss that Catullus – as a public poet in a stylized role with conventional expectations – wished and portrayed for him. And of course it is precisely the safety, social sanction, and frequency of marital sex, however rightly celebrated in poem 61 and wanted for in 68b, which constantly threaten to render it poetically (and otherwise?) banal. Poem 68b then hints that if Mallius wants the edgier, more exciting version, Catullus can tell that one, too.

But Catullus has other accounts to settle as well. Looking back at the beginning of the love affair now, after his troubled history with Lesbia and after his brother's death, naturally turns his gaze back on the poems commemorating that beginning. The resonances on offer are in any case irresistible: after 51, 68b makes a second poignant reminiscence to an initial moment: from "as soon as I saw you" to "as soon as we touched." It also makes for a reprise of Catullus' rival: *ille*, the godlike man who enjoys her presence, is now her husband (*uiri*, 146). After 11, 68b is the second dramatization of a pseudo-marriage: poetic divorce becomes poetic nuptials. After poem 8 and the moralizing conclusion of 51, 68b is the third moment of reflective interiority, of the poet evaluating his circumstances and deciding what to think and do. And finally, of course, the two poem-

[93] Rankin (1967).

pairs 2/3 and 5/7 are the direct, occurrent witnesses of the beginnings looked back on collectively by 8, 11, 51, and 68b.

Here at the end of 68b, the moralizing caution at the end of 51 is recalled and repudiated:[94]

> quae tamen etsi uno non est contenta **Catullo**,   68.135
> rara uerecundae furta feremus erae,
> ne **nimium** simus stultorum more **molesti:**
>
> otium, **Catulle**, tibi **molestum** est;   51.13
> otio exsultas **nimiumque** gestis
> otium et reges prius et beatas
>   perdidit urbes.

Catullus' resolution at 68.137 not to be *molestus* is the resolution not to be troublesome to *her*, the *mulier potens* who has options and need not suffer too much trouble from too many people; this concern overrules the conservative moralizing implicit in his earlier assertion that erotic leisure provokes trouble for *him*. This is especially so given the exemplary lesson Catullus might have taken from 68b, which points implicitly but clearly at *perdidit urbes*. Just after the brother passage at the heart of the poem (91–100), the narration returns to the mobilization of Greek youth to Troy, on the following mission:

> ne Paris abducta gauisus libera moecha   68.103
> otia pacato degeret in thalamo.

The close of 68b likewise picks up the rhetoric of poem 8, specifically its recollection of the "brilliance" of the affair. This time, however, Catullus does not offset the affair's earlier brilliance with a dark present. The nearly identical lines 8.3 and 8.8 read:

> **fulsere** quondam **candidi** tibi soles   8.3
> . . .
> fulsere uere **candidi tibi soles.**   8.8
> nunc iam illa non uolt; tu quoque, impotens, noli

Compare

> quam circumcursans hinc illinc saepe Cupido   133
> **fulgebat** crocina **candidus** in tunica.

and

---

[94] The comparison of gods and men and the godlikeness of *ille* at 51.1–2 are likewise present in the difficult 68.141; this, however, aids our understanding. Note that Lesbia is the divinized member of the same love triangle here (*mea . . . diua*, 68.70).

> quare illud satis est, si **nobis** is datur unis   147
> quem lapide illa **dies candidiore** notat.

The same events in Catullus' life are described in either poem, with *fulgeo* and *candidus* collocated; but where the reprise in poem 8 draws the contrast with the present reality of Lesbia's rejection, the reprise in 68b looks forward to whatever future brilliance she might permit.[95]

Meanwhile, the sparrow is present at the moment of the lover's first embrace, with an overtly erotic valence now acknowledged or activated:

> lux mea se nostrum contulit in **gremium**,   132
> quam **circumcursans hinc illinc** saepe Cupido . . .

> nec sese a **gremio** illius mouebat   3.8
> sed **circumsiliens modo huc modo illuc**
> ad solam dominam usque pipiabat.

Dominam at 3.10 is also picked up in 68b by *erae* a few lines later (136). Finally, the way in which the kiss poems reappear is heartbreaking. Catullus' concluding comment in 68b on the affair, specifying the frequency of sex he expects, resonates not only with the far greater frequency of Manlius' conjugal episodes in 61, but also with the stated requirements of the not yet disillusioned Catullus at the end of poem 7, just before the unforeseen disruption of his love:

> sed **furtiua** dedit mira munuscula **nocte**,   145
> ipsius ex ipso dempta uiri gremio.
> quare illud **satis** est . . .

> aut quam sidera multa, cum tacet **nox**
> **furtiuos** hominum uident amores.
> tam te basia multa basiare
> uesano **satis** et super Catullo est.

Conclusions to §6

What follows? How does the end of poem 68b now read, given all that has preceded? In this final section I will argue for an extraordinary mimetic correspondence between the literary experience of completing a sequential reading of poems 61–68b (and 1–51, 61–68b) and the specific content found at the point of textual completion.

---

[95] For *dies* picking up *soles*, compare 5.4, *soles occidere et redire possunt*.

Whether or not a strong dichotomy between "the gifts of the Muses" *qua* scholar-poetry and "the gifts of Venus" *qua* love poetry is correctly ascribed to Catullus in 68a, it is clear that some such distinction is usefully applied to the different kinds of responses the Catullan long poems evoke; we might characterize these as cognitive and sexual responses, respectively. As inelegant a characterization of the distinction as this may be, I make it for the sake of clarity.

The presence of cognitive response is too obvious to require argument or enumeration. As to sexual response, there is no question that the narrative pacing and build-up of poem 61 strive to provoke a sympathetic reaction (both among actual readers and the imagined spectators at the wedding *qua* internal readers) to the bride and groom's anticipation and desire. To be entirely unmoved by this is to take the poem to fail at one of its evident goals.[96] Poem 64 counts as well, though more ambiguously: the woven image of the topless Ariadne (63–67), spectated upon by the human guests at the wedding (*spectando*, 267–68), and clearly the central interest of the voyeuristic narrator of the ecphrasis (50–266),[97] is primarily a metapoetic focalization of artistic arousal, perhaps only secondarily an instance of it.[98] Not unlike the narrator of 64, that of 66 takes a clear interest in the spectacle of marital consummation she witnessed (13–32), nor does she fail to imagine the disrobing and bared breasts (79–81) of the wives whom she demands pour her libations before sex (82–83).[99] The Door and her interlocutor in 67 have a different sort of third-party sexual fascination.[100] And finally, as I have argued, the erotic narrative of 68b succeeds at least in provoking the corresponding response in the composing/narrating Catullus[101] – as it

---

[96] Wedding guests are a perfect correlate for the reader of love poetry as a participant "ritually sanctioned" to indulge in vicarious erotic response.

[97] Within 64, cf. the Argonauts' and especially Peleus' glimpse of topless Nereids (12–21) outside the ecphrasis, the evident motivation of Bacchus within it (Jupiter hears Ariadne's prayer at 204, but Bacchus has surely *seen* her), and the more oblique references to the bridal couple in the song of the Parcae (330–32, 371–80).

[98] That is to say, we readers are asked to devote our attention to various less erotic aspects of Ariadne's narrative, rhetoric, and the like. We should remind ourselves that these are mental suppletions of a sexualized image, where the poet and his embedded human viewers primarily see her partially naked figure, and need not think through her story any more than they care to.

[99] See Höschele (2009) for the pointedness of these remarks in light of the gender inversion of the Catullan Lock.

[100] As do we, to the extent we appreciate this. The capacity for lurid fascination with sexual horror is surely part of how poem 63 works as well – and no doubt many engaged readers of the poem have at some point literally shuddered at its content.

[101] Of the non-introductory poems in the sequence, only 62 has gone unmentioned here; does it similarly implicate either the reader or its speakers? I think not. Even if the Lock is titillated by the

well might, since he is virtually the only sexual narrator in the sequence who cannot be called a voyeur (and just as Mallius is the only internal reader who escapes that characterization, in respect to his first gift-poem, 61).[102]

Reading through the eyes of the represented Catullus as composer of this sequence of erotically potent poems, for whom the conclusion of its concluding piece is easily the most potent, we infer that the climax of 61–68b is just that, a literary mimesis of sexual climax. The return of the groom and the house in poem 61 complicates but does not contradict this picture. It is true that, absent the framing, the poem that closes the doors on readers' voyeurism just before the groom's consummation is the most potent of the series. Yet the framing not only of Catullus as self-narrating poet but also of Mallius as now erotically deprived reader/voyeur mimetically borrows the erotic charm of that earlier poem. Mimetically, that is, because the dual framing focalizes not only the vexed correspondence between poetry and the poet's experience, but that between poetry and the reader's experience as well: how else would Mallius mentally realize the image Catullus paints-with-words for him, if not through his own commemorated memory of a woman's similar entry into the same house?

So too for external readers. The four poems of **B** take the reader progressively away from his world, whether this is understood as the Roman Republic of his lived reality or the fictionalized version of it presented in poems 1–51.[103] Readerly sympathy or identification with Ariadne et al. is of course not made impossible by this progression – far from it – but it is indeed complicated by it. Moving to **C1**, poems 66 and 67 return them, again by stages, to the dramatized social world they are invested in, though the death of the brother revealed in poem 65 alienates them from the content of the inset 66 and 67, and their joint reading of 65 with 68a points toward a poet whose love is now grief, who is no longer capable of handling the most unforgettable story and theme of poems 1–51. It is thus an extraordinary reversal when Catullus now brings back his sexiest poetic invention, to inform us simultaneously of her real marriage

---

feigned sexual reluctance of brides (66.15–22), where this marks an obvious reprise of the boys' reaction to the girls' anti-marriage case at 62.36–38, poem 62 seems in general too abstract and disembodied to come off as plausibly depicting or striving for such responses.

[102] "Virtually," because both Attis (63.64–67) and Ariadne (64.147–48) obliquely relate their earlier experiences, naturally in a very different mode.

[103] Here too we have a representative in Mallius, to the extent that 68a reveals him to be, as I have argued, a maximally competent reader of the Lesbia-inflected poem sequence at the end of **A.**

and to make us guests at her pseudo-wedding, allowing us to watch him make love to her for the first time.

   This, in turn, is where the cognitive experience of reading the end of 68b at the end of the sequence of long poems becomes crucial. We have learned by now to draw inferences forward and back, to see one poem as the realization or renunciation or explanation or continuation of another. We have learned how "external" poems construct metapoetic frames through which inset poems take on interpretively different, privileged aspects. Even if poem 64 has disoriented us and shaken our confidence – its mimetic labyrinthine threads constantly presenting us an excess of paths but a deficiency of sight[104] – and even if 68a here and there seems to say the opposite of what we need it to say, we are now entitled to think that we know something about how these poems mean. And there is one thing in particular that the end of 68b and its comparanda mean with alarming clarity.

   We have already seen it all. First, the irresolution of Catullus' resolution to let Lesbia go in poem 8: in spite of vacillating there, he indeed carries through with his "divorce" in poem 11. Somehow this is reversed in 36, a reversal that is immediately reversed in turn in poem 37. At book-end of **A**, 51 reveals that Lesbia is his enduring *dolor*, but also shows Catullus moralizing to himself about the danger she represents. We then turn from 51 to 61, where the message is confirmed: Venus without the marriage god's blessing is infamous for the individual (61–65), causes the dissolution of the family (66–70), and threatens the military conquest of the land (71–75); this in turn leads to the enslavement and rape of its inhabitants (62.24). A ruinous, quasi-sexual and nuptial-by-negation obsession follows (poem 63), followed by a human/divine wedding which leads, both by its deadly progeny and via the extratextual myth of the *Streitapfel*, to the master story of both adultery and catastrophe. We turn to **C**i; the brother is now dead. Two more inset poems intervene, which respectively warn against adultery (66.84–86) and performatively punish it (67, *passim*). We now flash back to the adulterous lovemaking; although it has already happened, the composing and self-reflective Catullus (as opposed to the lovemaking Catullus) is the present one, who since then has sown all of the intratextual warnings we occurrently reap. The power of the gods to punish, their mercilessness, Helen and Paris themselves – all are here, everything Catullus needs to see the truth. But Catullus thinks with Laodamia, whose ritual heedlessness had already caused her catastrophe. The exemplary value of his brother is

---

[104] Gaisser (1995).

now the erotic persuasion with which Lesbia had been wooed and won ("once we're dead, baby, you know ... "). Why doesn't he see? The Lock has put the question to Berenice: *quis te mutauit tantus deus?* But the Lock knew, just as we knew and know, this god's identity: Amor, the other god flitting about in Mallius' house.

Our readerly work and its cognitive result at this moment of textual climax thus effect a still deeper level of mimetic parallelism between us and the Catullus in the house. This mimesis feeds back into the poem's erotic potency both for the remembering/composing Catullus and for us. Simple, really, and obvious: it's sexy because we know it's wrong. We are free to read the remembering Catullus' postcoital rationalizations, if we choose, with all the smug superiority and analytic delectation with which later readers will read the moral self-suasions of Seneca's tragic villains – and just like those readers, we would not want the represented mental pathology any other way.[105] Or we may, like many readers of Vergil's Dido, allow ourselves to endorse his mistaken self-suasion without denying the mistake (*Aen.* 4.6–55: the suasion facilitated, but just barely, by her sister Anna). From some points of view it hardly matters; Mallius can enjoy the poem, even as he wishes for nothing more fondly and deeply than the restoration of his marriage with his *uita*. So can we. This is Catullus' gift to us all.

7 Résumé of Narrative Time in B and C1

The previous chapter argued for the belatedness of **C** as a whole relative to **A**, as well as for the dramatic sequentiality of poems within **A** and **C2**, with a few exceptions (1, 14b, 31, 46, 50, and possibly 116). From indications in this chapter we have seen that Catullus represents himself composing **B** during the composition of **A**: by the dramatic date of poem 35, poem 63 has existed in partial draft for some time. The sequence 34–36, I have also argued, hints that Catullus has at least foreseen the eventual contents and sequence of **B** by that time. Sometime, presumably after the completion of **B**, the brother dies, and Catullus suffers a partial loss of his ability to compose. He nonetheless manages to compose poem 65 to Ortalus as cover letter for 66 and 67 (whose composition had preceded the brother's death), as well as a *recusatio* to Mallius, 68a. Some time passes, and on regaining his faculties Catullus composes 68b, which acquits his obligation by (M)allius

---

[105] And just as one needs to be a sort of left-handed moral genius to be a Senecan Medea or Atreus, so is the Catullus who makes so strong a case out of Laodamia and Juno's exemplarity.

and rekindles his love for Lesbia; 69–116 follow sequentially thereafter, with only the final poem arguably out of sequence. The three Catullan books coherently and fully dramatize their own composition.

A few questions of relative chronology are left indeterminate. We cannot deduce any details about the relative composition for the long poems preceding the brother's death (61–64, 66–67); we might conjecture that the elegiac 66 and 67 would not have been begun until after **B** was finished, but this is uncertain and changes nothing. Only one question matters: when was the wedding of Manlius Torquatus? For the composition of the long poems, this event provides the sole dramatized event preceding the brother's death.[106] On this question an important aspect of the overall Catullan plot turns.

To be clear, the relative composition and literary order of 61–64 do not turn on this question. Poems 62–64 do not (as far as we can see) have or presuppose occasions within the depicted Catullus' world. Regardless of when 61 was composed or performed, there is no compelling reason why it could not be arranged with poems 62–64, in any order Catullus might have wished. The generic distinctness of poem 61 sufficiently relieves us of the worry that it should be arranged at its proper temporal moment in **A**, for it does not belong in **A** at all; the fact that 62–64 are "purely literary" and ungrounded in Catullus' social fiction renders him free to craft a "purely literary" order for all four poems in **B**.

What *does* turn on the dramatic date of 61 is the relative sequence of the two entrances of women into Mallius' house. Had Catullus and Lesbia already made adulterous love when Catullus, speaking in the publicly and ritually conditioned voice of poem 61, warns of the dangers of extramarital sex? Or did he (and Mallius) later agree to forget those words, in jointly arranging for the assignation with Lesbia? There are provocative – and incompatible – ironies and implications in either possibility.

I do not think we can answer this question, but I also am far from certain that no definitive answer exists. The literary sequentiality of **A**, **B**, and **C** and the dramatic sequentiality of **A** and **C** might encourage our guess that the wedding day falls between the completed circulation of **A** and the death of the brother, but the plausibility of imagining one poem with an

---

[106] Hutchinson (2003) 210 suggests that poem 61 may be significantly earlier than 1–60 on the basis of the identification of its groom with L. Manlius Torquatus, praetor in 50 or 49, as *c.* 55 would be too late for his first marriage. I regard both the identification and reasoning here as too uncertain to rule much in or out; nor can we exclude that the historical chronology is bent by the poems for Catullus' own literary purposes.

earlier date of composition being later combined on a roll with thematically similar "purely literary" poems rules out any conclusive judgment.

On the other hand, we must also allow the possibility that the historical
date of Manlius Torquatus' marriage counts as an interpretively valid fact
for Catullus' intended readership. Most readers will probably agree that
there are *some* purely fictional figures in the poems (Ipsitilla at the very
least); on my reading, as we have seen, a large proportion of the characters
may be fictitious. But there is no question that there are indeed historical
figures about whom fully competent readers must have independent
knowledge.[107] The problem, however, is not so much that we cannot
clearly determine which characters are real and which are fictional, but
rather that we have very little evidence for how much we are expected to
know about those figures whose historicity is certain.[108] It would not be my
guess that knowledge of the historical date of Manlius' wedding is assumed
by the text, or that a reader who did know this date and read it into the
poems would necessarily be correct in doing so. I do think that Catullus
could have fictionalized this date, if it had served his purposes. But I frankly
admit that he might in fact not have done so, and the poems might expect
historically accurate knowledge on this score. Judgment should be
withheld.

To conclude, then: the dramatic date of poem 61 is an open question.
Internally, for the narrative to work, the wedding day need only precede
the brother's death and be "some time ago" by the time of 68a. The
wedding could have preceded not only Catullus' affair but also his
Bithynian service; if so, it will be on my reading the only poem that does
so. But it may also have taken place after the circulation of **A**. Depending
on the answers to questions taken here as unanswerable, we might be
authorized to imagine Catullus' urbane amusement or conservative discomfort as he performs the contradiction between his "life" and his "verse"
in this house he knows, warning of the dangers of extramarital sex. We

---

[107] An utterly minimal list would of course include Caesar, Pompey, Cicero, Calvus, and Cornelius
Nepos.

[108] It is not clearly wrong that Catullus, if not writing for eternity, is at least writing with enough
posterity in mind that the required knowledge about the historical figures rarely goes further than
essential biography. For instance, I tend to think that the mysteriousness of Catullus' thanksgiving
to Cicero (49) is an integral feature of the poem, even if there is a real answer which some readers
had extratextual access to. The poems might well tell us all we need to know without giving us an
answer.

On the other hand, one could well ask why an extremely small, functionally omniscient in-group
could *not* have been the only fully competent readers of the poems. Nor, of course, will it be widely
agreed whether Catullus' intentions and assumptions are competent to determine what a reader
needs to know.

might do well to imagine Catullus and the groom exchanging glances (or avoiding eye contact) at these moments. But we cannot know.

It may, however, be fruitful to entertain one possibility: what if we trust the sequence, and what if we are right to do so? Catullus' last recorded words in respect to his love had been the moralizing self-suasion of 51.13–16 (*otium, Catulle*...). He may still be in this mindset; he may well have taken himself to have learned from his mistakes and mended his ways. It might then be authorized for us to imagine him intoning these words with a pointed look not at the groom but at a certain guest. She understands what his look is conveying ("it's over"), and her eyes make an instant reply ("I've heard that one before"). He looks away, briefly losing the beat. He knows she is right.

To be sure, imagining Lesbia among the guests in poem 61 is far from mandatory, and the particular way I have imagined her pointed presence above is at most an intelligent indulgence of private fancy.[109] What I claim as point of scholarship is more restricted. Placing the dramatic date of poem 61 after the self-suasion of 51.13–16 but before the reevaluation occasioned by the brother's death is the single best hypothesis; on it, the relationship in those two poems between Catullus' words and his values is an authorized site for intelligent speculation. The same goes for the similar anti-adultery content of poems 66 and 67. At the dramatic moment of the end of 68b, the backward-glancing Catullus repudiates all of this.

Finally, a literary point. Catullus' elegiac book opens with a cover letter introducing his translation of the final poem of Callimachus' *Aetia*; it ends with a poem intertextual with the *Aetia* preface. It is sometimes said that poem 68 (as a putative unity, or else 68b alone) is programmatic for this book.[110] This, however, seems too weak: since the connected drama of 68a and 68b itself is half of half of the book, it is better to say that it is deeply constitutive of the book, and that its poetics constitute much of the book's poetics. At any rate, like 65, 66, and 116, poems 68a–b are thoroughly etiological. The initial consummation of desire 68b looks back upon is explanatory for the Lesbia-drama of **A**; the earlier poetic nuptials of **B** and **C**1 offer explanatory conclusions for us to apply *to* 68a–b; the death of the brother explains why the poem has *this* peculiar form (*hoc tibi quod potui*), as well as why the retrospective Catullus of its end thinks through his own

---

[109] The parallel of 64.31–37, where "everyone" in Thessaly attends Peleus and Thetis' wedding, does offer some encouragement – even, perhaps, if Roman invitation-customs and hypothetical enmities between the families would have kept Lesbia's historic correlate away. Again, we do not know just how fictional Catullus' fictionalized world is.

[110] So Hubbard (2005) 271.

exemplary images in the way he does. No less does his resolution there explain his amatory future in **C2**: the Catullus who has interpreted Lesbia as his sole reason to live (*qua uiua*, 160), his sole protection from a Laodamian erotic abyss (*barathrum*, 107–18), is one who must suffer the personality-shattering disaster that awaits him (poems 75, 85, 92). Poems 68a–b are the causal vortex of the Lesbia drama.

CHAPTER 4

C2 (poems 69–116)

1 Structure of C2

The basic division between the two halves of **C2** – that is, poems 69–92 and 93–116 – is of a different sort from the midpoint division in **A**. There is no unfolding drama of composition or textualization in these poems,[1] and the reality of the break at this point is one determined by the content of the poems rather than by overt signs of programmaticity or other forms of metapoetry. Again, the thematic connections that guide us through these poems is significantly less rich, particularly in the second half, than is the case in **A**. But this is a different kind of collection with a different and rougher poetics; once it is allowed that this shift in the artistry of Catullan poems plausibly tracks this shift in the artistry of Catullan poem-arrangement, the motivation to despair of finding *any* patterning for want of perfect pattern-ing, or to hunt for truly cryptic patterning, is thoroughly undermined. And, to recall the most important earlier result, the global response to the fussier 25 + 25 (give or take one) collection **A** in this scrappier 25 + 25 (give or take one) collection **C2** has already vindicated overall authorial control.

Transition between C1 and C2

It has been observed that the motif of marriage to Jupiter in poems 70 and 72 links these poems (the first and second Lesbia poems in **C2**) to the end

---

[1] On Ferriss' (2009) metapoetic reading of poem 71, **C2** all but does begin with something like a drama of composition, namely a comment on the metrical incompetence of Rufus (figured as gout, *podagra*, with a pun on metrical feet), a "stinking" poet (per the "goat" both in 71 and the initial 69). While the foot-pun she argues for itself strikes me as highly plausible, I worry that her reading of *quotiens futuit* (71.5), on which "whenever he fucks" encodes "whenever he composes," is inadequately signaled by the text. Her reading is nonetheless evocative, and it would certainly be welcome on my thesis, tidying up the correspondence between terminal points and metaliterary moments.

of **C1** (68b.138–40), where Catullus cites Juno as an *exemplum* for his need to accept Lesbia's infidelity to him.[2] What deserves sharper notice, however, is that *nubere* at 70.1 effects a (humorous) transition between the conceptual world of poems 61–68b and 69–116. Like Greek γαμέω and cognates, *nubo* and *nuptiae* are attested of sexual intercourse as well as formal marriage.[3] The mythological precedents for Jovian behavior in 68b obviously encourage the thought that this is the sense in which Jupiter might contract nuptials with Lesbia; the great marital theme of **B** and **C1** is thus acknowledged, while the humorous turn away from it is marked by the semantic slippage from formal marriage to sex.[4] Further confirmation of this slippage comes between the two Lesbia–Jupiter marriage poems: the lovers in poem 71 are inferably Lesbia and Rufus, and their love is now characterized as "fucking" (*futuit*, 71.5).

One might, however, still worry about poem 69: how, if at all, does this first poem in **C2** handle the transition from **C1**? To my knowledge it has not been seen that 69 can also be mapped onto 68b, humorously marking the turn from the mythological and heroic to Catullus' social fiction and invective:

> Noli admirari, quare tibi femina nulla,
>   Rufe, uelit tenerum supposuisse femur,
> non si illam rarae labefactes **munere uestis**
>   aut **perluciduli** deliciis **lapidis.**
> laedit te quaedam **mala fabula** qua tibi **fertur**   5
>   **ualle sub alarum** trux habitare **caper.**
> hunc metuunt omnes, neque mirum: nam mala ualde est
>   **bestia,** nec quicum bella puella cubet.
> quare aut crudelem nasorum **interfice pestem,**
>   aut admirari desine cur fugiunt.   10

At 68b.109–16, Hercules is said to have dug a drainage ditch to drain a swamp (*siccare emulsa pingue palude solum*) and killed monsters (*Strymphalia monstra perculit*). He had two motivations, deification and marital consummation (*Hebe nec longa uirginitate foret*). The myth or *fabula* in 68b devolves in 69 into self-performing defamation (*mala fabula . . . fertur*): a comical monster/beast (*caper . . . bestia*) needs killing (*interfice pestem*), Catullus kindly informs Rufus, for his erotic bliss to be

---

[2] Wiseman (1969) 25.

[3] Adams (1982) 159–61; for this reading of poems 70 and 72, see Newman (1990) 248–49. Miller (1988) 130–31 thinks rather of formal marriage.

[4] So too for *tenere Iouem* at 72.2, where we hear "erotically embrace" at least as clearly as "be married to."

achieved. The serious matter of gift-exchange in 65–68b is comically cheapened by Rufus' ulterior motives (*munus* 8x in **C1**, only here and – seriously again – at 101.3 in **C2**; *uestis* 3x in **C1**, only here in **C2**). The valley of Rufus' armpits in need of drainage is verbally similar but otherwise quite unlike the one watered by the mountain spring at 68b.57–59:

> qualis in aerii **perlucens** uertice montis
>   riuus muscoso prosilit e **lapide**,
> qui cum de prona praeceps est **ualle** uolutus . . .

Given these connections, readers are now off and running, with a good sense of what poetic/generic landscape they now occupy and how they arrived in it.

Poems 69–92

First, there are questions of character-identity and the conceptual problem of the "Lesbia poem" to sort out. It is clear that no more than a handful of these poems is unrelated to Lesbia, either directly or via Catullan invective against a man erotically involved with her: but which are these non-Lesbia poems? Then, some but not all of the invective rivalry poems mention Lesbia or attack the rival *qua* rival for Lesbia. Lesbia herself seems more present in poem 85 (*odi et amo*), where she is not mentioned by name or epithet, than in the following poem 86, where she is. How can we speak of the distribution of Lesbia poems?

The table below represents the addressees and principal characters in each poem. In parenthesis are inferred characters, with cross-referencing diction establishing their identities indicated, in bold type for Lesbia.

Poem	Character(s)	Identifying language
69	*Rufe*	*caper*
70	(Lesbia)	**mulier mea**
		dicit . . . **Iuppiter**
71	(Rufus)	*hircus* . . . *aemulus*
	(Lesbia)	**uestrum amorem** . . . **illam**
72	*Lesbia*	**dicebas** . . . **Iouem**
		dilexi tum te . . . **amare magis sed bene uelle minus**
73	(Rufus)	*unicum amicum*
74	*Gellius*	*patrui perdepsuit ipsam uxorem*
75	*Lesbia*	**nec bene uele queat tibi** . . . **nec desistere amare**
76	(Lesbia)	**non iam** . . . **me ut diligat illa**
77	*Rufe*	*pestis amicitiae*

(*cont.*)

Poem	Character(s)	Identifying language
78	*Gallus*	
	(Gellius)	*patrui . . . adulterium*
78b	(Lesbius)	
	(Lesbia)	**purae . . . puellae suauia . . . saliua tua**
79	*Lesbius*	
	Lesbia	**suauia reppererit**
80	*Gellius*	
81	*Iuuenti*	
82	*Quinti*	
83	*Lesbia . . . uiro*	
84	*Arrius*	
85	(Lesbia)	**odi et amo**
86	*Quintia*	
	Lesbia	
87	*Lesbia*	**mulier**
88	*Gelli*	*patruum non sinit esse maritum*
89	*Gellius*	
90	*Gelli*	
91	*Gelli*	
	(Lesbia)	**hanc . . . cuius me magnus edebat amor**
92	*Lesbia*	

To begin with the easier inferences: The identity of Rufus in 71 is secured by mention of a goat and body odor, as in 69. The network of cross-references above makes Lesbia's presence in poems 70, 71, 76, 78b, 85, and 91 clear: the *mulier* in 70 speaks of "preferring Catullus to Jupiter," as Lesbia does in 72; the unnamed object of the love/hate relationship in 76 and 85 is obviously Lesbia, who plays the same role in 72, 75, and 92; consecutive references in 78b and 79 to impurity, kisses, and a "girl" or Lesbia leave little doubt as to their character's identity. Controversial or at least non-trivial inferences here are Rufus in 73, Gellius in 78, and Lesbius in 78b. But each of these identifications is supported by verbal/thematic recalls and Occam's razor. The betrayed friendship of 73 ties the poem to Rufus in 77, while 71 specifies the nature of the betrayal; the man who cuckolds his uncle in 74 fits into the vignette of uncle-cuckolding in 78, with Gallus the uncle Gellius is *not* (yet) cuckolding; Lesbius, Lesbia, and befouled kisses in 79 point back to the same in 78b, with the poem serving as advance warning of the revelation to come (*nam te omnia saecula | noscent*, 78b.3–4). The denial of Lesbia's (or Juventius') presence in 82 will be somewhat surprising. The warning not to "seize away" (*eripere*, 82.3) what is dear to Catullus points to Lesbia (cf. *eripuisti*, 77.4 and 5), but the preceding poem's address to Juventius, especially combined with the neuter gender of Catullus' "dear item" here, frustrates the identification. I propose below linking Quintius in 82 and Quintia in 86 to the Aufillena sub-plot in 93–116.

On this set of identifications, 14 of the 25 poems attack Catullus' rivals for Lesbia: Gellius in seven poems (74, 78, 80, 88–91), Rufus in four (69, 71, 73, 77), Lesbius in two (78b, 79), and Lesbia's husband in one (83). Another seven poems (70, 72, 75, 76, 85, 87, 92) address or primarily concern Lesbia. Lesbia is also (perhaps merely) mentioned in poem 86; the comparison of her beauty to that of "Quintia" there presumably ties poem 86 to "Quintius" in 82. These correspondences account for all but two poems in 69–92: the Juventius poem, 81, and 84, the witty attack on Arrius' misplaced aspirations.

Taking our cue from the sequence itself, and in particular from its expectation-setting opening, it is clear that "Lesbia poems" come in degrees:[5] there is an obvious ABAB pattern of Rufus and Lesbia in the first four poems (69–72), even though Lesbia is present in the second Rufus poem (71), while Rufus is at least explanatorily present in the second Lesbia poem (72). To the extent that rivalry for Lesbia underlies and explains the invective, some 22 out of the 25 count as Lesbia poems; omitting those in which she is not directly in question cuts out the first Rufus poem (69) and all but the final Gellius poem (91), leaving 15. Some subjectivity is inevitable in seeking to classify poems against Catullus' rivals, such as 71, where Lesbia is a presence but a less dominant one; on my count, this group consists of six poems (71, 73, 77, 78b, 86, 91).[6] This leaves nine "core" Lesbia poems (70, 72, 75, 76, 79, 83, 85, 87, 92).

Barring some cryptic identification, poem 84 will remain an isolate in 69–92; depending on one's preferred principle of unity for the rest, it may be the only such.[7] As we have seen, no terror need attach to the prospect of an isolate or two in a series of poems as thematically tight as these. In concrete terms, then, how are these tightly related poems arranged?

[5] Compare the marginal cases of poems 13, 39, and 43 in **A**.

[6] Less than obvious judgments here concern poem 83 (a core Lesbia poem, because unlike Furius and Gellius, the husband is of no interest considered on his own), and Lesbius in 78b and 79 (the latter a core Lesbia poem because the Lesbia plot is incomplete without the unmasking it effects, the former not because it specifically focalizes Lesbius as object of eternal infamy).

[7] Choosing the specific motif of Lesbia and rivals for her love as unifying principle would isolate 81 and 82 from the others; the broader characterization of love rivalries would keep them. Lesbia's appearance in 86 is somewhat unique; the characterization of her and Quintia as rival beauties, while Catullus and Quintius in 82 share some other rivalry, might be useful to think with.

The most useful characterization, I claim, is that the center of the collection is the narratively crucial 78b–79, in which Catullus unmasks Lesbia to take his great revenge, while the two primary male invective targets, Rufus and Gellius, are anchored at the two respective ends of the sequence. Rufus is at first arranged in alternating sequence (69, 71, 73) but his final poem skips a beat (77); the Gellius material is by contrast concentrated for maximum effect at the end (88–91),[8] with the complication that his first appearance (74) interrupts the opening Rufus–Lesbia alternation, while his remaining two poems frame the central Lesbius/Lesbia ones (78 and 80).

A heterogeneous principle of arrangement is also discernible, namely poem-length. Longer poems are carefully spaced out, presumably to prevent the (narrative as well as literary) tempo from flagging. There are four poems containing more than eight lines: 69 and 91 have ten lines apiece, 84 has twelve, and 76 extends transgressively to 26 lines. These four **L**onger poems are fit into the sequence as follows:

L > six poems > **L** > eight poems > **L** > six poems > **L** > final poem

Even more neatly, the longest poems after these are the three eight-line poems (72, 80, 88); each of these is located at the center of one of the "short" sequences above (the third of six, the fifth of eight, and the fourth of six).[9] Additionally, the six four-line poems (70, 75, 79, 82, 87, 92) are separated respectively by 4, 4, 2, 4, and 4 poems (again assuming the lacuna in 78b).

On a broader scale, one can plausibly see odd–even alternation throughout the sequence, by which the core Lesbia poems fall on the even beat. This is admittedly subverted by 92 (the final poem in the sequence), and by 74, which disrupts the ABABA pattern of Rufus–Lesbia alternation. Excluding 75, the core Lesbia poems fall second, fourth, eighth, twelfth, sixteenth, eighteenth, and twentieth; the twenty-fourth poem (91) ties Gellius to Lesbia, and the sequence closes with Lesbia on the odd beat.

I must note, however, that I find small need or interest in demonstrating arithmetically perfect patterning, though this may exist; what matters here is that the pacing or tempo is clearly important to these poems and how their sequence works, and that authorial care has been taken on this point. The table below offers a schematization of this sequence's movement parallel to those given in Chapter 2 for the components of **A**. In general,

---

[8] For the gradual increase in intensity of the Gellius poems, see Fordyce (1973).
[9] For this scheme to be arithmetically perfect, only a single distich would need to be missing from 78b, but I certainly do not claim that the pattern constitutes an argument for that being the case.

the narrative continuity is clear, though the thematic overlap (that is, themes P, P+Q, Q in three consecutive poems) frequent there is less evident at transition points between addressees here; it is convincingly present over the sequence 78–81, probably not otherwise.

69——71: Goats, sex, body odor, Rufus
   70——72: Lesbia, marrying Jupiter
      71——73: Rufus
            74————————78: Gellius
    71–72–73——75–76–77: Rufus, Lesbia's betrayal of Catullus
            74————————78–78b–79: in-family sex
                   78b–79: dirty kisses, Lesbius, Lesbia
            74————————78————————80: Gellius

78b–79–80: polluted mouths
    80–81: male/male couples
        82: Quintius
            83——85: Lesbia, contradictory sentiments
               84: Arrius
            83——85–86–87: Lesbia
        82————————86: Quintia, -us
    80————————————88–89–90–91: Gellius
           87————————91–92: Lesbia

Finally, the sequence is notably specular at its terminal points: Rufus/Lesbia in the first two, Gellius/Lesbia in the final two poems. The first and final Lesbia poems (70 and 92, the second and final for this section) draw a palpable ring both verbally (*nulli se dicit mulier mea nubere malle ~ Lesbia mi dicit semper male*) and thematically, with the unreliability of her speech at issue in both. This last is particularly artful: her unreliability is a wary Catullus' *fear* at the beginning and becomes his post-disillusioned *wish* at the end.

Poems 93–116

To repeat, there is no question but that this sequence is looser and more puzzling than those previous. Nonetheless, there clearly is internal organization here. The differences in extent and kind between the organization of these poems and those pose serious and open questions; the fact of the matter can and should be put beyond doubt.

Most notable here is consecutive grouping: the initial single-distich epigrams on Caesar and Mentula (93–94) form a clear pair, as do Cinna and Calvus, the poet-friends of Catullus (95 and 96; if 95b is separate, as

I think, that makes three such poems).[10] The filthy mouths of Aemilius and Victius in 97 and 98 are clearly paired, and Juventius' rejection of Catullus' kiss in 99 does unto Catullus as Catullus had done unto Aemilius and Victius. We find three more obvious pairs: two more single-distichs in 105–06, one of them on Mentula, as in 93–94; Aufillena in 110–11, and Mentula's dispraised real estate in 114–15. Meanwhile, the only clear case of alternating arrangement is found in the Lesbia poems: 107 and 109 are the paired reconciliation poems, and although two poems intervene between 104 and 107, the fact that these are the single-distich poems keeps the separation between 104 and 107 minimal, arguably rendering 104, 107, and 109 virtually alternating poems. The majority of poems (93–94; 95–96; 97–99; 105–06; 110–11; 114–15: 14 of 25 on my count), then, are clearly linked to adjacent poems; the three Lesbia poems 104, 107, and 109 instantiate alternating sequence.

Connections between the two- and three-poem consecutive units above are again fainter, but still present. Mentula makes sense as the hinge between the opening political invective (93–94) and the subsequent poems on poet-friends (95–96) in the light of poem 105, the attempted rape of the Muses which mocks Mentula's poetic pretensions; the last of these, 96, contains a form of *quisquam* in its first line, a feature shared with the next two of the three subsequent poems on polluted mouths, 97–99.

In the cases of poems 96 and 101, the existence of local correspondences, rather than their absence, is arguably more troubling. Poems 97–103 make for a particularly rough sequence: the first two of these are among the most aggressive and obscene Catullan poems, and the last two especially come off as slight, prosy, and forgettable.[11] For the *Trostgedicht* to Calvus to precede these poems and the infinitely moving and memorable farewell to the brother to fall in their midst is hard to understand. This, one could (probably *must*) say, is pointed contrast; I nonetheless cannot help wishing that Catullus had not threaded *frater* (3x) and *fraterno fletu* in poem 101 to the pedestrian quip *fraternum . . . sodalicium* in poem 100, or Catullus the "silent friend" (*tacito . . . fido ab amico*) in poem 102 to the brother's mute ash (*mutam . . . cinerem*).[12] That I fail to understand this moment of

---

[10] Following King (1988) and Claes (2001).

[11] In defense of 102, see Edwards (1990). For the possible association of Catullus 105's *Pipleium montem* with Pipla and its implication for the attempted rape of the Muses, see Deuling (1999) 191.

[12] The fraternal fidelity shown in 101 may also be transferred to the *fides* Catullus shows in keeping the secret entrusted (*commissum*) to him in poem 102 – a secret which, whatever it is, poem 102 probably in fact reveals. Whether that link between 101 and 102 is accepted or not, the metaphorical financial/fiduciary language of 102 does indeed turn literal in poem 103: *redde decem sestertia*.

Catullan craft, however, seems to be the fact of the matter: this is *my* (or *our*) aesthetic problem.

From here on, there are certainly linked poems, but it is not obvious that there are links *between* the links. Interpretation is frustrated on multiple points by our uncertainty that we have unraveled the epigrammatic *pointe* of poems 106, 108, and 112 especially. It seems highly likely that the combined motifs of sexual and political misdemeanor run through the poetic singletons in this final stretch; all of this would then be tied to the recurring figure of Mentula in the closing words of poem 115 (*mentula magna minax*), in which his speaking name ties the villa-criticism of 114–15 to the political connections that have enriched him and the appetites responsible for his perpetually negative cash flow.[13] As with the brother in 101, the presence of Lesbia's textual farewell in the midst of this material will provoke and possibly unsettle: we might draw our own conclusions, or we might refrain from doing so.

The following table summarizes local correspondences:

93–94: single distichs, Caesar and Mamurra
  94–95–95b–96: poems and poets
      96–97–98: *quisquam* in opening line
        97–98–99: polluted mouths
          99–100: male/male couples
            100–101: fraternal themes
              101–102: silence
                102–103: good and bad credit

104————107————109: Lesbia
  105–106: single distichs, Mamurra and ?
      108: Cominius
        110–111: Aufillena
        112: Naso
          113: Pompey
            114–115: Mamurra's real estate
  105–106————108————————112–113————115: "sexual politics"?
            116: Gellius

We are better served by terminal patterning.[14] Most conspicuous is the ring formed by 116 and 65 (*carmina . . . Battiadae*). Moreover, the status of

---

[13] See Skinner (2003) 131–42 on the ubiquitous conflation of political and sexual delinquency in these poems.

[14] The patterning of poems by line-count is evident here only in the semi-adjacent distribution of the three longest poems in 93–116: 97 (12 lines), 99 (16), and 101 (10).

Gellius as addressee recalls also the closing sequence of 69–92, in which he is the dominant figure, and there is a clear verbal recall ringing 93–116 itself: *studioso animo* at 116.1 recalls the equivalent poetically loaded term at 93.1: *nil nimium studeo, Caesar . . .*[15] Within either side of this outer frame, then, we find *Mentula* and his explicitly speaking name, forming an inner frame (*Mentula moechatur . . . mentula magna minax,* 94.1 and 115.8). With four of twenty-five poems devoted to him (94, 105, 114–115), Mentula is the left-handed star of this show; these poems are arranged in a recognizable variant of first-middle-last patterning.[16]

For many readers, I expect, the sense of a weak ending for **C2** – if not also the sense that **C2** itself constitutes a weak ending for the corpus – has long presented one of the principal grounds for skepticism about authorial design. The belated recognition of the metapoetic and framing functions of poem 116 certainly helped here, and the further framing responses just seen, between 115–16 and the close of 69–92 and opening of 93–116, should also help.

We can go further still. Accepting, as we all but must, the identification of "Mentula" with Mamurra,[17] the penultimate pair of poems 114–15 are also resonant with both sides of the medial division in **A** (as, of course, the drama of composition in 116 resonates strongly with the end of **A** and clearly with its beginning). The first half of **A** had ended with mockery of poor Furius' *uillula* (poem 26); next, the prologic poem 27 leads immediately to Catullus' poor friends Veranius and Fabullus (28), followed by his rich enemy, Mamurra (29; *ista uestra diffututa mentula* at 29.13 grounds the identification and assures the recollection). The geminated real-estate "villafication" of 114–15 recalls this same device as closural motif for the first half of **A**, while the concurrent recollection of poems 28 and 29 (at the opening of its second half) pointedly displays Catullus' dialectical flexibility, if you will. Poem 26: Furius is poor (shame on him for it); 28: Veranius and Fabullus are poor (shame on their propraetor for it); 29: Mamurra the *mentula* is rich (shame on his proconsul for it); 114–115: Mentula is rich (shame on his greed). The poetics of hypocrisy create a knowing distance between the poet and his invective craft, or the logocratic *dictator* takes positive delight in his supereminence to the rule of law.

---

[15] I might venture that *nil nimium studeo* can be understood as a self-conscious marker of the roughness evident in these poems. Picking this up, *saepe tibi studioso animo* at 116.1 would then inform Gellius that Catullus has been mulling a return to more respectable verse – but no such luck, and by Gellius' own fault.

[16] If 95b is separate, the return of Lesbia in poem 104 is the middle poem, the thirteenth of twenty-five; assuming unity, she in 104 and Mentula in 105 fall on either side of the middle by poem.

[17] Following e.g. McDermott (1983) and Fratantuono (2010) 101 n. 2.

Finally, the closural sequence we posited for **A** (46–51) can be extended to include the four final poems of **C2**. Poem 113 runs:

> Consule Pompeio primum duo, Cinna, solebant
> Maeciliam: facto consule nunc iterum
> manserunt duo, sed creuerunt milia in unum
> singula. fecundum semen adulterio.

So close to book-end, mention of Pompey's second consulship (55 BCE) handily dates the entire book. Mention of contemporaneous political events for dating purposes is a feature of the *sphragis*, as exemplified by *Georgics* 4.560–61 (*magnus dum Caesar ad altum* | *fulminat Euphraten bello* . . .); more closely, the consulship of Lollius and Lepidus (21 BCE) dates Horace's first book of *Epistles* (1.20.28, its final line).

2   Narrative Time in C2

Our examination of **C1** in the previous chapter included its temporal framing; for the current section, the relevant assumptions are that the plot of **C2** is later than that of **A** and follows directly on 68b, that the brother is dead, and that the series is introduced by Catullus' resolution at the end of 68b (135–48) to accept Lesbia's love on whatever terms she offers it. Once again I postpone a full discussion of the Lesbia chronology until other recurring characters (at least three of whom are said to be her lovers) have been discussed. Besides her, there are seven or eight characters recurring within **C2**. In order of appearance, they are: Rufus (69, 71, 73?, 77), Gellius (74, 78, 80, 88–91, 116), possibly "Lesbius" (78b?, 79), Juventius (81, 99), Quintius (82, 100), Mentula (94, 105, 114, 115), Cinna (95, 113), and Aufillena (82?, 100, 103?, 110, 111).

Rufus

As this storyline is plainly sequential, it is particularly important in that Rufus is the first character we meet in **C2**. As in **A**, a reader of **C2** is immediately informed that she must assume narrative sequentiality to understand these poems. In poem 69 Rufus cannot find a woman to sleep with him; the reason, Catullus helpfully informs, is his malodorous underarms. In poem 70, a woman identified as *mulier mea* prefers Catullus even to Jupiter, though Catullus has his doubts; in 71 a malodorous man now enjoys the favors of Catullus' lover; in 72, the woman who once claimed she preferred Catullus to Jupiter is identified as Lesbia and vilified for an *iniuria* she has committed. The identification of *aemulus iste* in 71 with *Rufe* in 69 should no more be resisted than that of *mulier mea* and *Lesbia* in 70 and 72, and the four poems constitute a temporally-ordered alternating sequence.[18]

The following poem, 73, is a self-address about an unnamed friend's faithlessness. That this is Rufus is strongly hinted at least; the ABAB patterning of the first four poems would predict another Rufus poem, the story of betrayal fits perfectly, and there are clear verbal connections with poem 77, the final poem addressing him. His story thus runs: he is mocked by Catullus (69) but gets the best possible revenge, sex with Lesbia (71); discovering this, Catullus first soliloquizes about his faithlessness (73) and then attacks him in direct address (77).[19] With this last address proclaiming Rufus the *pestis* of Catullus' friendship (77.6), the final poem also explains why we find no further mention of him.

Gellius

By contrast, the poems dealing with this other principal rival figure in **C2** hardly develop in terms of ongoing story; the development seems entirely on the side of our discovery of the circumstances attending Catullus' campaign against him. We first see him in poem 74, which interrupts – uniquely so – the coherent love-triangle story of 69–77. He is probably an unnamed character in 78, and is addressed in 80. The information given in these poems is limited and unrelated: he has committed adultery with his uncle's wife and fellates a man named Victor. He then reappears in four consecutive poems just before the close of 69–92, an unprecedented invective barrage. In order: he cuckolds his uncle – as before, but now he also practices incest on his mother and sister, and may even self-fellate (88);

---

[18] These poems also contain chiastic (ABBA) formal patterning: 69, invective address to a man with no lover > 70, soliloquy doubting Lesbia's faithfulness > 71, soliloquy after discovering their affair > 72, invective address to Lesbia for her faithlessness.

[19] The rhetoric of friendship in poems 73 and 77 cannot be sincere, since the only information we are given about Rufus before his affair with Lesbia comes in an attack on him by Catullus: the poems "play dumb," with the added invective payoff of the claim that Rufus has no other friend than Catullus (73.6; that is, he never had *any* friend at all). Of course it is suspicious to have Catullus attack someone "for no reason" and *then* immediately find he is sleeping with Lesbia; the story and its chronology would probably best be taken as lies (by the Catullus-character), except that Catullus embarrassingly eats his words about Rufus' erotic loneliness. The fact is that the poems cohere when taken chronologically (Catullus in 69 thinks Rufus has no lover, in 70 he merely suspects Lesbia's words are unreliable), and not otherwise; the best solution is to take Lesbia's offense against Catullus – beyond the mere fact of her infidelity – to consist in an affair with someone this sexually repulsive, and someone Catullus had "publicly" identified as such.

he is thin, for the same reason (89); he ought to father a *magus* on his mother (90); and he carried on with Lesbia, even though his only "incestuous" tie to her is his close friendship with Catullus (91). He then disappears until the final poem, the abortive gift-exchange of 116.

As we have seen, there is careful patterning throughout the sequence, but not in narrative terms: the discontinuous earlier poems (74, 78, and 80) introduce two sexual accusations (cuckolding his uncle, fellatio) that are both picked up in the first of the consecutive ones (88), with a new accusation added, incest; these are then the theme of the two following poems (89–90), to which the accusation of sex with Lesbia in 91 is humorously tied. Gellius then disappears until the end of the book; now we find he is an invective poet himself, whom Catullus has (with open insincerity, of course) sought to win over through the gift of poetry. Gellius' final appearance in 69–92 reveals the textual Catullus' real invective motivation in the entire series, namely erotic rivalry with Lesbia. Or so we think: poem 116 returns us to Catullus the poet, the dramatized figure who himself depicts, and partially fictionalizes, his love for Lesbia. Could it be that Gellius' role in the Lesbia plot is explained by grievances standing outside it? Meanwhile, just as poem 91, the final Gellius poem of 69–92, explains the previous ones, so does the penultimate Gellius poem there, 90, hint that Gellius is himself a poet, thus pointing forward to 116.[20]

In terms of narrative sequence, the (only) real question is in regard to poem 116: Do the retaliatory verses promised there refer back to the previous invective, or forward to more?

Lesbius, Juventius, Mentula, Cinna

Lesbius is included here in that I propose to understand the fragmentary 78b as addressed to him, a separate poem meant to strike terror in him (and Lesbia) by promising to reveal his identity for all ages, appropriately building up anticipation for the bombshell *Lesbius est pulcer* (79.1). Obviously this would constitute narrative sequence if true; otherwise, Lesbius appears only once. The two Juventius poems of **C2** are 81 and 99; the former scarcely helps, but the latter is a renunciation, and thus ought to be final.[21] Mentula and Cinna, however, seem inert: no detail in the four Mentula poems seems to imply any temporal order at all, while

---

[20] Thomson (1997) 519–20: *accepto . . . carmine* (90.5) is overtly the "spell" of the future *magus*, Gellius' incestuous son; *omentum* (90.6), a synonym for *membrana*, hints at the physical book (cf. 22.7).

[21] Unlike what we see in the Lesbia poems, there is no indication of any reunion.

Cinna, the celebrated author of the *Zmyrna* in poem 95, seems to be the purely ornamental addressee of poem 113 (Maecilia's adulterous career, from Pompey's first to second consulships).[22]

Quintius and Aufillena

I print the first of two appearances of Quintius, poem 82:

> Quinti, si tibi vis oculos debere Catullum
> aut aliud si quid carius est oculis,
> eripere ei noli, multo quod carius illi
> est oculis seu quid carius est oculis.

One's initial impression is that, like the majority of poems in 69–92, this one involves one of Catullus' rivals for Lesbia. Or else, taking as a hint the appearance of Juventius in poem 81, that Juventius is the one "dearer than his eyes" to Catullus. If either of those plausible readings is true, Quintius amounts to very little: he is an erotic rival of Catullus' (82), who has a not-quite-beautiful female relative (86), and is a Veronese youth in love with one Aufillena (100); Catullus, however, favors Quintius' love for Aufillena less than he does Caelius' love for Aufillena's brother, Aufillenus. The problem here is not that there is too little information, but rather that the two scraps of information fail to amount to anything.[23] I propose instead that the rivalry in question in poem 82 looks forward to poem 100 and beyond for its object: Aufillena. Nonetheless, while this reading yields a sequential storyline, it is too speculative to *substantiate* the narrative sequentiality of **C2** on its own.

Now we have no evidence anywhere that Catullus feels any affection at all for Aufillena; how will she be "dearer to him than his eyes"? She will not be; but the information we do receive suggests a reinterpretation of "dearer" – money has changed hands, with Catullus understanding that Aufillena owes him sex, which she then fails to provide (poem 110). Between her first named appearance in poem 100 and her second in 110, there is 103: Catullus asks Silo, whom he abusively calls a *leno* or pimp, for

---

[22] It might – just slightly – contribute to the case for the belatedness of **C2** that the poet-comrade mentioned once in **A** (10.30) has now completed the *Zmyrna*, nine years after its inception.

[23] This Caelius is even more obscure: since he too is clearly indicated to be Veronese, there is little prospect of identifying him with M. Caelius Rufus, and thus potentially with the Rufus of poems 69, 71, 73, and 77. He is merely a Veronese youth, who is (sarcastically?) credited with demonstrating *unica amicitia* (100.6) for Catullus in his erotic troubles. See Arkins (1983).

the return of ten thousand sesterces. Commentators are quick (and correct) to assert that this Silo is not literally a professional pimp, since he would then be socially irrelevant to Catullus and beneath his poetic notice. The same, however, is true of any female target of Catullan invective: it is no more absurd for Catullus to accuse Silo of pimping than it is for him to accuse Aufillena of prostitution. Taking the hint that Catullus' demand that a "pimp" return his money and his vilification of Aufillena's business practices refer to the same incident, we have a story: to Catullus' distress, Quintius has his eyes on Aufillena, in whom Catullus is "invested" (82); Catullus accordingly favors Caelius' suit for Aufillenus, lest Quintius' interest in Aufillena interfere with his own (100). Later, seeing no return on his investment, Catullus demands his money back from Silo (103), rebukes Aufillena for breach of contract (110), and accuses her of incest for good measure (111).[24]

The following table sums up the various non-Lesbia storylines:

Character	69–92	93–116	Sequence
Rufus	69, 71, 73?, 77		69 > 71 > (73, 77)
Gellius	74, 78?, 80, 88–91	116	ambiguous
Lesbius	78b?, 79		78b > 79 (dub.)
Juventius	81	99	81 > 99
Quintius	82	100	82 > 100 (dub.)
Mentula		94, 105, 114, 115	unknowable
Cinna	95	113	unknowable
Aufillena	82?	100, 103?, 110, 111	82 > 100 > 103 > (110–111) (dub.)

Lesbia

I now turn to Lesbia, beginning with the thirteen poems in the first half of **C2** (69–92) that comment on her. The table below summarizes the content of each poem (omitted are poems about rivals in which she does not directly appear), focusing on the presence or absence of aggressive or hostile comment against her. What I think has gone underappreciated is how tightly localized the invective is, and *where* it is located: unleashed by her affair with Rufus (from 71), it escalates brutally until it culminates in Catullus' great act of vengeance, the

---

[24] Silo is a fairly common cognomen, and it is possible that this figure is addressed elsewhere by his *gentilicium*. Perhaps he is Caelius in poem 100: his *lenocinium* might count as the friendship shown to Catullus in his hour of erotic need – or so Catullus then thinks. Note, however, Case and Claes' (1995) observation that Silo the *leno* is treated in the same manner as Aufil-*lena* in 110.

revelation of her identity (79);[25] thereafter it stops. Though he remains angry and hurt (85, 92), Catullus now has second thoughts: he compliments Lesbia's beauty (86), declines clear opportunities to attack her (87, 91), and interprets her actions in both willfully optimistic (83, 92) and implicitly exculpatory ways (92: exculpatory because common to him as well).

Poem	Summary	Hostile language
70	L claims to prefer C even to Jupiter	C suspicious but not hostile
71	L "fucks" Rufus, justly "catches" his disease	*futuit; malum; ulciscitur; odore*
72	C recalls L's words in 70, now betrayed; he once "esteemed" her, but now feels "hate/love"	*nunc te cognoui; multo mi tamen es uilior et leuior; iniuria; bene uelle minus*
75	L's fault has driven C mad, makes him "hate/love" her	*tua culpa; si optima fias; omnia si facias*
76	C soliloquizes about his devotion to L, expects divine reward, resolves to be free of his love, prays to gods for release	*ingratae . . . menti; hanc pestem perniciemque; suprepens ut torpor . . . expulit . . . laetitias; quod non potis est, esse pudica uelit; taetrum hunc . . . morbum*
78b	C threatens to expose the man who has polluted L's kisses	*purae pura puellae suauia comminxit spurca saliua tua*
79	L practices incest with her brother Clodius	*quem* [sc. fratrem] *Lesbia malit*
83	L's husband foolishly infers from L's anger that she has "forgotten" C	None
85	C's "hate/love"	none
86	unlike Quintia, L is truly beautiful	none[26]
87	C superlatively loved and was superlatively faithful to L	implicit contrast obvious but unstated (withheld?)
91	Gellius betrayed C with L	(arguably) none[27]
92	L's curses of C prove she loves him, as he speaks ill of but loves her	none

---

[25] A nice parallel: recall that Catullus uses the metapoetic framing of 50–51 to connect the Lesbia plot to the less fictional world of the poem-composing Catullus and his real poet-friend Calvus; on my reading in Chapter 2, the signal effect of this is not so much to emphasize the literariness of his love for Lesbia but its reality. Just so here: Catullus wishes to show Lesbia his grief, as he wished to show Calvus in 50–51. Here too he does so by breaching the boundary between his textual world and the extratextual reality of Lesbia's identity.

[26] Unless there is coded promiscuity in *omnis surripuit Veneres.*

[27] The image of Lesbia having sex with a man described as a voracious pervert would not be flattering, but the poem omits reference to sex, and is in fact compatible with Gellius merely attempting to seduce Lesbia; she, meanwhile, is neutrally described as *hanc . . . cuius me magnus edebat amor.* The *amor* itself is *misero hoc nostro, hoc perdito amore* (91.2); it is not clear that this counts as abusive speech about Lesbia.

Notice especially the content of poem 83, the first Lesbia poem following the revelation of her identity: this is also the first time we hear that *she* is angry with and speaks ill of *him* (repeated only in poem 92; the only *comparandum* for her displeasure is poem 36, where she wishes no longer to be the target of invective). The grounds for her anger are explained precisely by poem 79, the revelation of her identity: everyone, both intra- and extratextually, knows who she is. Catullus there takes extraordinary care that the revelation not be missed: 79 is one of the few poems to mention both lovers by name, and one of the few poems to geminate their names.[28] Within the text, that world crucially includes her husband, whose relief at Lesbia's maledictions of Catullus implies both his discovery of the affair and his decision to overlook it. Catullus at 68.135–48 is thus not the only man to overlook Lesbia's infidelity, and not the only man who must deceive himself in doing so (68.135–48 again, poem 83 itself, 92).

Another possibility arises: are we to read Catullus' negotiation of Lesbia's "infidelity" to him as an indication that he expects her to read or hear poem 68b? This would explain the motif of marriage to Jupiter in the first two Lesbia poems in **C2**. Accepting his acceptance of her sexual independence, she would also accept his mapping of their relationship in 136–40 (Juno : Jupiter :: Catullus : Lesbia) and his understanding that her marriage to another means he can expect even less from her (143–48). In response she warmly or politely says, "I wish we *could* be married," and returns Catullus' Jovian serve, reversing his gender inversion: "I'd take you over him, too." Her rhetoric comes off as overdone and rings false to Catullus, explaining the suspicion of poem 70. Catullus now discovers her affair with Rufus, setting up the following poem 71 and all invective pyrotechnics to come. Lesbia has an excellent lover's argument against him; she points out his hypocrisy in that he can figure her as Jupiter, but not the other way around, and his self-contradiction in attacking her just after admitting he had no right to expect her fidelity. The self-righteous indignation that follows will be the greater for Catullus' suppressed knowledge that she is right.

In this reading of the Lesbia plot in the first half of **C2**, we are closely guided by the reflection it makes with the equivalent plot in the first half of **A**. Poem 8, as disillusioned lover's soliloquy, has long been recognized as the specular pair with 76 that it is; among many similarities, the Catullus of

---

[28] *Lesbius . . . Lesbia . . . Catulle . . . Catullum*. Besides poem 79, only poem 8 (and 52, including **Ax**) also repeats the poet's name, only poem 92 (and 58, including **Ax**) also repeats hers; only poems 7 and 51 (and 58) contain both lovers' names.

either poem (thinks he) knows what must be done, but also vacillates. In **A**, the subsequent Lesbia poem (11) executes the dismissal that the soliloquy (8) resolves upon; his "divorce" from Lesbia is performative, with the requested agents Furius and Aurelius miming the requirement of Roman family law for *nuntii*, by whose agency and speech-act the husband's repudiation becomes public.[29] So here do 78b and 79 execute the irresolute resolution of poem 76, by which Catullus determines to be freed from his wretched love. No vengeful lover in a secret and adulterous affair could fail to see the power she or he has over the other; the Catullus of poem 76 is both vengeful and keenly *aware* of his habitual irresolution in respect to Lesbia. He has even just informed her of these facts: the previous poem informs us and her that Catullus has "lost his mind" (*huc est mens deducta*, 75.1–2), that he is maliciously disposed toward her (*nec bene uelle queat tibi*, 75.3), and he still loves her (*nec desistere amare*, 75.4). The only solution, poem 76 now concludes, is to be done with Lesbia permanently, by any means possible (or impossible: 76.13–16). He now finds, so he thinks, the obvious expedient to burn his bridges forever. Any of the three under-handed weapons (the revelation of her adultery, the notorious incest accusation, the breach of her pseudonymity) poem 79 hurls at Lesbia might, should, suffice to alienate her forever; surely, he thinks, all three together will work.

But, at least on rereading, *we* think: surely not. On Catullus' side at least, the second thoughts are found from the very following Lesbia poem, 83 – as they should be, after the consecutive statement and demonstration (in 75 and 76) of Catullus' ambivalence, his hate/love for Lesbia. Just as his malice, madness, and misery in 75 and 76 had set up and explained the vengeance taken by 78b–79, so does his perduring love in those poems explain 83; just as that vengeance had also been an act of madness (75.1–2), so does his willful deduction of Lesbia's perduring love (*uritur*, 83.6) now look like the act of a *mens deducta* (75.1). Following this, we have the bare fact of the poet's hate/love (85), his fair words about Lesbia's beauty (86), the pulled punch of his assertion of *fides* (87), the tie-in between the Gellius and Lesbia plots (91), and the last word, the blatantly self-serving invalid-syllogism-*cum*-ironic-text -interpretation of poem 92, with ring composition for the Lesbia plot in **C2** thus far (*nulli se dicit mulier mea*, 70.1 – *Lesbia mi dicit semper male*, 92.1).

From poem 93, as we have seen, the Lesbia plot goes on hiatus, returning about halfway through the sequence, in poem 104. In that poem, the unnamed addressee who expects Catullus to speak ill of his (estranged)

[29] Mayer (1983).

love is compellingly taken as an embedded incompetent reader of the Lesbia poems, just as Furius and Aurelius had been: she or he has not read carefully enough, providing Catullus a strategic opportunity (is Lesbia listening? are these poetic utterances so public that all inhabitants of this world hear everything?) to proclaim that he will not speak ill of the woman who is life itself to him.

Just following, they are back together. Catullus' reasoning in poems 83 and 92 had been flawed, but its conclusion, that Lesbia's love also remains, now seems correct:

Poem	Summary	Well-disposed language
104	C refuses to speak ill of his "life" who is "dearer than both eyes"	*meae ... uitae; carior est oculis*
107	L has restored herself to C!	*gratum; carius auro; te restituis, Lesbia, mi cupido; o lucem candidiore nota!; quis ... uiuit felicior*, etc.
109	L says their love will be eternal; let her be sincere!	*iucundum, mea uita ... amorem; hoc sanctae foedus amicitiae*

The sequence: a troubled and suspicious lover (70) who is cheated on (71); the spectacle of his self-righteous pain (72–76); his savage act of revenge (78b–79); her reaction to the same (83, 92) and his calmer, rationalizing, conflicted second thoughts (83, 85, 86, 92); a hiatus of some time (93–103); his fair words, hoping to be overheard (104); the lovers reunited (107); a troubled and suspicious lover, hoping that *this* time it's forever (109, with another closural recollection of the lovers' vow theme in the initial Lesbia poem, 70). This is a sequential narrative.

3 Conclusion: The C2 Problem

It is also an explanation. The account of these poems and their arrangement given here has offered a neat rhetorical talisman against the reasonable worries these poems occasion: If these poems individually come off as rougher or weaker (as the case may be for any given reader) than the short poems of **A**, why should the ensemble of **C2** not come off likewise rougher or weaker than the ensemble of **A**? But perhaps this line is all too neat. So, I confess, it seems to me. We should, and can, do better.

In **A**, the turn from polish in poems 1–14 to *horror* in 14b–26 is signaled by the Saturnalian drama of composition in poem 14; if the account of **Ax** as the improvised wax scribblings *chez* Calvus is accepted, that stretch of roughness is similarly explained, and both stretches held at authorial arm's length, presented repectively as meta-invective and meta-doggerel. Here, it will not be authorial distancing of this kind, but the plot of Catullus' life circumstances which signals and explains the generic turn: the Catullus who returns to love (poetry) and to Lesbia in 68b is a traumatized man reasoning badly; when the Catullus in uneasy dialogue with her in poem 70 discovers Lesbia's "infidelity" just thereafter, the poetic vehicles for his displays of self-pity and vengeance bespeak his mental state just as surely as his inability to compose love poetry in poem 65, the (self-)hobbled poetics of 68a, and the grief-infused erotics of 68b do. Unlike the equivalents in **A**, these poems cannot plausibly feature a witty and confident poet winking at his own splenetic displays: such a Catullus would not be the Catullus that his poetic self-plotting needs him to be.[30] The clipped and concentrated expression of epigrammatic point, however, is perfectly suited for the developing sketch of the wounded Catullus' one erotic obsession and his many invective ones.

Does this answer suffice? Are we satisfied with it, for example, in respect to the quite rough invective stretch between Lesbia's farewell in poem 109 and the closural drama of the non-composition of "poem 117"? Answers here will vary with one's sense of these poems and their artistry, and my own answer, I say with anxiety rather than embarrassment, remains somewhat equivocal.

That is, it makes sense that Catullus should have come to his project in **C2** with a conception of their form along the lines of what we in fact read: poems "like this" are a recognizable genre, and they are one of a number of genres this poet thinks of as fitting for him to work in. They impose strict limits on what he can say and how he can say it; he will have fully understood that they do not constitute the most prestigious poetic medium available to him. Yet even if we grant that these limitations are professionally exciting to him, and even if we sensibly deny a reverse-engineered quasi-biographical intentionality by which *our* last Catullan words are *his* final poetic testament, I still think it is odd to end **C** with its last few poems. It is fine to say, and I do assert, that the persistence of this same poetic tenor before, during, and after the final reconciliation drama with Lesbia correctly and helpfully points us away from the face-value optimism of its "happy ending." More broadly, it is fine to see the

---

[30] The contrast is not, of course, intended to deny that the represented Catullus' control slips in **A**, as it surely does in poem 8 at the very least. Rather, the point is that **C2** is *pervasively* the product of represented psychological turmoil, while the same is not the case for **A**.

sputtering, cage-rattling political rage of so much of poems 93–116 as dramatically caused and explained by their creator's unhappy mental state and the "madness" occasioned by his unhappy love: discontinuous, momentary shards of epigrammatic wit and perceptiveness, but within an overarching consciousness incapable of achieving any sustained or coherent (self-)perspective. I do see that in these poems. But this may or may not yet be enough.

What may, however, be enough, or might gesture at a sufficient answer, is to show how not only the supervenient Catullus plot but the three Catullan books as a poetic whole come together with brilliant and unforgettable effect, as consummated by the poems of **C2**. I now turn to the conclusion of this work, the first of whose two parts aims at just such a demonstration.

Two Interpretive Applications

1 Troy as Catullan *Ariadnefaden*

Were he a more practical man, (the represented) Catullus would have married; a poem 61 would have been sung for him and his bride, who would have gone on to hold a little Catullus in her lap, assuring the continuity of his *domus*. Instead he falls for Lesbia. Their love may endanger her husband's *domus*, but it is certain, especially after the brother's death, to destroy his own.

Catullus knows this, sometimes well enough that he can say it (51.13–16 and 76; he knows less, and about less, in poem 8). In 68b, he must produce brilliant irrationality in order to deny it to himself; the hopelessness of his hope in the final Lesbia poem (109), by contrast, is so manifest that either he knows he is deceiving himself or he has lost his powers of discernment entirely. The latter is not impossible: these poems are co-written by a force that hijacks and destroys those powers, *amor*.[1] That they are also co-written by anger and hatred is paradoxical enough to be presented as such in poetry, but learned poetry knows that their conjunction is not only possible but paradigmatic – in fact, inevitable. And the represented Catullus who undergoes these upheavals is a learned poet. We would know that he knows this even if we had not read poem 64, at whose center is Ariadne's deadly anger/love for Theseus, and which is framed by the deadly love of Peleus and Thetis, fated to bring forth one birth in Thessaly and innumerable deaths at Troy.

The comparison between the Trojan deaths, funeral rites, and tombs prophesied by the Parcae (64.343–70) and the brother's Trojan death, funeral rites, and tomb (65.5–8, 68a.19–24, 68b.91–100, poem 101) would

---

[1] The most frequently appearing noun in the corpus (53 times). See Fraenkel (1980) 213, Putnam (2006) 88, and Horace, *Odes* 1.15 and 2.16.

be there for the noticing, even if this study has failed to show that the end
of poem 64 is the end of one artfully arranged book and poem 65 the
beginning of another. So too would the following correspondence (51.13–16
~ 68.101–04):

> **otium**, Catulle, tibi molestum est:
> **otio** exsultas nimiumque gestis:
> **otium** et reges prius et beatas
>   perdidit **urbes**

> ad quam [*sc.* **Troiam**] tum properans fertur <lecta> undique pubes
>   Graeca penetralis deseruisse focos,
> ne Paris abducta gauisus libera moecha
>   **otia** pacato degeret in thalamo.

"Idleness has destroyed kings and rich cities in the past." Since it is typically
military conquest that destroys cities, and since *otium* can mean political
tranquility, there is a whiff of sinister paradox to 51.15–16: peace has caused
(defeat in) war. With *otium* in 51.13–16 clearly negative, the referent of its
conservative moralizing ought to be either Catullus' idle poetic or erotic
pursuits; although the responsion with *otiosi* at 50.1 points to the former,
both the immediate context of poem 51 and the more distant intratext with
68b.104 (the sole appearance of *otium* or *otiosus* outside **A**) point to the
latter. Troy is in any case a paradigmatic city destroyed by wrongful erotic
otium; a reader is authorized by this at least to consider a reference to Troy
in *perdidit urbes*. The intratext with 68.101–04 is then sufficient demonstration that this reference is real.

But of course this study has now concluded that *perdidit urbes* are the
closing words of an authorial book, and that **C**, in which the intratext is
read, is another, belated book. And now we recall that **C** begins with
a reference to Troy and the Trojan war:

> Etsi me assiduo confectum cura dolore
>   seuocat a doctis, Ortale, uirginibus,
> nec potis est dulcis Musarum expromere fetus
>   mens animi, tantis fluctuat ipsa malis –
> namque mei nuper Lethaeo gurgite fratris   65.5
>   pallidulum manans alluit unda pedem,
> **Troia Rhoeteo** quem subter **litore tellus**
>   ereptum nostris obterit ex oculis.

The great calamity which has befallen Catullus is a Trojan calamity; the
tomb on the Rhoetean shore likens the brother to Ajax, rendering Catullus
the overshadowed second son Teucer. **A** ends with a warning of what on its

own we may take as a disaster potentially (for Catullus) Trojan in scope. The opening of **C** reaches immediately back and alters the meaning of the close of **A**, rendering this possible or potential reading of *perdidit urbes* now mandatory. The explicit intratext in 68b above, which is itself interwoven with the recurrence of the brother at the heart of the ring-structure of 68b (Troy at lines 85–90, the brother at 91–100, Troy again at 101–04), merely elaborates what has already been put beyond doubt.

Yet poem 51 and *perdidit urbes* have a further Trojan resonance *within* **A**:

cum suis uiuat ualeatque moechis,		otium, Catulle, tibi molestum est;	
quos simul complexa tenet trecentos,		otio exsultas nimiumque gestis,	
nullum amans uere, sed identidem omnium		otium et reges prius et beatas	51.15
Ilia rumpens.	11.20	**perdidit urbes.**	

Neither the twinned status of the two Sapphic poems and Lesbia poems 11 and 51 nor the imbrication of military and imperialistic themes with eros in the former can be reasonably doubted. Nor can we resist the reference to Troy in *perdidit urbes*. Comparing the two poems again with this knowledge, we now see that "destroying Troy" lies before us in poem 11 as well, similarly at stanza end, requiring for Catullus' readers not even the upper case letter added here to make plain what is being said. One could translate, interpretively:

> farewell and fuck off with her adulterers, taking them three hundred at a time, loving none truly, a repeated She-who-destroyed-Troy for them all.

Once again we recall that Furius and Aurelius are delivering a *diuortium per nuntios*: Catullus' fake Troy-themed divorce from Lesbia, textually preceding his Troy-themed and brother-themed fake marriage to her in poem 68b. She is identified with Helen,[2] thus casting Catullus as a modernist Menelaos, irresolutely and temporarily letting her go. He claims here that he will not go after her to Troy; at book-end of **A**, once again occurrently struggling against his vast *amor* for Lesbia, he warns himself: "careful: Troy could come after you." When next we meet him speaking freely in his own poetic voice, at the beginning of **C**, we see that it has.

I have argued above for one other reference to Troy in **A**, at 46.6: *ad claras Asiae uolemus urbes*. Again, Troy is the most illustrious Asian city,

---

[2] Horace clearly reads 51.13–16 and 68.101–04 together in *Odes* 1.15, Nereus' prophecy to Paris aboard the ship conveying him and Helen to Troy (Putnam (2006) 87–89). Compare also Propertius: naked with Cynthia, he and she *longas condimus Iliadas* (2.1.14), punning on "compose long *Iliads*" and "bury my long *ilia*"; 2.34.87–88 mention *scripta Catulli* | *Lesbia quis ipsa notior est Helena*. These references frame our Propertius 2 and could therefore plausibly point to each other, whether these poems were originally one book or two.

and its site is indeed on Catullus' itinerary. This reference points in a literary direction, to Catullus' more ambitious future poetry: his poetic *mens* longs to roam (*auet uagari*), he exults in the growing vigor of his poetic prowess (*laeti studio pedes uigescunt*). He thinks of his poetic mission to Troy as a bank holiday lark, as perhaps it would be, absent the poetic disruption that his brother's death will occasion.

We now recall how **B** picks up the Troy theme. Poem 61 is framed by the myth: the pre-Iliadic Judgment appears in its opening simile (16–20), the Odyssean and post-Odyssean Penelope and Telemachus at its end (219–23). Venus without Hymenaeus causes ill repute (61–65), the loss of the *domus* (66–70), and military defeat (71–75); all of these do indeed result from her visitation of Paris, the *Phrygius iudex* (18–19). Manlius too is visited by Venus (189–98), but with the marriage god ritually present; he will not be tempted away from his bride (97–101).

Turning to the remainder of **B**, it bears mention that there is a reference to a sacked city in the following epithalamium (62.24),[3] and it is evocative to reflect that poem 63 narrates the disastrous sequelae of a Greek Attis' arrival at the Troad, after which he "tore off the weights of his *ilium*" (*deuolsit ili . . . pondera*, 63.5).[4] Yet it is naturally poem 64 which substantially engages with the Troy myth.

Catullus' epic negotiates between extremes of inclusion and exclusion: its universalizing chronological and mythic sweep on the one hand, and the minute focus of its descriptions and narratives on the other. The central narrative is of the wedding of Peleus and Thetis, and the central description is of a single item in Peleus' house; yet even as the description alone constitutes a majority of the work, the poem not only mentions but deeply engages with the myths of the Argonauts and the Fleece, Theseus and Crete, and the Trojan War. With Troy and the *Argo* especially standing as mythic nodes, the great majority of heroes and heroic narratives thus fall either within the poem's scope or at one remove from it.

All three of the poem's central myths are approached through focalizations on their eccentric or peripheral elements. This is clear enough for the first two: Peleus' vision of the naked Thetis and betrothal to her displaces the rest of the Argonautic expedition, as Ariadne's abandonment and plaint dominate the Theseus/Cretan myth. As for the Trojan War, the

---

[3] Memorably reworked by Vergil at *Aen.* 2.746: where Catullus' chorus of maidens had argued that marriage itself is as cruel as the sack of cities, Aeneas compares the loss of *his* marriage to the sack of Troy.

[4] The noun is heteroclite, with forms belonging to an unattested nominative singular *ile* along with the attested *ilium*.

prophetic account of Achilles' heroism at Troy (343–70) elides narrative elements, such as his quarrel with Agamemnon and slaying of Hector, focusing instead on Achillean deaths, tombs, and funerals. The Trojan stanzas of the song move as follows:

1) Achilles will be without heroic equal at a besieged Troy soaked in Trojan blood (343–46).
2) Trojan mothers will admit his heroism, tearing their disheveled hair and bruising their exposed breasts at their sons' funerals (348–51),
3) for he will *cut down* Trojans as a reaper levels a field (353–55)
4) while he *piles up* their corpses, as the river Scamander, its course clogged with the slain, will attest (357–60),
5) and a funeral mound *piled up* upon his death will receive the corpse of a maiden as a prize, as she will attest (362–64),
6) for as soon as the Greeks sack Troy, Polyxena will be slaughtered over the *lofty* tomb, *collapsing* over it and wetting it with her blood (366–70).

All of this in turn leads to the shocking inference drawn by the Parcae: the marital union that will occasion all of this should now begin, and for these reasons (*quare*, 372). The birth of Achilles begets deaths as the wedding of his parents begets funerals:[5] *comme il faut*, the Parcae believe.

Thinking now in terms of characters, just as Peleus and Thetis rather fade into the background of their own story, so does Theseus fade away (quite literally, his boat barely visible on the ecphrastic *objet*) from his, while the Argonautic protagonist Jason – and with him Ariadne's typological correspondent Medea – are subject to complete narrative erasure. Ariadne dominates the larger myth that dominates Peleus and Thetis' wedding myth, but Peleus and Thetis had just crowded out Jason and Medea from their myth as well. Likewise for Achilles at Troy: he is merely a producer of corpses and then a (still corpse-producing) corpse himself. The princess who upstages the hero is Medea in the suppressed Apollonian model, Thetis in Catullus' narrative *praeteritio* thereof, Ariadne in his ecphrastic centerpiece, and now Polyxena in the prophetic finale.

Turning now to etiology: the *Argo* causes the wedding; the wedding causes Troy. Ariadne and Theseus reflect and illustrate these cause-and-effect sequences. But just as Ariadne's most conspicuous reflex is the entirely suppressed Medea rather than the Thetis she matches in the

---

[5] The last of which is an explicitly non-nuptial ritual; see for instance Polyxena calling herself an "un-wedding-hymned un-bride" in Euripides' *Hecuba* (416, cf. 612).

narrative (Ariadne is Medea's fellow vengeful abandoned princess, and like Medea, she has traded her brother's life for a romantic relationship with a Greek), so is the more conspicuous causal link from wedding to war (the advent of Eris or Discord at Thetis' wedding) suppressed, leaving the crucial but not causal Achilles in his narrative place.

Eris' provocation, as mentioned above, leading to the Judgment of Paris, is suppressed in Catullus. As the song of the Parcae ends, the bride has not yet arrived at the house; the moment Catullus' narrative ends (or breaks off) is the moment for the *Streitapfel* to roll.[6] While it is true that one needs strong justification to argue convincingly for an absent, suppressed presence, the evidence is there: first, the poem already requires us to read the absent presence of Medea;[7] then, the Parcae give the game away, framing their prophecy with the assertion of unprecedented *concordia* between the bridal pair (336) and the denial of Thetis' future discord (*discordis . . . puellae*, 379).[8]

This sharpens the Troy-themed framing of **B** as a whole: the opening simile of 61.16–20 likens the bride Iunia to Venus at her Judgment, which will now be brought about just after the epic narration of 64 comes to a close. Poem 61, however, also closes with Troy: the issue of this marriage, *Torquatus paruulus*, will be, Catullus' speaker proclaims, the Telemachus to Iunia's Penelope (219–23); the boy's resemblance to his father will prove his mother's modesty (214–18). This too has a reflex in the song of the Parcae, though we should be cautious not to take it too far: the stratagem by which Penelope preserves her *pudicitia* (217) and *fama* (223) is the *femineus labor* the Parcae carry out as they sing: namely, textile manufacture.

The issues raised here are too many and too complicated to treat responsibly at this point, and in any case the matter has attracted a wide and distinguished body of comment. My point can be stated in less controversial form: any extent to which the thread spun by the Parcae *is* poetry, whether their occurrently sung song alone and/or in conjunction with other tales and texts, is an extent to which **B** virtually ends with a drama of composition, just as **A** and **C** do; both the drama itself and the question of its referent(s) must then, as elsewhere, be interrogated.

---

[6] Townend (1983). The Judgment and Eris' role in it are ancient, going back at least to cyclical epic, specifically the *Cypria*; the first literary attestations of the apple are post-Catullan. All that turns on my assumption that Catullus' audience knows the story is the argument in Chapter 1 that nuptial apples are read at the beginning of **A** and **C** and an absent presence at the beginning of **B**.

[7] The poem begins with the *Argo*, which is destined to bring Medea back from Colchis; Ariadne's reaction to her situation cannot help but recall Medea's reaction to Jason's second wedding. For further parallels between Medea-related texts and Catullus 64, see Gaisser (1995), Claire (1996), Morwood (1999).

[8] O'Hara (2007) 48 n.34.

The Parcae are uniquely authoritative spinners: the "fates follow their threads" (326–27), producing their own truth and thus apparently closing off the logical space between their "words" (*qua* text/textile) and "deeds."[9] The woven *puluinar* which precedes their song is a textile representation of threads they have, on the day of Thetis' wedding, already spun.[10] As they sing, then, it should not be thought they are occurrently spinning only their prophetic song itself. That they are spinning the *subtegmina* of Fate, which is to say, the future, is the given here; if their spinning is metaphorically represented as song, it will be song *as well as* the future the song represents, not instead of it.

The deeds they are here producing and the words that represent them, of course, will "later" be represented in the *Iliad*, the most celebrated poem of all. Besides the post-Iliadic events (Achilles' death and burial, the fall of Troy, and Polyxena's sacrifice) with which it ends (362–70), the account of Achilles' career maps specifically onto the climactic books of the *Iliad*. While in isolation the mention of Achilles "laying low" Trojan corpses (355) might refer only generally to his fighting at Troy,[11] the clogged Scamander in the following stanza (357–60) picks out the equivalent scene in *Iliad* 21. This ties the "laying low" just before to Achilles' *aristeia* starting in book 20, continuing through the Scamander incident in 21, and culminating in the slaying of Hector in book 22. The stanza just before these two (348–52) is the description of Trojan mothers bereaved by Achilles' deeds; each of its elements is paralleled by the Iliadic Hecuba. She does indeed "admit Achilles' great deeds" (348–49) upon the repatriation of Hector's corpse (24.748–59; the slaying of so many of her sons), just before the funeral rites for him which close the poem. And she had earlier torn her hair and thrown down her veil upon his death (20.405–07; she tears her hair again at 24.710–11), as Catullus' matrons will "loosen

---

[9] See O'Hara (2007) 47–54 on the problem of the song's veracity. I would however caution that while the song may well be prima facie misleading, oracular interpretation need not be straightforward, and there is little prospect of catching the Parcae in a formal lie, rendering false the narrator's and their own asseverations of truthfulness. If their concluding denial of Thetis' discord (379–80) is taken to contradict e.g. Apollonius' account of her separation from Peleus (4.869–79), we can say that Catullus polemically contradicts Apollonius rather than that he makes his Parcae speak falsely. But in fact those lines do not promise marital concord for the rest of Peleus' life; they merely promise his mother's (or mother-in-law's) unextinguished hope for grandchildren. Note too that the assertion of the couple's *concordia* at 336 is in the present tense (*adest*): it is not even a prediction.

[10] Weber (1983) notes the chronological irregularity: Medea traditionally came to Athens before Theseus came of age; how can Theseus' affair with Ariadne then predate the voyage of the *Argo*?

[11] The reaper simile (353–54) is taken from earlier in the poem (11.67–71); Achilles is absent from the fight, and the simile refers to the Greek and Trojan sides as a whole. It is useful for my claim that *Discordia* is implicitly present here that the fighting illustrated by the simile has been instigated by Eris (11.1–14), who now rejoices to behold it (11.73).

disheveled hair from a gray head" (350).[12] While she does not beat her breasts in mourning (351), she movingly exposes her breast to Hector just before his death (22.80), invoking her nursing of him to dissuade him from confronting Achilles. The Parcae emphasize the matrons' age in respect to both their hair (*cano . . . uertice*) and breasts (*putrida*); the aged Hecuba, unlike the young or immortal Greek women Homer describes beating their breasts (18.30–31, 18.50–51, 19.284–85), plainly answers well here.

The point of this is not to claim that the Parcae are composing the *Iliad*, but rather that they are pointedly *not* composing the *Iliad*. They are bringing about the future which Homer will describe and praising its most accomplished warrior, but they prefer to mention the near-madness of his *aristeia* to his victory over his most accomplished foe, just as they prefer to stress the grief he inflicts on enemy mothers rather than his courageous acceptance of his own mortality, let alone his sympathetic response to Priam in book 24. They suppress Priam entirely and down-grade Hector and Hecuba to one slain warrior and one bereaved mother out of many; continuing beyond the moment at which the *Iliad* ends, they finally come to a mortal who to them rates mention by name: the sacrificed maiden Polyxena. All of these veridical prophecies are, for the Parcae, positive grounds for the wedding to proceed.

It is anything but clear that the song fails to be *ueridicus* or is an instance of *perfidia*,[13] and there is a consistent set of values by which it all makes sense. It is indeed hard, and I would say highly implausible, to attribute these values to poem 64 or Catullus, but grounds for denying them to the Parcae are not clearly met. And in fact there is great explanatory power in ascribing to them attitudes and motivations upon which they reasonably produce the song.

How do the Parcae think? What are their values, their goals? Just as Catullus' tight focalizations on narrative and descriptive details and his complex and polemical manipulations of his intertexts provide points of entry into his composition of his poem, so do those of the Parcae for theirs. They have given us a wealth of information about themselves: dramatic necessities may force them to collapse *Iliad* 20–24 into a dozen or so lines, but it is their choice to collapse it into *these* dozen or so lines.

Their choice of content, then, tells us much. For one thing, the Parcae *like* death. They're good at producing it, and they respect quantity over

---

[12] If it is objected that *soluent* refers to the "loosening" rather than the Homeric "tearing" of hair, the removal of the veil will have presumably achieved the former.

[13] Could it be *ueridicus qua* "technically true" but still *perfidus qua* "misleading?" I doubt one could successfully press such a charge (recall the judicial metaphor in *arguet*) before a court competent to hear the case.

quality (as well they might: their shears kill *everybody*). Much of their descriptive *enargeia* is expended upon the bodily realities of violent death (359–60, 368–70).

For another thing, they are moralists. They respect *uirtus* above all, and they hold to a perfectly recognizable, heroic-age characterization of it. Its reward is κλέος or *fama*, and they are pleased to contribute to the *fama* of their deserving honorands. And they are not unsympathetic: they warmly felicitate Peleus on his unprecedented nuptial achievement (334–36), vicariously participate in his expected conjugal pleasure (328–32, 372–74), and celebrate the affectionate sentiments of the bride and groom and their families (336, 376–80). With their sympathy focalized entirely through the couple and their son, and with heroic *uirtus* their master value, they do not view the suffering heroically inflicted by their honorands as a negative cost that heroism must pay, but as one of its positive payoffs. In their estimation, tactful omission dictates that they pass over Achilles' gallant sympathy for the elderly Priam.

Finally, we know that their temporal horizon is a long one. All human beings die, sooner rather than later. A grand tomb on which a terrible, heroic offering is made therefore yields a greater share of *kleos* than most heroic deeds achieved in life. Why would they omit mention of it?

All of these results follow from simply reading the song, taking it as true and sincere, and reconstructing the beliefs and values from which such a song could sincerely emerge. The song, however, is not the only text to inform us of their values. The reason for this, of course, is that the Parcae compose every mortal birth and death: they spin the human cosmos. They do not merely condone Polyxena's terrible death; her death *is* their creative idea. The answer to the interpretive puzzle of why the Parcae mention child sacrifice in a wedding song thus stares us in the face: the set of values on which this puzzle puzzles is one that would not have sanctioned the sacrifice of a child in the first place. When we ask this question, we are not thinking as the Parcae do. The question dissolves as soon as we realize this.

And if the simultaneous spinning and singing of the Parcae is a figure for the song's performativity, for the equation of their words with their deeds, we are left to consider that not only their song but also its narrative content and facticity constitute the noble favor they are performing for the happy bridal pair. Their son's story, in both senses, is their nuptial gift. All of Greek culture ratifies its success: this is the best tale the Parcae ever spun, the best gift they could give.

Poem 64, then, sets for itself a problem of theodicy – as is generically appropriate for an epic poem to do. If the gods write the world, why have they written *this* one? On any version of this problem, you can explain what is bad in the world by redirecting blame away from the gods (onto human agency, say, and/or the refractory nature of sublunary matter), or you can deny that there *is* anything bad about the world. If the latter, you will have to offer a revisionist account of what is good. The Parcae are committed to a complementary solution along these lines: the senses of "good" which pick out what is truly good are the artistic and the heroic ones. They compose the best μῦθος about the best ἥρως.

The Parcae resemble human poets in further ways, beyond composing songs, singing arms and the man, and taking care to sing well. For one, their textile songs are, and must be, the theoretical limit-cases of intertextuality. No song of theirs can be explained without reference to their other songs; if the endlessly ramified intertextuality of poem 64 is a figure for this, it is a most effective one. And one of their signal uses or applications of intertextual technique is seen at the highest levels of poetic structure: they compose by pattern, constructing typological correspondences for their characters and plots, which they then play upon artfully. They are narrative traditionalists. They write the same story over and over again: a man goes on a journey, meets a princess, and falls in love so immediately and intensely that he and his beloved ignore the consequences of their actions until, eventually, disaster strikes.[14]

Most crucial of all, I claim, is the "characters" for whom these disasters are *fatal.* These are usually not the lovers, but usually are their kin: the fathers Aegeus and Priam; the brothers Absyrtus, the Minotaur, Hector and the rest; the child Polyxena and the more distantly alluded to post-Argonautic children of Medea and Theseus. Achilles' death is more profit than loss, and Paris' death is far less and far later a price than others in his story pay. Jason, Medea, Theseus, Ariadne, and Helen join Peleus and Thetis in personally escaping the violence their love sets into motion. Considering the summed burden of guilt these figures bear, the Parcae are authors of

---

[14] That is: Peleus goes to Colchis and meets Thetis; Jason goes to Colchis and meets Medea; Theseus goes to Crete and meets Ariadne; Paris goes to Sparta and meets Helen; Achilles goes to Troy – and meets Polyxena, a perverse twist on the repeated bride-and-groom motif. The thematic repetitions don't stop there: Achilles kills Polyxena's brother Hector; Theseus, the Minotaur; Jason, Absyrtus – the killing of the brother, is, in all three stories, a necessary condition for the hero's "getting the girl." In four of the stories, disaster ensues in the form of a breakup (Jason and Medea, Theseus and Ariadne) or the death of one partner (Polyxena, Paris) or their children (Jason and Medea's sons, Thetis and Peleus' son Achilles) or other relatives (Theseus' father Aegeus, Paris' parents and siblings). These disasters are the consequence of the couple's actions: betrayal of the princess' homeland (Medea, Ariadne, Helen), fratricide (Medea, Ariadne), theft (Jason and Medea stealing the Golden Fleece), adultery (Helen). Hence the narrator of 64 is amazed that Thetis' marriage to Peleus is *not* a betrayal, but rather sanctioned by her divine/royal family (25–30).

a retributive justice that is not only terrifying, but also – once again befitting their nature as poets – relentlessly ironic. And, finally, the Parcae never stop spinning (*aeternum . . . laborem*, 310).

Once again, this is not to say that the Parcae write poem 64. They did not, for instance, write the words which constitute Ariadne's plaint. In poetic terms, they write the *plots*, especially those of the death scenes; creative agency over speeches and reactions belongs to mortals alone. What they wrote, then, is Aegeus' death: Theseus would forget to unfurl the white sails because he forgot, because Jupiter made him forget, because he granted Ariadne's prayer, which she utters because Theseus abandoned her. They write the patterns, plots, and outcomes – for everyone, and thus for Catullus. Catullus writes them here but they wrote him first.

Consider the plot of **A**: a man arrives from a foreign journey (poems 4, 10, 31, 46).[15] He meets a Roman aristocrat, a republican princess;[16] it is love at first sight (51.6–7: *nam simul te, Lesbia, aspexi . . .*). Consequences are ignored (5.2: *rumoresque senum seueriorum . . .*); Catullus either fails to follow his own good judgment or hits upon it too late (51.13–16: *otium, Catulle . . . perdidit urbes*), depending on whether we emphasize the retro-jected dramatic moment of poem 51 in respect to its *otium* stanza, or, as I prefer, the book-final moment of its composition for Calvus.

And now the poet of **A** has composed **B** as well, when the news comes: his brother has died at Troy. The Parcae have played to form, spinning Catullus into the design he recalls them spinning. Recalling the very last temporal moment of **A**, we reflect that Catullus indeed anticipated a poetic instance of the *lex talionis* (50.20–21):

> . . . ne poenas Nemesis reposcat a te.
> est uemens dea: laedere hanc caueto.

Having already written of love at first sight, having mapped Lesbia onto Helen and Rome/Bithynia onto Sparta/Troy, the Parcae now implement the disaster phase of their Catullus-song upon the brother, burying him in the common tomb of Europe and Asia. The author of **C** will be their plaything, forced to endure and vainly rationalize a predicament he lacks the power to break free from.

---

[15] Armstrong (2013) 45 rightly points to 46.10–11 (Catullus' comrades had sailed together to Bithynia and now will make separate Roman returns from there) as correlate to the Greek heroes' expedition to Troy and their post-Iliadic *nostoi*. The poem complicates expedition and return in any case, with its flight to the famous cities of Asia (and hence Troy) balancing the homecoming it ultimately anticipates.

[16] Syme (1939) 12: "The *nobiles* were dynasts, their daughters princesses"; quoted of Lesbia/Clodia by Wiseman (1969) 59.

Before turning to **C**, we should note that the thread of the Troy myth is not only a figure for the composition of the Parcae but also a readerly heuristic for **B**, just as the *Ariadnefaden* in poem 64 (112–15) had already implicitly figured any hypothetical reading strategy by which we might unwind, like Theseus, its textual labyrinth. The Odyssean simile ending poem 61 refracts the Iliadic song of the Parcae in an ideologically pointed way: speaking in his own voice, or a voice negotiating between his personal sentiments and the values of his honorands and community, Catullus' wish for Iunia and Torquatus is an Odyssean one: the birth of a son who will enjoy the *fama* of a Telemachus born to a Penelope. By contrast, the divine powers exercising control not over Catullus' values but his fate end their Iliadic prophesy (and thus virtually end poem 64 and **B**) with the murder of a child reinforcing the *fama* of Achilles.

This tips the balance on a core interpretive question in poem 64: what should we think of the poet-narrator's awestruck enthusiasm for the heroic age he felicitates at its beginning (22–30) and judges so superior to his own at its end (384–408)? Taking poem 64 on its own, there is already a compelling case that the moral stance of these passages collapses upon inspection. The culmination of the allegedly glorious heroic age is child sacrifice, conducted amid piles of corpses. The heroes felicitated by the narrator behave unjustly, and the injustices with which he taxes his own age have all too conspicuous mythological parallels.[17] Taking poems 61 and 64 together, and considering each poem's Troy-themed references to its bridal pair's future, Roman readers will have seen their own ideals, values, and wishes (and surely Catullus') reflected in the Odyssean wish of 61 but not the Iliadic prophecy of 64: no murdered Trojan child's blood wetting a Greek tomb, but a living Roman Telemachus in the lap of a faithful Roman Penelope, reaching out with a cute, open-mouthed infantile face to his father, a Roman [Odysseus] who has not suffered overly much on land or sea.

However we wish to understand individual detail, then – and crucial interpretive problems do turn on this question – there is a gap between the values expressed by the narrator of poem 64 and those which we can

---

[17] Fratricide (399): Eteocles and Polynices; Thyestes and Atreus, though indirectly, through Aegisthus; in 64 itself Ariadne aids the killing of her brother (150), as the suppressed Medea kills Absyrtus. Fathers against sons (400–1): Laius and Oedipus, Hercules and his sons – though in neither case is this intentional; more straightforwardly, Tantalus and Pelops; though their immortality of course rules out death, the generational succession from Uranus to Saturn to Jupiter is hardly a story of filial piety or parental duty. Mother–son incest (403–4): Jocasta and Oedipus, though in their case both parties are (probably) ignorant. It does, however, seem clear that Jocasta realizes the truth before Oedipus, and at least possible that she would be content to continue their relationship if he would only drop the matter (Soph. *Oed.* 1060–68).

reasonably attribute to the Catullus who speaks elsewhere.[18] Further strengthening this sense are the epilogic lines just preceding poem 64 (63.91–93), in which the narrator reacts in an opposite way to his own story of human/divine relations, praying to the goddess in question precisely to leave him and his loved ones alone.[19] If the authorial voices of **B** are to be integrated with themselves, let alone those of **A** and **C**, it will not be in favor of the epilogic speaker of 64 taken at face value.

To summarize, then: both **A** and **B** embed the Troy myth, either book balancing its more optimistic, Odyssean elements with more minatory, Iliadic ones. Catullus' *nostos* from Bithynia brings him to the acquaintance of a woman belatedly seen as a Roman Helen who brings "Troy," erotic ruin, to her lovers. In the less first-personal poetry of **B**, his great themes of marriage and humans and gods are limned by the Troy myth, with his Odyssean wishes for Iunia and Manlius' marriage in 61 set off against his exploration of darker realities of sexual and marital union in 64. The *telos* of these darker realities is Troy and death; their Iliadic darkness is in fact hyper-Iliadic, a revision of its violent story stripped of its elements of noble pathos. That this revision is presented in an entirely glorious light would be troubling enough; that the creative agency which presides over human destiny crafts that destiny in accordance with these values is terrifying. And now, looking back at **A**, we see how well the represented Catullus' story maps onto these goddesses' template of erotic disaster. If their creative agency presides also over Catullus and his fate, catastrophe is certain.

Now **C** opens, and the catastrophe has come. The tomb of Achilles we have just read (64.362–70) is now joined by the other senior Greek hero's Trojan tomb, as the brother's Rhoetean tomb (65.7) maps onto that of Ajax, son of Telamon.[20] That death has come to lovers' kin rather than the lovers themselves fits the pattern; likening himself to Procne sorrowing for the son who dies at her own hands, but as vengeance for another's sexual wrongdoing (65.13–14), Catullus poses an interpretive problem. We may be confident in the fit between the mythological plots of erotic disaster in poem 64 and Catullus' own Trojan love affair: this fit is an artistic reality, and its reality

---

[18] The question is too large to consider properly at this point. One strategy would be to take the narrator's epilogic stance as openly insincere, perhaps even approaching the jocular insincerity or "bullshit" argued for in **A**. On another, one could read Catullus as sincere in all of these instances, with his consciousness divided against itself in ways he cannot resolve and may not see.

[19] Nor is there, in contradistinction to poem 64, the slightest internal tension between the narrative content of 63 and its narrator's concluding reaction. Readings on which Catullus reacts negatively to the foreign cult of Cybele, as opposed to the respectable Greco-Roman gods (Wiseman (1985) 200–6), must confront Cybele's cultic status as the mother of those gods.

[20] Thomson (1997) 445.

proposes an explanatory relationship between the brother's death and Catullus' love. But does Catullus know this, or even suspect it? Or is this explanatory relationship, like the creative control of the Parcae over it, merely the poet's moral/theological interpretation – and not necessarily a literally or sincerely meant interpretation – of the course his life has taken? A mere figure for the plight of an unhappy lover unexpectedly struck with familial grief? Or a delusion we would do best to pity him for? In other words, is Catullus so mad that he thinks his brother literally died for his erotic sins?

I will not argue for the solution presented here, on the grounds that the evidence does not determine a single correct realization, and can richly sustain different ones; there are also ways in which substantially different interpretations partially converge.[21] That said, I propose that the represented author Catullus is ignorant of, or at most dimly suspects, the metaphysical realities that we readers agree to take for true. Catullus wrote the Parcae correctly in poem 64: the world of the Roman social fiction is also a world in which circumstances of life and death are made to fit typological patterns, for artistic and moralistic reasons. But the Catullus of **C**, most of the time and in most respects, writes himself wrong: his failure to locate himself on his own poetic map is explained by the spectacle of his motivated reasoning, his all-too-partial perspective. He is quite his own ecphrastic Ariadne: viewing the woven image on the *puluinar*, the Thessalian wedding guests see that she is poised between abandonment by the pseudo-husband Theseus who sails away, and rescue by the approaching Bacchus who will be her real husband. But she looks in one direction rather than the other, and wrongly maps herself as the unburied victims of the wrath of Achilles (64.152 ~ *Il.* 1.4–5). If she looked the other way, she would see that she maps as both parties to the wedding she has been woven to celebrate, the parents of Achilles: as mortal spouse to a divinity, Peleus represents her immediate future, while Thetis is her present reality *qua* unclothed maiden in the sea, gazed upon with nuptial result.

It is important to note the resonance of this reading with the exculpatory ending of poem 22, which proclaims that our self-evaluative gaze is universally mistaken:

> nimirum id omnes fallimur, neque est quisquam
> quem non in aliqua re **uidere** Suffenum
> possis. suus cuique attributus est error;   20
> sed **non uidemus manticae quod in tergo est.**

---

[21] For example: whether you think that Catullus is mad to map himself onto his myths, or that Catullus is mad not to see how he maps onto his myths, you are likely to posit the superordinate perspective of "the text" or "Catullus the author," on which this mapping is an artistic construction.

Catullus' version of the beam in one's own eye appeals to our ability to see some parts but not others of a self-exemplary textile object; if this is felt to be evocative, we might consider taking the *mantica* as a mantic anticipation of the similar item to come. One naturally scruples to insist on the point: in any case, Catullus' comment about flawed self-insight invites us to look into his blind spots as well.

Returning now to poem 65, the brother's Trojan death has now cut Catullus off from his poetic craft; we have already seen how the concluding simile characterizes the gift to Ortalus as previously composed, newly-repurposed verses. He is still alienated from poetry when Mallius asks for gifts of the Muses and Venus, and Catullus must refuse the request (68a). When he later fulfills it (68b), Troy and the brother are literally at the center of his thoughts. Forced by social necessity to send poems 66 and 67, the Catullus of 68b will not wish to reflect how deeply their content tells against him. Legal marriage, proper religious observance, and safe return from foreign campaigning in poem 66 set off adultery, Protesilaus' overlooked sacrifice, Lesbia's ill-omened foot on the threshold, and the brother's Trojan death in 68b. The divinized Callimachean Lock celebrates conjugal desire and its fulfillment as thoroughly as Catullus had. She notably shares his and his male characters' enthusiasm for the bared breasts of wives (and wives-to-be), using the image of the husband in their presence to heighten the disavowal of adultery, just as Catullus had done (66.79–88 ~ 61.97–101); unlike Catullus there, she characterizes adultery as a specifically religious impropriety. And poem 67 in its entirety, of course, relies upon and provokes social disapproval and individual disgrace for *malum . . . adulterium* (67.36). The *domus* itself is ashamed to give admittance to adultery in 67; in 68b, Allius' house receives Catullus' benediction for the same (155–56), and he even prays to Nemesis that he might never be so pleased by something as to undertake it against divine will (75–76). He is as forgetful of vital precept as his Theseus becomes, in the divine vengeance which takes his father Aegeus' life (64.202–48).

It is, nonetheless, Ariadne's rhetoric that Catullus' self-suasion at the end of 68b resembles. In figuring himself as erotically enslaved to Lesbia as mistress (*erae*, 136), and in admitting that her father did not lead her to his house in marital union (143–44), Catullus' resolve to accept her love at any cost figures him as a kind of concubine. Ariadne puts a virtually identical, though counterfactual, case to the apostrophized Theseus: if he did not intend marriage (158) because of his father's wishes (159), he still might have led her to their house, so that she could be his slave (161).[22] Her expectation that she would be his concubine on this arrangement is clear, though not explicit, presumably in keeping with a modest self-presentation.[23] The difference is that where Ariadne has nothing to lose and a rhetorical point to score in counterfactually proposing this servile indignity, Catullus is actually committing himself to such a future.

I now turn to a final way in which the Catullus of poem 68b maps onto the mythological template of 64, namely the shocking conclusion to both narratives proper, in the sense of both textual closure and argumentative inference: *quare* (64.372 and 68b.147). Just as the Parcae had done, Catullus has presented what readers have every reason to take as an overwhelming case against the erotic relationship in question; just like them again, he endorses the relationship not in spite of this case but because of it. The justice of the Parcae (and their agents *Venus* and *Amor*), then, is particularly cruel in Catullus' case: they strike down the poet's brother as they did Theseus' father, and then they make him reason as madly as Ariadne did, and as they do themselves.

Turning now to **C2**, the principal Trojan text is poem 101: the Odyssean journey to the brother's tomb, balancing the Iliadic 68b. Before turning to it, however, a few elements of the Lesbia drama in poems 69–92 should be considered. I have already argued that poem 79 (and 78b, on the assumption that its addressee is Lesbius/Clodius) is Catullus' principal action in 69–92, the words of which are more richly taken as a collective speech act. In **A**, the post-breakup soliloquy, poem 8, establishes Catullus' resolution to repudiate Lesbia, a decision then publicly realized by poem 11, Furius and Aurelius' commission to deliver the repudiation. As reprise in **C2**, poem 76 is the soliloquy, 79 the execution of its resolution. In its unforgivable act of bridge-burning – or so Catullus hopes – poem 79 reveals Lesbia's extratextual identity and defames her and her brother, as (only) enemies of theirs do, by means of the incest accusation.

Parallels between Ariadne's lament and poem 76 are many and deep. Either poem is an anguished soliloquy which turns into a prayer for

---

[22] 64.158–60: *conubia, prisci ... parentis, attamen in uestras ... ducere sedes* ~ 68b.143–44: *nec tamen illa mihi dextra deducta paterna ... uenit ... domum*; 64.161: *quae tibi iucundo famularer serua labore* ~ 68b.136: *rara uerecundae furta feremus erae*.

[23] She refers to Theseus' promises of marriage (139–42) and sarcastically refers to him as her *coniunx* (182), but is otherwise euphemistic: her reference to men's "satiated desire" (147) makes the loss of her virginity to Theseus clear, and their intimacy is hinted at in *nulla ... res* at 136: "Could *nothing* change your cruel mind?"

redress,[24] accuses a lover of ingratitude and broken faith, is (dubiously) convinced of its speaker's own blamelessness,[25] is uttered "at the point of death,"[26] and is conspicuously marked in its poetic surroundings by its extraordinary length. On my reading of poem 76 in respect to poem 79, each text also sets in motion an act of vengeance against the lover, one which falls principally on the lover's kin. Theseus kills Ariadne's brother; Ariadne's revenge kills Theseus' father; either Jason or Medea kills *her* brother; Paris' adultery kills *his* brothers; Catullus has lost his own brother and now strikes Lesbia's brother, and his vengeance (*non impune*, 78b.3) will be rewarded with eternal fame (*omnia saecla ... fama loquetur anus*, 78b.3–4). Ariadne's revenge is carried out by divine will, but in the *hic et nunc* world of **C2**, Catullus must execute his own prayer.

Little though we may like it, Catullus' pious service for his brother in poem 101 is set in counterpoint with Lesbia's impieties with *her* brother in 79. Lesbia's brother is central, not only in explanatory terms but also textually, to the breakup drama of 69–92: though poem 80 falls in the middle by poem-count, the middle by line-count falls between 78b and 79.[27] Similarly, the Catullan brother is poem-medial in all three of his earlier appearances: he runs up to the middle of poem 65, straddles the middle of 68a, and runs up to the line-count middle of 68b, while also inhabiting the structural middle of its ring-composition scheme.[28] Within the second half of **C2**, 93–116, the exact mediality of poem 101 depends on the widespread but contested claim that 95b is fragmentary.[29] Whether the arithmetic centrality obtains or not – and the matter is certainly beyond conclusive demonstration – it nonetheless bears mentioning; it would be uncomfortable for Catullus to have arranged the brother passages in **C1** with precise attention to line-count but not to have done so with the equivalent sibling passages in **C2**. The transmitted text shows at least that

---

[24] The closest verbal parallels are found in either concluding prayer: *ego uae misera, extremis proferre medullis ... inops ... pectore ab imo* (64.196–98) ~ *extremam ... tulistis opem | me miserum ... imos ... in artus ... pectore* (76.18–22).

[25] Ariadne openly claims complicity in the killing of her brother, the Minotaur (150); she then asks "and for *this* I am to die without burial?" (152–53). Not all will agree that this is obviously unjust. For Catullus, the clearest self-indictment is to read his assertion of having performed all possible "benefactions" and "benedictions" to Lesbia (76.7–8) against 11.15–16: *pauca nuntiate meae puellae | non bona dicta.*

[26] 64.152–53, 186–89 ~ 76.18.

[27] A lost distich or two in 78b is all but certain; assuming it, the line-count middle falls within 78b, whose addressee, of course, I claim to be Lesbius/Clodius.

[28] 65: lines 5–12 of 24; 68a: 19–24 of 40; 68b: lines 91–100, the 51st to 60th of 120 transmitted lines.

[29] A three-distich poem 95b would place the end of 101 at the exact middle. For poems in the middle by line count as an alternative to the middle by poem count, compare Horace's "Parade" *Odes* (1.1–9), which are precisely bisected by line-count into 1.1–3 and 1.4–9.

the arithmetic may very well have been equally punctilious in **C2**, and is certainly not too far off; on these grounds, I will now argue for the thematic and explanatory centrality of poem 101, in respect to the reconciliation plot of 93–116.

To recall, Lesbia is absent from poems 93–103, reappears in 104, is reconciled with Catullus by 107, and has her textual *envoi* in 109. Two poems and eight lines separate the brother's farewell in 101 from Lesbia's return in 104. That Catullus' final expression of familial love and grief mediates the return of his erotic love has just been hinted at: 101 is clearly (and uniquely, within **C2**) paired with poem 96, the consolation to Calvus grieving his lover Quintilia, by the theme of death. Grief, says Catullus at 96.2–3, is "the longing by which we renew old loves and weep for friendships once dismissed." The reading *missas* ("dismissed" or "given up") is challenging here, prima facie harsh. Though some have sought to amend this to an easier *amissas*, "lost,"[30] the connection with Lesbia gives the transmitted reading a fine point: the affair certainly counts as *ueteres amores* (cf. *longum . . . amorem* at 76.13), Catullus has indeed "dismissed" her, and the final word of the final Lesbia poem describes their love as "friendship" (*amicitiae*, 109.6). Calvus' lover is gone; Catullus' brother is gone – but his lover is *not* gone. He thus promptly picks up the opportunity to refuse to speak ill of Lesbia, warmly refer to her as his *uita*, and proclaim her dearness (104). The gesture is noticed: two poems and four lines later, she has come back to him (107). Poem 101 marks the second time the poet's grief for the brother "makes an old love affair new," after 68b; after poems 3, 5, and 7, it marks the third time thoughts of death have mediated erotic persuasion between Catullus and Lesbia.[31]

Before turning to the Odyssean valence of poem 101, we must consider its Ariadnean intratext. We have seen how Catullus has already paralleled Ariadne-on-the-shore in the plot of 69–92, moving from anguished soliloquy to prayer in poem 76, avenging himself on his faithless lover by way of the lover's kin in 79. Now, in the central scene of anguish in 93–116, he plays Ariadne once again, and in fact even more so. Visiting the brother's tomb, he stands on the shore (per 65.7, *subter litore*), having just arrived there by sea. His brother has died. He speaks vainly to one who cannot hear his words, to whom he gives a belated send-off upon his departure. His circumstances map superabundantly onto hers; in addition, we now see

---

[30] Trappes-Lomax (2007) 273–74.
[31] Poem 5 above all: there can be little doubt that *da mi basia mille* is a persuasive inference from *nox est perpetua una dormienda*.

that nearly half of the poem's words are close verbal reminiscences of
Ariadne's:

101	64

conveyance & arrival

multas per gentes et multa per aequora **uectus**	aut ut **uecta** rati spumosa ad litora Diae
aduenio has miseras, frater, ad inferias,	**\<uenerit\>**, aut ut eam deuinctam lumina somno
	(121–22)

vain speech

ut te *postremo* donarem munere *mortis*	sed quid ego **ignaris nequiquam conquerar auris**,
et *mutam* **nequiquam alloquerer cinerem**,	exsternata malo, quae nullis sensibus auctae
	nec missas audire queunt nec reddere uoces?
	(164–66)

reasons for address

quandoquidem fortuna mihi tete abstulit	[**quandoquidem fortuna** mea ac tua feruida
ipsum,	uirtus
heu miser indigne frater adempte mihi.	**eripit** inuito **mihi te** . . .] (218–19)

paternal instruction

*nunc tamen inter*ea haec, **prisco quae more**	si tibi non cordi fuerant conubia nostra,
parentum	saeua quod horrebas **prisci praecepta parentis**
tradita sunt tristi munere ad inferias,	(158–59)

fraternal effluvia

accipe **fraterno multum manantia fletu**,	an patris auxilium sperem? quemne ipsa reliqui
atque in perpetuum, frater, *aue* atque *uale*	**respersum iuuenem fraterna caede** secuta?
	(180–81)

further diction

| | nulla fugae ratio, nullast spes: omnia *muta*, |
| | omnia sunt deserta, ostentant omnia letum. |

	non tamen ante mihi languescent lumina *morte*,
	nec prius a fesso secedent corpore sensus,
	quam iustam a diuis exposcam prodita multam,
	caelestumque fidem *postrema* comprecer hora.
	(186–91)

	(cf. 23–23b:
	heroes, *saluete*, deum genus! o bona matrum
	progenies, *saluete* iter\<um, *saluete* bonarum!\>)

The intratexts constitute a tight and consistent program: the poet-
brother begins with his own epic narrator's *praeteritio* of Ariadne's
conveyance/arrival, then passes to her acknowledgment of the uselessness
of unheard speech. The reason given for the address then switches to the
words of Aegeus, whose send-off speech to Theseus mirrors that of
Ariadne, at the structural center of the poem (132–201 ⁓ 215–37). Yet
this too recalls Ariadne's speech, and precisely the next reminiscence of it

in poem 101. Ariadne imagines her abandonment by Theseus as the dubiously pious observance of Aegeus' instruction on departure, namely that he not return with a Cretan bride; it is already an internal irony for poem 64 that we read Aegeus' actual instructions on departure, which now become the mechanism of the divine retribution by which he (rather than Ariadne) dies. In poem 101, *quandoquidem fortuna* ... (5–6) and *prisco quae more parentum* (7) thread those two passages together, deepening the already present textual invitation to read them together. The intratext also wondrously reflects the complexities of Catullus' piety: Theseus both is and is not responsible for his impious failure to carry out paternal precept, thus causing the death of his father, while Catullus both is and is not responsible for causing the death of his brother, whose funeral he now piously carries out, in accordance with paternal custom.

Finally, and however uncomfortably for those who have actually grieved with poem 101, there is one more brother: the Minotaur with whose blood Theseus is bespattered is reflected in the brother's offerings, seeping with Catullus' tears. Here it is Ariadne's impiety, her erotically-motivated complicity in her brother's murder, which implicates Catullus, though he is as blind to this fact as she is. That is to say, there is a most exquisite irony in the sibling funeral reflex in poem 64. In Ariadne's first mention of the Minotaur as brother (149–51), she indignantly reminds the absent Theseus that she saved him from death, even at the cost of her brother's life. The following lines (152–53) are the ones recalling the incipit of the *Iliad*:

> pro quo dilaceranda feris dabor alitibusque
> praeda, neque iniacta tumulabor mortua terra!

Ariadne helped Theseus kill her brother rather than fail him at the critical moment; as punishment, she claims, "I shall be preyed on by beasts and birds and go unburied!" Ariadne's shift to the passive voice here, after "I saved you" in 149–50, allows us to hear the justice in what she presents as unjust, less as "you have left me to die, after all I did for you" and more "I helped a man kill my brother and shall now die for it."

The justice of the Parcae, however, is not so linear: Aegeus will soon die, Theseus will attend a funeral; Ariadne is not punished but rather approached by a wedding party (251–65). So it is for Catullus in poem 101 and environs: the funeral for the brother there, the non-marital reunion causally imbricated with it, just after. And now we notice whose song Catullus is singing on his love's return: the Lesbia poems close with the closural words of the Parcae to Peleus.

quare agite **optatos animi** coniungite **amores,**
accipiat coniunx **felici foedere diuam,**
dedatur **cupido** iam dudum nupta marito.
  currite **ducentes** subtegmina, currite, fusi.
non illam nutrix orienti **luce** reuisens
hesterno collum **poterit** circumdare filo,
anxia nec mater discordis maesta puellae
secubitu **caros mittet sperare** nepotes.
  currite **ducentes** subtegmina, currite, fusi.   (64.372–81)

Si quicquam **cupido optantique** optigit umquam
    insperanti, hoc est gratum **animo** proprie.
quare hoc est gratum nobis quoque **carius** auro
    quod te restituis, Lesbia, mi **cupido.**
restituis **cupido** atque **insperanti,** ipsa refers te
    nobis. o **lucem** candidiore nota!
quis me uno uiuit **felicior** aut magis hac quid
    optandum uita dicere quopis **poterit**?   (107.1–8)

Iucundum, mea uita, mihi proponis **amorem**
    hunc nostrum inter nos perpetuumque fore.
di magni, facite ut uere pro**mittere possit,**
    atque id sincere dicat et ex **animo,**
ut liceat nobis tota per**ducere** uita
    aeternum hoc sanctae **foedus** amicitiae.   (109.1–6)

Although the text of poem 107 is quite uncertain, the remarkable extent of its self-repetition will not be an artifact of textual corruption. Dative *cupido* appears three times, forms of *opto* and *insperanti* twice apiece; all of these reflect the end of poem 64. So does the notorious *quare* of dubious erotic inference, back now for a third time. Catullus' *hoc est gratum* is performative: *gratum (est)* means "thank you" (*OLD s.v.* 2b), and so the poet is accepting Lesbia's return, saying yes. The form *poterit* is uniquely shared by these two Catullan passages; *lux* in the sense of "day," *felix, carus,* and *animus* round out the list, rather insistently.

After the interstitial poem 108, 109 is the last word on Lesbia, with further verbal recall of the last words on Peleus and Thetis (*foedus* above all). Catullus' wish corresponds to the mythological prophecy's close with the apparent happily ever after of Peleus and Thetis. Lesbia says their love will be pleasant, and it will be perpetual (lines 1–2); Catullus hopes her promises are true, as the Parcae's are true; he wishes the affair to continue, as a happy marriage would – though this is obviously and pointedly not a marriage – as long as they live. As first-time readers, we already knew that at least most of the prophetic content of the song of the Parcae was true, and we were given every reason to be horrified by it, to exempt ourselves from their favorable judgment, their "wherefore." So here, as intertextual readers at the end: these lovers will love each other forever, and their love will pile disaster upon disaster. Everything predicts this conclusion and nothing contradicts it. The most pitiable happy ending, ever.

2   One More Drama of Composition

A pressing Catullan problem for which I have no satisfactory theory or stable view is the matter of allegory: under what conditions should we say that a represented figure in the poems (sparrow, yacht, and so forth) "is" or represents some other sort of thing, and what sort of relation do we take this to be? What rules of inference apply here? Does the association of the sparrow with a penis, for example, imply that the sparrow is not (also) a pet bird? Why (not)?

I am pointing to this gaping interpretive *barathrum* here only to point out that no bottom can be seen and to disclaim the courage to rappel down in search of one. And the question, of course, can be broadened to encompass other sorts of metonymies as well. *Lesbius est pulcer* (79.1): on the compelling traditional identification, what follows from the assertion that Lesbia is a sister of P. Clodius Pulcher? Is any or every representation of Lesbia a representation of one of the three Clodiae? Is Catullus asserting that any or every detail given about Lesbia is a historical fact about this woman? Could the truth of the claim that Lesbia "is" Clodia cash out to no more than that the text invites readers to think of Clodia when they think of Lesbia?

With these questions appearing, at the least, too big to raise in a work's conclusion, we might seek out instead a question for which both obtainable and useful answers might plausibly be found. Without asserting the correctness of this policy in any strong sense, then, the question I would ask in the case of poem 4 is not whether the *phaselus* is a model of a yacht, but rather how well it fits to take the *phaselus* as a model of a yacht. If a threshold quantity of correspondence is met, we will find ourselves able to claim non-fortuitousness: that a given X-as-Y correspondence is too rich to have arisen by chance, that we cannot assume that it is simply spurious or mistaken.

By my lights, the notorious phallic interpretation of the *passer* meets that test easily: there is simply too much there for there to be nothing to it. The non-fortuitousness of the correspondences, though, is open to interpretation. The following are non-exhaustive families of interpretations:

1) The *passer* "is" Catullus' penis in a strong sense: reading it as a pet bird, or anything else, is wrong.

2) The *passer* "is" Catullus' penis, but in a weaker sense, such that it can be read as a penis, but also as a pet bird; the two options may be equally authorized, or one more so than the other.

3) The *passer* "is" something else, and the phallic correspondence is an artifact: the what-is-it riddle is real, and such riddles can be composed at a level of generality such that multiple putative solutions seem to fit.

4) The *passer* is a *passer*; its description in a way partially consistent with a phallic allegory is a characterization of Lesbia (the phallic way she plays with her pet bird, displaying her sexual desire) and/or of Catullus (the phallic way he describes his love interest, imagining her alone and at play, revealing his sexual desire and obsessiveness).

The only assertion I am inclined to defend at this point is that (1) is wrong. First, the phallic reading simply does not map well enough to justify so strong a claim, especially in relation to poem 3: at best, I think, we can *consider* mapping out the death of the sparrow as the poet's "impotence" (so Giangrande) or "post-coital lassitude" (Nadeau).[32] To be so persuaded by this equivalence as to reject readings of poem 3 that do not involve impotence is ludicrous. More importantly for me, however, is an interpretive consequence of (1) which I find flatly unacceptable, namely its marginalization of desire. That is, if the *passer* just "is" Catullus' penis, Lesbia's *desiderium* (2.5) is no more than the circumstantial background of the scene depicted: "*when* she is glistening with longing for [Catullus]" she simply and unproblematically avails herself of his *passer*. Lines 2–4 of the poem, then, physically describe the fulfillment of her desire, 7–8 intuit her motivation, and 9–10 pull what cannot fail to be a raunchy onanistic joke; only 5–6 refer to the desire itself – and even then, as something simply to be dealt with as needed.

It is when (and to the extent that) one reads the *passer* as an erotic signifier in a looser and more general sense that desire comes to the fore: the poet and his *puella* are now apart, and her distracted play with the *passer* is a proxy for what she and he really want.[33] Read this way, the poem does not

---

[32] Giangrande (1975), Nadeau (1980).

[33] The wish "if only I could play with you[, sparrow,] as she does" is now tasteful understatement, as well as the (necessary) admission of his desire, in a poem which until then has only asserted the existence and potency of *hers*.

represent actual sex between Catullus and Lesbia, but rather the absence of sex. To the extent that poem 2 is about the sex itself, it is merely amusing; if it is about the absence or want of this sex, it engages us emotionally in a deeper way.

Just as the instances of successful fit between the text and the phallic reading make a strong case for non-fortuitousness, so too does the resonance between non-phallic readings of the *passer* resonate with the great Catullan themes of separation, longing, and *amor* of more than one kind. The obvious instantiation of those themes on a non-allegorical reading of poem 2 is vitiated if Catullus is and must be physically present when Lesbia plays with the *passer*. Writing off these clearly non-fortuitous resonances is a cost of the phallic reading in its strong version, and it is clearly a cost that the reading cannot hope to bear, given its own demerits. Simply put, if one of these readings has to go, it will have to be the phallic reading. The *passer*, then, is not univocally a penis.

It will be useful here to spell out the demerits of the phallic reading: (1) *cui primum digitum dare appetenti*: touching a penis with the tip of one's finger is not a characteristic mode of sexual interaction; (2) *et acris solet incitare morsus*: it is unclear how one "provokes a penis to bite sharply"; (3) *desiderio . . . solaciolum sui doloris . . . credo ut tum grauis acquiescat ardor*:[34] when desirous of a boyfriend's penis, one might well avail oneself of it, true; but "a little solace for one's pain[ful desire]" is an insufficient and dubious characterization of the attainment of one's desire: an abandoned lover, for instance, would not call reunion with her or his beloved "a consolation" for their earlier loss; (4) *tecum ludere sicut ipsa possem*: Catullus *can* play with his penis (proponents will turn this into a joke about masturbation, but the plausibility of such a joke is itself not beyond dispute);[35] (5) *passer mortuus est*: Catullus' penis is not dead. Of course, proponents think of impotence or post-coital lassitude. But then (6) *qui nunc it per iter . . . unde negant redire quemquam*: these sexual conditions, unlike death, are not irrevocable;[36] finally, (7) *suamque norat ipsam tam bene quam puella matrem*: it is not obvious that the comparison to

---

[34] It is important to recall that our textual uncertainty here is considerable.

[35] For Giangrande (1975) and Nadeau (1980), both reading 2b as the conclusion of poem 2, the point is that Catullus cannot play with his sparrow *sicut ipsa*, that is, "as satisfyingly" as Lesbia does. The gratification Catullus receives from masturbation is then compared to the apple that led to Atalanta's marriage, on the understanding that she was not in fact gratified by this turn of events at all.

[36] One will probably have to see another joke here: Catullus and Lesbia lamenting that his penis is "gone forever" when in fact we know that all will soon be well. The problem here is not that this is unthinkable but that it imposes a further theoretical cost rather than, as allegorical readers would hope, providing an interpretive benefit to the text. If we are sufficiently motivated to play at

a daughter and her mother make much sense as correlates for a boyfriend's penis and his girlfriend; even if it did, it is more than possible that contemporaries would find this to be in such overwhelmingly poor taste as to render it unthinkable.[37]

Before proceeding to the alternative allegory I will defend, I would like to pause briefly to consider a different option: what if the *passer* is not Catullus' penis, but Lesbia's clitoris? Remarkably enough, this idea seems at present to be utterly familiar to working Latinists, but never to have been mentioned in the scholarly literature.[38]

This proposal maps rather better onto the text: three of the seven difficulties surveyed above for the phallic reading are resolved entirely by it: (1) Lesbia's touching the *passer* with the tip of her finger now makes sense; (3) as an erotic proxy for what Catullus thinks she really wants, namely him; (4) Catullus, being apart from Lesbia and desiring her as she does him, could indeed be pleased to play with the "sparrow" *sicut ipsa*. And (7), the unacceptable mother/daughter comparison seems far less difficult: one's naturally close acquaintance with the parts of one's own body might well be described in a familial way, without necessarily evoking unpleasant thoughts.[39] Indeed, if *matrem* at 3.7 evokes Greek μήτρα ("womb," but words for womb are regularly used more broadly of genitalia[40]), the allegorical meaning is almost the literal one: " . . . the way a girl knows her private parts."

The "death" of such a *passer* still needs explaining away, but if post-coital lassitude is a possible understanding for the phallic reading, an equivalent understanding is not impossible here (what is at issue is not the existence of a female equivalent to the male "refractory period," but rather the like-lihood that Catullus or his readers believed there was one). At any rate, the permanence of the sparrow's departure (6) is no less a problem for the male reading. Some of the textual elements which could support either reading particularly support a female one: *in sinu tenere* and *nec sese a gremio illius*

---

allegorizing, we can accept this sort of cost – but needing to do so tells against the case that we are sufficiently motivated.

[37] Jocelyn (1980) 428, Adams (1982) 32–33.

[38] Internet searches in mid-2018 turn up dozens of open-source discussions but not a single peer-reviewed one; well-informed colleagues have been surprised to the point of incredulity on being told of this silence. On more than one occasion students of mine have independently proposed and defended this reading.

[39] One worries slightly that contemporary English slang wrongly encourages us here, e.g. in that a woman can refer to her breasts as "the girls" and a man can call his testicles "my boys." I am aware of no personifications of this form in Latin; nor does Adams (1982), for instance, offer parallels.

[40] Wombs: Adams (1982) 80, 103–5. On *matrem* ~ μήτρα see Nadeau (1980), offered in support of the phallic reading,

mouebat make literal sense; *quem plus illa oculis suis amabat* becomes amusingly appropriate, creating an "apples to apples" comparison between organs; *ad solam dominam usque pipiabat* indicates that she has no lover – or, at any rate, none that knows how to please her sexually. The allegorical mapping, in short, is unmistakably closer.[41]

It would be tempting, at this point, to declare the male reading of the *passer* interpretively dominated by the female one: textual elements that fit the male reading fit the female one too, and fit it better; at least some elements that do not fit the male reading do fit the female one. This seems clearly true, but one's sense of the improbability of a male poet staging a cryptic address to his beloved's clitoris remains. References to female genitals in ancient poetry are so often crudely misogynistic and derogatory; men's disgust at the physical realities of the female bodies they desire is an all too familiar story, in antiquity and otherwise. I can cite no ancient reference to female genitals as parallel for how these poems would read. Worse, to the proposition that no status-conscious Roman man would ever represent the clitoris as the object of his desire, I cannot offer the slightest counterevidence. To put the matter in terms of Bayesian statistical reasoning, one's "prior probability" on the presence of an allegorical desired penis in ancient poetry will be undoubtedly greater than one's prior for such a desired clitoris.

On the other hand, a bare 150 lines after the *passer*, we read a sexualized metaphor of a nicked flower and a passing plow (11.21–24). And of course Catullus is the flower, Lesbia the plow, and many more such inversions will follow. This too requires that we adjust our priors, now in the opposite direction. The proper size of these adjustments seems to me no easy determination to make.

It is not my intention to defend or contradict either allegorical referent, and in point of fact I think that the insistence in poem 3 that the sparrow "will never return" hints that anatomical allegory will never quite furnish us with a stable solution here. It may be the case, as some have argued, that allegorical mapping is too crude an analytical tool for the erotic/symbolic content of the sparrow poems, as the failure-cases of the phallic reading arguably demonstrate.[42] To reduce this to a slogan, the sparrow can be

---

[41] Although it might be the case that *passer* is slang for penis, ancient references to the clitoris readily note that it and the penis are phenotypically analogous (*Priap.* 12.14, Mart. 1.90). In any case, *passer* would not be the only term capable of referring to the genitals of either sex (Kronenberg (2015) 193, 201).

[42] Janan (1994) 46–50, Oliensis (2009) 12–13, 123–24.

a sparrow without the sparrow being about a sparrow. Yet this is not quite my position, either: allegorical mapping works too well simply to be a mere error recurring from Martial to Poliziano to our day. It might be an illusion but it is not a delusion; and if it ends up an illusion, it will be because the poems are in some way *trompe l'oeil* compositions.

As I see it, then, the data are these: the sparrow poems are erotic poems soaked in erotic language. The *passer* is a proverbially lascivious bird, and its Greek equivalent is slang for penis. Martial's Catullan sparrow is certainly phallic. When you try the allegory out, you get some conspicuous matches. But it only goes so far: first you have to do some inventing, then defend those inventions from Occam's razor, and finally wave your hands in respect to the worst-fitting evidence. Next, a feminine allegory has signal advantages over a masculine one. Yet this worries us: if understanding an allegorical penis in this sort of text is like a textual editor restoring the high-frequency phrase "man on the moon" to a corrupt text, an allegorical clitoris would be rather the unattested "woman on the moon." Yet such probabilistic reasoning, typically valid as it is, worries us, too: in Catullus, you would almost expect "woman on the moon," if ever it scanned.

I come now to my understanding. Lesbia is not masturbating, but she is by herself doing something erotic, and something women do, even if Roman readers tended to think it more characteristic of men. She is writing poetry, love poetry. This explains her literary pseudonym: she earns the comparison with Sappho.[43] It explains why Catullus' love for and obsession with her are so great. Writing poetry is sexy in Catullus. People fall in love with poets (poem 35), and they do so with his understanding (*ignosco tibi*, 35.16). Poetic prowess can make a short and bald *uir* the object of Catullus' erotic burning (50). Poetry, Mallius knows, is also a therapy for erotic longing, a proxy for sex (68a). Poetry in Catullus is love and sex; marriage, courtship, and adultery; pregnancy, miscarriage, and birth; fetus, child, traveler, and old woman. It is intercourse with a divinity, and can be its immortal progeny; so we hope.

So let us try it. *Deliciae meae puellae*: poetry is certainly a delight, and Catullus and Calvus compose together having "agreed to be *delicati*" (50.3). *Quicum ludere*: likewise of Catullo-Calvan composition (*ludere* 2x in poem 2 and in poem 50). *Quem in sinu tenere*: that is how you hold a papyrus *charta* or a *codicillus* made of wood and wax. *Cui primum digitum dare*

[43] Rankin (1976b) 8 and Hallett (2006) suggest that Lesbia may have been a poet, in order to explain her Sapphic pseudonym; Holzberg (2000) sees no evidence for the possibility. Zarker (1973) 108 and Hallett (2002) point out Cicero's invective against Clodia *qua* poetess. To my knowledge, however, no scholar has ever identified the *passer* with poetry.

appetenti: using a stylus, the tip of the index finger comes quite close to the writing surface. *Acris solet incitare morsus*: most easily of the "biting" wit of satirical or invective verse,[44] though I note that "biting" is surprisingly well attested of abrasive literary erasure, the counterpoint to composition in the previous line.[45] *Cum desiderio meo nitenti ... lubet iocari*: compare *per iocum* (50.6) and the "day after" Catullus, composing on waking from his night of erotic longing for Calvus (50.14–17). *Solaciolum sui doloris*: compare, of course, *ex quo perspiceres meum dolorem* (50.17). *Tecum ludere sicut ipsa possem*: Catullus wishes to read the inchoate composition. *Tristis animi leuare curas*: this is Mallius' wish as well; reading poetry as emotional therapy is well attested outside Catullus.

Now to poem 3. *Veneres Cupidinesque et quantumst hominum uenustiorum*: all gods and mortals interested in love poetry are addressed, because they are all affected by what has happened. *Passer mortuus est*: Lesbia has abandoned and destroyed her composition. Compare the prophesied "death" of Volusius' *Annales*; outside Catullus, note that Augustus' abortive *Ajax* is said to have "fallen on its sponge."[46] *Quem plus illa oculis suis amabat*: why wouldn't she? *Mellitus erat*: poetry as honey is easy. *Suamque norat ipsam tam bene quam puella matrem*: indeed! Lesbia *is* her composition's mother, just as Catullus in poem 65 is a mother to *his* compositions. *Nec sese a gremio illius mouebat*: Lesbia was always at work on it. *Circumsiliens modo huc modo illuc*: easiest to take this of the wide, polygeneric ground covered by the poetic content. *Ad solam dominam usque pipiabat*: no one but Lesbia ever saw it; in its unfinished state, the composition "chirped" (recall the birdsong to which Catullus likens his own poetry at 65.13–14) for her alone. *Qui nunc it per iter tenebricosum* and following: the rest of the poem continues on the death theme, ending with Lesbia's grief; there are certainly no difficulties to be found here. Note that poetry that endures is a contrivance for immortality, something that successfully avoids *malae tenebrae Orci*; perhaps there is some sort of visual pun with *opus* in *tuā ... operā*, though I would not press the point.

Why should the composition have "died"? The more recognizable and present a historical Clodia might be for the poems, the more Catullus

---

[44] Hor. *Ep.* 6.4, *Serm.* 1.4.93, Ov. *Trist.* 2.1.563: *mordaci carmine*.

[45] Ovid *Pont.* 1.5.19: *lima mordacius uti*; Mart. 5.80.12–13: *(libellus) quem ... docti lima momorderit Secundi*. The "biting" file here nicely activates both "erasure" and "criticism." Note also 6.64.16–17: *cor limante Minerua acrius* and 8.72: *morsu pumicis aridi politus*, of a *libellus*; the imitation of Catullus 1 is evocative here in respect to Catullus 2.

[46] Suetonius, *Divus Augustus* 85: *nam tragoediam magno impetu exorsus, non succedenti stilo, aboleuit quaerentibusque amicis, quidnam Aiax ageret, respondit Aiacem suum in spongiam incubuisse*.

might feel obliged to "kill off" a fictional poem of hers: it is flattering to present her as writing learned poetry, and face-saving for it not to work out. Here too, "the *Ajax* of Augustus" is a good parallel to think with. More broadly, we might say that the Catullus who mocks his acquaintances' girlfriends for their lack of wit (6, 41, 43) and is himself stung by the wit of another's girlfriend (10), calibrates the *doctrina* of his beloved perfectly: she is learned enough to obsess him, not so learned as to threaten him *qua* poet. She is also learned enough to appreciate and be obsessed with him, as the girlfriend in poem 35 is obsessed with the putative author of the *Magna Mater*; if the Lesbia plot in **A** makes us wonder if the love between them is one-sided, the reconciliation at the end of **C2**, brought about unexpectedly and by her own agency, in spite of everything, tells against that suspicion.

Lesbia is often treated as the paradigm case of the *docta puella* in Roman poetry.[47] Indeed she *should* be; but with the possible exception of the beginning of her story, only in poem 36 do we have any evidence at all of her learning. Her vow there to Venus and Cupid (36.3–8) is presumptively to be taken as free indirect discourse, indicating her use of elegant under-statement (*electissima scripta* for the invective against her) and a learned periphrasis for fire (*tardipedi deo*) which also alludes to her addressee Venus' marriage to Vulcan. Let us grant that this is certainly enough to establish that Lesbia is educated. But it is one isolated and belated instance. It would be helpful if the text had established this fact already. The textually difficult opening of **A**, with either its difficult ending to the first of its paired Lesbia poems or its lacunose trilogy of initial Lesbia poems, would be the place to establish this. And if, as Johnson suggests, Lesbia is the speaker of the fragmentary lines of 2b, we would have it: she would be commenting on her wooing by Catullus, and doing so by means of a learned mythological reference. She would also be an intratextual artist to match her boyfriend: likening herself at the beginning of her love to a *pernici puellae*, the "swift girl" Atalanta at the beginning of hers, she would alter the reference to *tardipedi deo*, the "slow footed" (and unhappily married, she hints) "god," after that love had gone bad. That would be brilliant of her.

I can't prove this. But the reason I can't prove it is that there is probably a lacuna after poem 2; if so, whatever it conceals will have been crucial to the poems. As for the allegory, I will say this: this entire work has sought to build the case that you can read the sequence of the poems, that you can

---

[47] E.g. by Arkins (1979) and Johnson (2003). See also Johnson (2008) 152 on Laodamia as a *docta puella* in Catullus.

rely and presume on it. With the great exception of my reading of 68b (as recalled consummation of the affair), I have mostly avoided doing so myself, out of a concern to avoid question-begging arguments. Now that case is made. The allegory itself, taking poems 2 and 3 alone, maps onto the text without the slightest difficulty. Not a single element embarrasses; it is rich and richly coherent. To rule out the fortuitousness of this fit, I probably need the larger thesis of this work to be true: *these* books, *these* dramas of composition at *these* terminal moments. If all of that is true, we are invited to see the sparrow as poetry; if the nexus of terminal responsions we have seen is for anything at all beyond marking itself as such, it will be for this. We will have our crucial second fact: the reading is externally suggested as well as internally coherent. This will not be accidental.

This will also render the drama of poems 50 and 51 even richer, and blur the line between love and verse even further. The seriocomic poem 50 presents to Calvus the conceit that poetic composition is erotically potent. Calvus knows the Lesbia poems; he is a brilliant poet and our brilliant poet's dear friend: anything we see in them, we should imagine that he saw first and more fully. His friend's opening verses to his literary beloved had compared her to Sappho; perhaps Calvus even heard Catullus' wish for ludic access to her poetry

> tecum ludere sicut ipsa possem

as if it were "as if it were Sappho's":

> tecum ludere sicuti psapos ...
> tecum ludere sicuti ΨΑΠ[Φ]ΩΣ ...[48]

Now Catullus has created a creation so Calvus can see his pain: a translation of the beloved poetess the poet has mentally constructed *his* beloved poetess to be. When poem 51 addresses Lesbia, there is now hardly any way to determine which woman is being addressed, and hardly any need to: Catullus' pain in respect to his Roman Sappho cannot be absent as soon as he looks at Sappho of Lesbos. And his composition, on the familiar metonymy of author for work, obviously requires him to look at her. Now he translates the first stanza:

φαίνεταί μοι κῆνος ἴσος θέοισιν	Ille mi par esse deo uidetur,
ἔμμεν' ὤνηρ, **ὄττις ἐνάντιός τοι**	ille, si fas est, superare diuos,

---

[48] Admittedly a venturesome claim. Yet nowhere else in the corpus does the syllable *sa* (let alone *psa*) precede *po*, either within a word or over a word break.

ἰσδάνει καὶ πλάσιον ἅδυ φωνεί-	qui sedens aduersus identidem te
σας ὑπακούει	spectat et audit

Our Calvus almost sheds a tear for Catullus, knowing the mental association his friend will never fail to make, and did not fail to make "today," when he opened his Sapphic roll to make his Latin Sapphics address his Roman Sappho. If it has already been established that Lesbia "is" Sappho, the relative clause at 51.3–4 reads in two ways:

> QVI.SEDENS.ADVERSVS.IDENTIDEM.TE [*id est, Lesbiam mulierem Romanam*]
> SPECTAT.ET.AVDIT

but also

> QVI.SEDENS.AD.VERSVS.[49]IDENTIDEM.TE [id est, poetriam Lesbo ortam pro opere]
> SPECTAT [id est, legit] ET.AVDIT [id est, recitans uocem suam, eius uerba audit]

That man is nearly a god to Catullus, for Catullus could not possibly hope to do this any more: whenever he looks at Sappho, his tongue grows numb and his eyes are covered in twin night. The *otium* stanza will then admit a hard truth: for a learned lyric poet and lover, that is quite the predicament.

3   Envoi: *quis te mutauit tantus deus?*

In fact it is worse than difficult to be this kind of poet and lover, the kind of poet and lover the young Catullus of **A** is. As is already present at its end, this kind of love (and) poetry are constituted by the *a priori* impossibility of their end: to experience overwhelming *amor* is to overwhelm the capacity to experience it, just as to lose power over language is to cease being a poet. Catullan desire is the desire to undergo the *petite mort* of eros fully sensate, to cross its event horizon and report the view from beyond. The nature of this desire likewise explains **B** and **C**. Marital love is the perfect foil for this desire, the sane and sacred compromise of its intensity in favor of its stability. Catullus approves, in his way, but does not or cannot follow: his wedding songs end not so much with marital consummation as because of it. Finally, Lesbia's return in 68b turns out to be Catullus' ill-counseling recollection of his adulterous consummation with her, whose reason-perverting power brings him, in **C2**, first to grief and then to the

---

[49] The metrical impossibility would not keep Calvus from seeing this.

catastrophic success of Lesbia's last recorded reconciliation, attended by Catullus' prayer for the perpetuity of their holy pact. Poor Catullus fails to see that he had been right in poem 51: what he seeks is beyond mortal or even divine aspiration. For him and us and even the gods, the poems argue against their poet, the holy pact of lifelong love is marriage.

Why does Catullus fail to see this, what god intervenes? The poems contemplate an array of divinities as possible agents of human woe. Cupid and Jupiter excepted, most of these are female: Venus, Cybele, the Eumenides, the Parcae, Themis, Thetis, Nemesis, Eris, the catasterized Lock; by courtesy, Lesbia and Sappho too. Above all of these, perhaps, are the Muses: Catullus' failure to marry and settle down can explain the fertility of their intercourse with him, in that it is indisputably better, poetically, to burn than to marry. It can also be explained *by* the same poetic given: their poet's ambition to conceive in his mind their sweet offspring explains his life choices. In the end, though, I would appeal to how small a portion of the Lesbia plot is unaffected by her first rejection of Catullus (only poems 2, 3, 5, and 7) to argue that neither he nor the poems desire anything so faithfully as to *repeat* the adulterous consummation with Lesbia: they seek to make love to her for the first time forever, again and again. And so I would look just beyond the Muses for the principal divine explanation of Catullus' narrative fate, to their all powerful mother.

Bibliography

Acosta-Hughes, B. (2010). Preserving her Aeolic song. In *Arion's Lyre: Archaic Lyric into Hellenistic Poetry* (12–61). Princeton, NJ: Princeton University Press.

Adamik, T. (1995). Catullus' urbanity: c. 22. *AAntHung*, 36, 77–86.

Adams, J.N. (1982). *The Latin Sexual Vocabulary*. Baltimore, MD: Johns Hopkins University Press.

Adler, E. (1981). *Catullan Self-Revelation*. New York, NY: Arno Press.

Agnesini, A. (2011). Catull. 67.1-s.: incipit della Ianua o explicit della Coma? *Paideia*, 65, 521–40.

Arkins, B. (1979). Catullus 7. *L'Antiquité Classique*, 48, 630–35.

——— (1983). Caelius and Rufus in Catullus. *Philologus*, 127, 306–11.

Armstrong, R. (2013). Journeys and nostalgia in Catullus. *CJ*, 109, 43–71.

Baehrens, E. (1885). *Catulli Veronensis liber*. Leipzig, Germany: Teubner.

Barchiesi, A. (2005). The search for the perfect book: a PS to the New Posidippus. In K. Gutzwiller (Ed.), *The New Posidippus: A Hellenistic Poetry Book* (320–42). Oxford, UK: Oxford University Press.

Barrett, A.A. (1972). Catullus 52 and the consulship of Vatinius. *TAPA*, 103, 23–38.

Barwick, K. (1928). Zu Catull c. 55 und 58a. *Hermes*, 63, 66–80.

Batstone, W.W. (1998). Dry pumice and the programmatic language of Catullus 1. *CP*, 93, 125–35.

——— (2007). Catullus and the programmatic poem: the origins, scope, and utility of a concept. In M.B. Skinner (Ed.), *A Companion to Catullus* (235–53). Malden, MA: Blackwell.

Beck, J.W. (1996). *"Lesbia" und "Juventius": Zwei libelli im Corpus Catullianum. Untersuchungen zur Publikationsform und Authentizität der überlieferten Gedichtfolge*. Göttingen, Germany: Vandenhoeck & Ruprecht.

Bellandi, F. (2007). *Lepos e pathos: Studi su Catullo*. Bologna, Italy: Pàtron.

Biondi, G.G. (1998). Il carme 35 di Catullo. *MD*, 41, 35–69.

Brunér, E.A. (1863). De ordine et temporibus carminum Velerii Catulli. *Acta Societatis Scientiarum Fennicae*, 7, 599–657.

Butrica, J.L. (2007). History and transmission of the text. In M.B. Skinner (Ed.), *A Companion to Catullus* (35–54). Malden, MA: Blackwell.

Cairns, F. (1975). Catullus 27. *Mnemosyne*, 26, 15–22.

Case, B.D. and Claes, P. (1995). Notes de lecture. *Latomus*, 54, 875–77.

Claes, P. (2001). Concentric composition in Catullus. *CW*, 94, 379–83.

(2002). Concatenatio Catulliana: *a new reading of the Carmina*. Amsterdam, Netherlands: J.C. Gieben.

Clare, R.J. (1996). Catullus 64 and the *Argonautica* of Apollonius Rhodius: allusion and exemplarity. *PCPS*, 42, 60–88.

Clark, C.A. (2008). The poetics of manhood? Nonverbal behavior in Catullus 51. *CP*, 103, 257–81.

Clark, G.W. (1968). The burning of books and Catullus 36. *Latomus*, 27, 575–80.

Clausen, W.V. (1976). Catulli Veronensis liber. *CP*, 71, 37–43.

Clay, D. (1998). The theory of the literary persona in antiquity. *MD*, 40, 9–40.

Connely, W. (1925). Imprints of Sappho on Catullus. *CJ*, 20, 408–13.

Conte, G.B. (1992). Proems in the middle. In F.M. Dunn and T. Cole (Eds.), *Beginnings in Classical Literature* (147–59). Cambridge, UK: Cambridge University Press.

Copley, F.O. (1951). Catullus, c.1. *TAPA*, 82, 200–06.

(1958). Catullus c.4: The world of the poem. *TAPA*, 89, 9–13.

Coppel, B. (1973). *Das Alliusgedicht: Zur Redaktion des Catullcorpus*. Heidelberg, Germany: Winter.

Courtney, E. (1996). Catullus' yacht (or was it?). *CJ*, 92, 113–22.

Curran, L.C. (1969). Catullus 64 and the Heroic Age. *YCS*, 21, 171–92.

D'Angour, A. (2006). Conquering Love: Sappho 31 and Catullus 51. *CQ*, 56, 297–300.

Dettmer, H. (1984). Catullus 2B from a structural perspective. *CW*, 78, 107–10.

(1997). *Love by the numbers: form and the meaning in the poetry of Catullus*. New York, NY: P. Lang.

Deuling, J.K. (1999). Catullus and Mamurra. *Mnemosyne*, 52, 188–94.

Döpp, S. (1993a). Saturnalien und lateinische Literatur. In S. Döpp (Ed.), *Karnevaleske Phänomene in antiken und nachantiken Literaturen* (145–77). Trier, Germany: Verlag.

Du Quesnay, I. (2012). Three problems in poem 66. In I. Du Quesnay and T. Woodman (Eds.), *Catullus: Poems, Books, Readers* (153–83). Cambridge, UK: Cambridge University Press.

Du Quesnay, I., and Woodman, T. (Eds.). (2012a). *Catullus: Poems, Books, Readers*. Cambridge, UK: Cambridge University Press.

(2012b). Epilogue. In I. Du Quesnay and T. Woodman (Eds.), *Catullus: Poems, Books, Readers* (255–72). Cambridge, UK: Cambridge University Press.

Dyson, J.T. (2007). The Lesbia poems. In M.B. Skinner (Ed.), *A Companion to Catullus* (254–75). Malden, MA: Blackwell.

Edwards, M.J. (1990). The secret of Catullus 102. *Hermes*, 118, 382–84.

Ellis, R. (1876). *A Commentary on Catullus*. Oxford, UK: Clarendon Press.

Fantham, E. (1991). Stuprum: public attitudes and penalties for sexual offences in Republican Rome. *Echos du monde classique*, 10, 267–91.

Fantuzzi, M., and Hunter, R.L. (2004). *Tradition and Innovation in Hellenistic Poetry*. Cambridge, UK: Cambridge University Press.

Fedeli, P. (1972). *Il carme 61 di Catullo*. Freiburg, Germany: Edizioni Universaire.

Feeney, D. (2010). Fathers and sons: the Manlii Torquati and family continuity in Catullus and Horace. In C. Kraus, J. Marincola, C. Pelling, and A. Woodman (Eds.), *Ancient Historiography and its Contexts: Studies in Honour of AJ Woodman* (205–23). Oxford, UK: Oxford University Press.

(2012). Representation and the materiality of the book in the polymetrics. In I. Du Quesnay and T. Woodman (Eds.), *Catullus: Poems, Books, Readers* (29–47). Cambridge, UK: Cambridge University Press.

Ferriss, J. L. (2009). Catullus poem 71: another foot pun. *CP*, 104, 376–84.

Fitzgerald, W. (1995). *Catullan Provocations: Lyric Poetry and the Drama of Position*. Berkeley: University of California Press.

Fordyce, C.J. (1961). *Catullus: A Commentary*. Oxford, UK: Oxford University Press.

Forsyth, P.Y. (1970). The marriage theme in Catullus 63. *CJ*, 66, 66–69.

(1976). Catullus: the mythic persona. *Latomus*, 35, 555–66.

(1977). Comments on Catullus 116. *CQ*, 27, 352–53.

(1987). Muneraque et musarum hinc petis et Veneris: Catullus 68A.10. *CW*, 80, 177–80.

Fraenkel, E. (1980). *Horace*, revised ed. Oxford, UK: Clarendon Press.

Frank, R.I. (1968). Catullus 51: otium versus virtus. *TAPA*, 99, 233–39.

Frank, T. (1914). A rejected poem and a substitute: Catullus LXVIII A and B. *AJP*, 35, 67–73.

Frankfurt, H.G. (2005). *On Bullshit*. Princeton, NJ: Princeton University Press.

Fratantuono, L. (2010). *Nivales socii*: Caesar, Mamurra, and the snow of Catullus *C. 57. Quaderni Urbinati di Cultura Classica*, 96, 101–10.

Fredricksmeyer, E.A. (1965). On the unity of Catullus 51. *TAPA*, 96, 153–63.

Fröhlich, J. (1843). Über die Anordnung der Gedichte des Q. Valerius Catullus. *Abhandlung der königl. bayerische Akademie der Wissenschaften*, 3, 691–716.

Gaisser, J.H. (1995). Threads in the labyrinth: competing views and voices in Catullus 64. *AJP*, 116, 579–616.

(Ed.). (2007). *Catullus*. Oxford Readings in Classical Studies. Oxford, UK: Oxford University Press.

(2008, October 30). Review of the book *Lepos e pathos: Studi su Catullo*, by F. Bellandi. *BMCR*. Retrieved from http://bmcr.brynmawr.edu/2008/2008-10-30.html

Giangrande, G. (1975). Catullus' lyrics on the *passer. London Philological Museum*, 1, 137–46.

Godwin, J. (1999). *Catullus: The Shorter Poems*. Warminster, PA: Aris & Phillips.

Goold, G.P. (1973). *Interpreting Catullus: Inaugural lecture delivered at University College, London*. London, UK: H. K. Lewis.

(1983). *Catullus*. London, UK: Duckworth.

Griffith, J.G. (1983). Catullus Poem 4: A neglected interpretation revived. *Phoenix*, 37, 123–28.

Griffiths, A. (2002). The *Odes*: just where do you draw the line? In T. Woodman and D. Feeney (Eds.), *Traditions and Contexts in the Poetry of Horace* (65–79). Cambridge, UK: Cambridge University Press.

Gutzwiller, K. (2012). Catullus and the Garland of Meleager. In I. Du Quesnay and T. Woodman (Eds.), *Catullus: Poems, Books, Readers* (79–111). Cambridge, UK: Cambridge University Press.

Hallett, J.P. (1978). Divine unction: some further thoughts on Catullus 13. *Latomus*, 37, 747–48.

(2002). Women's voices and Catullus' poetry. *CW*, 95, 421–24.

(2006). Catullus and Horace on Roman women poets. *Antichthon*, 40, 65–88.

Harkins, P.W. (1959). Autoallegory in Catullus 63 and 64. *TAPA*, 90, 102–16.

Harvey, A.E. (1955). The classification of Greek lyric poetry. *CQ*, 2, 157–75.

Haupt, M. (1853). *Catullus, Tibullus, Propertius*. Leipzig, Germany: Hirzel.

Hawkins, S. (2014). Catullus 60: Lesbia, Medea, Clodia, Scylla. *AJP*, 135, 559–97.

Heck, B. (1951). Die Anordnung der Gedichte des Gaius Valerius Catullus (Unpublished doctoral dissertation). Marburg University, Marburg, Germany.

Henderson, J. (1999). *Writing Down Rome: Satire, Comedy, and Other Offences in Latin Poetry*. Oxford, UK: Clarendon Press.

(2004). *Morals and Villas in Seneca's Letters: Places to Dwell*. Cambridge, UK: Cambridge University Press.

Hermann, L. (1957). *Les deux livres de Catulle*. Collection Latomus 29. Brussels, Belgium: Latomus.

Heyworth, S.J. (2012). The elegiac book: patterns and problems. In B.K. Gold (Ed.), *A Companion to Roman Love Elegy* (219–33). Malden, MA: Blackwell.

Holzberg, N. (2000). Lesbia, the poet, and the two faces of Sappho: "womanufacture" and gender discourse in Catullus. *PCPS*, 46, 28–44.

(2002). *Catull: Der Dichter und sein erotisches Werk*. Munich, Germany: Beck.

Höschele, R. (2009). Catullus' Callimachean 'hair'-itage and the erotics of translation. *Rivista di filologia e di istruzione classica*, 137, 118–52.

Hubbard, T.K. (1983). The Catullan libellus. *Philologus*, 127, 218–37.

(1984). Catullus 68: the text as self-demystification. *Arethusa*, 17, 29–49.

(2005). The Catullan libelli revisited. *Philologus*, 149, 253–77.

Hunink, V. (2000). Some thoughts of a friend: Catul. 35, 5–6. *MD*, 45, 133–36.

Hunter, R. (1993). Callimachean echoes in Catullus 65. *Zeitschrift für Papyrologie und Epigraphik*, 96, 179–82.

Hutchinson, G.O. (2003). The Catullan corpus, Greek epigram, and the poetry of objects. *CQ*, 53, 206–21.

Ingleheart, J. (2014). Play on the proper names of individuals in the Catullan corpus: wordplay, the iambic tradition, and the late Republican culture of public abuse. *JRS*, 104, 51–72.

Itzkowitz, J.B. (1983). On the last stanza of Catullus 51. *Latomus*, 42, 129–34.

Janan, M. (1994). *"When the Lamp Is Shattered": Desire and Narrative in Catullus*. Carbondale: Southern Illinois University Press.

Jocelyn, H.D. (1980). on some unnecessarily indecent interpretations of Catullus 2 and 3. *AJP*, 101, 421–41.

(1999). The arrangement and the language of Catullus' so-called polymetra with special reference to the sequence 10–11–12. In J.N. Adams and R.G. Meyer

(Eds.), *Aspects of the Language of Latin Poetry* (335–376). Oxford, UK: Oxford University Press.

Johnson, C. (2008). Mistress and myth: Catullus 68b. *Classical Outlook*, 85, 151–54.

Johnson, M. (2003). Catullus 2b: the development of a relationship in the *passer* trilogy. *CJ*, 99, 11–34.

Johnston, P.A. (1983). An echo of Sappho in Catullus 65. *Latomus*, 42, 388–94.

Khan, H.A. (1967). The humor of Catullus, Carm. 4, and the theme of Virgil, Catalepton 10. *AJP*, 88, 163–72.

King, J.K. (1988). Catullus' Callimachean *carmina*, cc. 65–116. *CW*, 81, 383–92.

Kinsey, T.E. (1967). Some problems in Catullus 68. *Latomus*, 26, 35–53.

Krebs, C. (2008). Magni viri: Caesar, Alexander, and Pompey in Cat. 11. *Philologus*, 152, 223–29.

Kroll, W. (1924). *Studien zum Verständnis der römischen Literatur*. Stuttgart, Germany: J. B. Metzler.

(1968). *C. Valerius Catullus, herausgegeben und erklärt* (5th ed.). Stuttgart, Germany: Teubner. (Original work published 1923.)

Kronenberg, L. (2014). Me, myself, and I: multiple (literary) personalities in Catullus 35. *CW*, 107, 367–81.

(2015). The rise of Sabinus: sexual satire in *Catalepton 10*. *CJ*, 110, 191–212.

Kutzko, D. (2006). Lesbia in Catullus 35. *CP*, 101, 405–10.

(2008). Catullus 69 and 71: goat, gout, and venereal disease. *CW* 101, 443–52.

Lateiner, D. (1977). Obscenity in Catullus. *Ramus*, 6, 15–32.

Lavency, M. (1965). L'ode à Lesbie et son Billet d'envoi (Catulle, L et LI). *L'Antiquité Classique*, 34, 175–82.

Lefèvre, E. (1991). Was hatte Catull in der Kapsel, die er von Rom nach Verona mitnahm? Zu Aufbau und Aussage der Allius-Elegie. *Rheinisches Museum Für Philologie*, 134, 311–26.

(1998). Alexandrinisches und Catullisches im Attis-Gedicht (c. 63). *Rheinisches Museum für Philologie*, 141, 308–28.

Leitao, D. (2012). *The Pregnant Male as Myth and Metaphor in Classical Greek Literature*. Cambridge, UK: Cambridge University Press.

Lenchantin de Gubernatis, M. (1928). *Il libro di Catullo*. Turin, Italy: Chiantore.

Lieberg, G. (1962). *Puella Divina: Die Gestalt der göttlichen Geliebten bei Catull im Zusammenhang der antiken Dichtung*. Amsterdam, Netherlands: Schippers.

Lindsay, R.J.M. (1948). The chronology of Catullus' life. *CP*, 43, 42–44.

Littman, J. (1977). The unguent of Venus: Catullus 13. *Latomus*, 36, 123–28.

Lyne, R.O.A.M. (1978). The neoteric poets. *CQ*, 28, 167–87.

Maas, P. (1942). The chronology of the poems of Catullus. *CQ*, 36, 79–82.

MacLeod, C.W. (1973a). Catullus 116. *CQ*, 23, 304–09.

(1973b). Parody and personalities in Catullus. *CQ*, 23, 294–303.

Marsilio, M., and Podlesney, K. (2006). Poverty and poetic rivalry in Catullus (C. 23, 13, 16, 24, 81). *Acta Classica*, 49, 167–81.

Maury, P. (1944). Le Secret de Virgile et l'architecture des Bucoliques. *Lettres d'Humanité*, 3, 71–147.

Mayer, R.G. (1983). Catullus' divorce. *CQ*, 33, 297–98.

(2003). Persona<l> problems: the literary persona in antiquity revisited. *MD*, 50, 55–80.

McDermott, W.C. (1983). Mamurra, *eques formianus*. *Rheinisches Museum für Philologie*, 126, 292–307.

McKie, D.S. (2009). Language and the poetic voice: Catullus 68a. In *Essays in the Interpretation of Roman Poetry* (191–248). Cambridge, UK: Cambridge University Press.

Merkelbach, R. (1957). Sappho und ihr Kreis. *Philologus*, 101, 1–29.

Miller, P.A. (1988). Catullus, C. 70: a poem and its hypothesis. *Helios*, 15, 127–32.

Morwood, J. (1999). Catullus 64, Medea, and the François vase. *Greece & Rome*, 46, 221–31.

Most, G. (1981). On the arrangement of Catullus' *carmina maiora*. *Philologus*, 125, 109–25.

(1996). Reflecting Sappho. In E. Greene (Ed.), *Re-reading Sappho: Reception and Transmission* (11–35). Berkeley: University of California Press.

Nadeau, Y. (1980). *O passer nequam* (Catullus 2, 3). *Latomus*, 39, 879–80.

(1984). Catullus' sparrow, Martial, Juvenal and Ovid. *Latomus*, 43, 861–68.

Nappa, C. (2003). Num te leaena: Catullus 60. *Phoenix*, 57, 57–66.

Nauta, R.R. (2004). Catullus 63 in a Roman context. In R. R. Nauta and M. A. Harder (Eds.), *Catullus' Poem on Attis: Texts and Contexts*. Mnemosyne 57 (596–628). Leiden, Netherlands: Brill.

Németh, B. (1974). Catullan twin-poems (c. 50–c. 14). *ACD*, 10–11, 45–53.

Neudling, C.L. (1955). *A Prosopography to Catullus*. Oxford, UK: Oxford University Press.

Newman, J.K. (1983). Comic elements in Catullus 51. *Illinois Classical Studies*, 8, 33–36.

(1990). *Roman Catullus and the Modification of the Alexandrian Sensibility*. Hildesheim, Germany: Weidmann.

Nuzzo, G. (1994). Le rotte del phaselus: Per un'interpretazione del c. 4 di Catullo. *QCTC*, 12, 41–66.

O'Hara, J.J. (2007). *Inconsistency in Roman Epic: Studies in Catullus, Lucretius, Vergil, Ovid and Lucan*. Cambridge, UK: Cambridge University Press.

Oliensis, E. (2009). *Freud's Rome: Psychoanalysis and Latin Poetry*. Cambridge, UK: Cambridge University Press.

Page, D.L. (1955). *Sappho and Alcaeus: An Introduction to the Study of Ancient Lesbian Poetry*. Oxford, UK: Clarendon Press.

Palmer, A. (1879). Ellis's Catullus. *Hermathena*, 3, 293–363.

Pearcy, L.T. (1980). Catullus 2B – or not 2B? *Mnemosyne*, 33, 152–62.

Port, W. (1926). Die Anordnung in Gedichtbüchern augusteischer Zeit. *Philologus*, 35, 280–308, 427–68.

Porter, J.I. (2011). Against λεπτότης: rethinking Hellenistic aesthetics. In A. Erskine and L. Llewellyn-Jones (Eds.), *Creating a Hellenistic World* (271–312). Swansea: Classical Press of Wales.

Prescott, H. W. (1940). The unity of Catullus LXVIII. *TAPA*, 71, 473–500.

Putnam, M.C.J. (2006). *Poetic Interplay: Catullus and Horace.* Princeton, NJ: Princeton University Press.

Quinn, K. (1973). *Catullus: The Poems.* London, UK: Macmillan.

Rankin, H.D. (1967). Water and Laodamia as catalysts of emotions in Catullus 68b. *Latomus,* 26, 689–94.

 (1976a). Catullus and incest. *Eranos,* 74, 113–21.

 (1976b). Catullus and the 'beauty' of Lesbia (poems 43, 86 and 51). *Latomus,* 35, 3–11.

Richlin, A. (1992). *The Garden of Priapus: Sexuality and Aggression in Roman Humor.* Oxford, UK: Oxford University Press.

Richter, R. (1881). *Catulliana.* Leipzig, Germany: Edelmann.

Rothstein, M. (1923). Catull und Lesbia. *Philologus,* 78, 1–34.

Ryan, F.X. (1995). The date of Catullus 52. *Eranos,* 93, 21.

Sandy, G.N. (1971). Catullus 63 and the theme of marriage. *AJP,* 92, 185–95.

Santirocco, M.S. (1986). *Unity and Design in Horace's Odes.* Chapel Hill: University of North Carolina Press.

Schäfer, E. (1966). *Das Verhältnis von Erlebnis und Kunstgestalt bei Catull.* Hermes Einzelschriften 18. Wiesbaden, Germany: Steiner.

Scherf, J. (1996). *Untersuchungen zur antiken Veröffentlichung der Catullgedichte.* Spudasmata 61. Hildesheim, Germany: Olms.

Schmidt, B. (1914). Die Lebenzeit Catulls und die Herausgabe seiner Gedichte. *Rheinisches Museum,* 69, 267–83.

Schmidt, E.A. (1973). Catulls Anordnung seiner Gedichte. *Philologus,* 117, 215–42.

Schwabe, L. (1862). *Quaestiones Catullianae.* Giessen, Germany: Ricker.

Segal, C. (1968a). Catullus 5 and 7: a study in complementaries. *AJP,* 89, 284–301.

 (1968b). The Order of Catullus, Poems 2–11. *Latomus,* 27, 305–21.

 (1996). Eros and incantation: Sappho and oral poetry. In E. Greene (Ed.), *Reading Sappho: Contemporary Approaches* (58–75). Berkeley: University of California Press.

Selden, D. (1992). *Caveat lector:* Catullus and the rhetoric of performance. In R. Hexter and D. Selden (Eds.), *Innovations of Antiquity* (461–512). New York, NY: Routledge.

Shackleton Bailey, D.R. (1966). *Cicero: Epistulae ad Atticum* (Vol. 5). Cambridge, UK: Cambridge University Press.

Shapiro, S. O. (2011). The mirror of Catullus: poems 12, 22, 39, 41, 42 and 84. *SyllClass,* 22, 21–37.

Skinner, M.B. (1971). Catullus 8: the comic "amator" as "eiron." *CJ,* 66, 298–305.

 (1981). *Catullus' Passer: The Arrangement of the Book of Polymetric Poems.* New York, NY: Arno Press.

 (1984). Rhamnusia Virgo. *CA,* 3, 134–41.

 (1997). *Ego mulier:* the construction of male sexuality in Catullus. In J.P. Hallett and M.B. Skinner (Eds.), *Roman Sexualities* (129–50). Princeton, NJ: Princeton University Press.

 (2003). *Catullus in Verona: A Reading of the Elegiac Libellus: Poems 65–116.* Columbus: Ohio State University Press.

(2007). Authorial arrangement of the collection: debate past and present. In M. B. Skinner (Ed.), *A Companion to Catullus* (35–54). Malden, MA: Blackwell.

Skutsch, O. (1963). The structure of the Propertian *monobiblos*. *CP*, 58, 238–39.

(1969a). Metrical variations and some textual problems in Catullus. *BICS*, 16, 38–43.

(1969b). Symmetry and sense in the *Eclogues*. *HSCP*, 73, 153–69.

Snell, B. (1931). Sapphos Gedicht *phainetai moi kenos*. *Hermes*, 66, 71–90.

Steenkamp, J. (2011). The structure of Vergil's *Eclogues*. *Acta Classica*, 54, 101–24.

Stevens, B.E. (2013). *Silence in Catullus*. Madison: University of Wisconsin Press.

Stroh, W. (1990). Lesbia und Juventius: ein erotisches Liederbuch im Corpus Catullianum. In P. Neukam (Ed.), *Die Antike als Begleiterin* (134–58). Munich, Germany: Verlag.

Stroup, S.C. (2010). *Catullus, Cicero, and a Society of Patrons: The Generation of the Text*. Cambridge, UK: Cambridge University Press.

Süss, J. (1877). *Catulliana*. Erlangen, Germany: Junge.

Syme, R. (1939). *The Roman Revolution*. Oxford, UK: Oxford University Press.

(1956). Piso and Veranius in C. *C&M*, 17, 129–34.

Syndikus, H.P. (1984). *Catull: Eine Interpretation: Erster Teil: Einleitung, Die kleinen Gedichten (1–60)*. Darmstadt, Germany: Wissenschaftliche Buchgesellschaft.

Tanner, R.G. (1972). Catullus LVI. *Hermes*, 100, 506–08.

Tatum, W.J. (1997). Friendship, politics, and literature in Catullus: Poems 1, 65 and 66, 116. *CQ*, 47, 482–500.

Theodorakopoulos, E. (1997). Closure: the book of Vergil. In C. Martindale (Ed.), *The Cambridge Companion to Vergil* (155–66). Cambridge, UK: Cambridge University Press.

Thomas, R.F. (1982). Catullus and the polemics of poetic reference (poem 64.1–18). *AJP*, 103, 144–64.

(2011). *Horace: Odes Book* IV *and Carmen Saeculare*. Cambridge, UK: Cambridge University Press.

Thomson, D.R.S. (1997). *Catullus, Edited with a Textual and Interpretative Commentary*. Toronto, Canada: University of Toronto Press.

Townend, G.B. (1983). The unstated climax of Catullus 64. *Greece & Rome*, 1983, 21–30.

Traill, D. (1981). Catullus 63: rings around the sun. *CP*, 76, 211–14.

Trappes-Lomax, J.M. (2007). *Catullus: A Textual Reappraisal*. Swansea: Classical Press of Wales.

Trimble, G. (2013, April 5). Serious Games [Review of the book *Catullus: Books, Poems, Readers*, by I. Du Quesnay and T. Woodman (Eds.)]. *TLS*. Retrieved from www.the-tls.co.uk/articles/private/serious-games/

Tsantsanoglou, K. (2009). The λεπτότης of Aratus. *Trends in Classics*, 1, 55–89.

Tuplin, C.J. (1981). Catullus 68. *CQ*, 31, 113–39.

Väisänen, M. (1984). *La musa poliedrica: Indagine storica su Catull. carm. 4*. Annales Academiae Scientiarum Fennicae, Series B, 224. Helsinki, Finland: Suomalainen Tiedeakatemia.

Van Sickle, J. (1981). Poetics of opening and closure in Meleager, Catullus, and Gallus. *CW*, 75, 65–75.

Vine, B. (1992). On the "missing" fourth stanza of Catullus 51. *Harvard Studies in Classical Philology*, 94, 251–58.

Volk, K. (2010). Aratus. In J. Clauss and M. Cuypers (Eds.), *A Companion to Hellenistic Literature* (197–210). Malden, MA: Blackwell.

Watson, L. (1990). Rustic Suffenus (Catullus 22) and literary rusticity. In F. Cairns and M. Heath (Eds.), *ARCA Classical and Medieval Texts, Papers and Monographs 29, Papers of the Leeds International Latin Seminar 6* (13–33). Leeds, UK: Francis Cairns.

(2006). Catullus and the poetics of incest. *Antichthon*, 40, 35–48.

Weber, C. (1983). Two chronological contradictions in Catullus 64. *TAPA*, 113, 263–71.

Wheeler, A.L. (1934). *Catullus and the Traditions of Ancient Poetry*. Berkeley: University of California Press.

Wilamowitz-Moellendorff, U. von (1913). *Sappho und Simonides*. Berlin, Germany: Weidmann.

Williams, C.A. (1999). *Roman Homosexuality: Ideologies of Masculinity in Classical Antiquity*. Oxford, UK: Oxford University Press.

Wiseman, T.P. (1969). *Catullan Questions*. Leicester, UK: Leicester University Press.

(1974). *Cinna the Poet and Other Roman Essays*. Leicester, UK: Leicester University Press.

(1979). *Clio's Cosmetics: Three Studies in Greco-Roman Literature*. Leicester, UK: Leicester University Press.

(1982). *Pete nobiles amicos:* poets and patrons in late Republican Rome. In B. K. Gold (Ed.), *Literary and Artistic Patronage in Ancient Rome* (28–49). Austin: University of Texas Press.

(1985). *Catullus and His World: A Reappraisal*. Cambridge, UK: Cambridge University Press.

Witke, C. (1980). Catullus 13: a reexamination. *CP*, 75, 325–31.

Woodman, T. (2012). A covering letter: Poem 65. In I. Du Quesnay and T. Woodman (Eds.), *Catullus: Poems, Books, Readers* (130–52). Cambridge, UK: Cambridge University Press.

Wray, D. (2001). *Catullus and the Poetics of Roman Manhood*. Cambridge, UK: Cambridge University Press.

Yatromanolakis, D. (1999). Alexandrian Sappho revisited. *Harvard Studies in Classical Philology*, 99, 179–95.

(2007). *Sappho in the Making: The Early Reception*. Cambridge, MA: Harvard University Press.

Zarker, J. W. (1973). Lesbia's charms. *CJ*, 68, 107–15.

Zetzel, J.E.G. (1983). Re-creating the canon: Augustan poetry and the Alexandrian past. *Critical Inquiry*, 10, 83–105.

Index

For EU product safety concerns, contact us at Calle de José Abascal, 56–1°,
28003 Madrid, Spain or eugpsr@cambridge.org.